Sierra
Nevada
Birds

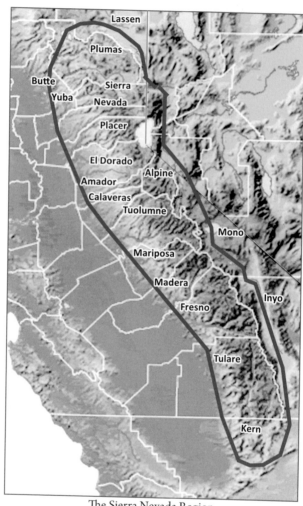

The Sierra Nevada Region

Sierra Nevada Birds

by David Lukas

LUKAS GUIDES

BIG OAK FLAT

COPYRIGHT © 2011, 2013 DAVID LUKAS
PUBLISHED BY LUKAS GUIDES
P.O. BOX 231, BIG OAK FLAT, CA 95305
415-320-5413

www.lukasguides.com
david@lukasguides.com

DESIGNED AND PRODUCED BY DAVE COMSTOCK
PRINTED AND BOUND IN DEXTER, MICHIGAN,
BY THOMSON-SHORE, INC.

ISBN 978-0-9834891-0-8
LIBRARY OF CONGRESS CONTROL NUMBER:
2011905951

THIRD PRINTING

Cover photo: May Lake and Mt Conness in the
upper Tuolumne River Watershed, Yosemite
National Park. By David Lukas

Table of Contents

Acknowledgments ✕ *vii*
Introduction ✕ *ix*
Ducks and Geese ✕ 1
New World Quail ✕ 24
Grouse and Allies ✕ 27
Loons ✕ 31
Grebes ✕ 32
Cormorants ✕ 37
Pelicans ✕ 39
Herons and Egrets ✕ 40
New World Vultures ✕ 45
Ospreys ✕ 46
Hawks, Kites, Eagles and Allies ✕ 48
Falcons ✕ 59
Rails ✕ 63
Cranes ✕ 69
Plovers ✕ 70
Sandpipers, Phalaropes and Allies ✕ 71
Gulls and Terns ✕ 79
Pigeons and Doves ✕ 84
Roadrunners ✕ 88
Owls ✕ 90
Goatsuckers ✕ 100
Swifts ✕ 101
Hummingbirds ✕ 106
Kingfishers ✕ 112
Woodpeckers ✕ 113
Flycatchers ✕ 130
Vireos ✕ 143
Corvids ✕ 147
Larks ✕ 160

Swallows ✗ 161
Chickadees and Titmice ✗ 170
Bushtits ✗ 174
Nuthatches ✗ 176
Creepers ✗ 180
Wrens ✗ 181
Gnatcatchers ✗ 188
Dippers ✗ 189
Kinglets ✗ 191
Wrentits ✗ 193
Thrushes ✗ 195
Thrashers ✗ 203
Starlings ✗ 205
Pipits ✗ 207
Waxwings ✗ 209
Silky-Flycatchers ✗ 210
Wood-Warblers ✗ 212
Sparrows ✗ 223
Cardinals and Allies ✗ 244
Blackbirds ✗ 249
Finches ✗ 260
Old World Sparrows ✗ 272

Appendices
1. *Rare and Unusual Birds of the Sierra Nevada* ✗ 274
2. *Glossary of Place Names* ✗ 281

Index ✗ 284

Acknowledgments

When I started this project in early 1996—a mere 15 years ago—I had no idea it would go through so many phases, involve so many people, or take so long to complete. I originally imagined that this book would take two years to research and write, but even as I put more and more time into the project it kept growing in scale.

I cannot begin to thank the amazing people I have had a chance to work with while researching this book. Or the inspiring places I have had a chance to explore. For the past 15 years, I have lived in beautiful remote areas and have hiked over 15,000 miles and spent more than 15,000 hours studying birds in the Sierra Nevada. Every summer I live out of my car, for months at a time, traveling and teaching bird classes and leading hikes all over the Sierra Nevada for organizations like the Yosemite Conservancy, Mono Lake Committee, and the Sierra Nevada Field Campus. I also work as a naturalist hiking guide and birding tour leader for YExplore, a professional guiding service in Yosemite National Park, and have seen some amazing country.

Over the past 15 years, I have been in the field with more than two thousand different naturalists and biologists who have helped me see, interpret, and understand Sierra Nevada birds in more ways than I ever thought possible. Together we have explored, investigated, and pondered the status of Sierra Nevada birds in every month and in every corner of the mountains. What a life-changing experience this has been!

There is no way to acknowledge everyone, but I want to thank some of the many folks whose perceptive feedback and insights have most significantly enriched this book: Ted Beedy, Ryan Burnett, Dave DeSante, Jon Dunn, Keith Hansen, Sacha Heath, Tom and Jo Heindel, Jack Laws, Mac McCormick, Chris McCreedy, Suzanne McDonald, Joe Medley, Martin Meyers, Kristie Nelson, Lew Oring, Alison Sheehey, Dave Shuford, Rodney Siegel, Jim Steele, John Sterling, Emilie Strauss, Jerry Tecklin, and Bob Wilkerson.

In particular, I want to thank Sarah Stock at Yosemite National Park, Bob Barnes in the Kern River Valley, and Will Richardson at Lake Tahoe for graciously and tirelessly answering my endless questions, and for their singular contributions to our understanding of Sierra Nevada birds.

Thanks to Steve Medley at the Yosemite Association, Malcolm Margolin at Heyday Books, and Phyllis Faber at University of California Press for their support and guidance through the different phases of this book. And thanks in part to a grant from the Highfield Foundation, which helped fund a portion of the work in an early stage of the project.

This book would not have been possible without the cheerful and skillful assistance of David Comstock at Comstock Bonanza Press. Thank you David.

And thank you Nicole, for your patience, generosity, and willingness to spend so much time reading all those drafts of the manuscript.

This book is a song of love for the Sierra Nevada as told through the prism of birds. It is dedicated to Jeff Maurer, an outstanding Yosemite biologist and friend to many, who tragically died in a climbing accident in 2009.

DAVID LUKAS, 2011

Introduction

The Sierra Nevada is one of the world's foremost mountain ranges, a mix of high peaks, cliffs, rugged canyons, and vast wildernesses that capture the imagination and attract millions of people every year. Most visitors are drawn to the region's premier attractions—including Lake Tahoe, Yosemite National Park, and Sequoia & Kings Canyon National Parks—but there are an incredible diversity of other equally interesting destinations to explore in this immense and complex landscape.

To fully explore the Sierra Nevada would take a lifetime, but even a short visit is enough to feel the spirit of this place. Everywhere you go there are mountains upon mountains, forests and meadows, tumbling rivers, and lakes of pure water. And for birding enthusiasts and naturalists, a wealth of plants and animals wait to be discovered around every corner.

Spanning 400 miles in length, the Sierra Nevada differs little from the forests of Oregon and Washington at its northern end, and desert scrub habitats at its southern end could just as easily be found in Mexico. This is the place covered by this book, everything from the broad sweep of landscape to the intimate bend in the trail where you might suddenly run into a family of Sooty Grouse. While the Sierra Nevada is a big place, this guide will help you scratch the surface.

This book gives fully-detailed accounts for the 207 bird species that are most characteristic of the Sierra Nevada. These birds are common residents or common migrants, and can be found in reasonable numbers every year. Shorter accounts are given for an additional 115 species that are very rare visitors to the Sierra Nevada, or else breed or migrate in very limited areas.

AREA COVERED   Although it is easy to find the Sierra Nevada on a map, no perfect boundaries circumscribe the region and different experts use different criteria. My goal is simply to encompass the areas that best characterize the experience of birdwatching in the Sierra Nevada. Wherever possible, and for ease of use, I have drawn the boundaries of the area covered by this book along easily recognized features.

At its northern end, the Sierra Nevada disappears in a densely-forested, geologically complex area around Lake Almanor where the granites of the Sierra Nevada dip under the volcanic rocks of the Cascade Mountains. For convenience, I have chosen as the northern boundary a line drawn west along Hwy 36 from Susanville, over Fredonyer Pass to the community of Westwood, then across the southern half of Lake Almanor to Butt Valley Reservoir and down the canyon of the North Fork Feather River (Hwy 70) to Oroville.

Along its western perimeter, the Sierra Nevada slope dives under the accumulated sediments of the Central Valley, shifting almost imperceptibly from gentle slope to flat valley bottom. In general, the western boundary is defined as the lower edge of oak woodlands, where oaks give way to the annual grasslands of the Central Valley. In some areas, and especially around the Sacramento region, this boundary is obscured by suburban neighborhoods and planted nonnative trees.

In the south, the mountains come to an end visually at the South Fork Kern River Valley (including Isabella Lake), but technically the Sierra Nevada region continues southward into the low desert hills north of Tehachapi Pass. The southern boundary is drawn along Hwy 58 to the town of Tehachapi then north along Hwy 14, but these highways take in stretches of desert terrain that are not really part of the Sierra Nevada. For the purposes of this book, I've largely limited my discussion of bird distribution to a boundary drawn at the South Fork Kern River Valley, with a few references to the lower desert hills to the south (e.g. Breckenridge Mountain and the Piute Mountains) because this area is little known and ripe for new discoveries.

The eastern boundary line can be conveniently drawn along Hwy 395 even though the highway does not perfectly trace the complexities of the eastern side of the Sierra Nevada region. It is arguable whether east-side locations (like Owens Valley, Lake Crowley, and Mono Lake in the south, or Sierra Valley and Honey Lake in the north) should be included in the Sierra Nevada region, but for the purposes of this book they are considered part of the Sierra Nevada both in terms of experience and ecology.

Wherever possible, or useful, an attempt is made to distinguish between "west slope" and "east slope" as divided by the crest of the Sierra Nevada. In most cases, the distinction is clear cut and based on the distinctly different geography, vegetation, climate, and bird distribution patterns found on each slope. But in other cases, such as north of Donner Pass or south of Walker Pass, where the crest is lower and the same vegetation can be found on both slopes, this distinction is less important. And in other cases, some birds are so common and widespread that their distribution and seasonal patterns are almost identical on both slopes.

HABITATS AND ZONES Due to its immense size and length, the Sierra Nevada has a bewildering diversity of habitats ranging from arid deserts to icy alpine peaks. To add to this complexity, the west slope and the east slope of the Sierra Nevada have very different environmental conditions and distinct floras.

Depending on the classification system used, there might be dozens or even hundreds of habitat types in the Sierra Nevada. To avoid needless jargon and to keep the book as straightforward as possible, I distilled habitat descriptions down to 5 broad zones (following the system used in the guidebook *Sierra Nevada Natural History*), and wherever possible, I refer to specific elevations and habitat features rather than to zones. For instance, rather than saying that a bird lives in the "Upper Montane Zone," my preference is to say that the species can be found in "red fir forests around 7500 ft."

Most vegetation in the Sierra Nevada occurs in distinct zones (or belts) based on elevation. These are best observed on the west side, where the slope is gradual, but the east side is so steep and rocky south of Lake Tahoe that the vegetation zones are not so clearly marked. However once learned, these broad zones are easily recognized and can help visitors understand the ecology of the Sierra Nevada. They are not perfect categories because there are many exceptions due to local geology, climate, and hydrology, but they are still a useful tool.

Foothill Oak Zone: On the west side, annual grasslands of the Central Valley begin giving way to oak woodlands around 500 ft in elevation. This zone is primarily composed of oaks—mostly valley, blue, and interior live oaks—and extends from 500 ft to around 3000 ft (perhaps as high as 5000 ft in the southern Sierra Nevada). In places, oaks form a continuous cover while in other places they grow in open woodlands interspersed with grasslands. On dry, rocky slopes oaks are replaced by impenetrable chaparral habitats of dense shrubs like manzanita, ceanothus, and toyon. At the upper edges of the Foothill Oak Zone, ponderosa pines become increasingly common, forming an intermediate forest type between the Foothill Oak Zone and the Mixed Conifer Zone.

Mixed Conifer Zone: This is the main forested belt on both slopes of the Sierra Nevada, characterized by lush forests of big trees. On the west slope this zone occurs from about 3000 ft to about 6000 ft, but on the east slope it is shifted somewhat higher. At its lowest edges, ponderosa pines are the dominant trees, but most of the zone consists of sugar pines, incense-cedars, Douglas firs, white firs, black oaks, and canyon live oaks. In the northern Sierra Nevada, the Mixed Conifer Zone occurs broadly on both slopes, but on the east slope south of Lake Tahoe these forests are increasingly fragmented and consist mainly of Jeffrey pine.

Upper Montane Zone: Above 6000 ft, the harsh winters, deep snow packs, and short growing seasons limit the diversity of plants. Forests from about 6000 ft to about 8000 ft (or as high as 10,000 ft in the southern Sierra Nevada) are characterized by dark, somber stands of red firs, with some areas dominated by lodgepole pines, western white pines, Jeffrey pines, and quaking aspens. These forests occur on both slopes but are found at higher elevations on the east side, where they are the primary forests of the upper slopes south of Lake Tahoe (where some experts combine them with the Mixed Conifer Zone and call them the Eastside Zone). A very common habitat within the Mixed Conifer Zone and the Upper Montane Zone is montane chaparral, which resembles chaparral habitats of the Foothill Oak Zone but is comprised of different species, including different manzanitas and ceanothus, as well as chinquapins and huckleberry oaks.

Subalpine Zone: The uppermost limits of forest in the Sierra Nevada ("treeline") differ from area to area but generally occur around 8000 ft to 10,000 ft. This zone of sparse, high-elevation forest is dominated by mountain hemlocks in the north, and a mix of lodgepole pines, western white pines, and foxtail pines in the south. The highest trees, often stunted and twisted by extreme wind and snow conditions, are whitebark pines. This zone is characterized by small, scattered pockets of trees, usually in close proximity to moist montane meadows.

Alpine Zone: The highest peaks and ridges of the Sierra Nevada, above 9000 ft in the north and above 11,000 ft in the south, are treeless. This zone consists of rocky slopes with scattered pockets of sparse alpine grasses, sedges, herbs, and dwarf shrubs.

SEASONS The first signs of spring arrive in the Sierra Nevada in February and March, mostly at the lowest elevations, as resident birds begin to sing and act territorial. A few hardy migrants such as swallows and raptors show up while overwintering birds such as ducks become restless.

Migration peaks in April, with large numbers of songbirds arriving at low elevations and many ducks and geese flying north. Species that breed at higher elevations migrate north along one or both slopes of the Sierra Nevada at low elevations, increasing in numbers as they wait for snow to melt at higher elevations.

Many species begin nesting in the foothills during April, while other species push upslope day by day, beginning to nest in late April, May, or even in June at the highest elevations. At the same time, foothill habitats become fairly dry by late May so species that have completed their nesting season move upslope as soon as their young have fledged, essentially following the arrival of spring as it begins at higher elevations.

In July and early August, large numbers of birds are found in high-elevation forests and meadows, feasting on insects and seeds in preparation for their migration south. As meadows dry up in late August and September, most of these birds either leave or head downslope again. Some species linger at high elevations until pushed downslope by the first cold storms in late October or November.

Increasingly cold and snowy conditions in November and December force all but the hardiest species down to middle or lower elevations. In mid-winter, the foothills of the Sierra Nevada can be surprisingly "birdy," while lower elevation lakes and reservoirs attract large numbers of ducks and other waterbirds that linger through the winter.

ABUNDANCE When trying to find birds, it can help to have an understanding of how abundant a species should be. Is it common or rare, for instance? Unfortunately, every checklist and bird book has a different sense of what constitutes the abundance categories, and it is even more difficult to compare the abundance of different types of birds. Does a single flock of 1000 ducks make that species common? And how would you compare this to 5 pairs of California Towhees found along a chaparral trail?

In this book, the following categories are used. They are simply meant as helpful guides, one way to assess whether a particular sighting is expected or exceptional.

Common or Abundant: Both terms suggest that a bird is nearly always encountered in the proper habitat, often in moderate to large numbers.

Fairly Common: Just a notch down from common, this category suggests that a bird may be found in low to moderate numbers, or may require some searching, but can usually be found.

Uncommon: A bird is usually present in small numbers but not always found, even with some searching.

Rare: This category suggests that a bird will be very hard to find, either because it is present in very small numbers, or else in a very limited area, or for a very limited period of time. A flock of 1000 ducks that are only seen one day out of the year would probably be rare, for instance.

In addition to these abundance categories, a few other terms are used in the bird accounts.

Resident: These birds occur year round in the Sierra Nevada. They may remain in the same location or may move to different areas at different seasons. While permanent residents are found every month, it is not always clear whether the same individual birds remain all year or whether breeding birds are replaced by different birds that are migrating or spending the winter.

Wintering/Overwintering: Birds that arrive in the winter and linger until the following spring are considered wintering or overwintering birds. Most of these are merely seasonal visitors, but breeding birds that linger over the winter could also fit into this category (though they are likely to be residents at that point).

Breeding/Nesting: A large number of birds in the Sierra Nevada arrive in the spring and leave in the late summer. Because they come to the Sierra Nevada to breed and nest, they are called breeding birds, which usually implies that this is the primary reason they are in the region.

Nonbreeding/Postbreeding: For species that breed in the region, there may be a cohort of immature birds or adults that do not breed in a given year. These nonbreeding birds occur individually or gather in small groups, and sometimes they have unique behaviors or habitat choices that distinguish them from breeding birds. Birds that have finished breeding (postbreeding) may also move into new habitats or vegetation zones, or exhibit unique behaviors that separate them from breeding birds.

Migrants/Transients: Many species only pass through the region, either migrating or in transit to some other destination. Migration implies a long-distance, traditional movement from a specific wintering area to a specific breeding area, repeated by many individuals of the same species; transients, on the other hand, may be off-course or making some other type of movement, but usually on an individual and non-traditional basis. From an observer's point of view, it is hard to tell whether a bird is a migrant or a transient, so the two terms are used somewhat interchangeably in this book.

TAXONOMIC SEQUENCE AND SOURCES   The taxonomy of birds is in constant flux and is interpreted differently by various authorities. This book follows the taxonomic sequence adopted by the American Birding Association as of November 2010.

No guidebook like this can exist in isolation; it is by its very nature a compilation derived from many sources. For life history information, I drew from dozens of excellent books, both old and new; but for the final word, I always turned to the Birds of North America, an online project of the Cornell Laboratory of Ornithology, http://bna.birds.cornell.edu/bna/. For range information, I referred to many sources including the excellent and well-documented *Birds of Yosemite and the East Slope* by David Gaines, and *California Birds: Their Status and Distribution* by Arnold Small, as well as a stack of local and regional bird checklists. Although these sources are static and somewhat outdated, they still provide a framework for understanding the status and distribution of Sierra Nevada birds.

Fortunately, in the 15 years since I began this project, there has been a veritable explosion of online resources, with hundreds of observers now documenting and sharing up-to-the-minute local observations and feedback through online discussion groups. In particular, a general discussion group on birds of the Sierra Nevada is at http://groups.yahoo.com/group/sierra-nevadabirds/, and a discussion group specific to Inyo and Mono County, sponsored by the Eastern Sierra Audubon Society, is at http://groups.google.com/group/easternsierrabirds.

Equally important are the amazing maps being created at California eBird, http://ebird.org/content/ca/, a site where anyone can add their sightings to constantly updated maps that are being generated for each species in California. These immensely valuable maps can be searched county by county, or month by month, to reveal the local movements of birds in ways never before possible.

I also reviewed a huge number of scientific reports and papers, but of special significance were a number of excellent surveys conducted by the Institute for Bird Populations, http://www.birdpop.org/, in Yosemite and Sequoia & Kings Canyon National Parks, and in Devils Postpile National Monument.

AN INVITATION   This book attempts to summarize patterns in bird distribution and abundance over a very large region and over decades of time, but it is important to remember that birds are individuals and there are still many patterns and behaviors that have not been discovered or described. It is surprising to realize how few birds have been studied in the Sierra Nevada, and in many cases almost no information exists on even the most basic aspects of birds' lives in the Sierra Nevada.

This book is merely one contribution to an ever-evolving exploration and discussion about Sierra Nevada birds rather than being a final statement. And every person who watches birds in the Sierra Nevada has an opportunity to be part of this discussion, maybe by posting observations on one of the online sites mentioned above, or by closely watching birds in your local neighborhood. If you have suggestions or feedback on the book, or if you find any errors, please send comments to me at david@lukasguides.com.

May you enjoy your time in the Sierra Nevada and see lots of birds!

DUCKS and GEESE (Anatidae)

Canada Goose *Branta canadensis*

LIFE HISTORY There are two faces to this familiar bird, a population of relatively tame, permanent residents that hang out in city parks and golf courses, and a population of wild brethren that migrate vast distances to their northern and boreal nesting grounds. Year-round residents are primarily the offspring of a large subspecies from the Great Basin and Midwest that, partly due to capture and release programs and partly due to the creation of productive manmade habitats, have lost the urge to migrate and are now so widespread that some people consider them a nuisance. The mixing of these two populations creates such a complex set of seasonal movements and behavior that one's perspective on what the geese are doing might change with the location.

Throughout the winter these geese gather in both large and small flocks, roosting each night on open bodies of water or in large marshes, then spending the day grazing on newly emerged grass shoots and fallen seeds in nearby meadows and pastures. They are strong walkers and runners, appearing more comfortable on land than many other waterfowl species though they still keep close to open areas, far from bushes where predators might hide. Their stout, flat bills are ideally suited for clipping vegetation and nearly their entire diet consists of plant material, ranging from seeds and leaves to aquatic roots that they find by tipping up while swimming and reaching underwater with their long necks.

Large flocks are comprised of multiple family groups and individuals that assemble for safety and company, but if you watch a large flock land you might notice that as they alight, they briefly split into family groups then mingle together again. By February, increasingly restless migratory groups begin to gather in key staging areas, and this is a time when large flocks may be seen passing north and east over the Sierra crest. Although they can fly 2000 miles in marathon 48-hour flights, they tend to head north in smaller increments with many stopover points along the way. Many of the geese that winter on the east side of the Sierra Nevada seem to be resident breeders rather than part of the migratory population.

Canada Geese are solitary or loosely colonial nesters that build their nests in a wide variety of habitats, with a preference for locations that are near water and have commanding views of the surrounding terrain, such as meadows or islands. Most geese form life-long pair bonds in their second year of life, so they typically arrive on their breeding grounds already paired up. With males standing guard, females select nest sites and make simple scrapes on the ground that they line with dry grasses and downy feathers. Females lay an average of 4–5 eggs that they incubate for 25 days. Chicks hatch synchronously and within 24 hours leave the nest already walking, swimming, diving, and feeding themselves. Young birds can fly when 7–8 weeks old, but the entire family remains together as a small flock until the following breeding season.

> **Note:** *Canada Goose taxonomy is complex and not entirely settled, but there are at least 11 subspecies that fall into two subgroups: the larger forms, lumped together as the Canada Goose; and the smaller forms, recently split off and lumped into the* **Cackling Goose.** *Hybridization and overlap in features makes identification of intermediate sizes extremely difficult though it is relatively easy to separate races at the extremes (the largest subspecies weighs as much as 10 times the smallest one). Migrating and wintering Cackling Geese sometimes show up in the Sierra Nevada but only in small numbers among larger groups of Canada Geese.*

RANGE The complex mingling of multiple subspecies that occur in California has two basic components: a fairly small resident population that breeds here in the spring and summer, and an enormous migratory population that arrives and leaves each winter. In the winter, Canada Geese are abundant and widespread in low-lying areas west of the mountains, less so on the east side. Spring migration probably peaks in February though flocks of what are likely migrating geese continue moving through for another month or two. Return migrants begin arriving in August, and there is a big movement in late September and October though many linger to the north or on the east side until cold winter storms finally nudge them into the warmer Central Valley. **WEST SLOPE:** Uncommon to rare visitors in the southern end of the Sierra Nevada but otherwise common to abundant around large reservoirs and rivers in the lower foothills, with hundreds to thousands being reported each winter on Christmas Bird Counts in the region. Some remain to nest in the region, often in close association with humans, from the foothills to as high as Lake Van Norden at Donner Pass. **EAST SLOPE:** Common to abundant migrants and winter visitors, especially in the northern half of the Sierra Nevada. Small numbers may hang out around large lakes in the south, but one measure of their overall scarcity is that only 1–2 dozen are reported on about half of the

Bishop Christmas Bird Counts, while thousands can be found at places like Lake Tahoe and Honey Lake. In suitable habitats they are generally common and widespread breeders, with pairs nesting everywhere from the edges of popular reservoirs to large marshes to patches of meadow along small streams.

WOOD DUCK *Aix sponsa*

LIFE HISTORY Remote ponds, marshes, and slow-moving rivers hidden by screens of vegetation and tall trees are the favorite haunts of these lovely feathered gems. During the breeding season you might hear the squeaky ascending whistles of males before you see them because these ducks have a knack for keeping out of sight and then exploding into noisy flight as females give their loud *oo-eek* calls of distress. Such anxious behavior may be a result of the extreme hunting pressure they have faced; at one point so many were slaughtered that it was predicted they would go extinct, and they are still the second most hunted duck in the eastern United States.

Careful management and nest-box programs ensure that they are once again common and familiar ducks, and because their favorite foods are acorns, they are especially abundant among oak woodlands on the lower west slope. Here they use overgrown ponds and wooded marshes scattered throughout the foothills, and are also regular visitors to city parks and reservoirs.

Wood Ducks are well-adapted for wooded habitats, with slim bodies so they can nest in narrow tree cavities and large eyes that help them navigate as they fly among dense branches and trees. When feeding on both land and water they move rapidly, deftly picking up seeds, fruits, and invertebrates with their narrow bills, but they may also dive several feet to collect waterlogged acorns. Their highly elastic esophagus is designed to hold 20–30 acorns at a time.

During the fall and winter, Wood Ducks often feed and roost in large groups, using this time to form pair bonds. Pairs split off to find their own nesting sites in March, but due to their unusually long breeding season (5–6 months), females may lay eggs anytime between March and late June. About 10 percent of females have second broods, so newly hatched chicks have been seen as early as mid-April in the foothills of the central Sierra Nevada or as late as the end of July at Lake Almanor.

A male fiercely guards a female as she searches for a suitable tree cavity, but he plays no role in the nesting effort and loses interest in the female as soon as she begins incubating her 10–13 eggs. Usable cavities are often created in the decayed wood where big branches break from mature trees, so these ducks require the presence of large trees that are over or near water. These cavities are scarce, so Wood Ducks readily use artificial nest boxes.

Wood Ducks are frequent victims (and perpetrators) of "egg-dumping," during which females indiscriminately lay eggs in each other's nests, with some females laying eggs in other nests first then starting their own nests later. Perhaps for this reason females sit on their eggs almost all day long, with only short feeding breaks at dawn and dusk. Chicks hatch in 30 days and soon thereafter the female entices them to jump out of the nest with soft *kuk* calls. She leads them to water, sometimes over a mile away, and stands guard to protect them from predators like bullfrogs, Great Horned Owls, or raccoons for 30 days or more.

RANGE The majority of Wood Ducks in California are resident west of the Sierra Nevada. Their sudden arrival on various ponds and lakes in the fall and spring indicates that there must be a fairly significant migration, but an overlap in resident and migratory populations makes this hard to gauge. **WEST SLOPE:** During the winter they are common in the lower foothills everywhere except at the northern and southern ends of the range, where they occur in the single digits on about 1 in 6 Christmas Bird Counts at Lake Almanor, and in the single digits on about half of the counts in the Kern River Valley. In the breeding season they are so widely distributed that it is hard to say whether they are uncommon or common, but single pairs or small numbers breed in suitable habitats along the full length of the Sierra Nevada. At all seasons they occupy large and small bodies of water in oak woodlands and mixed oak forests below 3000–4000 ft. **EAST SLOPE:** Very rare in the winter except for a few locations, such as Bishop City Park, where a few pairs are now annual visitors. Most arrive in March and April, and either continue onward or remain as uncommon breeders at scattered locations such as in Sierra Valley and around Bishop. Fall migration stretches from late August into November, with a few lingering into December.

Gadwall *Anas strepera*

LIFE HISTORY Gadwalls are the characteristic nesting ducks of Great Basin marshes along the east side of the Sierra Nevada, but they are also common migrants and wintering visitors on low-elevation lakes and reservoirs throughout the region. Recent Christmas Bird Counts even hint at a surge in their population starting about 2000–2001 since they are now annual on many counts where they were formerly sporadic.

Throughout the winter Gadwalls forage on the stems and leaves of aquatic plants in the shallow waters of ponds, marshes, and slow-moving streams then retreat to the safety of large open bodies of water to rest and sleep. They mostly feed by dabbling at the surface or tipping up to reach underwater plants, but they also readily forage in agricultural fields with other ducks. Pair bonds form in November, a full 4–5 months before they start breeding, with the male defending the moving female until she starts laying eggs. Even after settling on their breeding grounds, most wait another month before females lay their 7–12 eggs. At this point males depart and gather with other males to molt their wing feathers and huddle nervously in the center of open bodies of water until they can fly again.

Nests are simple grass and feather-lined scrapes in the soil that are located in dense emergent or upland vegetation near the water's edge. Nests in the Great Basin may be located in stands of sagebrush away from water. Females incubate almost continuously for 26 days, with very short breaks to feed. As soon the chicks hatch, females lead their new broods to productive feeding areas and guard them until they are independent at 10 weeks of age. Females with young can be seen as late as mid-August.

RANGE The core of North America's breeding population stretches from the north-central United States across northern Nevada and down the east side of the Sierra Nevada, with many birds wintering in California's Central Valley. In the Sierra Nevada they begin arriving on their breeding grounds in March, are uncommon to common through the summer, then are briefly abundant in September and October when many fall migrants arrive. On the east side some linger into November, but depart by the end of the month. Except for a few late-summer wanderers to high elevations, Gadwall are primarily restricted to low-lying areas, mainly below 3000 ft, although large lakes like Lake Tahoe may attract a fair number of migrating and nonbreeding birds. **WEST SLOPE:** Fairly common winter visitors to marshes, ponds, and lakes with numbers varying from year to year at any one location. Breeding is confirmed or suspected at a handful of the region's large reservoirs, but they are probably not very common at this season. **EAST SLOPE:** Formerly scarce or irregular winter visitors on the east side but now found annually at many locations and maybe even in greater numbers (though maybe only a dozen or so birds in most places). Starting in March, they are abundant migrants, with many apparently staying to breed. Common breeders through the summer, when they might be found at almost any body of water ranging from single stock ponds to huge marshes. Their numbers increase and they move to larger, open bodies of water when southbound migrants appear in September.

AMERICAN WIGEON *Anas americana*

LIFE HISTORY Roughly 50 percent of North America's wintering American Wigeons can be found west of the Cascade-Sierra axis, so it is no surprise that these ducks are common wintering birds and abundant migrants in the Sierra Nevada. Across their entire wintering range, however, their numbers vary dramatically, suggesting that the population shifts its patterns of movement and residency from year to year. For example, observers on Lake Almanor Christmas Bird Counts have recorded wild swings from three wigeons one winter to 46,000 another winter, and many other winter counts in the Sierra Nevada swing from single digits to hundreds of birds in different years.

In many ways, wigeons are our most unusual dabbling ducks. They breed further north, have one of the earliest fall migrations, have unusually strong pair bonds, and eat more vegetable matter than almost any other duck. In the winter, they spend much of the day grazing quietly in fields with cows and Canada Geese. They can also be aggressive and opportunistic in their feeding behaviors, and when they are on the water they follow coots and diving ducks trying to steal pieces of aquatic vegetation that those birds bring back to the surface to eat. Their bills are adapted for a grazing lifestyle, with a unique shape that concentrates force at the tip, where they clip leaves and stems.

Note: *The Eurasian Wigeon is a very rare winter visitor that has become increasingly common and may now show up every year in the Sierra Nevada; should be looked for among large groups of American Wigeons.*

RANGE Huge numbers of American Wigeons winter in California west of the Sierra Nevada, where they can be found in all types of habitats from large lakes, rivers, marshes and mudflats, to agricultural fields and city parks. They prefer large bodies of water next to grassy fields. Spring migration begins in February, but peak numbers move north in the first half of April, showing up in places as diverse as Lake Tahoe and Sierra Valley. Except in the north, they are scarce to absent through the summer. Fall migration begins in the far northern parts of their North American range in late August, but the main influx of birds does not arrive in California until October. Large numbers of fall migrants linger in the north and on the east side of the Sierra Nevada and may even stay unless lakes freeze over and cold storms push them into the warmer Central Valley. **WEST SLOPE:** Common migrants and winter visitors on foothill reservoirs and lakes up to 4000 ft though numbers vary considerably from year to year. Some observers even suspect that wigeon might show up in the foothills on a daily basis when duck hunters are hunting in the Central Valley. **EAST SLOPE:** Common to abundant migrants with winter numbers dependent on location and local weather conditions. In the Owens Valley they were once sporadic and rare winter visitors but are now annual, with several hundred birds staying through the winter. Have nested at Bridgeport Reservoir, Lake Crowley, and the Hot Creek Fish Hatchery at the far southern end of their range, and in the north may nest at Honey Lake.

MALLARD *Anas platyrhynchos*

LIFE HISTORY If someone only knows Mallards from city parks, they might be shocked to find wild Mallards at some remote Sierra Nevada lake they had just backpacked 3 days to reach. In fact, the human-mallard association is so extensive and stretches so far back in time that most people do not even know there is such a thing as a wild Mallard. But there are thousands of lonely little lakes and marshy wetlands scattered throughout the Sierra Nevada where the only birds you might see are a pair of Mallards or a female with a line of bright yellow ducklings trailing along behind. And during migration flocks of noisy, unruly Mallards descend upon larger lakes and marshes by the hundreds or thousands, on route to and from their wintering grounds in the Central Valley.

Mallards are the most abundant ducks in North America and they are correspondingly widespread and common in the Sierra Nevada. Not only are they particularly abundant during migration, but they endure cold weather and can tolerate snow and ice as long as there is a dependable supply of food and pockets of ice-free water where they can sleep at night. Migrants and wintering birds forage for bits of tender leaves and stems in all types of shallow wetlands and flooded fields, with a strong preference for agricultural lands where there is an abundance of leftover grains. Their bills are lined with sieve-like lamellae that filter food particles out of the water, while the sharp nails at the tips of their bills help them grasp small items.

They are highly gregarious during migration and through the winter, and most find mates during the winter, with courtship signaled by increasing levels of chasing and squabbling as the winter progresses.

Only females give the familiar quacking calls while males make much quieter raspy calls. Their entire mating ritual is rather chaotic because males try to mate with multiple females; in addition, females use "inciting" behavior to get males to chase them, thus ensuring that they end up with the fittest males that have the greatest stamina.

Mallards nest in a vast array of habitats from sea level to treeline as long as they have access to water (which can be up to half a mile away) and dense vegetation where females conceal their nests; but even these conditions are not absolute, for they have been found nesting on the open forest floor on the slopes above Tioga Pass at 10,000 ft. The nesting season begins as early as late February, but extends into June in the high mountains or if females have to renest because they have lost their first broods. Males intensely guard their mates until the females begin incubating their eggs; then males leave to hang out with other males that are also done breeding.

Nests—which are simple scrapes in the soil lined with bits of dry grasses, leaves, and twigs—may be simple bowls or elaborate structures, to which females continue to add downy feathers throughout the 28 days of incubation. Females incubate their 1–13 eggs for 23 hours a day with only furtive breaks to feed in the early morning and late afternoon, and because they are well camouflaged and do not move, they are very hard to spot unless they flush up in fright. The morning after the chicks hatch, the female leads her brood to the nearest suitable feeding pond, which may be over a mile away. Ducklings spend most of their waking hours foraging for invertebrates for their first month of life, gradually shifting to a plant-based diet until they start flying at 50–70 days old.

RANGE Mallards are ubiquitous in North America and are year-round residents almost everywhere in the United States. They are likewise common and widespread in the Sierra Nevada though they retreat from higher elevations in the winter. Nesting birds can be found from early March through June. They are abundant migrants, but in most areas they are already so common that this movement can be hard to detect though the pulse of fall migrants is more noticeable. There is some variation in numbers of wintering birds, probably in response to local weather and to conditions in the north (where they linger until pushed south by winter storms), but dozens to hundreds can be found on any given day. **WEST SLOPE:** Generally common migrants and winter visitors to 3000 ft but scarcer at increasingly higher elevations, with only small numbers of fall migrants showing up on high mountain lakes. Breeding birds are common but thinly distributed over the entire west slope, with breeding records as high as 10,000 ft. **EAST SLOPE:** Wintering birds may either be more or less numerous than on the west slope, probably depending on the severity of winter conditions. Migrants begin arriving as soon as ice starts to thaw in early March. Most move on but large numbers remain to nest near lakes, marshes, and streams up to 10,000 ft, usually in dense marsh vegetation but also in sagebrush thickets away from water. Numbers pick up again in late summer, with a large pulse of migrants in September that may linger into December.

CINNAMON TEAL *Anas cyanoptera*

LIFE HISTORY These slim, attractive birds are not only one of the most abundant nesting ducks in the Great Basin marshes along the east side of the Sierra Nevada, but also one of the earliest spring migrants and thus an exciting indicator of the coming change in season. Even better, they are one of the few ducks that almost completely disappears in the winter so their sudden appearance is particularly noteworthy. And once they arrive, they are a lively and welcome presence, adding their peculiar splash of brilliant color to any pond or marsh, or at least until mid-summer when they molt into a drab eclipse plumage that makes them virtually indistinguishable from the closely related Blue-winged Teal (see note below).

Surface waters in the land-locked basins of the east side are often brackish or even highly alkaline, but Cinnamon Teal seem to thrive in these waters. They are active feeders in the shallow waters at the edges of ponds and marshes, dabbling in search of nutritious seeds that are the mainstay of their diet, then supplementing these with a wide variety of invertebrates and snails to meet their increased energy needs during the breeding season. Pairs have already formed on their wintering grounds, but pair formation and courtship may continue through February and March until females start laying eggs in May and June. Among the dabbling ducks, male Cinnamon Teal are unusually attentive, though they still leave at the tail end of the incubation period and fly to nearby marshes where numerous males gather and molt into their drab, late-summer plumages.

Nests are located in dense, concealing vegetation alongside ponds and slow-moving waters, and females are so skittish about revealing the nest's location that they will sneak through 100–200 ft of thick grasses and reeds to avoid flying directly to their nest. Their 4–16 eggs hatch after about 23 days, usually in June to mid-August. Females quickly lead their newly hatched broods to the nearest water, maintaining constant vigilance until the ducklings fledge about 50 days later.

Note: Blue-winged Teal *are very scarce, even casual, visitors to the Sierra Nevada though they breed in low numbers at Honey Lake and Sierra Valley (and maybe in the Owens Valley) on the east side, and have bred in Yosemite National Park and in the Kern River Valley on the west side. Their status in the fall is disputed due to the difficulty of separating birds in their drab eclipse plumage from the much more common Cinnamon Teal.*

RANGE Cinnamon Teal are permanent residents in the San Joaquin Valley and along the coast, but they are otherwise absent in California in the winter. Spring migrants begin appearing in late January and are common to abundant breeding birds on the east side of the Sierra Nevada from March to August, thereafter decreasing steadily in numbers until nearly all have left by mid-October. Very rare in winter. **WEST SLOPE:** The proximity of the Kern River Valley to wintering populations in the San Joaquin Valley means that more winter visitors show up there than anywhere else in the Sierra Nevada (though fewer than a half dozen birds may be seen about 1 out of every 3 winters). Single birds show up on central Sierra Nevada reservoirs about once every 5 years, and about once every 15 years at Lake Almanor during the winter. Commonly breed at Kern River, but uncommon breeders elsewhere in the lower foothills. Occasionally observed above 3000 ft during migration. **EAST SLOPE:** Absent in winter, but common to abundant as soon as migration begins in late January and persisting in these numbers as a breeding species through the summer and into early fall. Even nests in higher elevation lakes such as Lake Tahoe, where this species was once the most common nesting duck. It is one of the 3 most common nesting ducks at Honey Lake, as it probably is all along the east side.

NORTHERN SHOVELER *Anas clypeata*

LIFE HISTORY Northern Shovelers are notable for their ridiculously large bills that are specially modified for straining small swimming crustaceans (mostly *Daphnia*) from the water. These types of crustaceans favor warmer, shallower waters so shovelers spend most of their time foraging at the edges of ponds, marshes, and mudflats. After feeding, they retreat to deeper waters to rest and sleep, but they seldom spend much time on large, open bodies of water, even during migration.

Shovelers leave relatively late in the spring and arrive relatively early in the fall, but they apparently do not linger to breed, so few of their intervening breeding and nesting behaviors are observed in the Sierra Nevada.

RANGE Shovelers are fairly common wintering birds in California, but they do not winter here in the enormous numbers that some of our other dabbling ducks do. They breed in the far northeastern corner of the state but are rare elsewhere in the summer. They are only abundant in the Sierra Nevada during migration, but their migratory patterns are confusing and hard to sort out. On the east side, for example, they are abundant in Sierra Valley during spring migration but with no noticeable migration in the fall, while at Mono Lake and in the Owens Valley to the south they are uncommon in the spring and abundant in the fall. In the past they were rare and irregular winter visitors, but according to Christmas Bird Count records, they have become fairly common winter visitors at almost all low-elevation Sierra Nevada locations during the past 10–15 years. **WEST SLOPE:** At best, shovelers might be considered uncommon migrants, but there are scant records of migrating groups so there are few dates and few numbers from which to draw conclusions. They are rare during the breeding season, except at Isabella Lake where they are uncommon in the spring and may even breed. The only exception on the west slope is Lake Almanor, where they are not known to breed but remain fairly common throughout the year. They are now annual winter visitors to large lakes in the lower foothills, with numbers ranging from single digits into the hundreds of birds. **EAST SLOPE:** As on the west slope, they have become annual winter visitors east of the crest though in similarly low numbers. This situation changes in mid-March and April when they become abundant migrants, especially in the productive marshes of Sierra Valley. During this same period they range from being rare migrants at Lake Tahoe to uncommon migrants further south, but large numbers are possible anywhere as when 3100 stopped at Owens Lake in mid-April. Large numbers linger into early summer at Sierra Valley and the presence of pairs raises the possibility that they might be breeding locally, but in general shovelers are rare or absent in the summer, at least until the influx of fall migrants starts in late August. Peak numbers occur in September and October but drop off quickly by the end of the month.

Northern Pintail *Anas acuta*

LIFE HISTORY These elegantly-attired ducks are the most abundant of all the wintering and migrating waterfowl found in California and are likewise seasonally abundant in the Sierra Nevada. They often gather in large flocks on open, shallow wetlands and on adjacent agricultural fields where they feed on leftover grains and the seeds of diverse marsh plants. Although they ultimately number in the millions when they reach their final destination in the Central Valley, their numbers at intermediate stopover points like the Sierra Nevada are highly variable and probably depend on whether weather conditions and limited food supplies drive them south or allow them to linger in the north. Christmas Bird Counts at Lake Almanor have recorded as many as 46,000 but years might go by without a single pintail.

Pintails form pair bonds on their wintering grounds, but males are also highly promiscuous on their breeding grounds, where they aggressively chase females and display by burping, grunting, and lifting their rear ends so their tails stick straight up. During the period when females are fertile and laying their eggs, up to 16 males at a time may pursue a single female in fast acrobatic flights that may last over 30 minutes at a stretch—and all this while males try to keep their eyes on their own females so that they do not get chased as well. Males lose interest in their mates as soon as incubation begins, retreating to open bodies of water where they molt their feathers and begin heading south in August.

Females nest among low grasses and shrubs near water (up to a mile from water and sometimes in sagebrush where you least expect to find a duck). Pairs scout out potential locations by circling low over suitable habitats though the male is simply guarding the female and following her. After making several simple scrapes on the ground, she finishes one by lining it with dead vegetation then laying 3–12 eggs that she incubates for 23 days. During the entire incubation period, she takes only very quick predawn breaks and slightly longer ones in the late evening, making herself inconspicuous by flying low to and from the nest and walking the final stretch back to the nest. Nesting females and young chicks feed heavily on aquatic and terrestrial invertebrates, and they stick together for 4–6 weeks until the chicks start flying in July or August. Females with new chicks have been seen as late as August 31 on Lake Tahoe, but this is exceptional because few breed at such high elevations.

RANGE The core nesting area for Northern Pintails is the Prairie Pothole Region of the northern Great Plains, with huge numbers of migrants and wintering birds moving to the Klamath Basin and Central Valley in the fall and winter. In the Sierra Nevada, they range from being completely absent, to being rare, to being locally common at different times and over different years. These fluid, local movements can obscure the beginning of spring migration, but sometime in March it is obvious that large numbers of pintails are moving through. By the end of April, only breeding birds have been left behind until their numbers pick up again with the arrival of migrants after mid-August. Peak numbers occur in September and October, thereafter declining to a small winter population. **WEST SLOPE:** Wintering birds are present in the single digits or low dozens (rarely into the thousands) on some of the large foothill reservoirs but they are not present every year. In the summer, they are uncommon but confirmed breeders at Isabella Lake; fairly common but not confirmed breeders at Lake Almanor; and unknown as breeders elsewhere. **EAST SLOPE:** Winter status as on west slope though in the south they are rare after early December with single birds or small groups being found less than half the winters. They are common to abundant migrants (particularly in the fall). Dozens breed at Honey Lake and Sierra Valley, but they probably only breed in the single digits at Lake Tahoe, Mono Basin, Lake Crowley, the Owens Valley, and perhaps in other patches of suitable habitat.

GREEN-WINGED TEAL *Anas crecca*

LIFE HISTORY These small teal, the smallest dabbling ducks in North America, are so readily overlooked among groups of their larger cousins that it sometimes takes many minutes of scanning flocks of mixed ducks to find them. This task is a bit easier when males are in their breeding plumage because the green streak on their chestnut heads and the white vertical bar on their sides are such distinctive marks. Green-winged Teal may also gather in conspicuous groups that roam in search of favorable places to feed and roost. They favor shallow water and mudflats where they search for a wide variety of invertebrates and seeds of grasses and rushes, eating whatever items are most readily available.

Although it is far easier to find Green-winged Teal when they are abundant migrants and winter visitors, there is a special thrill in having a pair swim into view when you least expect it, as occasionally happens at open bodies of water and marshes during the summer. At this time, most teal have traveled north to breed in the boreal forests of Canada, but a few find similar sites to breed on the east side of the Sierra Nevada, as in the pairs that have bred on beaver ponds among aspen trees in Lundy Canyon at 8200 ft.

Pairs form while teal are in their winter flocks, so courtship displays begin in October and November then continue into early spring with up to 25 males at a time surrounding a female and trying to woo her by burping, grunting, and tilting their heads up. As in other dabbling ducks, male Green-winged Teal lose interest as soon as females begin incubating their eggs in May.

Females prefer to nest on wooded ponds, thoroughly conceal-ing their nests in nearby meadows or thickets, but on the east side of the Sierra Nevada they may end up breeding in marshes or around the edges of lakes and ponds where there are few trees. Nests are simple scrapes on the ground, but as soon as the first egg is laid, a female will begin pulling vegetation around her to build up a protective rim, and then when the last egg is laid she lines her nest with downy feathers. Females incubate 6–9 eggs for about 22 days, but little is known about the lives of chicks once they hatch.

RANGE   Green-winged Teal are abundant wintering birds in the rela-tively warm Central Valley, but they readily linger on the east side of the Sierra Nevada and in the northern parts of the state because they tolerate all but the most extreme cold weather. Migrants are in transit March–April and September–October, with few remaining to breed in the state. **WEST SLOPE:** Winter visitors and migrants are uncommon at low elevations but their numbers are oddly variable; on Christmas Bird Counts they either show up in single digits or by the hundreds, with few numbers in between, and they are present only one out of ev-ery 3–4 years at any given location. They may be very uncommon to rare breeders but there are few records. **EAST SLOPE:** Often the most abundant ducks during fall migration, first appearing in late August and remaining numerous until October then dwindling in numbers by December. Spring migration begins as soon as ice starts thawing in February, then peaks in March and April. Uncommon nesters in the marshes of Honey Lake and Sierra Valley, with scattered records as far south as Owens Valley.

Redhead *Aythya americana*

LIFE HISTORY   Redheads are the most notorious parasitic ducks in North America, which means that females "dump" eggs in nests that are not their own, both in other Redhead nests and also in the nests of other species of ducks, bitterns, rails, and even Northern Harriers. In fact the sight of a nest with eggs is such a trigger for female Redheads that some "dump nests" accumulate dozens of wasted eggs (the records is 87 eggs in one nest). Females that lay eggs in other nests may or may not end up laying their own clutch, and some females do not parasitize at all. As many as 70 percent of all Redhead nests in some locations are parasitized but the typical percent may be around 50 percent.

Redheads forage in shallow waters, usually less than 3 ft deep, where they dive and feed on the stems, leaves, tubers, and seeds of aquatic plants, as well as on a mix of invertebrates and mollusks. Courtship begins as they mingle in their winter flocks and may continue during migration. Courting birds are aggressive and act nervously with much chasing as males display by kinking their necks, throwing their heads back, and making meowing calls.

Nesting females seek out dense patches of cattails and bulrushes, occasionally nesting in wetlands where the vegetation is so dense there is no open water. A male will wait in nearby open water while his mate checks out potential sites where she will eventually build a solidly woven nest of dry and fresh cattails and bulrushes that is placed over standing water. About half of all nests have a loosely woven roof and two-thirds have a ramp leading into the water. An average clutch is 7–8 eggs but parasitized nests may end up with more. Males leave as soon as the female starts sitting on eggs; incubation lasts 24 days, and then the female leads her newly hatched chicks to water, guarding them another 6–8 weeks until they start flying.

Note: *Larger* **Canvasbacks** *are uncommon to rare migrants and winter visitors, usually seen alone or in small groups on large lakes and reservoirs. Breed only in Sierra Valley.*

RANGE North America's population of nesting Redheads are centered on the Prairie Pothole Region of the northern Great Plains and most Redheads winter along the Gulf of Mexico coast, with fewer numbers wintering along the Pacific coast. Limited numbers breed or winter in the Sierra Nevada; and migration peaks in March–April and September–October. **WEST SLOPE:** Uncommon migrants in the Kern River Valley, where they also breed. Except at Lake Almanor, where they are fairly common migrants and may breed, they are probably uncommon to rare migrants at other low-elevation lakes. Wintering birds number in the single digits to several dozen at some of the large foothill reservoirs, especially at Lake Almanor and at the Thermolito Afterbay in Oroville; but after years of being annual to near-annual visitors in the central and southern Sierra Nevada, they have not been counted on Christmas Bird Counts at Folsom Lake or Isabella Lake for the past 15 years or so. **EAST SLOPE:** Abundant migrants, with fall migrants lingering into December some years. Hundreds at a time may be seen, making them the second most abundant diving duck after the Ruddy Duck. Breeding is centered on the marshes at Honey Lake and Sierra Valley, but they formerly nested at South Lake Tahoe and have at times bred near Mono Lake and in the Owens Valley.

Ring-necked Duck *Aythya collaris*

LIFE HISTORY These perky diving ducks with their distinctively marked bills add a welcome splash of elegance to Sierra Nevada ponds and lakes during the winter. Small numbers may unexpectedly show up on otherwise unremarkable patches of water, and on larger lakes they sometimes gather by the hundreds. Much of their food is gathered during shallow underwater dives, so a group of feeding Ring-necked Ducks is an entertaining sight as they dive and bob to the surface repeatedly. They seek whatever types of seeds and aquatic tubers are most available but will not hesitate to snack on invertebrates, especially during the breeding season when nesting females and growing chicks have higher energy needs.

Ring-necked Ducks prefer shallow wetlands with both floating and submerged plants and abundant patches of emergent vegetation, but on migration and in the winter they readily use large reservoirs that lack these features. In March–April, nearly all of California's abundant wintering population leaves to breed in Canada, but there is an intriguing and growing realization that some remain to nest in the Sierra Nevada. Scattered breeding pairs around Lake Almanor, around Lake Tahoe, and as far south as Meiss Lake near Carson Pass simply hint that others might be discovered in the future. For example, they have bred at Lake Crowley, and there is a steady trickle of summer records from other southern Sierra Nevada lakes where they might breed.

Ring-necked Ducks breed on small wooded ponds or marshes, and in the Sierra Nevada probably move to their breeding sites sometime in May. Males closely guard females as they scout out potential nest sites and build flimsy platforms of bent-over stems in dense sedges or other marsh vegetation, but as soon as females begin incubating their 6–14 eggs, males depart. After 26 days, the chicks hatch and immediately head for open water, where females guard them until they are independent at 50 days of age.

RANGE Ring-necked Ducks are widespread and common in California from mid-September to late April, with some lingering through the summer to breed in the Sierra Nevada and northern California. **WEST SLOPE:** Fall migrants arrive at many sites in October, and through the winter they are found on a wide variety of lakes, ponds, and reservoirs as high as 3000 ft. Some begin heading north in late February but most depart in March–April, with a handful staying to breed in the northern Sierra Nevada. Oddly, at Isabella Lake, in the southern Sierra Nevada, they were common winter visitors until the early 1980s, but in the last

20 years they have only been reported in the single digits on about one of every 4 Christmas Bird Counts. **EAST SLOPE:** Depending on location, they are uncommon to abundant migrants; in northern locations like Lake Tahoe and Sierra Valley, they occur in much higher numbers in spring migration while at southern locations they may be more common in fall migration. In all cases, they are found on both low and mid-elevation lakes, ponds, and marshes, often mingling with other diving ducks like Common Goldeneyes. Breed in the Lake Tahoe Basin and at Meiss Lake, and may breed at Sierra Valley and other locations. Wintering birds seem to be increasingly common from north to south, being found in the single digits at Honey Lake, in the dozens at Lake Tahoe, and into the hundreds around the Owens Valley.

LESSER SCAUP *Aythya affinis*

LIFE HISTORY These gregarious diving ducks may be seen in large numbers, especially at traditional staging areas along their migration routes, and on their wintering grounds. Much of their diet consists of aquatic insects, crustaceans, and mollusks so they are probably restricted to locations rich in these foods. Because they only feed 4–6 hours a day in the winter, they spend most of their time sleeping and loafing in large rafts, often loosely mingling with other ducks.

Nearly all Lesser Scaup in North America breed on lakes in the boreal forests of Canada and Alaska, but there is a small breeding population in southeastern Oregon and northern California's Klamath Basin. The proximity of the Klamath Basin to the northern Sierra Nevada raises the possibility that this species might occasionally breed here, and there are currently nesting records from Honey Lake and Mountain Meadows Reservoir.

Note: *It takes a fine eye to separate out the very similar* **Greater Scaup**, *which are much less common in the Sierra Nevada but should be looked for amidst any group of Lesser Scaup. In the fall and winter, they are occasionally more numerous than the Lesser Scaup at some locations.*

RANGE Common wintering ducks in California, and particularly abundant at places like San Francisco Bay. Spring migrants move northward in March–April and begin returning in late September. **WEST SLOPE:** Widespread but uncommon winter visitors on numerous ponds, lakes, and reservoirs up to at least 4000 ft, with greater numbers showing up during migration. Christmas Bird Counts hint that these uncommon annual visitors have become scarce or absent in the last 10–15 years in the central and southern Sierra Nevada; while at Lake

Almanor in the north their numbers have increased into the hundreds over the same time period. **EAST SLOPE:** Rare winter and uncommon migrants at a wide variety of marshes, lakes, and ponds. Absent during the summer at Sierra Valley and Lake Tahoe but occasionally seen anywhere south of Lake Tahoe as high as 9000 ft. Reported to breed at Honey Lake.

BUFFLEHEAD *Bucephala albeola*

LIFE HISTORY Boldly patterned black-and-white and almost constantly active, Buffleheads are a welcome sight wherever they are found. Popping to the surface like corks then diving again almost immediately, Buffleheads spend their entire day foraging on small lakes and ponds in search of insect larvae, crustaceans, and mollusks. They are the smallest diving ducks in North America so must eat a lot in order to meet their high metabolic needs.

And if they are not feeding, they are probably actively courting or mingling with other Buffleheads. Courtship can be observed at almost any time of the year, consisting of energetic, ritualized displays as males bob their heads rapidly, erect their crests, and lift their wings up and forward. They then fly over a female, landing and "skiing" past her with legs extended to show off their pink feet and flashy plumage.

Nearly the entire population breeds in the boreal forests and aspen woodlands of Canada and Alaska, but since 1996 an increasing number of breeding Buffleheads have been discovered nesting at small mountain lakes in the northern Sierra Nevada. Because pairs may remain together for several years and females often reuse the same nest sites, it is likely that many of these new locations will continue to be used for years to come.

Buffleheads lay 6–11 eggs in tree cavities made by nesting Northern Flickers, and it has been suggested that these ducks evolved to be the smallest duck so they could use abundant woodpecker cavities that larger cavity-nesting ducks cannot fit into. Although Buffleheads rarely leave the water, females are able to cling to branches and tree trunks while searching for suitable cavities. Due to their small size, females may take up to 3 days between each egg they lay (an unusually slow laying rate), and as soon as they start incubating, the male leaves. Eggs hatch in 30 days, and by late June females begin leading newly hatched chicks to the nearest water. Females remain with their ducklings for 3–6 weeks but abandon them before they can fly.

RANGE Uncommon to common wintering ducks in California, with all except for a few breeding pairs leaving the state in March–April and reappearing in late October. In the Sierra Nevada, they may be seen on all types of small wooded ponds and large, open lakes up to 9000 ft, and since they are surprisingly hardy, they are little fazed except by the fiercest snow and ice. Breeding has been reported at more than a dozen sites including the Lake Almanor area, the Lakes Basin, Henness Pass, Loch Leven Lakes, the south Lake Tahoe Basin, Red Lake on Hwy 88, and others. **WEST SLOPE:** Buffleheads are a particularly delightful presence during the winter when they are often the only ducks found on thousands of tiny rural ponds scattered throughout the Sierra Nevada foothills. Many remain through the entire winter, but there may be some local movement between ponds or to larger reservoirs and rivers. **EAST SLOPE:** Smaller numbers winter on the east side, varying each year from the single digits to the hundreds on different Christmas Bird Counts though there has been a notable increase in numbers on the Bishop count in the last 15 years. Abundant migrants, but they have intriguing patterns like being more abundant at Lake Tahoe in the spring, versus more abundant in the fall at nearby Sierra Valley.

Common Goldeneye *Bucephala clangula*

LIFE HISTORY These hardy visitors tend to fly quickly over much of inland California heading to productive coastal bays and estuaries where they spend the winter diving for shellfish and fish in shallow waters along mudflats. They are common in the Sierra Nevada all winter, but it would be hard to tell if individual birds linger or whether there is a constant shuffling of late-arriving migrants in the fall and early-departing migrants in the spring. It is unlikely that ponds and lakes in the Sierra Nevada offer an adequate supply of the rich food they need for their long migration and breeding season.

Note: Barrow's Goldeneyes *formerly bred at a handful of high-elevation lakes as far south as Fresno County, including at Lake Tahoe, but are now far less common and eagerly looked for in the Sierra Nevada. They have the same basic life history and range as Common Goldeneyes and the two species are often found together.*

RANGE Common Goldeneyes occur in California only as a wintering bird with the entire population heading north in mid-March to April to breed in the boreal forests of northern Canada and Alaska. Most winter on the coast and must migrate north over the northern end of the Sierra Nevada because spring migrants are rarely observed in the south. They are one of California's scarcest ducks in the summer. In the fall, they arrive fairly late with an influx of juveniles in late October, but the majority of the population heads south only as northern lakes begin to freeze in November and December. **WEST SLOPE:** Fairly common winter visitors below 3000 ft, appearing on both large and small bodies of water. Rare migrants in the southern end of the range, but fairly common migrants elsewhere. **EAST SLOPE:** After the big push of fall migrants arrives in early November, goldeneyes linger through the winter; they are generally common but their numbers decrease in proportion to the degree of cold. It may be a sign of warmer temperatures that in the past 15 years their numbers have increased on both the Honey Lake and Bishop Christmas Bird Counts, and they are now annual where they were once only present every couple years.

HOODED MERGANSER *Lophodytes cucullatus*

LIFE HISTORY Sadly, these stunning little ducks breed and winter in the Pacific Northwest and are only relatively uncommon visitors to California. With their perky crests, flashy colors, and odd little bills, they are a surprising and lovely sight, but they are skittish and it is difficult to approach and get a good look at them. Their preferred habitats are wooded ponds, where they readily hide in the vegetation or fly off with a noisy commotion, but overwintering and migrating birds may be found on larger open bodies of water mixed with other ducks. Hooded Mergansers are expert divers, readily catching fish, insects, and crayfish. They have an ability to alter the refractive properties of their eyes during a dive, so it is believed they have excellent underwater vision.

Courtship behavior may be observed in the winter but the specific timing of their pair bonding is unknown. Males have energetic and entertaining courtship displays that include raising their crests, pumping their heads, and flipping their heads back with their bills pointing up. Hooded Mergansers nest in tree cavities and females scout out potential nest sites the year before, returning to the same locations the following year to use the cavities that catch their eye. Like other cavity-nesting ducks, they are brood parasites, and Hooded Mergansers, Common Mergansers, and Wood Ducks regularly lay eggs in each other's nests.

Females add some downy feathers to the tree cavity but otherwise make no modifications before they begin laying eggs. Their clutch size is unknown, and the vague estimate that they incubate their eggs for 26–41 days simply reflects our limited knowledge of this species. When eggs hatch, the female first scopes out the surrounding area then gives her chicks the all-clear signal that they should climb out of the nest, jump to the ground, and follow her to the nearest water. Chicks start diving and feeding themselves right away; however, it is not known how long the female stays with them.

RANGE Most wintering Hooded Mergansers congregate in the northern half of California, first arriving in mid-October then leaving by late April; some begin moving northward in late February, but peak migration occurs March–early April. There are scattered, and perhaps an increasing number of, breeding records south to about Lake Tahoe, but only a couple of nesting pairs are discovered each year. **WEST SLOPE:** Uncommon migrants and winter visitors, thinly dispersed below 4000 feet, with single birds or pairs (rarely larger groups) found on many types of forested wetlands, small rural ponds, rivers, and larger reservoirs. Most common in the north, where up to 400 have been found at Lake Almanor in mid-winter and 280 in early March. Once rare in the southern Sierra Nevada, they have become annual visitors in small numbers over the past 10 years. **EAST SLOPE:** Although generally rare and not present every year on the east side, they are annual and locally common winter visitors (averaging 1–2 dozen birds) at South Lake Tahoe starting in mid-October and in the Owens Valley by late October. Many of the ones in the Owens Valley may leave by December because they are found on less than half of the Bishop Christmas Bird Counts, but the ones at Tahoe seem to linger through the winter nearly every year. Other than at Lake Tahoe, where a pulse of migrants appears in March–early April, they seem to be rare spring migrants with only a few scattered records in early March.

COMMON MERGANSER *Mergus merganser*

LIFE HISTORY Although most ducks lead lives peripheral to the Sierra Nevada, either wintering in adjacent lowlands or merely passing overhead in migration, Common Mergansers are one of the few ducks that personify the mountain landscape. Lonely males, pairs, and females with their young are all familiar sights to anyone who spends time in the mountains, and these are the ducks most likely seen on wilderness backpacking trips, river-rafting expeditions, and family campouts around mountain lakes. On the water they present a streamlined, low-slung profile, while in flight they shoot up and down river canyons like sleek arrows.

After the breeding season, they are anything but solitary mountaineers, for they readily gather by the hundreds or even thousands on large lakes and rivers in the foothills. In groups, they preen and bathe at the same time, and when feeding they use a "follow-the-leader" technique, diving and coming to the surface in quick succession like falling dominoes. The serrated edges on their long, narrow bills help them grab and swallow fish up to a foot long, but they just as readily eat insects, mollusks, frogs, small mammals, and birds.

Common Mergansers are remarkably hardy birds that linger on cold mountain lakes late in the winter then push back into their breeding habitats even before the snow and ice melts. Males precede females by several weeks, which is noticeable because they have such dramatically different plumages. Courtship begins as soon as females arrive, with several males courting one or more females at the same time.

Females typically nest in tree cavities such as old Pileated Woodpecker holes, but they also nest on the ground or in rock crevices, and readily use nest boxes. They usually return to the nest they used the year before, but they continually keep an eye out for other potential future nest sites while raising their chicks. Nests may be modified somewhat with the addition of nesting material, and they incubate their 9–12 eggs for 32 days. Females call newly hatched chicks out of the nest and lead them to water, which can be nearly a mile away, where the chicks feed on aquatic invertebrates until they start catching their own fish at 12 days old. Females increasingly lead their broods downstream towards larger rivers and lakes but abandon them in 1–7 weeks, well before the chicks start flying at 60–75 days old. There is a remarkable range of nesting dates in the Sierra Nevada (even at the same locations), females with young chicks being seen from late May to late August.

Note: *It is not easy to distinguish similar* **Red-breasted Mergansers**, *but they are uncommon migrants and winter visitors to the Sierra Nevada, especially on the east side and most consistently at Lake Tahoe.*

RANGE Common Mergansers are found on forested lakes and rivers throughout the Northern Hemisphere, and in North America they winter further north than almost any other duck. Common during all seasons in the Sierra Nevada with so much overlap in their breeding and wintering ranges that it is hard to tell whether our local populations simply shift around with the seasons or whether there are separate wintering and migrating populations as well. In the spring, there seems to be no particular peak movement, with males and females gathering and shifting constantly as they begin nesting at lower elevations in mid-April or wait until mountain lakes thaw in May or June (some may wait to begin nesting until early July). Fall migration is slightly more obvious, at least on the east side, where numbers pick up noticeably in late October then drop off significantly by the end of December. **WEST SLOPE:** Common but widely dispersed breeders on lakes and rivers to 7000 ft. Large numbers begin to accumulate on foothill lakes and reservoirs in mid-November and as many as 5000 have been counted at Isabella Lake in late winter, with dozens to hundreds appearing on other large bodies of water. **EAST SLOPE:** Not very common during the breeding season due to the relative scarcity of larger rivers and wooded lakes on the steeper, more rugged east side. Large numbers stage on Lake Tahoe by mid-April, perhaps waiting for breeding sites in the higher mountains to thaw out; for example, a few hardy pairs were observed in nearby Coldstream Canyon as soon as snow started to melt in early May. They appear in large numbers at lakes, rivers, and reservoirs all along the east side by mid-October and remain common until departing in December. Relatively scarce and irregular in winter, usually in small numbers and absent some years.

Ruddy Duck *Oxyura jamaicensis*

LIFE HISTORY The first time you see male Ruddy Ducks in the breeding season you might think there is something wrong with their bills because that sky-blue color looks fake. But then, little is average about these odd, perky ducks. Males first arrive on their breeding grounds in late March still wearing their bland gray winter plumage (they are one of the only ducks to have separate winter and summer plumages), and must wait until they molt into their startling breeding colors before they can court newly arriving females. Their courtship is one of the most comical bird behaviors in the Sierra Nevada. Males puff themselves up, lift their crowns and tails, beat their bills against their necks faster and faster until they are sitting in a mass of bubbles, then wrap things up by burping. Even though pair bonds may only last a few days or weeks, males are astonishingly pugnacious on their breeding grounds, aggressively chasing away other Ruddy Ducks and even animals coming to the water to drink.

Three to 5 weeks after arriving, females build ill-formed nesting platforms of dead or green stems amid dense stands of tall cattails and bulrushes. Then as their 7–9 eggs are laid, they progressively reinforce the nest structure, keeping its location secret by approaching underwater then surfacing next to the well-hidden nest. Eggs are the largest relative to the body size of any duck, and take so much energy to produce that when females begin egg-laying one-third of their body weight is fat. Egg-laying peaks in mid-June and most broods hatch in mid-July to early August. Females abandon their chicks when they are 3 weeks old, well before they can fly at 7–8 weeks of age. A small percentage of females lay some eggs in the nests of other marsh birds.

Although these specialized diving ducks have a harder time walking on land than any other duck and must lie on their bellies while pushing themselves along with their legs, females still frequently lead ducklings over land to reach new feeding ponds. Ruddy Ducks feed by diving underwater then sweeping their heads back and forth in the mud while rapidly opening and closing their bills to sift out aquatic invertebrates. Their primary foods are midge larvae, but they consume other invertebrates and some plant materials.

RANGE Both breeding and wintering Ruddy Ducks are widespread in western North America and common in the Sierra Nevada. **WEST SLOPE:** Fairly common at low-elevation lakes and reservoirs, first arriving in September then lingering until March–April. Groups of hundreds and even thousands (up to 8000 have been reported at Lake Almanor) are possible at the lowest elevations but numbers drop off quickly above 2000–3000 ft. Winter numbers have decreased dramatically at Isabella Lake over the past 20 years (where they are rare breeders) but seem stable elsewhere. **EAST SLOPE:** Large numbers begin arriving in late August and remain by the hundreds or thousands until November, then linger in variable numbers through winter until spring migrants begin streaming back in late March. Wintering totals often reach the hundreds at Honey Lake, Mono Lake, and Owens Valley. Breeding birds are common at Honey Lake and Sierra Valley, and they have nested in much smaller numbers at South Lake Tahoe, Bridgeport Reservoir, and Mono Lake.

NEW WORLD QUAIL (Odontophoridae)

MOUNTAIN QUAIL *Oreortyx pictus*

LIFE HISTORY These hardy mountaineers are one of the Sierra Nevada's most iconic birds and while everything about them is enchanting and evocative, woe to the observer who harbors a desire to see one. During the breeding season their loud calls ring out from brushy slopes but from a hundred yards away you can hear the furious scurrying of little feet if you dare approach closer. A reasonable rule of thumb when trying to identify fleeing quail is if they wait until you get close then they are California Quail, but if they scatter while you are still at a distance, then they are Mountain Quail.

Their elusive nature and fondness for dense brush means that much of what we know about their biology and seasonal migrations is purely speculative. Although details are slim, it is clear that Mountain Quail spend their winters in brushy thickets on the lower foothill slopes. Coveys of a dozen or so quail stay well hidden and reluctantly venture across small openings in their constant search for food. Throughout the year they specialize on the seeds, fruits, and flowers of perennial plants, but they also dig up bulbs, eat acorns in the fall, snack on mushrooms in the winter, and occasionally grab insects.

There are numerous records of calling males as low as 1000 ft, and some may breed at low elevations, but as soon as the snow starts melting at higher elevations, nearly all pairs and single birds begin pushing upslope as quickly as they can. Their growing excitement is transmitted through the far-carrying *quee-ark* calls of males, which begin in earnest in April and reach a crescendo in May and June. These calls serve as advertisements of the male's presence and readiness to breed, but they also function to strengthen pair bonds with males continuing to call until chicks hatch.

Both sexes apparently contribute to the nesting process, and it is thought that males may sometimes incubate one set of eggs at the same time as their mates lay and incubate another set of eggs. There is scant data, but 6–14 eggs may be a typical clutch and eggs hatch in about 24 days. Some eggs hatch in April at lower elevations, but most hatch in June or early July at higher elevations.

In early September, families become restless and either start heading downslope right away or else linger into late October (exceptionally into early November) before making this journey. It has been said that they walk downslope to their wintering grounds rather than flying, but this has never been verified. Winters are spent below the snow line.

RANGE Mountain Quail are restricted to mountainous terrain from Washington to Baja California, and are fairly common residents along the entire length of the Sierra Nevada. **WEST SLOPE:** Typically found among manzanita and ceanothus brushfields below 4000 ft in the winter, then move upslope into montane chaparral during the breeding season. Calling males have been heard from 1000–9000 ft but it is not clear whether these are the actual limits of their breeding range. **EAST SLOPE:** Breed from 7000–10,000 ft in the southern Sierra Nevada but at lower elevations in the north. It is thought that breeding birds cross the crest to spend the winter on the lower west slope, but scattered records from the lower east slope and adjacent desert hills suggest that at least some groups overwinter on the east side.

CALIFORNIA QUAIL *Callipepla californica*

LIFE HISTORY California Quail are one of the most diagnostic birds of foothill oak woodlands on the lower west slope, where their ringing *chi-CA-go* calls can be a very common sound. These distinctive calls help members of a covey find each other when they get separated in dense brush and tall grasses, which seems to be fairly often judging from their frequent calls. Coveys of 12 to 50 or more quail start gathering in August after the breeding season winds down (in the southern Sierra Nevada their breeding season must start much earlier because coveys can be found in June). These flocks then stay together for safety through the fall and winter, sticking closely to any habitat with significant amounts of scattered brush thickets mixed with grassy clearings. They even frequent rural neighborhoods, city parks, and adjoining patches of undisturbed habitat, and may become daily visitors to backyard bird feeders along with juncos and mourning doves. They regularly feed in open areas but need nearby thickets for roosting, resting, and escape. Much of their diet consists of seeds, leaves, flowers, berries, and grains, with some insects; but acorns can be one of their primary food items in the fall and winter. Feeding lasts for an hour right after sunrise, then picks up again half an hour before sunset so that the quail can go to sleep at night with full crops.

Coveys begin breaking up in February–March, with pairs first splitting off from the flock then initiating nest-building a month later. Males typically advertise for mates with a prolonged version of the final *goo* note of their winter calls. Their 1–28 eggs are laid in April–May, some as late as mid-July, in a well-concealed ground nest lined with dry grasses. Females incubate for 22 days with males standing guard nearby, and after the eggs hatch males continue to act as lookouts while females protect the precocial chicks and guide them to food sources with soft calls. Females occasionally hand newly hatched chicks off to the male then lay another clutch with a new male. Coveys reassemble as soon as chicks near adult size.

RANGE California Quail are widespread and common birds in low-lying areas west of the Sierra Nevada. Their range is greatly limited east of the Sierra Nevada due to their intolerance for deep snow, but one unique subspecies is found in the White Mountains and from Benton south through the Owens Valley. **WEST SLOPE:** Common residents below 2000 ft, but occasionally found as high as 4000 ft. Populations may be locally abundant, and they are always found within walking distance of drinking water. **EAST SLOPE:** Intermittently introduced as game birds east of the crest, making it hard to tell if quail in any given location are introduced or naturally occurring; many introduced populations simply die out in the harsh winters but pockets of quail are still found in many areas. Quail south of Mono Lake could be a desert subspecies that periodically reaches the Sierra Nevada foothills. Uncommon summer visitors to the Tahoe Basin but in the winter they disappear. Uncommon, but locally abundant further north.

GROUSE and ALLIES (Phasianidae)

CHUKAR *Alectoris chukar*

LIFE HISTORY The introduction of these stocky, colorful Himalayan game birds has been successful enough that Chukars now persist on both slopes of the Sierra Nevada. Although continually successful in some locations, their exact distribution is somewhat uncertain because large numbers die off after cold winters and because they continue to be released in new areas. First introduced to California in 1932, and in Inyo County in the mid-1930s, Chukars have thrived because so many arid areas had already been overrun by an invasive Himalayan weed called cheatgrass, which just so happens to be the Chukar's favorite food.

It still takes a lot of work, or a bit of luck, to find Chukars. They are heavily hunted, live high on remote, rocky slopes, and are extremely wary. You are more likely to hear their alarm calls, loud piercing squeals *whitoo whitoo*, or the namesake contact calls that keep flocks together, rising *chuck-chuck-chuck* notes that turn into *per-chuck* then loud *chuck-ar* and *chuckara* calls. When alarmed they run uphill, and if pressed further they escape by flying downhill and arcing off around the hillside at great speed.

Pair formation occurs in mid-March with eggs being laid in April, but females renest if their first brood is lost so new chicks may be seen in late August. Very few nests have been found, but they are simple depressions in the ground lined with dry grasses and a few feathers. Males remain through all phases of nesting, but it is believed they do not help the female. Based on limited data it is thought that 10–21 eggs are a normal clutch with the female incubating 24 days. Chicks take care of themselves, being able to fly within two weeks, reaching 50 percent of adult size in 40 days, and reaching adult size in just over 70 days. Families stick together until they split up to find mates the following spring.

One or more family units form the nucleus of winter coveys that wander dry, rocky hillsides during the day, ducking into sheltering ravines when the weather is windy or moving onto south-facing hillsides when cold or snowy, but always staying close to a dependable source of drinking water. Their preferred foods are tender, green grass shoots, but they also eat dry grasses, seeds, and insects (which are mainly eaten by young birds).

RANGE Populations of introduced Chukars have been most successful in the Great Basin, including desert slopes mere miles from the Sierra Nevada, but they are only marginally successful here. **WEST SLOPE:** Best known from the foothills of the southern Sierra Nevada but they are occasionally reported north of Fresno County. Widespread in Kern County, from desert slopes to the higher elevations of the Kern Plateau. **EAST SLOPE:** Found on the east side, up to about 7000 ft, from Tehachapi Pass to at least Mono Lake, then north from Reno to Susanville.

Sooty Grouse *Dendragapus fuliginosus*

LIFE HISTORY Sooty Grouse may be fairly common in the sprawling mixed conifer and red fir forests of the Sierra Nevada, but it is difficult to tell for sure because they stay incredibly well hidden. The only good time to detect them is from April to late June when males give eerie, booming calls that resonate all day through the somber forests. Their calls are ventriloquial and deep in pitch, sounding somewhat like someone thumping on a waterlogged tub in the distance. They usually call from big branches in the upper third of large, prominent conifers but they do not move and blend in perfectly. You might have better luck finding females with chicks (one of the easiest and most dependable spots to find them in the Sierra Nevada is next to the concession stand at Glacier Point, in Yosemite National Park, in mid-July).

Sooty Grouse have very complex seasonal movements that have not been well documented in the Sierra Nevada. Even the limits of their breeding range are not clearly understood because booming males have been recorded from 4600 ft to over 9000 ft, but that does not mean this is where they are finding females; and females with broods start moving upslope soon after the chicks hatch, so scattered records of females with chicks of unknown ages have not helped advance our knowledge of this species.

It seems likely that most breeding occurs between 4000 ft and 8000 ft, with males heading upslope as soon as they have finished breeding, and females with their broods following soon after. Late summer and early autumn are spent in open subalpine forests and montane meadows (one female with chicks was found at 10,800 ft) gorging on a steady diet of berries, fruits, and insects. With the first snows they retreat downslope into dense conifer stands and spend the winter eating the tips of conifer needles. Then in late March to early April males begin booming, mating with as many females as they can attract with their distinct calls.

Nesting females make a simple scrape on the ground, loosely lined with bits of vegetation and usually placed under the cover of some overhanging branches or objects. Females incubate 2–10 eggs for about 26 days with only a few breaks each day. Chicks are very mobile and can start flying in 8 days; they feed themselves while the female stands guard and flushes up angrily if an intruder approaches.

Note: *Alpine meadows of the central Sierra Nevada are home to introduced* **White-tailed Ptarmigans,** *separable from grouse by the white feathers on their legs, wings, and tails. First released at Mono County's Twin Lakes in 1971–72, they have since colonized scattered high peaks and passes from Carson Pass in the north to Pine Creek Pass in the south. They should be looked for around boulders in alpine meadows, particularly on north-facing slopes where grasses and forbs grow more luxuriantly.*

RANGE Fairly common residents in a narrow band of mid- to high-elevation forests on both slopes of the Sierra Nevada (with a distinct subspecies formerly found in forests of the Piute Mountains). **WEST SLOPE:** Reported as low as Yosemite Valley (4000 ft) and regularly heard and seen by hikers in Yosemite National Park, particularly around subalpine meadows in late summer. Southern limit of its known range is Sunday Peak in the Greenhorn Mountains. **EAST SLOPE:** Males may be heard calling in many types of mixed conifer forests, from dense forests in the northern half of the range to isolated pockets of trees on open, rocky slopes in the south.

Wild Turkey *Meleagris gallopavo*

LIFE HISTORY In a way it is a shame that Wild Turkeys are not native to the Sierra Nevada because they are such a colorful and dynamic presence. They are wily and evasive birds when hunted, but in the absence of hunting pressure they become as fearless as backyard chickens, wandering among neighborhoods, city parks, and grassy roadsides with all their quirky and complex behaviors in full view. First introduced to California in 1908, large flocks of foraging turkeys are now a prominent sight among low-elevation woodlands and grasslands almost everywhere on the west slope.

Flocks are first noticed in late summer as females with their broods of growing chicks increasingly gather into groups that may reach 200 birds by the fall. In late fall–early winter, older and younger males wander off to form separate male flocks of 1–10 birds. The breeding season begins in early March when flocks of males start giving loud gobbling calls to attract distant females and also to challenge other nearby male flocks. Both sexes develop elaborate dominance hierarchies; the hierarchies within female flocks are highly stable while those within male flocks are constantly shifting. Not only do males develop hierarchies within each flock, but each male flock acts together as a unit to form hierarchies in relationship to other neighboring flocks.

By April, female winter flocks break up into smaller breeding harems that will be constantly attended and courted by multiple males until every female has bred and departed to build an isolated nest. Courting males can be noisy and conspicuous from April to June. The bare fleshy parts (the "snood") on the faces of dominant males become inflamed with brilliant reds, blues, and whites that change color as males droop their wings to the ground, broadly fan their tails, ruffle out all their feathers, and pull their heads back to emphasize their snoods. While making these flamboyant displays, males strut stiffly back and forth past the females making odd thrumming sounds, loudly rustling their feathers, and making false charges at each other. However, females tend to look disinterested and even bored by this entire routine.

Nests are shallow scrapes in the soil among dense brush. Females incubate their 4–13 eggs about 26 days, and raise their young chicks in isolation until they join up with other females and their broods as the summer progresses.

Flocks of turkeys forage in loose groups in the morning and then again for a few hours in the afternoon until they fly to their nighttime roosts in large trees. All feeding is done on the ground, where they scratch in a distinctive 1-2-1 rhythm with their strong legs and claws. They kick aside leaf litter to expose acorns, seeds, fruits, insects, and a wide variety of small vertebrates. They consume an enormous quantity of acorns as well as every large insect, lizard, and small snake they can catch. Each large turkey is reported to eat one pound of food per meal, and the widespread introduction of these birds to the Sierra Nevada must have a huge ecological impact.

RANGE The distribution of Wild Turkeys in the Sierra Nevada is due to numerous introductions and the subsequent spread of these highly successful birds. They are now widespread almost everywhere in the lower foothills of the west slope, though they are relatively scarce in the more arid southern foothills and scarce but increasingly abundant at higher elevations. On the east slope a few smaller populations seem to gaining footholds around Quincy, Loyalton, and Markleeville, while hunters regularly lobby for the California Department of Fish and Game to introduce them at additional locations.

LOONS (Gaviidae)

COMMON LOON *Gavia immer*

LIFE HISTORY Heavy bodied and low slung, loons are awkward and helpless on land but masters of their aquatic kingdoms. With their large-lobed feet set to the rear of their bodies to provide them with powerful swimming strokes, loons have skeletons and muscles highly adapted for the fast, agile underwater pursuit of the fish that comprise the primary portion of their diets. Loons only occur on large bodies of water because their high wing-loading (narrow wings on a big heavy body) means that they need up to 600 ft of open water for a long running start in order to get airborne. Here they hunt for fish in relatively shallow waters (usually less than 15 ft deep) near shorelines and sleep on the open water at night. Loons find their prey by peering underwater while swimming at the surface, then diving in quick pursuit when they spot some food. In the absence of fish, they prey on crayfish and mollusks, completely crushing both bones and shells in their large, muscular gizzards. Loons have a hard time catching trout and salmon, so they specialize on slow-moving fish like bluegills.

> **Note:** *Slightly smaller and slimmer* **Pacific** **Loons** *are occasionally observed on large bodies of water, mainly in fall, winter, and spring.*

RANGE North America's sizable population of Common Loons breeds on freshwater lakes north of the Canadian border then winters along ocean shores. Most loons migrate both north and south along the coast, but significant numbers also fly across the interior of western

North America and may stop at almost any large freshwater lake, reservoir, or river. In particular, look for migrants on windy days when they seek out bodies of water to avoid fighting the wind. Spring migration is a headlong rush that starts with a trickle in early April then peaks from mid-April to mid-May, with scattered individuals lingering through the summer (principally immature birds that do not breed until they are a couple years old). Fall migration is protracted, stretching from mid-September into December, with most loons passing through the region after mid-October and then remaining on local lakes and reservoirs (as high as the Sierra Nevada crest) until freezing temperatures and storms arrive in December. **WEST SLOPE:** Uncommon during migration, with individual loons occasionally reported in the summer. Possible on any large body of water, though likely to linger only where there are sufficient numbers of fish to eat. Numbers are variable in winter, but a dozen or more loons have been observed on some of the large, low-elevation reservoirs. **EAST SLOPE:** Uncommon to fairly common during migration, but more are found here than on the west slope because Great Basin lakes east of the Sierra Nevada seem to be part of a major loon migration route. One of the best places to see them is at Lake Tahoe in April. Rarely reported on the east side during the summer, and irregular during the winter (single birds present some years but not in others).

GREBES (Podicipedidae)

PIED-BILLED GREBE *Podilymbus podiceps*

LIFE HISTORY These stocky, dusky grebes are a solitary presence on smaller ponds and sloughs, often lurking just out of sight behind cattails and bulrushes. When startled on open water, Pied-billed Grebes may dive with a big splash or sink slowly out of sight so only their eyes and nostrils remain above the surface. During the breeding season, pairs are aggressive and highly territorial, chasing away other grebes and ducks by diving and attacking the intruder's feet from below. Pairs are more easily heard than seen, as they produce a variety of loud yelping *caow* and *wup* notes from the midst of marshes.

There is a significant movement towards larger bodies of water in the winter, but pairs may remain on their territories year round if the water does not freeze and enough food is available. The grebe's stout bill and strong jaw muscles are particularly well adapted for crushing the shells of crustaceans, but they are opportunistic and will eat any fish, frogs, and invertebrates they can catch under or above water (they will even snatch insects in mid-air).

Newly arriving grebes quickly pair up and noisily begin to build floating platform nests made from both freshly clipped and wet, rotting stems of larger marsh plants. Both parents work together on all aspects of nest-building and the care of eggs and chicks. An average of 6 eggs are laid, with some of the first eggs partially submerged in water at the bottom of the waterlogged nest (their eggs are extraordinarily porous so that water drains out of the shell). Incubation lasts 3–4 weeks, with parents leaving the nest in the daytime and letting the heat of decomposing nest materials keep the eggs warm. Within an hour of hatching, zebra-striped chicks clamber onto their parent's back where they hide among the warm feathers for the first week of their life. In their second week they begin to sprout unruly tufts of gray feathers and start to venture out on their first attempts to feed themselves. Soon thereafter, parents split the brood, with each parent caring for half of the brood until the chicks are independent at 1–2 months of age (though the parents may start a second nesting effort at the same time).

RANGE Pied-billed Grebes are widespread in North America and year-round residents everywhere in California except the high mountains. In the Sierra Nevada, spring migration (mid-March to mid-April) is obscured by the presence of resident birds though single birds or pairs might appear on formerly unoccupied ponds. During the breeding season they are thinly dispersed on isolated ponds or marshes below 6000 ft. At some locations, fall migration is obvious with large numbers occurring October through mid-November; individual postbreeding birds very rarely wander as high as 9000 ft. In the winter they are regular visitors to large bodies of water, and rare on small bodies of water. **WEST SLOPE:** According to Christmas Bird Count data, Pied-billed Grebes are fairly common below 4000 ft in the winter, with numerous counts reporting over 100 grebes each year. Scarcely reported during the summer, but breeding pairs likely occupy many of the region's small ponds and marshes. **EAST SLOPE:** Here the situation seems reversed. In the winter they are rare and irregular (not seen every year) on large bodies of water north of Mono Lake, and regular but in very small numbers from Bishop south. They seem fairly common in the breeding season, but they are primarily concentrated in the large marsh systems that occur along the base of the east slope.

Horned Grebe *Podiceps auritus*

LIFE HISTORY These winter visitors are fairly rare in the Sierra Nevada and occur in such low numbers that it is difficult to summarize their seasonal patterns here. They are nearly always observed on large bodies of water, often at such great distances they can be difficult to identify. They are usually alone, but have reached exceptional numbers at Lake Almanor (with up to 510 reported during Christmas Bird Counts). Horned Grebes forage in moderately shallow water up to 15 ft deep and probably specialize on bottom-dwelling crustaceans and invertebrates over the winter, though they also eat frogs and fish. Some may pair up during winter, but it is rare to see them in their breeding plumage or to witness their courtship behavior.

RANGE Horned Grebes breed on freshwater lakes across interior Canada, but winter along the coasts of North America. Fall migrants and winter visitors are uncommon in the Sierra Nevada, while only a few have been seen in the spring or summer. Nearly all records are from late September to late April, with most sightings in October and November. **WEST SLOPE:** Single birds or very small groups have been reported from a wide variety of low to mid-elevation lakes and reservoirs in the fall to early winter. In the winter they are scarce visitors in the southern Sierra Nevada, uncommon in the central Sierra, and fairly common in the northern Sierra (at least at Lake Almanor); though in all locations their numbers fluctuate from year to year. **EAST SLOPE:** It takes a lot of work but a diligent observer might pick out a few Horned Grebes among the million or so Eared Grebes that gather on Mono Lake each fall. They likewise appear in small numbers on other large lakes and reservoirs but with few exceptions they leave the region by mid-December. Up to a dozen may remain at Lake Tahoe but this happens about once every 5–6 years.

Eared Grebe *Podiceps nigricollis*

LIFE HISTORY These are the most abundant grebes in the world, and if you need proof then check out the annual gathering of over 1 million Eared Grebes on Mono Lake. This event has been given many superlatives, but visitors have described seeing so many birds that they could imagine hopping across the lake on the backs of grebes. Each fall, Eared Grebes gather here to feed on the lake's immense population of brine flies and brine shrimp, with each bird eating an estimated 8000–70,000 shrimp a day and becoming so fat they cannot fly. So important is this food source that Eared Grebes fly to Mono Lake as soon as they are done breeding, arriving from as far away as Canada, and stay on the lake from late July until the first storms push them further south, typically in late November. They molt their flight feathers and remain flightless for 3–4 months, growing new feathers in time for their journey to the Salton Sea where 2.5–3 million Eared Grebes spend the winter.

Most Eared Grebes breed on freshwater lakes and ponds of western North America to the east and north of California, but small numbers breed in suitable habitats along the eastern base of the Sierra Nevada. In particular they favor shallow waters with abundant emergent vegetation adjacent to large lakes and reservoirs. These remarkably gregarious grebes nest in colonies, sometimes by the hundreds or thousands. From late May into early July, both members of a pair cooperate to build nests, incubate eggs, and care for their young. Nests are flimsy and formed by bending over plant stems and heaping up pieces of decaying plants into sodden mounds. The 3–4 eggs sit in a puddle of cold water and hatch 3 weeks later.

Parents take turns carrying newly hatched chicks on their backs while the other parent collects aquatic invertebrates to feed the chicks. Parents split the brood (usually there are only two chicks remaining by this time) when the chicks are 10 days old and provide care for another 10 days until they abandon the chicks and fly to Mono Lake. The lives of immature Eared Grebes have not been studied, but they also head for Mono Lake as soon as they can fly.

RANGE Except for the phenomenal gathering at Mono Lake each fall, Eared Grebes are relatively sporadic and unpredictable in the Sierra Nevada. Small numbers breed in the region, becoming locally abundant around their breeding colonies. But on any given lake, migrants and winter visitors may occur in the single digits one year and in the thousands the next. Postbreeding visitors very rarely show up on small lakes near the Sierra Nevada crest, with several records near 12,000 ft. Spring migration begins in late March and extends into mid-May while fall migration abruptly begins in late July and continues into November. **WEST SLOPE:** Irregular fall, winter, and spring visitors to a wide variety of lakes and reservoirs, except at Lake Almanor, where they are fairly common breeders and may reside in high numbers year round. **EAST SLOPE:** Small breeding colonies occur in suitable habitat at Lake Crowley, Bridgeport Reservoir, Lake Tahoe, Sierra Valley, and a few other locations. Although the vast bulk of the population heads to Mono Lake from late July to late November, then continues south to the Salton Sea for the winter. Small numbers may stay behind at Mono Lake, Lake Tahoe, and other large lakes that do not freeze. Likewise, an estimated 25,000–30,000 nonbreeding grebes spend the summer at Mono Lake.

WESTERN GREBE *Aechmophorus occidentalis*

LIFE HISTORY Populations of these large, elegant grebes were hunted heavily in the late 1800s for their valuable breast feathers, then suffered from the effects of DDT in the mid-1900s, and today find their lakeside nesting sites impacted by recreational boat traffic. Although still common, they now breed in limited numbers in the Sierra Nevada.

In all seasons, Western Grebes favor large, open bodies of water. Nonbreeding, migrating, and wintering birds will loosely gather on open water far from shore, often sleeping with their heads tucked back into their shoulder feathers, while breeding birds spend much of their time in and near stands of emergent vegetation along remote stretches of shoreline. These expert hunters use their long, thin bills to catch fish, and they have a unique cocking mechanism in their necks that helps them spear fish with lightning speed. Like all grebes they keep their stomachs more than half full with feathers, perhaps as insulation against the sharp fish bones in their diets.

During the breeding season Western Grebes draw attention to themselves by giving loud, rasping calls day and night, creating one of the most distinctive summer sounds around the lakes where they breed. As if that was not enough, they perform some of the most flamboyant and complex courtship rituals in the bird world. Displays include a "weed dance," during which members of a pair hold wet vegetation in their bills and rise up out of the water so their bellies meet; and their famous "water dance," in which pairs of birds run upright and side by side for 50–100 ft with their feet madly churning like roaring motorboats. Partly because their courtship rituals are so complex and their care of young so extended, they have a fairly lengthy breeding season lasting from about May into August.

Their floating platform nests are solidly built of green and decaying aquatic vegetation and are located in a loose colony with other Western Grebes amid emergent rushes and aquatic plants. Both sexes cooperate in all aspects of nest-building, incubation, and care of young; and unlike other grebes they rarely leave their nests unattended. After the 3–4 eggs hatch, the chicks clamber onto their parents' backs where they remain for 2–4 weeks, with parents taking turns brooding and feeding the chicks. When parents hand chicks over to each other, the new parent may help the youngsters climb aboard by stretching out its foot as a step up. The parents split the brood in half at two weeks, but they continue to care for the young until they are two months old; immature birds often stay with their parents until they all migrate.

> **Note:** *Although* Clark's Grebes *were formally designated as a distinct species in 1985, their habits and range almost exactly mirror Western Grebes. They differ primarily in their face and bill color, and in their advertising calls (a double note in Western, and a single note in Clark's). In general, Clark's Grebes prefer deeper waters and are scarcer in the Sierra Nevada, but much remains to be learned about their life history and relative abundance.*

RANGE Widespread and fairly common breeders on large lakes throughout the western United States, including in California. Many migrating, nonbreeding, and wintering birds stop briefly or linger for months on large bodies of water at any season, though by December the vast majority move to coastal areas for the rest of the winter. Spring migration begins in March, and by April or May they are common at their breeding locations. After the breeding season, some have been observed on large lakes as high as 10,000 ft. **WEST SLOPE:** Only known to breed at Isabella Lake, and at Lake Almanor (which hosts one of the most significant nesting colonies in North America), but regularly occurs at all seasons on any of the large foothill reservoirs. However, the abundance of nonbreeding grebes is highly variable with hundreds or thousands appearing one year and dozens or no birds the next year. **EAST SLOPE:** Single birds may occasionally linger or make a brief appearance in the winter, but most begin arriving in March and are then abundant from early April through November. Despite the recreational boat traffic, important nesting colonies persist at Lake Crowley and Bridgeport Reservoir, with smaller colonies possible at other lakes (for example, they nested at Topaz Lake until recently).

CORMORANTS (Phalacrocoracidae)

DOUBLE-CRESTED CORMORANT *Phalacrocorax auritus*

LIFE HISTORY Unlike their pelican cousins that are graceful in flight and ride lightly in water, cormorants always seem as if they were waterlogged, either sitting low in the water or flapping furiously trying to become airborne. They frequently perch on bare branches, clumsily spreading their wings to dry them. But cormorants are expert, fast swimmers, and with pelicans, they share the unusual trait of having all four toes webbed together on each foot.

When visiting the interior, Double-crested Cormorants favor large bodies of slow-moving and still waters where they dive repeatedly in search of schools of slow-moving fish. Although many cormorants must travel over the Sierra Nevada, they were until recently rare visitors to our region. With the construction of numerous reservoirs on virtually every west-slope river, cormorants have become increasingly common residents and may one day begin nesting in some locations. Their bulky nests are typically built of sticks and placed in large waterside trees, often in the vicinity of heron or egret nests, or on the ground on predator-free islands. Active nests can be found from April through July.

RANGE Double-crested cormorants principally breed on slow-moving rivers, lakes, and reservoirs in the heartland of North America, with a separate breeding range in extreme north-eastern California and south-central Oregon. Although cormorants traveling to and from their coastal wintering areas must pass over the Sierra Nevada in large numbers, they seem to be relatively uncommon visitors. In April–May and August–October small numbers of migrants may be observed resting on open waters or flying along rivers in west-slope canyons, while nonbreeding visitors may be scarce or common at different sites. **WEST SLOPE:** Occurs at any season in large reservoirs and lakes, sometimes in remarkable numbers. Wintering cormorants at Isabella Lake can approach 1000 birds, but this species is otherwise scarce as you head north, with an average of 100 wintering cormorants at Folsom Lake and only a handful at Lake Almanor. In the summer they are uncommon and thinly scattered, except at Lake Almanor where they are fairly common breeders (this is currently their only known nesting location in the Sierra Nevada, though they have tried nesting at Honey Lake and Bridgeport Reservoir). **EAST SLOPE:** Fairly common summer visitors at a few east-side reservoirs such as Bridgeport Reservoir and Lake Crowley, but in general they are uncommon to rare migrants, and seldom seen at any other time. Numbers drop off dramatically in November (which coincidentally is about the time their numbers pick up at Isabella Lake on the west slope), and they are exceptionally rare in the winter and early spring.

PELICANS (Pelecanidae)

AMERICAN WHITE PELICAN *Pelecanus erythrorhynchos*

LIFE HISTORY The sight of white pelicans soaring over the Sierra Nevada produces two reactions: disbelief at seeing these birds in the mountains, and awe at the spectacular way that the flocks circle in flawless formation. Gliding effortlessly on 9 ft wingspans, pelicans regularly cross back and forth over the Sierra Nevada crest on route to their ancestral breeding grounds at Nevada's Pyramid Lake. They do not breed in the Sierra Nevada but are regular visitors to numerous lakes and reservoirs, especially during migration and in late summer. Here they stop to loaf and feed on fish that they catch in shallow waters. Their feeding behavior is fascinating to watch because they repeatedly dip their lower bills and expandable throat pouches into the water and use them as nets to scoop up small fish, frogs, or crayfish. These large birds need to eat about 3 pounds of fish a day so they are active feeders, and groups of pelicans frequently cooperate by lining up shoulder to shoulder to chase and trap fish in shallow waters.

RANGE American White Pelicans breed in large scattered colonies across the interior of western North America then winter in California's Central Valley and along the coast of Mexico. They start crossing east over the Sierra Nevada in March, even before ice melts from some of their breeding sites, and they can be seen flying overhead or resting on almost any large body of water until November. A significant portion of the population does not breed each year and spends the spring, summer, and fall loafing and wandering widely in search of places to feed. Nonbreeding birds are frequently joined by breeding adults who switch nesting duties every 3 days and use their days off to find food; by early August newly independent, immature birds start dispersing as well. **WEST SLOPE:** Small groups of spring and fall migrants, as well as summer visitors, are an uncommon sight almost anywhere on the west slope, but they occasionally stop to rest on any large body of water. Isabella Lake seems to be a particularly good location for finding pelicans, especially in winter when they are very rare anywhere else. **EAST SLOPE:** Commonly observed from April to October at large lakes and marshes on the east side of the Sierra Nevada, even as high as Lake Tahoe where they are irregular and uncommon. They are regularly observed at locations like Sierra Valley, Bridgeport Reservoir, and Lake

Crowley. Some have lingered as late as December and a few have been seen on Christmas Bird Counts.

HERONS and EGRETS (Ardeidae)

AMERICAN BITTERN *Botaurus lentiginosus*

LIFE HISTORY Populations of these solitary, cryptically camouflaged wading birds have been dramatically reduced throughout their range due to widespread destruction of their marshy homes. On the east side of the Sierra Nevada, where freshwater marshes are already a limited habitat, they have been detrimentally impacted by water diversions, grazing, and agriculture though they return if a wetland site is restored.

Finding a bittern is another story altogether and little is known about their basic life history, much less their status and distribution. Hiding amid dense marsh vegetation and scarcely moving much of the day, bitterns are best looked for at dawn and dusk when they begin actively hunting. Even then their typical hunting strategy is to stand stock still, or to walk so slowly it is hard to tell they are moving. On rare occasions you might actually see one grab an insect or small vertebrate with an explosive stab of its bill, but most of the time they see you first and freeze in an upright position with their vertical streaks blending flawlessly into the shadows of tall marsh plants.

Bitterns are best detected in the breeding season, when their eerie thumping *pump-er-lunk* calls resonate across the marshes, and when they flush up in brief flights as they move around trying to find mates or chase away intruders. Eggs are probably laid in May or June, with the female building a well-hidden platform amid dense, emergent vegetation and tending to the eggs and chicks by herself. Incubation takes almost a month; chicks remain in the nest for 1–2 weeks then linger around the nest for another 2–4 weeks.

RANGE American Bitterns are widespread breeding birds across the northern United States and southern Canada, with most wintering west of the Sierra Nevada and south into Mexico. In the Sierra Nevada, they breed in low-lying marshy areas with extensive patches of cattails and bulrushes and occasionally on foothill slopes where suitable habitat exists. Formerly bred at South Lake Tahoe (6200 ft). Migrants (April to early June, and early August to mid-October) have been reported at higher elevations, such as one at Tuolumne Meadows (8600 ft) in late May. **WEST SLOPE:** Other than in the Kern River Valley, where they are considered rare breeders, there are very few breeding records from the west slope. Much of their potential habitat has been inundated by large foothill reservoirs, but there are still pockets of low-elevation marshes along the full length of the Sierra Nevada where they might breed. Nearly all bitterns retreat to warmer regions in the winter, but once in a while a few hardy individuals stay behind. **EAST SLOPE:** Migrants may show up in areas where they are otherwise scarce, such as at Lake Tahoe, but most start arriving on their breeding grounds in early April where they remain uncommon until they leave by early October. All known breeding sites occur in valleys along the eastern base of the mountains, such as at Sierra Valley (perhaps the best place to see them in the Sierra Nevada) and various marshes along Hwy 395 in Owens Valley. Exceptionally rare in the winter, with most of the handful of records from the Owens Valley.

GREAT BLUE HERON *Ardea herodias*

LIFE HISTORY Great Blue Herons are the most common and widespread wading birds in the Sierra Nevada and, because they wander extensively, they show up almost anywhere, especially after adults and young birds disperse from their nesting colonies in the summer. Their preferred habitats are shallow waters along the edges of ponds, lakes, and rivers, but they are readily seen in places as diverse as schoolyard fields, tiny neighborhood ponds, and grassy highway shoulders. On occasion they may be observed perched on tops of high trees or rock outcrops, seemingly in the middle of nowhere.

They are correspondingly universal in their food choices and eat just about any animal they can catch and swallow: everything from fish and frogs when hunting in water, to gophers and snakes when foraging in a field. Hunting herons walk slowly or stand motionlessly while looking for food, then make their captures with lightning fast strikes. They are mostly solitary due to their antagonistic behavior when hunting, but they are gregarious while nesting and are sometimes plentiful in areas of abundant food in the wintertime.

In California, Great Blue Herons begin returning to their nesting colonies (rookeries) surprisingly early, with males gathering in the vicinity of previously established colony sites as early as December. From early January into March you may see pairs engaged in their elaborate courtship rituals—including lots of bowing, feather ruffling, and stick shaking—with eggs being laid in late February to early March.

Nest-building is a cooperative effort with the male bringing sticks to his mate, who either tosses them aside or weaves them into a messy platform that after several years of use can grow to be a solid structure measuring nearly 4 ft across and 3 ft deep. Colonies are generally located on tall trees in marshy or flooded areas, or on islands, and are scarce in the Sierra Nevada.

Chick-rearing is an extended effort by both parents. They take turns incubating as soon as the first egg is laid, with an average of 4 eggs being laid that take about a month to hatch. Chicks remain in the nest until they are two months old, and then in late May they begin climbing out of the nest in progressively more adventurous forays even though they continue returning to the nest and being fed for another 3 weeks.

RANGE Great Blue Herons are common year-round residents virtually everywhere in the United States though there is considerable regional movement after the breeding season and in the winter. In the Sierra Nevada they are fairly common and found year round at lower elevations, with some wandering to treeline in summer and early autumn. They are particularly widespread in the winter but most probably move towards favorable breeding locations from January to June. However, few nesting colonies have been reported in the Sierra Nevada so either there are unknown colonies or perhaps many leave the region to breed elsewhere. **WEST SLOPE:** An uncommon to common resident, mostly below 3000 ft. Most obvious in the winter; one indication of how common they are is that dozens to over a hundred are reported from nearly every west-slope Christmas Bird Count. They nest at Isabella Lake and in the vicinity of a few other large foothill reservoirs and rivers, though there must be unreported colonies. **EAST SLOPE:** Although generally uncommon to common residents, Great Blue Herons are complexly distributed on the east slope due to freezing conditions over large areas in the winter and lack of ideal breeding sites in the summer. For example, up to several dozen are observed every winter at Honey Lake, but they are extremely rare at nearby Sierra Valley, where they are uncommon (but do not nest) from March to November. They are fairly common in Owens Valley, where there are several nesting colonies along the Owens River in the vicinity of Bishop and Lone Pine, and where many remain through the winter.

Great Egret *Ardea alba*

LIFE HISTORY These slightly smaller and slimmer versions of Great Blue Herons share many of the same life-history and range traits, and the two species are often seen feeding and nesting together. Egrets, however, are more closely associated with lowlands and coastal areas west of the Sierra Nevada, so they are primarily transient visitors in our region (although there is a separate breeding population in extreme northeastern California and south-central Oregon which may explain why they are sometimes fairly common at Lake Almanor).

Great Egrets frequent shallow waters in wetlands and at the edges of lakes and rivers, and like Great Blue Herons they also show up in fields, grasslands, and pastures in search of just about anything they can catch and swallow. They also nest in colonies and seek tall trees in or near water, but they are low-elevation birds so they very rarely nest in the Sierra Nevada. A colony of these white birds standing prominently exposed on high tree branches would be easily seen from a distance and should be reported. One small colony located in the upper branches of a huge, sprawling gray pine can be seen along Hwy 4 just west of Copperopolis. Eggs are laid in mid-April to mid-May,taking about two months for the eggs to hatch and the chicks to become independent.

Note: *The much smaller* **Snowy Egret** *has almost exactly the same status and distribution patterns as the Great Egret though they occur in much lower numbers and are rare visitors at any season.*

RANGE Great Egrets are year-round residents in low-lying and coastal areas west of the Cascade-Sierra axis, though migrating and nonbreeding egrets wander widely and can be uncommon to common anywhere around the base of the Sierra Nevada, with a few individuals straying to subalpine meadows and mountain lakes in late summer. There seems to be a pulse of migrants from April to early June and from late July through October, when they show up in areas where they are otherwise scarce, particularly on the east slope. WEST SLOPE: Great Egrets from the Central Valley frequently wander onto the lower slopes of the Sierra Nevada and can be observed in grassy and wet areas or around lakes and marshes at almost any time of year. Because of the proximity to their breeding habitats in the Central Valley, they may rarely nest in low-lying portions of the west slope but this topic has been little studied. According to Christmas Bird Count records, they are fairly common wintering birds in the central Sierra Nevada and irregularly rare to the north and south (every other year a few are seen at Lake Almanor and at Isabella Lake). EAST SLOPE: Rare to uncommon spring and fall migrants with some lingering through the summer and even into December. They can be fairly common around Lake Crowley in August and September. Most of the east slope's handful of winter records are from Owens Valley, where individuals are seen on average every other winter.

BLACK-CROWNED NIGHT-HERON
Nycticorax nycticorax

LIFE HISTORY It is hard to compete for food when you have lots of bigger, taller relatives around, so these stocky, little herons do much of their hunting at night when there is no competition. Cosmopolitan night-herons are highly adaptable and live almost everywhere in the world except Australia and Antarctica, and in areas where there are no tall herons around they even feed in the daytime. They nest in a phenomenal range of conditions and eat not only everything they can catch and swallow but also the eggs of marsh birds, carrion, plants, and garbage (at landfills). They are the ultimate survivors yet they are not particularly common in the Sierra Nevada.

By day, night-herons perch on tree branches and among dense vegetation at the edges of marshes, lakes, and rivers, and their presence may be revealed by their loud, squawking calls. They are gregarious and nest colonially, frequently in the company of other herons and egrets. Most colonies are in or near large wetlands, but they are otherwise not picky about their choice of nesting locations, and nests may be built on the ground or in trees up to 160 ft high. Successful colonies will be used for decades if they are not disturbed.

In the Sierra Nevada, they begin nesting in April as males arrive at their colony sites and engage in feather ruffling, bowing, and stick shaking to attract the attention of passing females. The males' elegant white head plumes are essential to their future chances, and a pair bond dissolves quickly if a male's plumes are lost or damaged at any point. With luck, a male gradually switches from shaking sticks at a female to laying the foundation of a nest, which an interested female continues building while he brings her more sticks. The pair cooperates in all aspects of raising their 2–3 chicks, including incubating eggs for 25 days and for the month or more it takes until chicks start scrambling out of the nest on their own. While feeding chicks the adults may fly miles to find food and will actively hunt in the daytime.

RANGE In western North America, Black-crowned Night-Herons are widespread breeders in the Great Basin. For this reason they are probably more abundant on the east side of the Sierra Nevada. Wandering birds, especially juveniles, boost numbers everywhere in late summer and fall, with some appearing over 10,000 ft. **WEST SLOPE:** Scarcely reported but probably rare to uncommon throughout the foothills be-low 3000 ft, with numbers dropping dramatically in winter when single individuals are rarely observed. Known to breed in the Kern River Val-ley, and likely breed elsewhere on the west slope. **EAST SLOPE:** Arrive around mid-April, and then their numbers remain fairly constant (with an influx of young birds in August) until most depart in October. They are locally common around known breeding locations, such as Hart-son Reservoir at Honey Lake, Sierra Valley, and Mono Lake, but they almost certainly breed at other sites including in the Owens Valley. In the summer, they are uncommon but do not breed at Lake Tahoe. In the winter they are extremely rare on the east slope.

NEW WORLD VULTURES (Cathartidae)

TURKEY VULTURE *Cathartes aura*

LIFE HISTORY   In all respects, Turkey Vultures are exquisite soaring birds able to read incredibly nuanced aspects of landscape and thermal uplift. So finely tuned is this ability that vultures may soar for hours and many miles without a single wingbeat simply by moving from updraft to updraft. Gliding so slowly that they wobble as if ready to tumble out of the sky, vultures are ever on the lookout for carrion that they detect both visually and by smelling drifting molecules emitted from decay-ing carcasses. Their remarkable sense of smell, one of the most refined of all birds, is so acute that Turkey Vultures can locate carrion buried under leaves in the forest or dead animals as small as tadpoles.

Since carrion is an unpredictable and widely scattered food resource, vultures are experts at conserving energy between meals. They are often seen perched with wings outspread, absorbing the sun's warmth as a way of warming up without using calories. Vultures rarely waste energy by fighting over food and they can gorge so heavily that they can go two weeks between meals. They are also very efficient at maintaining their body temperature, raising their ruff of neck feathers to warm up or lowering them to expose their bare necks and cool down.

About the only time that vultures use extra energy is during courtship "follow flights" in April, when males may spend anywhere from several minutes to an entire day flapping along behind females. Nests are located in dark recesses under boulders, on cliffs or rocky slopes, and occasionally in hollow stumps or logs, but they are rarely found. With both parents sharing incubation duties, the two eggs take about 40 days to hatch and the chicks are ready to leave the nest after another 70–80 days.

> **Note:** *Previously known from the foothills of the west slope,* **California Condors** *last bred in the southern Sierra Nevada in 1984. Fortunately, their numbers are once again increasing in the southern Coastal Ranges thanks to a successful reintroduction program, and it is possible that condors may one day find their way back to the Sierra Nevada.*

RANGE Deciphering the status and distribution of Turkey Vulture populations is tricky business. They occur year round at low elevations, but seem to drift around the landscape in no particular pattern, making it almost impossible to tell if they are local residents, if they are breeding, or whether they are just passing through. In fact, their breeding status in the Sierra Nevada is poorly documented and very few nests have been found. During the winter they retreat downslope, or disappear for weeks at a time, during stormy weather, but then return to the foothills as soon as the sun comes back. Large numbers of migrants, sometimes in groups of dozens or hundreds of birds, move through the region in March–April and in September–October. **WEST SLOPE:** Common, sometimes even abundant, at all times of year around open oak woodlands and grasslands of the lower foothills. On sunny days in the winter, and throughout the summer, they are common up to 3000 ft, but over coniferous forests at higher elevations they are scarce up to about 6000 ft. The fall migration of vultures can be impressive, especially in the South Fork Kern River Valley where nearly 40,000 are counted each fall. **EAST SLOPE:** Very rarely observed in November–December, but in January a few move into the Owens Valley and by February a handful have drifted north along the entire east side in advance of the major rush of migrants in March–April. They are uncommon during the summer below the main forest belt but rarely, if ever, nest on the east side. Fall migration peaks in September with the tail end of the migration passing through in October.

OSPREYS (Pandionidae)

OSPREY *Pandion haliaetus*

LIFE HISTORY Ospreys are almost always seen flying around large bodies of water, including lakes, reservoirs, and rivers. At first it seems that they are just flying by, but then without warning they might pull up on beating wings and dive 40–100 ft. Just before plunging into the water, they extend their legs and talons forward, reaching out to grab the small to medium-sized fish that are their main targets. Almost immediately they surge back out of the water with a single, powerful wing-beat and hopefully fly off with a struggling fish clenched in their talons.

Ospreys are the only North American raptors whose diets consist almost entirely of fish, so these unique raptors tend to stay near large bodies of clear water. However, they are powerful fliers so they readily fly long distances and can be seen over any type of landscape, and may even nest at some distance from their hunting grounds. It is not uncommon to see them flying over the forest carrying a fish in their talons, either taking it to their nest in the breeding season, or carrying it as a "snack on the wing" when they are migrating.

In their second year of life, Ospreys form pair bonds and make their first nests, but they delay their first nesting attempt until returning to use the same nest during their third year. Males perform elaborate climbing and diving courtship flights, with pairs copulating up to 400 times over a 3 week period prior to egg-laying. Nests are huge, bulky collections of large sticks built by males and lined by females atop towering snags, on cliff faces, or perched incongruously on buoys and electricity towers, usually near large bodies of water. The 2–3 large, whitish eggs are laid in April or May and incubated for just over a month, mostly by the female except when she takes breaks to feed on fish brought to her by the male. Young birds start flying at two months of age, and remain dependent on their parents for another 2–3 weeks.

RANGE Ospreys are primarily summer residents though a handful remain in California through the winter and are occasionally seen along Sierra Nevada lakes and rivers. Breeding pairs are thinly scattered throughout the Sierra Nevada except at Lake Almanor and just to the north at Eagle Lake, where several dozen Ospreys nest. During both spring and fall migration, Ospreys can be seen in fair numbers (up to several per hour visible from good vantage points). Northbound migrants first appear around mid-March, with nesting birds settling on their territories in late March or April. The southbound migration starts in late summer and continues through September. **WEST SLOPE:** Migrating and breeding Ospreys are commonly observed around large lakes, reservoirs, and rivers though they frequently fly over any type of habitat. **EAST SLOPE:** Due to a general absence of suitable nesting sites, breeding Ospreys are uncommon and sparsely scattered on the east side. Several pairs nest each year on tufa towers at Mono Lake even though they have to fly to distant lakes to find fish.

HAWKS, KITES, EAGLES and ALLIES (Accipitridae)

BALD EAGLE *Haliaeetus leucocephalus*

LIFE HISTORY Despite their formidable size, Bald Eagles are rather poor hunters and obtain much of their food by scavenging animal carcasses or stealing freshly caught items from other predators. They prefer fish but will eat any type of dead animal. They will catch their own fish by skimming over lakes and rivers and hooking the fish with their talons in passing, but whenever they can, they simply take fish that were captured by other hunters like Ospreys or Great Blue Herons. If food supplies are diminished in the winter, Bald Eagles may conserve energy by perching for long periods of time in one place.

In the Sierra Nevada, Bald Eagles gather at large lakes and rivers, resting in large trees near the places where they might find food. Migrating or moving birds are occasionally observed flying high over the landscape, but they are far less common than widespread Golden Eagles.

Nesting Bald Eagles are rare in the Sierra Nevada, but where they do nest, pairs typically use the same nesting platforms year after year, building them over time into gigantic stick structures (record-sized nests in North America have weighed nearly two tons and been up to 18 feet tall). Most nests are built in towering, older trees within half a mile of water. The 1–3 eggs are laid in March or April and incubated for 35 days, with both parents participating actively in all phases of nest-building and care of fledglings. Young birds wander extensively for at least 4 years, at which time they may breed for the first time or wait a couple years longer.

RANGE After a long absence in the latter half of the 1900s, Bald Eagles are once again reoccupying parts of their former nesting range in the Sierra Nevada, although dam construction and the subsequent loss of salmon runs (once numbering over 1 million fish in the Sierra Nevada) may preclude the species from ever returning to many of its former haunts. From October to March, they are uncommon winter visitors, but several at a time might be observed near large lakes or reservoirs (with 18 once seen at Crowley Lake in December), and they can be seen flying over any type of habitat. During the breeding season

(April to September) Bald Eagles are almost entirely absent except for scattered breeding pairs. **WEST SLOPE:** In just the past 10 years they have extended their breeding range south to Tuolumne County, and may expand even further southward in the future. Large west slope reservoirs along the full length of the range attract visiting Bald Eagles during the nonbreeding season, creating the possibility that new pairs will become established where conditions are favorable. In 2001, a pair successfully nested at Beardsley Reservoir, just northwest of Yosemite National Park, the first nesting in the region in 40 years and evidence of the species' return. **EAST SLOPE:** On the entire east side, a few pairs have nested or tried to nest as far south to Inyo County. In the nonbreeding season, they are uncommon or locally common around large bodies of water.

NORTHERN HARRIER *Circus cyaneus*

LIFE HISTORY Like owls, Northern Harriers have disks of specialized feathers around their faces that funnel sound into their large ear openings, giving them an extraordinary sense of hearing. Flying mere feet over the ground, harriers patrol grasslands and marshes searching for voles, birds, reptiles, and other small animals hidden in the deep grass then using sound to capture them with pinpoint accuracy. These hunting flights can be quite dramatic to watch because harriers are active hunters, systematically criss-crossing fields in grid-like patterns, and targeting prey with acrobatic pull-ups, cartwheels, drop-pounces, and other fancy wingwork.

Beginning in late March to early April, breeding males fly conspicuously over their territories, performing high-energy, roller coaster-like courtship flights that include up to 75 U-shaped dips in a row. While females incubate their 4–6 eggs, males bring a steady supply of prepared prey items (beheaded and skinned by the male) that are transferred to the female in dramatic mid-air handoffs. Nests are built on the ground in wet meadows and freshwater marshes, where they are very difficult to find amid tall grasses and are relatively safe from predators. As an added precaution against predators, the highly mobile chicks spend their days in hidden runways they construct into the surrounding vegetation. Both parents feed the young, but males sometimes mate with a number of females (2–5 females) and get spread thin on feeding duty, in which case they tend to favor one or two nests at the expense of others.

After young birds fledge, harriers wander widely, including

upslope into the mountains, where they can be found over open slopes near the Sierra Nevada crest until driven downslope by the first winter storms. Over the winter, much-larger females set up territories at prime feeding sites while males and juveniles roam widely hoping to find food in less productive areas.

RANGE Favoring lowland valleys and marshes, Northern Harriers breed and winter peripherally around the Sierra Nevada, where they are nearly always associated with open country. While harriers frequent fields, grasslands, and marshes, they are also found over sagebrush flats and other dry brushy or grassy areas. Populations of local residents are greatly augmented by the passage or arrival of migrant birds in March–April and September–October. **WEST SLOPE:** Primarily associated with Central Valley grasslands and marshes but edging onto lower foothill slopes up to the elevations where oak woodlands start to form extensive cover. During spring migration, harriers are frequently observed in transit over all habitats up to at least the Mixed Conifer Zone. Repeated observations of harriers on high mountain slopes in early June suggest a few may also nest in brushfields of the Upper Montane or Subalpine Zones, but this needs to be confirmed. Fall migrants are commonly observed flying over alpine meadows and peaks. **EAST SLOPE:** Breed locally in the Great Basin desert with scattered populations ranging westward up to the base of the Sierra Nevada. Formerly common in the extensive wet meadows and marshes flanking the Sierra Nevada, but grazing and development of these lucrative lands have greatly impacted and fragmented the best harrier habitats. Breed up to 7000 ft (rarely higher) in wet meadows or sagebrush flats. Wintering harriers are fairly abundant some years and totally absent in others.

SHARP-SHINNED HAWK *Accipiter striatus*

LIFE HISTORY Small forest birds scatter in terror at the appearance of Sharp-shinned Hawks, highly efficient and ruthless hunters whose diet is composed almost entirely of small birds. Anyone who maintains a backyard bird feeder will see these hawks on a regular basis and assume that they are fairly common, but in their native forest habitat they are relatively rare and seldom observed.

Sharp-shinned Hawks are impressive, dynamic fliers though they are scarcely larger than Steller's Jays. Using their short, broad wings to generate bursts of intense speed, and their long tails to maneuver, they appear out of nowhere, dart by like bullets, and disappear into tangled thickets in a flash. Their big eyes help them navigate through the vegetation, and they have extraordinarily long middle toes with needle-like talons so they can hook small birds out of the branches where they might try to get away. Still, they rely on the element of surprise, sitting on hidden perches or flying up from behind an obstacle until the last possible second, and they quickly give up a chase if they cannot catch their prey instantly.

Because these hawks spend so much of their lives in dense forests, little is known of their breeding biology and distribution. On the other hand, migrating Sharp-shinned Hawks are easily observed because they fly high over the forest canopy. In common with all *Accipiter* hawks, they have a characteristic "flap-flap-glide" style of flying that can be recognized even when they are at a great distance.

During their breeding season, from April–June, pairs often reveal their presence with sharp *kek-kek-kek* calls as they court and build nests. Pairs place their stick nests among obscuring clusters of leaves in the canopies of conifer or deciduous trees. Males may contribute twigs for the nest, but females put the nests together and incubate their 4–5 eggs for 30 days. Males supply food for incubating females and later for the nestlings as well, bringing beheaded prey to a nearby perch and calling softly for the females to come and take the food back to the nest. Much of their diet during the breeding season consists of the nestlings and fledglings of other birds, sometimes captured by the fistful. As soon as young Sharp-shinned Hawks begin to fly at 3 weeks of age, they fly out to grab food items dropped in mid-air by the arriving parents.

RANGE Sharp-shinned Hawks are uncommon to rare year-round residents with significant numbers of migrants moving through the region, especially in the fall when they are fairly common. Migration occurs over all habitat types, while territorial birds are closely associated with coniferous forests, oak-conifer forests, or riparian woodlands. Spring migration begins in early February, but peak numbers are observed in late March. Even as migrating birds continue to move through the region in April, some pairs stay behind to establish nesting territories and breed in May and June. In late spring and summer, Sharp-shinned Hawks are largely absent from the southern Sierra Nevada, an area where they are not known to breed. Numbers increase significantly in August, when many Sharp-shinned Hawks are reported at high elevations and over the Sierra Nevada crest, but it is not clear if these are resident birds that move upslope or newly arriving migrants from the north. Numbers diminish through the fall, and from November–March they are scarce in the mountains. **WEST SLOPE:** Uncommon to rare in both the breeding season and the winter, but fairly common during migration. In the winter, they are common in the Central Valley and regularly wander into nearby oak woodlands of the Sierra Nevada foothills, up to about 3000 ft. **EAST SLOPE:** Except for a brief pulse of fall migrants, they are thinly distributed and relatively rare on the east side. Migrating Sharp-shinned Hawks are concentrated at high elevations in August, but in September and October they seem to abandon the mountains and instead pass southward along low-lying valleys and foothill slopes. A few linger all winter around Bishop, Mono Lake, Lake Tahoe, and Sierra Valley.

COOPER'S HAWK *Accipiter cooperii*

LIFE HISTORY These crow-sized raptors are larger replicas of Sharp-shinned Hawks in nearly all aspects of their life history and seasonal movements, but being larger, they differ in eating mid-sized prey items like jays, robins, flickers, chipmunks, and ground squirrels. Like Sharp-shinned Hawks, they capture prey with lightning-fast, surprise attacks, but they also use other hunting techniques like stooping down from a great height, chasing on the ground, and drowning captured prey in water. These fierce hunters capture multiple food items each day and store surplus food on branches

Solitary and silent most of the year, Cooper's Hawks become very noisy in the breeding season, with pairs using loud *kak-kak-kak* vocalizations as a way of staying in touch in the dense forests where they breed. Females seem to dominate all interactions in the pair, so they use a more complex array of vocalizations to assert their dominance in different contexts.

The well-hidden nests are seldom observed but are located amid dense foliage in a wide variety of low to mid-elevation forests, including riparian woodlands, oak woodlands, and mixed conifer forests. In one California study, 97 percent of their nests were located in oaks. Pairs spend about a month together prior to egg-laying, with males providing females 2–3 food items a day as they court and build stick nests that they line with flakes of bark, and sprigs of greenery to help repel parasites.

Females lay 3–5 eggs in April or May, incubating them for 34–36 days. Males continue to feed females, leaving food items on a nearby branch then briefly sitting on the eggs as females eat. During the month it takes before chicks are ready to leave the nest, males never feed the chicks directly but bring food to females who divide up the food and feed nestlings themselves. Parents continue to care for the fledglings for a month after they leave the nest.

RANGE Like Sharp-shinned Hawks, the actual status and distribution of Cooper's Hawks is complex and not well understood. Cooper's Hawks are rare to uncommon (possibly fairly common in some areas) residents as high as the Mixed Conifer Zones on both slopes. After mid-August there is an increase in numbers as juveniles begin wandering on their own, followed by a pulse of fall migrants from mid-September to mid-October. During this time it is not uncommon to see Cooper's Hawks as high as the Subalpine and Alpine Zones. Counts of migrating raptors in the Sierra Nevada show that Cooper's and Sharp-shinned Hawks occur in roughly equal numbers. In winter, Cooper's Hawks disperse widely and even take up residence in areas where they are absent during the breeding season (e.g. open flats on the east side of the Sierra Nevada, or in residential areas with large numbers of bird feeders). **WEST SLOPE:** Widely scattered and hard to find during the breeding season, Cooper's are more readily observed during spring migration when, along with Sharp-shinned Hawks, they are the most abundant migrating raptors. More evidence is needed but some data suggests that spring migration is more pronounced on the west slope, and that fall migration is more pronounced on the east slope. **EAST SLOPE:** Rare to uncommon most of the year though migrants are commonly observed from mid-September to mid-October.

NORTHERN GOSHAWK *Accipiter gentilis*

LIFE HISTORY These bulked-up versions of Cooper's Hawks are ferocious hunters that use their mass to crash through branches and bushes in pursuit of terrified prey. Northern Goshawks are the size of Red-tailed Hawks and favor larger prey items like squirrels, rabbits, flickers, quail, grouse, and jays. One typical hunting strategy is to perch motionless for about 10 minutes then fly to a new perch, wait and fly to a new perch. They will also fly rapidly along forest edges, using bushes to hide their approach until the last second, and they have been observed chasing individual squirrels in trees, or rabbits on the ground, for up to an hour at a time. Unlike smaller Sharp-shinned and Cooper's Hawks, these larger hawks readily hunt in open areas.

Most of the year, Northern Goshawks are habitat generalists but during the nesting season they prefer stands of large, mature conifers (consequently, the widespread logging of these trees has led to declines in goshawk populations). After the breeding season, pairs split up and wander in search of food, reoccupying their previous nesting territories in March or early April, and breeding again with their previous mates if both return to the same area. Males provide all the food for their mates and nestlings so they hunt over very large territories, often hunting on separate territories far from their nests. Pairs may copulate over 500 times each nesting season, and it is thought that this is a way of ensuring the male's paternity since he spends most of his time hunting far away rather than guarding the female.

Pairs build bulky stick nests in the upper canopies of the tallest and largest conifers in their nesting territories, favoring conifers on gentle slopes where there is an open understory. They maintain up to 8 alternate nests and switch between different nests each year. Active nests are courageously defended with blaring *kak-kak-kak* calls and such intense attacks on potential intruders that popular hiking trails or campgrounds may be closed if there is a goshawk nest nearby. Females incubate 2–4 eggs for 32–34 days, and about 40 days after hatching the young birds are ready to leave the nest. Young birds spend 4–6 weeks hanging out in the nest area learning how to hunt before dispersing. After early August, family groups split up and seldom interact, except that juvenile females displace juvenile males from favorable hunting areas, forcing many young males to migrate.

RANGE Northern Goshawks are primarily associated with mature conifer stands, especially during the breeding season, but are often observed hunting in meadows or other openings. An estimated 500–700 breeding pairs are widely scattered throughout the Sierra Nevada and many of these birds are thought to remain year round though their winter movements are little known. Peak numbers are reported June–September, with most birds in August–September being seen at higher elevations or over alpine meadows. Rarely observed from November–February. Northbound spring migrants start to move through the region in late February, with migrating birds often flying high overhead. **WEST SLOPE:** Breed in extensive conifer forests at all elevations. During the winter, goshawks may be seen in foothill woodlands for brief periods. **EAST SLOPE:** Breed at mid- to high elevations where stands of large conifers reach their maximum extent, but also range down to the base of the Sierra Nevada slope where appropriate habitat exists, such as in the extensive Jeffrey pine stands between Mono Lake and Mammoth Lakes. Also breed in groves of mature aspens over a wide range of elevations.

RED-SHOULDERED HAWK *Buteo lineatus*

LIFE HISTORY Formerly restricted to wooded river bottoms and tracts of contiguous forest, Red-shouldered Hawks have adapted to nesting in the fragmented suburban and rural habitats created by humans, and now readily nest near houses and farms. These colorful and noisy raptors are an increasingly visible and auditory part of the landscape as they expand their range further into the Sierra Nevada each year. These small, active hawks spend more time in forests than other *Buteos*, and have a lot of behaviors in common with the *Accipiter* forest hawks. When hunting, their primary strategy is to perch in trees and watch for prey below, with small rodents, reptiles and amphibians, and insects being favored food items.

The breeding season is announced with clear, ringing *kee-ah* calls that peak from January–April. Red-shouldered Hawks are without a doubt our noisiest hawks, and anyone who has a pair nesting near their house may soon wish there was an "off" switch for the hawks. Their distinctive nests are located amid the main forks of large tree trunks in groves of trees. Though smaller than those of Red-tailed Hawks, their nests are still substantial and completely fill tree crotches. Unlike *Accipiter* nests, those of Red-shouldered Hawks are lined with many fine pieces of inner bark, lichens, or moss, as well as with sprigs of greenery. In March or April, both sexes share in the building of new nests or the relining of old nests, and both help incubate the 2–3 eggs (though the male's duties are restricted to procuring food then keeping the eggs warm while the female feeds away from the nest). Young birds leave the nest at 6 weeks of age and are soon proficient at catching their own small food items.

RANGE This lowland species is making a remarkable and recent incursion into the Sierra Nevada. Within a matter of one or two decades, Red-shouldered Hawks have not only begun moving out of the Central Valley and up the west slope to previously unrecorded elevations, but have become regular visitors and even breeders on the east side of the Sierra Nevada. It is not entirely clear whether this is the result of population increases or if it is a geographic shifting due to habitat loss in the Central Valley. Some have suggested that the development of small ranchettes, many of which have small stock ponds, in formerly dry oak woodlands have opened up new nesting possibilities on the west slope. From late summer through the winter, wandering individuals are regularly observed in the high mountains or crossing over the Sierra Nevada crest. **WEST SLOPE:** Mainly associated with dense riparian forests or adjacent upland slopes in the Foothill Oak Zone. While oaks are nearly always a component of their territories it is not clear whether this is a preference or a byproduct of the elevations where they nest. On the west slope they are rapidly expanding upslope into new habitats. In the central Sierra Nevada, for example, they pushed their upper breeding limits from 1500 ft to 3500 ft in as little as 15 years (1990–2005). **EAST SLOPE:** Starting with scattered records in the 1970s from Honey Lake, South Lake Tahoe, Reno, and Owens Valley, this species has become increasingly common and is now a regular breeder around the Owens Valley. They are primarily restricted to cottonwood stands along larger rivers in valleys or flats along the base of Sierra Nevada slope.

RED-TAILED HAWK *Buteo jamaicensis*

LIFE HISTORY These distinctive large raptors are the most widespread and common resident hawks in the Sierra Nevada, with huge numbers migrating to California in the winter and greatly swelling the resident population. Except at high elevations, resident pairs remain on or near their territories year round, preferring areas where tall trees with prominent lookout perches are located near open fields and grasslands. From these perches, and occasionally while hovering in mid-air, Red-tails scan open ground for small mammals ranging in size from mice to jackrabbits. Three-quarters of their diets are mammals, especially ground squirrels and gophers, supplemented with snakes and a few birds.

Any time they are not hunting from perches near the ground, Red-tails regularly patrol the air high over their territories, watching for intruders and advertising their territory with their presence. Their descending *keee-aaar* screams are given during territorial disputes while courting birds make sharp *chirk* notes. Courtship can occur in any month because resident birds mate for life and maintain their pair bonds all year, but their graceful "sky dances," in which mated pairs circle in tandem with dangling legs, are best seen in late February to early March.

Pairs typically reuse their large, bulky stick nests from previous years. Located in the crowns of tall trees, where they have commanding views, these nests are often decorated with sprigs of greenery. Both sexes help incubate the 2–4 eggs for about one month, but females do most of the incubating while males provide food throughout the entire nesting period. Young birds leave the nest in 42–46 days but stay in the vicinity of the nest for another 2–3 weeks, sometimes lingering near their parents' territories through the winter.

Note: *Three other species of large soaring hawks are peripherally or irregularly observed in the Sierra Nevada.* **Swainson's Hawks** *breed around annual grasslands and irrigated pastures in the Central Valley and sporadically in the Great Basin, including two pairs in Sierra Valley and about 20 pairs in the northern Owens Valley.* **Ferruginous Hawks** *and* **Rough-legged Hawks** *are migrants and irregular winter visitors, with dozens at a time possible in November–December around Sierra Valley (the best location in the region to see these two hawks).*

RANGE Red-tailed Hawks are commonly observed in all types of open country, with nesting birds using any mix of tall trees and open, grassy areas. Individuals seen flying over forested areas are likely in transit or venturing out from adjacent breeding territories. Red-tailed Hawks are year-round residents at lower elevations though they may briefly disappear from their territories during the winter. From mid-summer until late fall, many are observed at higher elevations, as high as the Alpine Zone, but these might be migrating hawks. At low elevations, where snow cover is minimal and prey readily available through the winter, dozens of local residents and winter visitors may be observed along any given stretch of road. **WEST SLOPE:** Resident of slopes and nearby meadow systems as high as the Upper Montane Zone, about 7000 ft. During the fall and winter, their numbers increase dramatically among the oak savannas and grasslands of the lower foothills. **EAST SLOPE:** Seasonal status and distribution similar to the west slope. Winter concentrations are notably high in east-side valleys that support agriculture like Honey Lake, Sierra Valley, Bridgeport Valley, and Owens Valley.

GOLDEN EAGLE *Aquila chrysaetos*

LIFE HISTORY Easily overlooked and unnoticed amongst the many vultures that drift over foothill slopes, Golden Eagles are the Sierra Nevada's most formidable avian predators. Eating mostly rabbits, ground squirrels, and marmots, these massive raptors with 7 ft wingspans can tackle Tundra Swans, Sandhill Cranes, and even full-grown deer. Mated pairs may work in tandem to corner fleeing animals, but they generally hunt alone by stooping down on unsuspecting prey while flying above.

These long-lived birds (up to 48 years in captivity) are thought to mate for life and remain year round on large territories that may be 50 square miles in size. Over time they gain such a highly detailed sense of their territories that they know the location of predictable updrafts and prime hunting areas, and will not kill prey items in areas of downdrafts because they know these are hard places to get airborne after they eat a full meal. Most food animals are crepuscular (active at dawn and dusk) so an eagle that does not find food in the morning may have to spend the day hunting or wait until evening for another chance, but once they have eaten a full meal, they spend hours circling high overhead, soaring comfortably on strong rising air currents and watching their territories.

Given their regal appearances, it is surprising that Golden Eagles seem so playful. Courtship displays, for instance, are quite lively and include a whole series of dives, tumbles, and flips. Young eagles seem to delight in chasing larger animals that they cannot kill, and eagles of all ages will repeatedly drop objects from great heights then dive to catch them in mid-air, often doing this in tandem with a mate.

Pairs begin refurbishing old nests or constructing new ones in the late fall or winter even though they do not begin laying eggs until February or March (and perhaps even later at higher elevations). Their bulky stick nests can become 6 ft across and 5 ft high after many years of use, and due to their great weight (up to a ton in some really big examples), they are built in large trees or on cliff ledges with expansive views of the landscape. Pairs are extremely sensitive to disturbance and the great majority of failed nests are due to human intrusion, so most pairs locate their nests in remote areas.

Females incubate the two eggs for 45 days, with males taking over during short breaks while females eat prey items brought to the nest. Young birds begin their first practice flights and leave the nest at around 10 weeks of age. In migrating populations, young birds disperse within a month but in resident populations they may linger around their parents for up to 6 months.

RANGE Golden Eagles might be seen at any elevation, particularly over open mountainous terrain where prey animals are easier to see and where there are strong updrafts. On both slopes, these wide-ranging birds may nest on rocky cliffs or in tall conifers at low to mid-elevations, then range upslope or downslope to hunt over open meadows, grasslands, or sagebrush flats. Numbers of eagles increase on lower foothill slopes and valley bottoms in the winter, probably due to both residents moving downslope to avoid deep snows and migrants arriving from the north.

FALCONS (Falconidae)

AMERICAN KESTREL *Falco sparverius*

LIFE HISTORY Nearly all of a kestrel's life is spent around open areas covered with little more than low grasses and scattered plants. These openings are critical places for finding prey, and kestrels will utilize patches of nearly any size or type, including parks, schoolyards, lawns and other urban habitats as well as wild habitats such as meadows, grasslands, or deserts. The majority of their hunting is done while sitting patiently on tree branches or power lines and watching for prey items, but in the absence of perches they hover with rapidly beating wings over open fields. Kestrels typically swoop down to grab insects and small mammals on the ground, but some individuals prefer to catch large insects or small birds in flight. Although there is a bit of regional variation, three-quarters of their diet consists of insects.

Nesting kestrels seek large trees or snags with woodpecker cavities, but in the absence of woodpecker holes they will use other natural cavities. Because cavities are a limited resource, people putting out nest boxes have had great success encouraging these small, confiding raptors to take up residence in areas that lack nest sites.

Although pairs mate for life, they do not appear to spend winters together and must find each other again each spring. Starting in April, males set out to inspect all potential nesting cavities on their territories, later escorting females to them so they can select ones to their liking. No special preparations are made to the nest cavity and the 4–5 eggs are sometimes simply laid on bare wood. Females take charge of incubating the eggs for 30 days while males provide food and short periods of incubation. Chicks leave the nest 30 days after hatching though they may stay with their parents as a family group until September.

RANGE Kestrels are fairly common breeders in open, grassy areas at low elevations around the perimeter of the Sierra Nevada. On both slopes they primarily breed below the extensive conifer forests, but some pairs nest around large meadows at higher elevations, very rarely to over 8000 ft amid lodgepole pines and other upper montane forests. Numbers of kestrels increase significantly after late July, probably due to the arrival of migrants. During this late summer influx, they are relatively common at all elevations and may be readily observed hunting over subalpine and alpine meadows and rocky slopes. By late October, most have left the mountains and settled on their wintering grounds in annual grasslands or agricultural areas.

MERLIN *Falco columbarius*

LIFE HISTORY Based on shape alone it is easy to confuse Merlins and American Kestrels, but the instant Merlins launch into flight all doubt is removed, for these tiny falcons are intensely powerful and awe-inspiring on the wing. Each wingbeat propels them forward with so much speed that in mere moments they are dots in the distance. Merlins use this prowess for their primary hunting specialty: taking down fast-flying birds in mid-air. They are particularly adept at pursuing shorebirds, but in the absence of shorebirds they will hunt other birds such as Horned Larks, and while migrating they catch large numbers of dragonflies.

Most hunting is done from perches, where they scan expansive, open areas until they spot potential prey. After leaving their perches, they often drop down and power along just over ground level, coming up on their prey with lightning speed, camouflaged against the backdrop of the ground. If their initial attack fails, they may arc up and stoop down repeatedly on their fleeing target.

RANGE After breeding in Canada and Alaska, Merlins migrate south each fall and winter and are regular but rare visitors to the Sierra Nevada foothills. Of the 3 races known to occur in the Sierra Nevada, only the "Taiga" race (*F. c. columbarius*) is widespread and expected regularly. Both the beautiful, pale "Prairie" race (*F. c. richardsonii*) and the hauntingly dark "Black" race (*F. c. suckleyi*) are extremely rare visitors. When they first arrive in the fall (late August–early September), Merlins may be seen over barren alpine slopes as readily as in low foothill valleys, but with the arrival of winter storms they descend below the snowline. Little is known about their winter habitats or patterns of movement. Most leave the state by the end of April.

PEREGRINE FALCON *Falco peregrinus*

LIFE HISTORY Thanks in large part to stringent legal protection and herculean efforts to breed these birds in captivity and then release them back into the wild, Peregrine Falcons have made a stunning comeback from the perilous lows they had reached by the 1960s as a result of DDT contamination. And nowhere is this comeback better illustrated than in Yosemite Valley where, after a 36-year absence, a pair of Peregrine Falcons nested on El Capitan in 1978. By 1995 there were 4 pairs nesting in Yosemite Valley, and in 2010 there were 8 pairs—a remarkable figure by any measure.

These beautiful birds are one of the world's most impressive avian predators. Much has been made of their ability to dive at over 200 mph, but just as impressive and far more common is their ability to take off after fast-flying birds in all-out pursuit that is breathtaking to watch. These falcons are master aerialists, and they seem to hunt and play for the sheer pleasure of the chase, even when they have just eaten a meal. Young falcons are particularly playful, and siblings practice all kinds of flying stunts together as they perfect their hunting techniques while waiting for parents to return with food.

Peregrine Falcons favor wild open country where there are abundant birds to hunt. They catch many types of birds, but some of their main targets are Rock Pigeons. During the nesting season, males provide most of the food for incubating females and hungry nestlings (though males sneak in a few snacks by eating the heads off the prey items before delivering them to the nest). Extra food is cached as a safeguard against bad weather and both sexes may visit the cache to feed.

Peregrines typically nest on remote cliffs where there are well-sheltered ledges that provide commanding views, and pairs often return to use the same nests each year. In March–April, females incubate 3–4 eggs until they hatch in 28 days. When they are 40 days old, young birds fledge and spend at least two months learning how to hunt, initially following the parents and catching preys items dropped to them in midair, then making their own tentative, playful chases that eventually lead to prey captures.

RANGE Far-ranging Peregrine Falcons are uncommon and sparsely distributed due to their large territories, but they are regularly encountered and can be expected in any location from the lowest valleys to the highest peaks. Migrants may be observed in areas where they are otherwise absent, but unlike many other raptors there is little noticeable movement of migrants. In the winter they usually leave the Sierra Nevada or move downslope.

PRAIRIE FALCON *Falco mexicanus*

LIFE HISTORY These sandy-brown falcons of dry, open spaces favor low-lying agricultural areas in the Central Valley and sagebrush flats in the Great Basin. Here, they specialize on hunting mammals and birds by flying 10–20 ft above the ground and swooping in on unsuspecting prey. Occasionally they will dive on prey from high above or scan for prey from nearby perches. During the nesting season, they almost exclusively eat fatty, calorie-rich ground squirrels then switch over to a diet of Horned Larks and Western Meadowlarks in the late summer and winter after ground squirrels have gone underground.

Breeding begins in March with a month of courtship and nest-site selection. A pair will visit numerous cliff faces and rock outcrops investigating ledges, cavities, and abandoned raven nests while performing stylized courtship behaviors. They are scarce breeders in the Sierra Nevada, but sometimes nest on cliffs overlooking their prime feeding areas.

The 4–5 eggs are laid in mid-April to mid-May and hatch a month later, just about the time that juvenile ground squirrels start emerging from burrows, thus ensuring that chicks hatch around the time of peak ground squirrel numbers. This ready supply of food is important because it takes a lot of calories to raise a large brood of hungry falcons. Young chicks leave their nests when they are 40 days old, but they are dependent on their parents for at least two more months.

RANGE Resident throughout California, Prairie Falcons don't migrate so much as wander nomadically in response to seasonal shifts in food supply. This becomes evident in the Sierra Nevada after ground squirrels at low elevations head underground to avoid the mid-summer temperatures. In July–August, many Prairie Falcons roam upslope in search of high-elevation Belding's ground squirrels that remain active around high-mountain meadows through the summer. Some falcons linger at these elevations until the first heavy snows drive them back downslope, but most head back downslope in September, just in time to capitalize on the big pulse of migrating Western Meadowlarks and, to a lesser degree, Horned Larks that arrive in late September. In the winter, Prairie Falcons roam widely across the annual grasslands of the Central Valley or the sagebrush flats of the Great Basin. **WEST SLOPE:** Uncommon winter visitors in the foothills, where they are primarily restricted to open grasslands and rarely observed above the line where grasslands drop out. Numbers start increasing in October and remain fairly high through the winter as juveniles and northern birds arrive and take up residence around ranches and agricultural areas. Some may linger in the spring to breed on cliffs either in the foothills or near the crest, but so few are observed during the breeding season that this needs further study. **EAST SLOPE:** Year-round residents though many Prairie Falcons seasonally wander upslope and downslope in search of food. A few may breed in the mountains on steep, rocky cliffs.

RAILS (Rallidae)

Black Rail *Laterallus jamaicensis*

LIFE HISTORY Formerly known in California only from salt marshes around San Francisco Bay and from another population along the lower Colorado River, Black Rails were unexpectedly found in Yuba County in 1994. As the world's smallest rails, Black Rails are incredibly elusive and almost impossible to see, but their loud *ki-ki-krr* calls are a dead giveaway.

Now the subject of a major University of California Berkeley study, this group of threatened rails has been characterized as a meta-population that moves fluidly among the hundreds of small, highly fragmented, permanent and semi-permanent wetlands that dot the low-elevation oak woodlands and annual grasslands of the central Sierra Nevada foothills. Black Rails occur in marshes and wet meadows, but they prefer muddy, densely vegetated sites with flowing water, and 75 percent of their known locations are fed by constantly flowing irrigation water. Remarkably, rails readily colonize spots where old, earthen irrigation ditches spring leaks on hillsides, allowing grasses and sedges to grow, and they will occupy patches as small as 40 ft across. Perhaps because so many ephemeral bodies of water dry up in the long hot summer, rails probably recognize that flowing water implies the presence of permanent water and food.

Black Rails have relatively short legs so they are narrowly restricted to shallow waters less than one-inch deep, where they slink unseen among a mix of dense cattails, rushes, and grasses in search of small invertebrates in the summer and a larger proportion of seeds in the winter. This is one of the least known birds in North America and even after thousands of days of fieldwork, researchers still know little about their life history and seasonal movements. Breeding may begin in early February with peak egg-laying in early May, but nests, chicks, and other aspects of their parental care are poorly documented.

Birds giving the distinctive *ki-ki-krr* calls (thought to be males) are best heard around sunrise and sunset though they may call spontaneously any time of day and night, especially in response to sudden loud noises. Highly agitated birds also make growling *grr-grr-grr* calls. Females lay 5–8 eggs in well-defined nests hidden among dense marsh vegetation, and they add a canopy of woven vegetation and a ramp leading into the nest. Juvenile birds appear to disperse widely, for they may briefly show up in unexpected locations until they move to suitable habitats for the winter.

RANGE At present, Black Rails are known only from the lower foothills of the west slope in Butte, Yuba, Nevada, and Placer counties, where they are both resident and transient among several hundred scattered permanent and semi-permanent wetlands ranging from tiny wet dots to sprawling marshes. Black Rails move frequently and quickly colonize new sites, and it is thought that some even regularly commute back and forth from salt marshes in the Bay Area. Most known locations on the west slope are on private lands, particularly on large cattle ranches, and a loose affiliation of these property owners continue to play a pivotal role in the continuing study and conservation of this threatened species. The best location for hearing Black Rails is at the spectacular and little-known Spenceville Wildlife Area, which straddles the Yuba-Nevada County line.

Virginia Rail *Rallus limicola*

LIFE HISTORY Virginia Rails are like an ever-changing, constantly adapting wave sloshing around the landscape, in some places temporarily or permanently pooling up, in other places ebbing and flowing like quicksilver. This capacity for movement, along with their broad use of muddy, wet habitats, gives Virginia Rails a unique ability to exploit highly ephemeral niches—shallow wetlands that appear briefly after spring rains, dry up in the summer heat, and sometimes freeze over in the winter. They are restricted to wetlands, sometimes as temporary visitors or becoming locally abundant in more favored locations; but unless they are calling, they are frustratingly hard to find and can be easily missed.

Virginia Rails prefer marshes with an equal mix of emergent vegetation and more open patches of shallowly flooded mudflats or matted vegetation; they avoid stands of dense, older vegetation in favor of marshes in early stages of succession. In many locations they coexist with Soras, but use parts of the marshes that are drier to avoid competition. They consume many more insects than Soras, as well as small fish, worms, slugs, frogs, and even small snakes that they capture with their long curving bills; in the winter, they replace many of these items with more widely available seeds.

Virginia Rails have narrow bodies, extremely flexible vertebrae so they can twist and turn (which makes them inefficient flyers), and feathers on their foreheads modified to resist the constant abrasion of pushing headfirst through vegetation. Like all rails they have the highest ratio of leg muscles to wing muscles of any bird, so in the face of danger they run away rather than trying to fly.

From early April to mid-June, the breeding season begins as pairs grunt in unison and then announce their actual courtship several weeks later with choruses of *tick-it* calls. The breeding season varies widely in the Sierra Nevada depending on whether the rails at a given location are year-round residents or arrive in migration after marsh vegetation begins to leaf out, but at all locations their loud, distinctive calls are one of the characteristic signals that spring has arrived in the marshes.

Nests are loosely woven baskets of marsh vegetation, which are thrown together in time to hold the first eggs then continually reinforced with additional materials as more eggs (up to 13) are laid. Up to 5 "dummy" nests are also built, either as sleeping platforms or backups in case the primary nest fails or perhaps to confuse predators. Both sexes incubate, trading off at the nest every 1–2 hours for 19 days, and share in parental care until the chicks start flying at 4–7 weeks of age. Newly hatched chicks have been reported in the Sierra Nevada from mid-May to July. Pairs split up after the young fledge, with many adults retreating to large marshes in late summer, where they molt all their flight and tail feathers prior to growing new feathers and beginning their fall migration.

RANGE Virginia Rails breed widely across the western United States, with most retreating south to Mexico or west toward warmer coastal regions in winter. On both slopes of the Sierra Nevada they winter in larger numbers in the southern end of the range, but because they rarely vocalize in the winter, their actual distribution is poorly known. **WEST SLOPE:** Although they winter in small numbers below 3000 ft, most arrive in mid-April or May and begin breeding in all types of marshy, wet areas and boggy meadows up to about 7000 ft. Fall departure is leisurely and they may show up in new locations as they meander towards their wintering grounds in September and October. **EAST SLOPE:** A few hardy individuals may rarely linger in milder winters, except in the Owens Valley where they have become almost annual over the past 10 years. Spring migration begins in mid-April then peaks a month later when they become uncommon breeders in marshes and wet meadows as high as 8000 ft. They breed at Honey Lake but are apparently rare, and they may even be absent at nearby Lake Almanor (on the west slope).

SORA *Porzana carolina*

LIFE HISTORY Although Soras differ in being able to forage over a wider range of water depths and in eating more plant material, Soras and Virginia Rails live in many of the same marshes and share many behaviors. While Virginias use their long, curved bills to probe and poke into mud and matted vegetation in search of food, Soras use their stocky, chicken-like bills to pick up surface foods like the seeds of grasses and rushes in the winter, or insects and snails in the summer. Even though their nesting territories frequently overlap, they are not known to compete for resources.

Like Virginia Rails, Soras announce the beginning of the breeding season with loud calls that help pairs find each other and then stay in touch in the dense marsh vegetation. Soras have a remarkable call that sounds like a horse whinnying *whee-hee-hee-hee-hee-hee* that doubles as a contact call and as territorial defense. When pairs duet, the female's whinny is shorter and higher pitched, and usually follows the male's call by a half-step. Soras also make plaintive *ker-wee* calls on migration and for a very brief period of time when they first arrive on their breeding grounds in the spring.

Based on their arrival dates, Soras probably pair up in late April to mid-May. The pair cooperates to pile up a crudely arranged mound of vegetation loosely woven over the water among the stems of tall emergent vegetation. Males continue to collect nesting materials and bring them to the females who strengthen the nest structure as they lay more eggs. Once their 8–11 eggs are laid, the pair cooperates in all aspects of incubation, in addition to brooding and feeding chicks. Eggs hatch after 19 days and chicks start flying about 4 weeks later. Like Virginia Rails, Soras move to large marshes in late summer, molting and growing new wing and tail feathers in preparation for migration.

RANGE Soras are the most abundant and widely distributed rail in North America, but nearly all of their known breeding range occurs east of the Sierra Nevada crest. Spring migrants begin trickling into the region in mid-April with most breeding birds on territory by mid-May. Fall migration begins in mid-September with some Soras lingering longer at different locations (though few remain through the winter). Almost nothing is known of their altitudinal limits during the breeding season, but there are mid-summer records from boggy meadows and lake margins as high as 8300 ft that suggest they may be breeding at these elevations. **WEST SLOPE:** Although small numbers of Soras are reported on Christmas Bird Counts, their overall distribution is problematic. For example, they were once very rare on the Auburn count, but in the past 15 years they have become annual visitors even though they have never appeared on the adjacent Grass Valley count. There are no records from the Lake Almanor count in the north, and they have been found on less than half of the counts at the Kern River Valley in the south. Very little is known of their breeding status on the west slope, but they are at least present on deeper water marshes. **EAST SLOPE:** Widespread but generally uncommon, known to breed at Honey Lake, Sierra Valley, Lake Tahoe, and Mono Lake, but they have been observed at other marshes where they might breed. Except for Bishop, where they have become annual in recent years, Soras are extremely rare winter visitors on the east side.

AMERICAN COOT *Fulica americana*

LIFE HISTORY At certain times of year, coot numbers surpass all other birds. In the nonbreeding season, coots can be counted by the hundreds, thousands, and even tens of thousands on some lakes. One mid-winter count at Lake Almanor tallied 122,000 coots, and numbers like this could be possible on other lakes. It goes without saying that these black, chicken-like birds, found on every type of water, from stagnant ponds on golf courses to popular recreational lakes, are familiar to almost everyone.

Despite their duck-like behavior, coots are gregarious, open-water rails that share many morphological and behavioral features with other rails. They are primarily plant-eaters, picking pieces of plants from the surface or diving underwater and bringing stems, leaves, seeds, and tubers to the surface. They may add a mix of insects, mollusks, crayfish, and small aquatic vertebrates to their diets during the breeding season.

Coots are notorious for their constant squabbles and fights, especially on their breeding grounds when you will see them lift up their wings to reveal white undertail patches as they chase each other back and forth for hours. Physical confrontations between males often escalate into pitched battles, with males leaning back in the water, kicking at each other with their claws, and sometimes even grabbing each other's feet; some may even continue fighting underwater as one tries to make its escape. Coots are no less aggressive if other birds, or even potential predators, come anywhere near their nests.

Most coots nest on lakes, ponds, and marshes that have a combination of open water and patches of emergent vegetation along some part of the shoreline. Both sexes cooperate to defend a territory, and almost immediately upon arriving on their breeding grounds begin constructing up to 7 floating structures that they use as display platforms during courtship. All this extra work probably helps strengthen the pair bond and has the added advantage of giving marsh vegetation time to fully leaf out and help hide their nesting activities. A female will eventually pick one of the floating platforms and modify it to her specific nesting needs, which is a time-consuming task because the wet vegetation she uses to make her nest becomes waterlogged, decays, and sinks at the same time. Any material she stacks up on the nest's rim might sink down to the water level within 4 days, requiring that she constantly add new material.

The 8–12 eggs are probably laid sometime between April and August, but these dates are not specific because there is little data from the Sierra Nevada and because a second batch of eggs is usually laid after the first chicks are independent. Males do most of the incubating, and because eggs hatch on different days, females will take the first chicks on feeding expeditions while males continue incubating the late-hatching eggs. Males also build separate brooding platforms that females and chicks sleep on at night. Young birds are aggressively guarded and actively fed by their parents for at least 30 days; then chicks become increasingly independent over the next 30 days, wandering further and further from their parents and feeding themselves. They fly at 75 days of age and are chased away by their parents when they start looking like adults at about 80 days. In July–August, adults molt their flight and tail feathers and are flightless for 4 weeks.

Note: *Distinguished by their reddish bills and white flank patches,* **Common Moorhens** *are uncommon residents in the Central Valley and rarely stray to low-elevation foothill ponds and rivers; they are casual on the east side.*

RANGE American Coots are year-round residents almost everywhere in California, often occurring in such large numbers that it may be difficult to detect their complex seasonal movements. Migration is best understood by examining patterns on the east side, where they are more clearly defined. Spring migration seems to peak in April, perhaps as early as mid-March in the southern Sierra Nevada. Coots are then common breeders on many marshes and open bodies of water from April–August. Numbers pick up again at some sites in late August, and might represent local migrations to molting locations or to staging areas, but the main passage of fall migrants peaks in late September or October. **WEST SLOPE:** Common breeders in the lower foothills but the upper limits of their breeding range are not well described. Abundant in migration and during winter up to about 4000 ft, with numbers reaching the hundreds or thousands at some large lakes and reservoirs, or dozens of coots in smaller bodies of water. **EAST SLOPE:** Relatively uncommon in the winter on the east side, with numbers varying in response to weather but often reaching the hundreds on larger lakes and reservoirs that do not freeze. Locally common breeders on a wide variety of ponds, lakes, and marshes, with nesting records nearly to 8000 ft.

CRANES (Gruidae)

SANDHILL CRANE *Grus canadensis*

LIFE HISTORY Residents of the northern Sierra Nevada are familiar with the noisy bugling of these distinctive birds migrating overhead each spring and fall. Large numbers of Sandhill Cranes that winter in the Central Valley migrate over the mountains to and from breeding grounds that stretch from southeastern Oregon to northern Canada. Migration may span several weeks but there always seems to be one day of peak numbers in which group after group of loudly calling flocks stretch across the sky. On the east side of the Sierra Nevada, they stage in the productive meadows and marshes of Sierra Valley, where feeding cranes can number in the hundreds in early March, and from late August into early September. Cranes use their long, stout bills to forage for a wide variety of plant and animal materials though they feed extensively on cultivated grains where available.

A few pairs of cranes remain in Sierra Valley to nest in wet meadows and marshes, building large mounds of cattails, bulrushes, or other marsh vegetation. Courtship displays, which are readily viewed when migrating groups visit in March, involve complex calls that include trills, purrs, rattles, and elaborate leaping and dancing rituals that are thrilling to behold. Pairs stay together year round, and young birds may wait 2–7 years before they begin breeding.

Although two eggs are laid, pairs rarely raise more than one chick to fledging because the chicks often fight for dominance until one dies. Eggs are incubated by both parents for 30 days. Chicks begin to fly at 70 days of age, and family groups stay together until the following March. Coyotes are probably the most common predators of young chicks, while adults are only rarely killed, as when Golden Eagles have been observed picking cranes from out of flying flocks.

RANGE Sandhill Cranes spend the winter in the Central Valley then migrate over the Sierra Nevada, where they can be observed flying overhead, mostly north of Donner Pass. **WEST SLOPE:** The long-distance flights of Sandhill Cranes make it unlikely that any would land on the ground on the west slope, unless injured or temporarily blocked by a powerful storm during migration. **EAST SLOPE:** Migrants are observed in the northern Sierra Nevada, with Sierra Valley being a significant staging site. Other east-side marshes and wet meadows of the northern Sierra Nevada may attract smaller numbers during migration. A few pairs nest in Sierra Valley and at nearby Kyburz Flat. Cranes formerly migrated through Bridgeport Valley and Long Valley east of Yosemite National Park, with some wintering in Owens Valley, but there are only a couple recent records of cranes in these areas.

PLOVERS (Charadriidae)

KILLDEER *Charadrius vociferus*

LIFE HISTORY These intriguing plovers are one of the few birds that have adapted favorably to the presence of humans. Formerly limited to nesting on narrowly restricted habitats like gravel riverbanks, Killdeer now readily nest and forage in a wide variety of similarly barren or exposed places like agricultural fields, gravel rooftops, athletic fields, highway shoulders, and city parks.

Towering high on relatively long legs, these alert birds constantly scan for food or the approach of potential predators. And like other plovers, their typical foraging strategy is to run forward a few steps, stop and scan, then run forward again, or turn aside to chase after grasshoppers, beetles, or worms. Their usual calls are a variety of *dee* or *dee-ee* calls, but when they are nervous they begin making trilling noises, and when they feel greatly alarmed they break into their trademark *kill-deer* cries.

Their eggs and chicks are highly vulnerable to predators on the open ground, so Killdeer do not rely solely on heart-wrenching cries to protect their nests. Parents will also run away and act as if they have a nest somewhere else, or attempt to distract intruders by pretending that they have a broken wing, flailing and crying as they draw attention away from their chicks. During many of these distraction displays they spread their flashy orange tails to create even more of a show.

Perhaps because they nest in such exposed locations, where

ground temperatures reach over 100 degrees Fahrenheit in the summer sun, Killdeer begin nesting in March. Pairs make simple dirt scrapes together as part of their pair-bonding rituals, eventually lining one with a mix of pebbles, shells, feathers, and bits of plastic to create a mottled appearance that blends into the surrounding ground surface. Both parents incubate 4 eggs, standing over them to create shade on hot days, or even wetting their breast feathers to help protect the eggs with evaporative cooling. Eggs hatch in 22–28 days, and the highly mobile chicks leave the nest within hours although they remain with their parents until they can fly at 20 days of age. Most pairs are thought to raise 2–3 broods each summer.

RANGE Killdeer are common year-round residents in the foothills though a few may nest from 5000 ft to treeline, moving upslope in April then remaining at higher elevations until early fall. Large numbers probably migrate through the region in April–May and August–October but they are hard to detect because Killdeer are already so common. **WEST SLOPE:** Readily observed in open areas below 3000 ft, becoming increasingly uncommon at higher elevations. At lower elevations, they are especially common when they gather by the dozens on agricultural fields and grassy meadows during migration or in the winter. **EAST SLOPE:** Fairly common year-round residents at lower elevations, but in cold and snowy winters they move further south or disappear temporarily. They sometimes breed at montane locations, like at Lake Tahoe where they are regular breeders as high as the upper limits of the Mixed Conifer Zone.

SANDPIPERS, PHALAROPES and ALLIES (Scolopacidae)

[**Note:** *At least 24 species of sandpipers and other shorebirds are observed annually in the Sierra Nevada, primarily as uncommon migrants; in addition, there are several other species that are very rare visitors. The most common migrating and breeding species are covered here while other species are discussed in Appendix 1.*]

SPOTTED SANDPIPER *Actitis macularius*

LIFE HISTORY Spotted Sandpipers are a lively presence along the shorelines of countless Sierra Nevada lakes and rivers. Constantly bobbing their rear ends up and down as if they were about to fall over, they chase each other, vigorously defend territories, and give *peet-weet* calls that ring loudly across the water. Much of this activity is part of a remarkable breeding strategy shared by few other birds, in which females arrive early and establish territories, then sing and fight other females in their attempts to attract males. Females may sequentially acquire up to 4 mates, building a nest and laying a clutch of eggs with each male, then leaving the males to care for the eggs and fledglings on their own. Their fighting is so intense that injuries are common, with adults sometimes breaking wings or legs, and chicks trapped in the skirmishes sometimes suffering fractured skulls.

This breeding strategy has added layers of complexity because some females are monogamous and help raise the eggs and nestlings; all males also defend their own territories; and some males sing to attract mates. Either sex may make a nest, which is a simple scrape in the dirt, using it as a place to sing and attract mates, or a paired male and female may make scrapes side by side.

In between bouts of courtship and territorial defense, Spotted Sandpipers walk along water edges scanning for aquatic or terrestrial insects, making quick runs to snap up food items. They move to new locations by flying with stiff, fluttering wingbeats, usually uttering a long series of *peet* calls as they fly and land.

Nests are located on the ground anywhere from the water's edge to 900 ft away, placed under protective branches or bits of vegetation and positioned to avoid whichever predators are most common in a given location. Females lay 4 eggs, but invest variable amounts of time into the care of eggs and fledglings, while males always do most of the incubation of eggs and care of young birds. Eggs hatch after 21 days and young birds leave the nest within hours of hatching, able to feed themselves but still tended by males (and sometimes females) for more than 4 weeks.

RANGE Breed along rivers and lakes from the lower edges of the conifer forests up to tree line (up to 11,000 ft). Peak numbers in the mountains occur from May and August. By October, they leave the mountains though a few may linger in the foothills and valley bottoms for all or part of the winter. **WEST SLOPE:** Locally uncommon summer residents up to tree line. During the nonbreeding season, they are widespread in the Central Valley and some wander into the lowest edges of the foothills. Year-round residents in the Kern River Valley. **EAST SLOPE:** Spring migrants appear along the east side in April, gathering in valley bottoms and then moving upslope in May. Large numbers reappear in valley bottoms in September, correlating with their departure from the mountains in late August and possibly with a pulse of southbound migrants from north of California. A few linger on the east side until October.

WESTERN SANDPIPER *Calidris mauri*

LIFE HISTORY When flocks of migrating shorebirds appear each spring and fall on Sierra Nevada mudflats, Western Sandpipers comprise the matrix in which rarer species mingle. These sandpipers are so common that they provide an ideal point of comparison for identifying other small shorebirds. They are frequently seen with Least Sandpipers though the longer bills on Western Sandpipers allow them to forage for aquatic invertebrates in slightly deeper waters, resulting in a subtle segregation between the two species.

RANGE Compared to other small shorebirds, Western Sandpipers appear to migrate in short flights and to stay longer at each stopping point. This may account for their predictable and widespread appearance throughout the Sierra Nevada while other shorebirds fly past the region. Western Sandpipers prefer mudflats at the margins of larger water bodies, but they may show up at virtually any wet area. As an example, they regularly visit the concrete spillway at Lake Van Norden near Donner Pass. Spring migration peaks in late April, with birds still moving north until mid-May. Fall migration begins when adults arrive in early July then continues as juveniles move through in early August. They remain common until mid-September, then are rarely observed into early winter. **WEST SLOPE:** Fairly common migrants that stop at lake margins, wetlands, and shorelines; restricted to lower elevations in spring, but possible at any elevation in fall. **EAST SLOPE:** Common to abundant migrants at traditional shorebird sites like Honey Lake, Lake Tahoe, and Mono Lake, but they are encountered at numerous other locations.

LEAST SANDPIPER *Calidris minutilla*

LIFE HISTORY Although numerous and widespread, the world's smallest shorebirds are easily overlooked as they pick their way through sparse vegetation at the upper edges of mudflats or forage with slightly larger Western Sandpipers. Often the first signs of their presence are the quick, high-pitched, trilling calls as single birds or small flocks flush briefly and resettle on another patch of mud. Tame and tolerant of close approach, Least Sandpipers provide rare opportunities for detailed observations of shorebird behavior. Unlike other shorebirds that run in pursuit of prey, Leasts seem to spend their time looking down with a characteristic hunched posture, pecking or probing at the soft mud for aquatic insects and worms. When not foraging, they settle inconspicuously in patches of short vegetation at the edges of mudflats. They seek mudflats at the margins of lakes, streams, and marshes but also visit flooded fields and other sites with shallow water. When mingling with other shorebirds, Leasts may segregate out due to their preference for drier sites further from the water's edge.

RANGE Migrating on a broad front across all of North America, Least Sandpipers readily show up at a wide variety of inland sites from valley marshes to high-elevation lakeshores. More so than other small shorebirds they tolerate cold conditions, arriving earlier in spring, staying later in autumn, or even overwintering in small numbers. Common to abundant spring migrants in April, with smaller numbers lingering into mid-May. Fall migrants return in mid-July and move through the region in relatively steady numbers until mid-September though never as abundantly as during spring migration. There are few winter records from the northern Sierra Nevada, but they occur in small numbers at some southern locations. **WEST SLOPE:** Widespread and possible at nearly any suitable location. However, they are seldom reported so their actual status and distribution is poorly known. **EAST SLOPE:** Readily observed at traditional shorebird sites such as Honey Lake, Lake Tahoe, and Mono Lake, but occur regularly at marshes and mudflats throughout the region.

Short-billed Dowitcher *Limnodromus griseus*

LIFE HISTORY See Long-billed Dowitcher below.

RANGE Although usually associated with coastal mudflats, Short-billed Dowitchers also show up in the Sierra Nevada, Central Valley, and Great Basin though in significantly lower numbers than their long-billed cousins. Overall they migrate slightly earlier than Long-billeds, both in spring and fall. Spring migration occurs in April. Southbound adults reach peak numbers during the latter half of July, followed by a peak of juveniles in late August. Some individuals linger until the end of September. Found along the margin of lakes, ponds, flooded fields, and streams with muddy shorelines. **WEST SLOPE:** Casual visitors, they may be more likely in fall, but it is hard to draw conclusions from the few records. **EAST SLOPE:** Fairly common during spring and fall migration from Mono Lake to Owens Valley, rare elsewhere.

LONG-BILLED DOWITCHER *Limnodromus scolopaceus*

LIFE HISTORY The two dowitchers are remarkably similar birds, sharing the same feeding behaviors and looking virtually identical in some plumages. Recent examination of their DNA reveals, however, that they are widely separated genetically and that they diverged from a common ancestor nearly 4 million years ago. Dowitchers are best known for their manic "sewing machine" or "stitching" feeding motions, and most birders are familiar with the sight of dowitchers hunched over, intently probing their long bills into soft mud. The tips of their bills possess countless sensitive nerves that enable them to instantaneously detect buried worms and larvae by touch.

Dowitchers are nearly always found in flocks on mudflats, with Long-billeds occurring in smaller groups than Short-billeds and showing more of a preference for muddy rather than sandy substrates. Long-billeds also differ in breeding further north and subsequently migrating south later than Short-billeds.

RANGE An estimated 30 percent of the world's migrating Long-billed Dowitchers pass through the Lahontan Basin, just 50 miles east of the Sierra Nevada. It is no surprise that dowitchers on this pathway spill over into the eastern Sierra Nevada in substantial numbers, showing up in wet areas from valley marshes to mountain lakes. While partial to the muddy margins of lakes or slow-moving rivers, they also frequent waterlogged agricultural lands and marshy areas of all types. Spring migration peaks from late April to mid-May. Southbound adults reach their peak numbers around the end of August while juveniles peak from late September through October (about one month later than Short-billeds). Individuals may linger into winter. **WEST SLOPE:** Uncommon migrant and rare in winter, both being periods of spillover from large numbers that use adjacent Central Valley habitats. **EAST SLOPE:** Generally common during migration though some sites such as Sierra Valley attract higher numbers in spring than fall, and at other sites like Mono Lake the opposite is true, with no apparent pattern.

WILSON'S SNIPE *Gallinago delicata*

LIFE HISTORY Most of their lives, snipes stay so well hidden that they are almost impossible find. Squat and streaky, they hide among the grasses of wet meadows, unseen until almost stepped on, then exploding up with a hoarse call in a short, erratically veering flight that ends when they drop back into the marsh grasses without warning.

Wilson's Snipes spend most of their time with their heads down, probing their extraordinarily long bills into soft mud in search of buried larval insects. The tips of their bills are flexible and packed with nerves, so they can feel their food items and open the tips of their bills to grab without having to pull their heads up. To help them see approaching predators, the eyes of snipes have been shifted towards the backs of their skulls, giving them excellent vision to the rear (and when they have their heads down they can look up).

Immediately after arriving on their breeding grounds in May, males sit on prominent outlooks, such as fence posts or rocks, in the middle of the wet meadows where they breed. Males announce their territories by flying overhead and making "winnowing" sounds as they dive steeply and veer sideways to send air rushing through their outer tail feathers to create a series of haunting *whi-whi-whi-whi-WHI-WHI-WHI* notes.

At the edges of marshes or flooded fields, females build tightly woven, well-concealed nests in dense grasses. Females tend their 4 eggs alone, but males stay close by, and when the young hatch after 17–20 days, the pair each takes half the brood and split up. This strategy of one parent not helping with incubation but sharing responsibility for the young birds is very rare in shorebirds. Adults feed the chicks for several weeks longer, and when they are 6 weeks old, young birds leave to form their own loose groups.

RANGE Wilson's Snipes are present all year but their numbers increase significantly on the east side in the breeding season, where moist meadows and marshes seem to offer optimal nesting habitat for snipes. They favor open marshlands, or even partly flooded fields, but avoid both open mudflats and dense vegetation. During migration and winter, they may appear in a wide variety of moist settings, even in locations with miniscule amounts of habitat. **WEST SLOPE:** Very local breeders at low elevations and maybe as high as the Mixed Conifer Zone, but so rarely reported that it is hard to tell if they are rare or uncommon. More widespread and occurring in greater numbers during migration and the winter. Fall migrants have appeared as high as 9000 ft. **EAST SLOPE:** Spring migrants arrive in May along the entire east side, but in June and July they are mainly found north of Mono Lake, where they are common around wet meadows and marshes. In August, they are once again found along the entire length of the east side. Their numbers slowly dwindle through the fall, but some linger all winter long, especially at Sierra Valley, Mono Lake, and the Owens Valley,

Wilson's Phalarope *Phalaropus tricolor*

LIFE HISTORY Each summer these diminutive trans-equatorial migrants make an impressive showing on the briny waters of Mono Lake where over 80,000 Wilson's Phalaropes appear in July and August. So important is the lake to the lives of these birds that Mono Lake has been designated part of the Western Hemisphere Shorebird Reserve Network. Over the course of weeks, individual phalaropes molt into their nonbreeding plumage then lay on enough fat reserves to make one mighty flight to the coast of South America. Some birds become so overweight that they cannot fly and have to wait several hours until they metabolize excess fat.

Phalaropes actively, sometimes almost hyperactively, feed on small aquatic invertebrates at or below the water's surface, picking them up with rapid-fire stabs of their fine, needle-like bills, and sometimes spinning like tops while feeding. This spinning motion creates an underwater vortex that sucks prey items up towards the surface. Such behavior is seldom observed at Mono Lake, where alkali flies and brine shrimp are superabundant, but may be observed on other lakes where it is harder to find food.

They nest throughout the interior of North America, reaching the Sierra Nevada at scattered sites on the east side. Like Spotted Sandpipers, phalaropes have reversed sex roles, with females being more colorful than the drab males and aggressively fighting each other for opportunities to mate with males. In dense vegetation around lakes and marshes, they build inconspicuous nests where females lay 4 eggs that they leave in the sole care of males. Females then find another mate or fly to molting areas that are rich in foods, such as Mono Lake.

RANGE Wilson's Phalaropes first appear in mid-April, and their numbers build by early May until they become common in some locations. Some linger to breed at low-elevation marshes around Honey Lake, Sierra Valley, Mono Basin, and Owens Valley, as well as at scattered locations in the mountains, including the south end of Lake Tahoe. After breeding, many phalaropes fly to Mono Lake, one of 5 major migration staging areas in North America. Females arrive first, followed by males then juveniles, and they are common from mid-June to mid-August. They are uncommon at Mono Lake until the end of September, and a few individuals linger into October. **WEST SLOPE:** Rare in spring and uncommon in fall, potentially appearing at any body of water. Numbers are generally low because the west slope is not on a significant migration route, except at Lake Almanor where they are fairly common migrants and remain fairly common through the summer (possibly breeding). **EAST SLOPE:** Widespread spring migrants, then locally common breeders at the sites listed above. Most birds move toward Mono Lake after breeding, but they can also be common at Honey Lake, Sierra Valley, and other intermediate locations until the end of July.

RED-NECKED PHALAROPE *Phalaropus lobatus*

LIFE HISTORY Despite the fact that these small and dainty phalaropes spend as much as 9 months of the year living on tropical oceans and then fly north to breed on arctic tundra, they still manage a fairly impressive showing in the Sierra Nevada during migration. Like other phalaropes, Red-necked Phalaropes possess dense breast feathers that hold pockets of air and keep the birds extremely buoyant. These types of specialized adaptations place phalaropes in their own subfamily within the shorebirds.

Very little is known about the winter ecology of these birds, and the little bit that is known about their migratory behavior derives from studies conducted at Mono Lake. Here, they stop briefly (1–2 weeks) to feast heavily on pupating brine flies that concentrate around submerged tufa formations. After morning feeding bouts near shoreline tufa, flocks of Red-necked Phalaropes move offshore to roost for the day or fly briefly to freshwater sites where they bathe and drink. While Wilson's Phalaropes linger long enough at Mono Lake to molt their feathers, Red-necked Phalaropes quickly move on to wintering sites off the coast of Central and South America.

RANGE The spring migration of Red-necked Phalaropes occurs primarily off the Pacific coast, but small numbers appear at inland sites, perhaps due to flocks flying north from the Gulf of California and crossing the Great Basin on route to Canadian breeding grounds. Females vacate their nesting areas after only a couple weeks and reappear in California around mid-July, joining small numbers that never make the journey north. Males, and then juveniles, return in August and September. Their short visits and their tendency to appear at nearly any water body suggest that fall migration consists of short hops rather than long-distance flights. Sewage ponds and saline lakes are preferred stops during migration. **WEST SLOPE:** Spring migrants are extremely rare visitors at low-elevation bodies of water. Fall migrants are uncommon in the Kern River Valley, with scattered records from other water bodies up to 10,000 ft. **EAST SLOPE:** Widespread during migration but they are best known and occur in the largest numbers at Mono Lake.

Spring migration is brief with most observations in the first half of May. Fall migration more protracted, beginning in mid-July and lasting until mid-October. During the peak from August to early September, tens of thousands may be seen at Mono Lake in a single day (a total of 65,000 are estimated to stop at the lake during fall migration).

GULLS and TERNS (Laridae)

[**Note:** *At least 15 species of jaegers, gulls, and terns are observed annually in the Sierra Nevada, many as scarce migrants or winter visitors. The species that regularly breed in the region are covered here, others in Appendix 1.*]

RING-BILLED GULL *Larus delawarensis*

LIFE HISTORY Ring-billed Gulls are best known for hanging out and waiting for scraps of food around parking lots, shopping centers, picnic areas, and viewpoints. They also congregate near agricultural fields, sewage treatment plants, and any body of water, where they search for insects, worms, fish, rodents, and grains. Like California Gulls, they primarily winter on the coast and breed in the interior of North America, but many Ring-billed Gulls linger longer at inland sites and can be found year round in the Sierra Nevada.

Ring-billed Gulls breed in large colonies on the sparsely vegetated islands of large lakes, including a colony that often reaches 2000 nests at Honey Lake. Pairs cooperate in building nests of twigs and plant materials on the ground next to low plants, and their nests are often mixed in among the nests of other waterbirds. Both sexes incubate their 2–3 eggs beginning in early to mid-May. Chicks are able to fly when about 35 days old, with family groups breaking up and beginning to leave their nesting colonies a week later, usually in late July to August.

RANGE Ring-billed Gulls are present in the Sierra Nevada at all times of the year, but most are migrants that only pause briefly from mid-March to mid-April as they fly from the coast to their breeding sites. There is a much bigger influx of adults and juveniles heading towards the coast in mid-August to mid-November. The only exception to this pattern occurs in valleys and marshes of the northeastern Sierra Nevada, where a large number gather from mid-March to mid-May, apparently in preparation for nesting at nearby Honey Lake. In late summer, both migrants and postbreeding birds from Honey Lake gather in agricultural fields and dry meadows almost anywhere in the Sierra Nevada to feast on grasshoppers. During migration they show up at any body of water, as evidenced by records from as high as 10,400 ft, while wintering birds may linger in any body of water that does not freeze. **WEST SLOPE:** Widespread throughout the year though typically in very low numbers. Large reservoirs and rivers at low elevations can sometimes attract significant numbers in mid-winter, with high counts of 600 birds each at Lake Almanor and Isabella Lake, and up to 4300 birds at Folsom Lake and the Nimbus Fish Hatchery. **EAST SLOPE:** Found throughout the year but seemingly in lower numbers than on the west slope. During migration, especially fall migration, single birds or groups of dozens to hundreds may suddenly appear at almost any location. Outside of migration many sightings are of single birds, but up to 1700 have been found at Honey Lake and 125 at Lake Tahoe in mid-winter. In the breeding season, thousands may gather to nest at Honey Lake from mid-May until late July, but these numbers vary from year to year, depending on lake levels and availability of food.

CALIFORNIA GULL *Larus californicus*

LIFE HISTORY Due to the well-publicized controversy of water being diverted from Mono Lake, it is possible that California Gulls have attracted more media coverage and more fans than any other Sierra Nevada bird. At one time, 50,000 gulls nested on Negit Island in Mono Lake, making it the second largest California Gull colony in the world, but after lake levels dropped when water was diverted to Los Angeles, coyotes started crossing a land bridge to the island in 1979, preying on eggs and chicks. Mono Lake levels have risen in recent years and the island has been reoccupied by nesting gulls once again, but it may take several generations for their numbers to rebound.

California Gulls nest on isolated islands in large lakes scattered around the arid interior West. Nesting colonies move from year to year based on lake levels and food availability, but several long-term colonies can be found along the eastern side of the Sierra Nevada. In addition to Mono Lake, nesting colonies are found at Honey Lake and Topaz Lake. During March and April it is common to see large groups of California Gulls crossing over the Sierra Nevada on route to their breeding colonies. Thousands can be found around their breeding sites, and adults regularly fly up to 40 miles to search for food in alpine lakes, schoolyards, irrigated farm fields, garbage dumps, or on sagebrush flats. Pairs cooperate in building simple stick nests on the ground and incubating their 2–3 eggs. Chicks are highly mobile but are fed by their parents for 45 days until they are able to fly. Fledglings disperse widely or head for the coast within weeks of their first flights while adults loaf and relax for a month or more before leaving the nesting area.

RANGE California Gulls are gregarious and usually occur in large numbers at traditional locations, but they also wander and can be and found almost anywhere in California. Winter mainly along the coast and in the Central Valley, then breed in approximately 13 isolated colonies in northeastern and eastern California. **WEST SLOPE:** Due to the proximity of their typical wintering areas in the Central Valley, California Gulls can be abundant at some large rivers and reservoirs on the lower west slope though numbers taper off sharply above the foothills. In the central Sierra Nevada, for example, up to 27,000 have been recorded on the Folsom Christmas Bird Count at 300 ft; while up to a 1000 (but generally much fewer) are seen on the Auburn Christmas Bird Count at 1200 ft; and the Grass Valley Christmas Bird Count at 2400 ft has one record of two birds. By April, groups of migrating gulls are regularly observed flying eastward over the foothills and crest. Nonbreeding adults and young birds may linger through the summer on the west slope at any elevation. **EAST SLOPE:** Present in very low numbers through the winter. Beginning in late March, numbers increase dramatically at breeding areas like Mono Lake, or at staging areas like Lake Tahoe and Sierra Valley. Most birds at staging areas leave for breeding sites by late April though some linger through the summer. During the summer, foraging gulls are found at diverse habitats from valley floor to alpine lake.

CASPIAN TERN *Hydroprogne caspia*

LIFE HISTORY Largest of the world's 44 tern species, Caspian Terns are as bulky and aggressive as some of the large gulls. In flight, they have little of the dainty, buoyant air of their smaller cousins, but are instead powerful, direct fliers with loud screeching calls. They come closest to being tern-like when they spot swimming fish and pause to hover lightly in mid-air before plunging into the water to catch their prey.

Caspian Terns nest in isolated colonies on desolate islands in large rivers and lakes scattered throughout the interior of North America. A few of these colonies exist on the eastern edge of the Sierra Nevada, but their suitability depends on water levels that change from year to year, meaning that colonies may be abandoned for years and new colonies may spring up at new sites. The largest colony, at Honey Lake, often hosts 250 pairs.

Caspian Terns typically nest with California Gulls, Double-crested Cormorants, and other large waterbirds starting in mid-May. Pairs of terns cooperate to scrape out simple nests in the sand, in some cases lining the scrapes with vegetation and constructing rims around their nests. The 2–3 eggs are incubated by both parents for 25–27 days, and both parents feed the chicks until they fledge 37 days later. Young birds remain dependent on their parents for several more months, and begging youngsters may be spotted hundreds of miles from their breeding colonies, causing confusion about "potential nesting records."

RANGE Caspian Terns winter along the southern California coast but are uncommon at inland sites. They migrate widely across California and breed on a handful of lakes on the east side of the Sierra Nevada and in northeastern California. **WEST SLOPE:** Seldom reported but possible at any large body of water, and they may actually be fairly common at some sites. Observed at low-elevation lakes and reservoirs from Lake Oroville to Isabella Lake in April, May, June, July, and September. Have been seen on two occasions on the Lake Almanor Christmas Bird Count. **EAST SLOPE:** Fairly common migrants in both spring and fall, while nonbreeding adults are uncommon throughout the summer in areas away from nesting sites. Caspian Terns may appear briefly in Owens Valley by late March, and at Lake Tahoe by late April, but then quickly establish themselves on nesting colonies at Honey Lake, Bridgeport Reservoir, and Mono Lake. By mid-August their numbers increase at large lakes as adults and their dependent juveniles abandon the nesting colonies and head south in stages. At this time, they wander widely and have been reported at lakes over 10,000 ft. They are rare on the east side after mid-September.

BLACK TERN *Chlidonias niger*

LIFE HISTORY These remarkable birds differ from other terns in being all black and in hunting insects as well as fish. They are lightweight terns, with an extremely buoyant, erratic flight. Highly social, Black Terns may be observed in large groups at traditional sites (50–100 at a time are not unheard of in the Sierra Nevada) but they are just as readily observed singly or at unexpected locations.

Black Terns nest semi-colonially in the emergent vegetation of shallow freshwater marshes, but they are highly susceptible to changing water levels and to habitat changes so their colonies are somewhat ephemeral. All the known nesting colonies in the Sierra Nevada are located on the east slope north of Lake Tahoe, mainly at Honey Lake and Mountain Meadows Reservoir, although they have also nested in Sierra Valley when habitat conditions suit their needs.

Nest building simply involves a pair tossing waterlogged vegetation into a pile to create a soggy, floating platform. Their 2–4 eggs are laid in late May and incubated by both parents. Young hatch in mid- to late June and most birds leave their nesting colonies by mid- to late July, when they all move to favorable feeding areas. Juveniles migrate south about a month after adults.

RANGE Black Terns are present in the Sierra Nevada from early May (exceptionally in late April) until mid-September. Despite the limited Sierra Nevada breeding population (maybe less than 50 pairs), they are encountered on the east side away from breeding areas in June and July with surprising frequency, indicating that some nonbreeding birds may linger at east-side lakes through the summer. Groups of 20 or more have been reported in June, July, and August. **WEST SLOPE:** Very rarely reported away from their breeding colony of about 20 birds at Mountain Meadow Reservoir in the northeastern corner of the Sierra Nevada. Even at nearby Lake Almanor they are rare in the spring and summer. They are likewise rare during spring and fall migration at Isabella Lake. **EAST SLOPE:** Uncommon but regular visitors from May to September at low-elevation lakes (Mono Lake, Crowley Lake, and large bodies of water around Bishop and Owens Valley) and at Lake Tahoe. A small colony (of perhaps 5 pairs) breeds at Honey Lake, and they also nest some years in Sierra Valley. Other groups may occasionally breed in the northeastern Sierra Nevada but they are readily overlooked.

FORSTER'S TERN *Sterna forsteri*

LIFE HISTORY These lanky, marsh-dwelling terns are the only terns restricted to North America throughout the year. In the winter, they retreat to the coast, but during the breeding season most of the population scatters to nesting colonies in the interior. They are usually observed swooping back and forth low over marshes and large bodies of water with their heads angled down as they scan for small fish. By late May, most breeding adults have gathered around wetlands and open marshes to begin breeding, and nesting efforts commence in early June. Their nesting requirements are fickle, so breeding populations may move from site to site over the years. Adults will also abandon their nests if disturbed by humans, boats, or dogs.

Both parents help construct a simple mass of soggy vegetation on floating reeds or occupy abandoned grebe nests where females lay 2–3 eggs. They may also nest in simple scrapes in the sand on isolated rocky beaches. Their precocial chicks leave the nest within a week of hatching and make their first flights at 4 weeks of age. Juveniles may continue to be fed for a month or more after they start flying, so an observation of parents feeding fledglings doesn't necessarily mean they nested nearby.

RANGE Early arriving Forster's Terns have been recorded at Lake Tahoe and at Bishop in mid-April, and within weeks large numbers show up at or near their breeding areas. They remain fairly common, mostly in the vicinity of breeding areas, through the summer, and then begin moving toward wintering areas in September. Nearly all leave by the end of September, but there are a couple of late fall and winter records. **WEST SLOPE:** There are only a few spring records from late April to early May, when they are possible at any large, low-elevation reservoir or lake. At Isabella Lake they are fairly common during spring migration but become rare by summer. Some nest at Mountain Meadows Reservoir. There are very few fall records from the west slope. **EAST SLOPE:** Nesting has been recorded at Leavitt Lake, Honey Lake, Sierra Valley, Lake Tahoe, and possibly at Bridgeport Reservoir, but they do not breed every year at all of these locations. Up to 135 have been reported from Lake Tahoe in mid-August, but they are more often seen in small numbers on east-side lakes and reservoirs during their September migration.

PIGEONS and DOVES (Columbidae)

ROCK PIGEON *Columba livia*

LIFE HISTORY Due to their long history of domestication and their confiding nature, Rock Pigeons have become such a familiar and ubiquitous part of the urban landscape that most people scarcely pay attention to them. Few birdwatchers record their presence in the Sierra Nevada, and oddly, their distribution in the region is poorly documented.

Rock Pigeons can be expected around most of the foothill towns and large ranches, as well as at other locations like railroad yards where grain cars are loaded and unloaded. Although they can survive in the wild by eating seeds, fruits, and some insects, their preference for cereal grains such as corn and oats keeps them largely confined to urban and agricultural areas. Complicating the picture even further, there is a constant mixing of feral and domesticated pigeons, so you never know if you are seeing wild pigeons or a group of free-roaming domestic pigeons out for a spin.

It is still fun to watch these flocks because they are constantly active and have a variety of vocalizations and behaviors; in fact, much of our fundamental knowledge about birds comes from scientists who have studied pigeons. And because pigeons usually breed year round, you can almost always see some type of courtship behavior. Look for pigeons bowing and cooing at each other, and after successful copulations males may fly up and loudly clap their wings together. Courting females beg for food and males demonstrate their ability to provide food by regurgitating ready-to-eat meals. Pigeons and doves are the only birds in North America that can drink water by suction without having to lift their heads up (much as humans drink water through a straw)—an adaptation that allows them to drink quickly, then fly to safety.

Pairs are monogamous and mate for life. They nest almost anywhere—on cliffs, in buildings, under bridges—as long as there is a flat surface and some sort of cover overhead. The female sits and calls as the male brings her nesting material one piece at a time. They have an average of 6 broods a year, typically reusing the same nest but adding new material each time to cover up the messy dried feces of the last batch of chicks, thus building up the nest substantially over the course of a year.

Pigeons feed their chicks a special, protein-rich "pigeon milk" that they produce from the lining of their esophagus, giving them the freedom to raise chicks at any time of year, even when there are no protein-rich insects available. Two eggs are laid in each clutch and they are incubated for 18 days, with females taking the night shift and males taking the day shift. Nestlings begin flying and depart at 30 days (in the summer) to 45 days (in the winter).

RANGE Rock Pigeons were first introduced to North America from Europe in the 1600s and soon spread across the continent. They are now widespread permanent residents almost everywhere in California. Their distribution is more limited at higher elevations, but this is probably due more to the absence of cities and agricultural grains than to an intolerance for cold. In the Sierra Nevada they seem to be locally common residents around most towns and agricultural areas, regardless of location or elevation, with a few wild flocks wandering into nearby canyons and forests. Because pigeons are such familiar and overlooked birds there have been no systematic surveys that document their distribution in the Sierra Nevada.

BAND-TAILED PIGEON *Patagioenas fasciata*

LIFE HISTORY Band-tailed Pigeons are strong-flying, highly mobile birds that roam great distances, mostly in search of their primary food, acorns, but sometimes in search of mineral-rich springs where they take long drinks. Because oaks produce copious crops of acorns some years, then very few in other years, Band-tailed Pigeon numbers are likewise highly variable, becoming locally abundant wherever they find a rich source of food, including flowers of dogwoods, madrones, oaks, and some shrubs in spring; various berries and fruits in summer; and grains and pine nuts in autumn.

Although these heavy-bodied birds are conspicuous in flight, they stay well-hidden when perched on tree branches and often reveal themselves in a noisy explosion of wildly beating wings when approached too closely. You may also hear soft, low frequency *whit-woooo* calls or drawn-out and guttural *caaaa* calls emanating from unseen birds on high branches. It is not surprising that they are skittish because in the early 1900s they were extensively slaughtered by market hunters and are still hunted in many areas. But these pigeons live up to 22 years and seem to have good memories because in areas where they are not hunted, they readily learn to trust backyard bird feeders and can become regular visitors.

In the Sierra Nevada, the nesting season begins in April when it is possible to witness courtship displays that include birds making short, floating flights with rapidly quivering wings and spread tails. But they have a long breeding season with pairs laying up to 3 separate clutches of single eggs. Eggs have been reported from late February to late October although the normal breeding season probably lasts from April–September.

Nests are loose platforms of sticks that do not look like they could hold an egg in place. Incubation lasts 16–20 days with females taking over at night and males in the day. Chicks are fed "crop milk" derived from the lining of their parent's esophagus, and they fledge in 22–29 days. The lives of juvenile pigeons have not been studied, but immature birds have been seen begging and being fed long after they have left their nests.

RANGE The highly mobile nature of Band-tailed Pigeons makes it difficult to separate true migrations from the movements of local birds, but the general pattern seems to be that they migrate north to Oregon and Washington, or upslope into the higher forests of the Sierra Nevada, in April. In the Sierra Nevada they nest mostly in mixed conifer forests, especially in the presence of black oaks, from 2000–7000 ft. They are frequently observed at higher elevations (8000 ft to over 9000 ft) in mid- to late summer and may breed there as well. By the end of September there is a strong movement downslope into oak woodlands and oak-lined canyons below 4000 ft, where they seem to wander widely in search of the best acorn crops. **WEST SLOPE:** Highly episodic winter visitors, absent many years and locally abundant other years. But they are present every year on the Grass Valley Christmas Bird Count, often by the hundreds, and are relatively regular on the Yosemite National Park count, even though they are very irregular and even scarce at many other locations. This either suggests that there is a core wintering area in the central Sierra Nevada, or that their winter distribution needs further study. **EAST SLOPE:** South of Lake Tahoe, where the east slope becomes steep and forests more highly fragmented, Band-tailed Pigeons are scarce and even casual, being unreported for years at a time in some areas. There is one nesting record from Mammoth, and only 70 sightings from Inyo County for example. North of Lake Tahoe, their breeding populations vary from uncommon to fairly common in various montane forests, especially those that have at least a small oak component.

Mourning Dove *Zenaida macroura*

LIFE HISTORY Mourning Doves have a whole collection of enduring attributes including gentle, confiding mannerisms; funny ways of bobbing their heads and bodies as they walk; and loving gestures shown by pairs as they perch side by side and tenderly nibble each other's feathers. In low-elevation towns, city parks, backyards, and open grasslands, they are among the most abundant of all birds and their plaintive *coo-OO-OO-OO* calls are a recurring element of the summer soundtrack.

Doves are found year round in the Sierra Nevada, but there must also be a huge movement of migrants and wintering birds into the region because a large portion of the Mourning Doves in the western United States are thought to spend the winter in California. Spring migration occurs in April and by the end of the month most have arrived on their breeding grounds and begun cooing to attract mates. They nest in almost every type of upland habitat except deep woods, but they prefer openings and edges, even along roadsides, and almost always near drinking water that they need to survive the dry summer.

Males that have successfully attracted females select potential nesting sites and call their mates over to help pick one. To build their nests, males collect twigs then stand on the female's back as she arranges the sticks into a flimsy platform that hardly seems capable of holding the pair's two eggs. Egg-laying probably occurs from April to August in the Sierra Nevada, and pairs rear multiple sets of eggs in an "assembly-line" fashion, laying new eggs while the previous chicks are still in the nest or just leaving the nest. Males incubate during the day, and females take the night shift until the eggs hatch in two weeks. To feed the chicks, each parent produces at least two batches of "crop milk" per day (see above accounts). Young doves can fly in 15 days but are fed until they are 30 days old.

Immature doves gather in flocks that grow larger as other young doves become independent and adults finish breeding in August. These flocks wander in search of drinking water and seeds, until they abruptly start heading south in mid-August.

Note: *Introduced* Eurasian Collared-Doves *first appeared in the Sierra Nevada in about 2000, and have aggressively expanded their range ever since, as they have elsewhere in North America. They are still rarely reported on the west slope but on the east slope they have already become common local residents around towns as far north as Lee Vining.*

RANGE Found all year in the Sierra Nevada though it is unknown if these birds are year-round residents, or if breeding birds are replaced by a different set of wintering birds. Large numbers arrive in April, remain common through the summer, then start heading south from mid-August to late September; uncommon through the winter in smaller numbers. **WEST SLOPE:** Thinly dispersed but uncommon to fairly common through the winter; most numerous at the lowest elevations then increasingly scarce up to about 3000 ft, but locally abundant around backyard bird feeders and other food sources. Breeding birds range from the foothills to 5000 ft. **EAST SLOPE:** Not as numerous in the winter as on the west slope but still locally uncommon to fairly common in valley bottoms or as high as Lake Tahoe. Breeding birds range up to 7000 ft and are perhaps more narrowly restricted to areas around water than they are on the west slope.

ROADRUNNERS (Cuculidae)

GREATER ROADRUNNER *Geococcyx californianus*

LIFE HISTORY The unexpected occurrence of roadrunners in the Sierra Nevada foothills is an indication of how many of the parched lowlands around the mountains consist of desert or desert-like habitats. These strange, terrestrial cuckoos possess many singular adaptations for life in a desert environment, including having black skin so they can warm up quickly while sunbathing on cold desert mornings. They are aggressive, opportunistic hunters, capable of running 20 mph for long distances though they usually forage by actively walking, running, and scanning to each side. Everything from insects, to birds, lizards, scorpions, spiders, rodents, and bats are snatched with powerful stabs and beaten furiously against the ground. They can even leap up and grab birds from backyard bird feeders, and pairs will cooperate to overcome large snakes.

In open habitats with scattered shrubs or trees, pairs establish long-term pair bonds and actively defend large territories. Pair bonds are renewed each spring through a remarkable series of courtship displays by males, who prance, bow, wag their tails, and offer food and nesting material to their mates. From high perches at sunrise, males give distinctive downslurred cooing calls *co-coo-coo-cooooo* while females often reply with loud coyote-like yelps.

Nesting may begin in April, or potentially any time after January. Nests are constructed in isolated thickets of shrubs, with males bringing thorny sticks to females who arrange them into a compact platform lined with grasses, feathers, shed snakeskins, and even bits of dried manure. The 3–6 eggs are incubated by both parents, females by day, males at night. Chicks hatch in 19 days and both parents feed them on the nest until they fledge at 2–3 weeks of age. Parents gradually coax fledglings from the nest by offering them food, and families stay together for another 4–5 weeks.

RANGE Greater Roadrunners are characteristic residents of the Southwest deserts that occur throughout southern California and are uncommon to rare residents in arid lowlands along both slopes of the Sierra Nevada. **WEST SLOPE:** Uncommon to locally common on low desert slopes of the Kern River Valley, including the Greenhorn Mountains, Piute Mountains, Breckenridge Mountain, and onto Walker Pass. They have been reported as high as 7500 ft in the Piute Mountains. Further north in the foothills they occur in open stands of chaparral and chamise but are rarely seen. They have been reported as far north as Butte County, but are not likely north of El Dorado County. **EAST SLOPE:** Many records from the desert slopes east of Tehachapi Pass north to Bishop, as well as a couple records from Mono Lake and one from Bridgeport.

OWLS (Tytonidae and Strigidae)

BARN OWL *Tyto alba*

LIFE HISTORY Because they are the most widespread of all owls, and perhaps one of the most widespread land birds in the whole world, Barn Owls are well known. These common owls readily take up residence around farms, or rural and suburban landscapes, where they can be found sleeping in tree cavities, deep within tangled tree branches, or in the rafters of barns and abandoned buildings. Traditional roosting sites can be identified by the dark gray, bone-filled pellets that pile up underneath. The pale, ghostly bodies and large, white, heart-shaped faces of Barn Owls make them instantly recognizable, as well as a little frightening.

Unlike many other owls, Barn Owls are very active hunters that search for rodents by systematically crisscrossing lower than 15ft over the tops of plants in meadows, agricultural fields, deserts, and marshes. Their primary foods are voles, but they eat all types of small mammals, including Norway rats around houses, and sometimes even sleeping birds. Although they hunt in complete darkness, they can be seen swooping through the glare of streetlights with deep, slow wingbeats. Barn Owls have extraordinary vision in low-light, and they have the most refined ability to locate prey by sound of any animal ever tested.

Their nesting season begins with display flights and harsh, grating screams given by males as they fly high over their territories in February and March. Pairs mate for life, and they will repeatedly use the same nest sites for as long as they live. The 5–8 eggs are laid in February–March, with females performing all the incubation duties while males provide the food for females and the chicks that hatch a month later. Young birds begin practicing flying at two months of age but stay close to their parents for at least another month.

RANGE Barn Owls are common residents near low-elevation meadows and grasslands, especially in agricultural and ranching areas. Rare visitors to montane meadows, especially in July. **WEST SLOPE:** Primarily found in the foothills where grasslands and open oak woodlands are widespread, but uncommon around meadows and rural landscapes up to 5000 ft. **EAST SLOPE:** Rare to uncommon below the Mixed Conifer Zone but may be locally fairly common near agricultural areas. Occasional sightings of groups of a dozen or more in otherwise unoccupied locations suggest seasonal movements.

FLAMMULATED OWL *Otus flammeolus*

LIFE HISTORY We have much to learn about Flammulated Owls in the Sierra Nevada. In fact, until biologists discovered that these owls responded to recordings, Flammulated Owls were thought to be very rare. They are now considered one of the more common owls in the Sierra Nevada's extensive stands of dry, open ponderosa and Jeffrey pine stands at lower elevations, but their overall distribution and seasonal movements are still little understood.

These diminutive and unique owls appear to migrate long distances. It is believed that they spend the winter in southern Mexico and Central America, but their lives in winter are a matter of pure speculation. One of the problems is that they are extremely well camouflaged on tree branches, making them virtually impossible to find unless calling.

Their calls are flat, melancholy hoots, given singly or in pairs every few seconds, that under ideal conditions can be heard up to half a mile away. Flammulated Owls have enlarged vocal chambers and produce hoots as loud as those given by large owls, creating a ventriloquial effect that makes them sound as if they are large owls a long distance away, when in fact they may be perched right overhead. Even more confusing, the presence of calling males in May–June does not necessarily mean that they are breeding locally because many males remain unmated and keep calling through the summer.

The long wings on these long-distance migrants prevent them from being agile hunters, which probably accounts for their occurrence in open forests where they can swoop to the ground unhindered. Much of their diet consists of moths, beetles, crickets, and other nocturnal insects which they capture in mid-air, on the ground, or while hovering near pine needles. They likely prefer ponderosa and Jeffrey pine forests because there are 4 times more moth species associated with these forests than other conifer forests.

Migrating Flammulated Owls first arrive in the southern Sierra Nevada in mid-April, and by May they have expanded northward along the full length of the Sierra Nevada. Pairs nest in the same abandoned Northern Flicker or Pileated Woodpecker cavities year after year as long as both members of the pair return. Prior to egg laying, females cease foraging and let males bring them food; by the time the first egg is laid in June or July, females may have gained so much weight that they have difficulty flying. The 2–3 eggs take 26 days to hatch and another 50 days until fledglings leave their parent's territory in August. Flammulated Owls are largely unknown in the Sierra Nevada after early October.

RANGE Breeding Flammulated Owls are primarily restricted to mature ponderosa or Jeffrey pine forests in a narrow altitudinal band below the Mixed Conifer Zone. Also thought to breed in patches of pines interspersed among various conifers of the Mixed Conifer Zone up to 6500 ft (or as high as 9000 ft in the southern Sierra Nevada). Status and distribution poorly known except in the few areas where researchers have worked extensively. **WEST SLOPE:** Scattered records from the length of the Sierra Nevada, but they seem to be locally common in some locations. **EAST SLOPE:** Likely nest in appropriate habitat, but the species is little known on the east side. Recent night trapping on the east rim of the Tahoe Basin has revealed that a fair numbers of these owls may be moving southward through this area in the fall, a pattern that may hold true for other locations on the east slope.

WESTERN SCREECH-OWL *Megascops kennicottii*

LIFE HISTORY In sheer numbers alone, these small owls reign the night in low-elevation oak forests of the west slope. They reputedly occur in the highest densities in riparian woodlands, but they are frequently encountered in forests on dry slopes and ridgetops as well. Western Screech-Owls do not screech but reveal their presence with a "bouncing ball call," a series of mellow whistles that accelerate in tempo. They also make other sounds, including trills, barks, whinnies, and chirps. In addition to calling, screech-owls strengthen their pair bonds by allopreening, with males and females sitting side by side, touching and preening each other. They engage in a significant amount of courtship feeding and vocalizing starting in January or February and lasting until eggs are laid in March or April.

Screech-owls nest in either natural tree cavities or those left behind by Pileated Woodpeckers or Northern Flickers (occasionally taking over already active woodpecker nests). They readily use artificial nestboxes put out by landowners who want to encourage these delightful owls to take up residence. Females incubate their 3–5 eggs for about a month while males find food for females, and later for the hatchlings as well. Young birds stay near their parents for 5 weeks, then begin increasingly wandering on their own as they learn to catch their insects, small mammals, and small birds.

RANGE Western Screech-Owls are one of the definitive birds of foothill oak woodlands but they also occur in cottonwoods and willows near water, as well as in stands of oaks mixed with ponderosa pines. In late summer, juveniles wander widely, sometimes as high as the Subalpine Zone. **WEST SLOPE:** Widespread and fairly common in oak woodlands, as well as in pockets of oaks in the Mixed Conifer Zone as high as 5000 ft. **EAST SLOPE:** Uncommon to fairly common resident in low-elevation woodlands though they have been found to 8000 ft in the nearby White Mountains. Screech-owls are generally much less common than on the west slope, which is interesting because they are widespread in the Great Basin.

GREAT HORNED OWL *Bubo virginianus*

LIFE HISTORY Great Horned Owls are extremely versatile in their choice of habitats and nest sites; in fact, they use a greater range of nest sites than any other bird in the Americas. Their preference, however, is for areas where they can hunt in large clearings or open forests, then roost in nearby groves of trees. Highly territorial pairs are permanent residents and make their presence known through persistent nightly hooting from January to March, and by attacking and killing other owls or diurnal raptors. In return, Great Horned Owls are intensely mobbed by crows, jays, and other birds when discovered at their daytime roosts. A frenzied cacophony of alarm calls is often a sure sign that the local birds are surrounding and mobbing an owl.

These owls are powerful hunters, fearlessly attacking any animal they can subdue and carry, from scorpions to skunks. They may even tackle birds as large as Great Blue Herons, but their preferred foods are rabbits and mice. While hunting, they generally sit on perches near open areas, and they are frequently observed on these same perches during the daytime, making Great Horned Owls the most commonly observed owls in the Sierra Nevada.

These owls are also conspicuous when nesting because they use the bulky stick nests of Red-tailed Hawks or the nests of other large birds in trees or on cliff ledges. They begin laying eggs in January or February, so in many cases they are nesting while tree branches are still bare of leaves. Females incubate two eggs for about one month as males provide food. Young owls make their first flights at 7 weeks of age but may remain with their parents into October (4–5 months after leaving the nest). They can live for 20–30 years if they survive their first difficult year of learning to hunt.

RANGE Though thinly distributed because of their fiercely territorial nature, Great Horned Owls are widespread in all parts of California below the Alpine Zone. Human activity and disturbance seem to favor this species, especially in areas where habitat destruction creates clearings that allow them to move into otherwise intact woodlands and forests, displacing other owl species. **WEST SLOPE:** They avoid large stands of dense coniferous forest but are otherwise widespread. Seem to be most abundant in the foothills, perhaps because this is where human disturbance has created many open areas favoring this species. **EAST SLOPE:** Fairly common permanent residents in all habitats below the Mixed Conifer Zone, and sparingly as high as treeline. In open, desert-like settings, Great Horned Owls frequently center their activities around homesteads and groves of tall trees, where they are easily spotted roosting during the day.

NORTHERN PYGMY-OWL *Glaucidium gnoma*

LIFE HISTORY Despite their diminutive stature, pygmy-owls are among the world's fiercest and most bloodthirsty birds, being well known for their astonishingly bold behavior. Preying extensively on other birds and to a lesser degree on mammals or insects, pygmy-owls attempt to kill by driving their talons into the throat of their prey and hanging on till the victim dies. They readily attack animals much larger than themselves, including quail, flickers, and woodrats—with records of them subduing large domestic chickens up to 64 times the owl's own weight. Often it seems that they kill more for the excitement of the chase than out of hunger since they may eat only the brain of their prey then discard the rest.

In behavior, pygmy-owls are alert and constantly active diurnal or crepuscular hunters. While hunting, they are often observed perching at the tips of trees or snags, commanding large views of meadows and open areas where they can quickly chase down their prey. They are rarely observed while breeding, so they are best found during the non-breeding season, especially when they are being mobbed by flocks of extremely agitated, loudly scolding songbirds.

Pygmy-owls nest in naturally-occurring tree cavities or those left by larger woodpeckers, often using the same cavities year after year. Females incubate 4–6 eggs for about one month while being fed by males. Young pygmy-owls have prodigious appetites, so males hunt almost continuously, bringing food items to females to be plucked and torn into bite sized pieces. After about a month on the nest, young owls leave the cavity and begin testing their wings for the first time.

RANGE Pygmy-owls are widespread in the Sierra Nevada but generally avoid the high mountains, dense forests, and open deserts. In most areas, they are year-round residents, but in the fall and winter they may irregularly wander outside their breeding range. **WEST SLOPE:** Fairly common but localized in foothill oak habitats, with smaller numbers in the Mixed Conifer Zone up to 6000 ft, and rarely as high as the Upper Montane Zone. **EAST SLOPE:** Uncommon to rare (in the south) residents of coniferous forests, occasionally observed in woodlands or residential yards at lower elevations.

SPOTTED OWL *Strix occidentalis*

LIFE HISTORY Roosting high overhead next to the trunks of tall conifers, these owls are difficult to see against the dappled texture of tree bark. Once located, however, they are easy to watch due to their gentle, relatively tame nature and utter lack of fear of humans. So calm is this species that females lifted off their nests do not protest or show interest but merely look around with big, dark eyes.

Pairs live year round on large territories in mature conifer forests though they only associate closely with each other during the breeding season (roughly February–June). After sleeping all day, they usually wake up just after sunset, hoot at each other with their distinctive barking calls, then spend the night hunting for woodrats and flying squirrels. Males launch the breeding season by seeking out nest sites in February, favoring broken-off snags, naturally-occurring cavities in trees, or old raptor nests. Females lay 2–3 eggs in March or April and incubate them for about a month while being fed by their mates. Young birds are fed on the nest for about a month, and then continue to linger with their parents and be fed until August (2–3 months after leaving the nest).

Unfortunately due to the cutting of mature forests, Spotted Owl numbers continue to decline despite urgent measures to safeguard the species. One survey estimated that there were just over 1100 Spotted Owl territories remaining in the Sierra Nevada.

RANGE "California" Spotted Owls (*S. o. occidentalis*) are entirely restricted to the mountains of California—the west slope of the Sierra Nevada and coastal mountains of southern California. **WEST SLOPE:**

Breed from 3000–7000 ft in the northern and central Sierra Nevada, and mainly limited to the Mixed Conifer Zone. In the southern Sierra Nevada, they regularly occur from oak woodlands at 3600 ft in the Greenhorn Mountains up to red fir forests at 9000 ft on the Kern Plateau. Many adults move downslope to spend the winter while some juveniles may be forced into low-quality habitats, like second-growth forests, because so few mature forests remain. **EAST SLOPE:** Extremely rare visitors to mixed conifer forests. Nesting may be possible in the Tahoe Basin or elsewhere in the northern Sierra Nevada where the crest is lower and birds from the west slope could spill over onto the east side.

GREAT GRAY OWL *Strix nebulosa*

LIFE HISTORY One of the Sierra Nevada's most majestic birds was awarded special recognition in 2010 when the population centered around Yosemite National Park was documented as a distinct subspecies ("California" Great Gray Owl, *S. n. yosemitensis*), found nowhere else in the world. Great Gray Owls are huge, awe-inspiring, mythical owls found only in the boreal forests of northern Europe, Asia, and North America, except for one lonely outpost, a small isolated population in the montane coniferous forests of the Sierra Nevada, where approximately 100–200 owls survive far from their northern cousins.

Nearly all of these owls—easily recognized by their massive facial disks and piercing yellow eyes—are found in Yosemite National Park and on National Forest lands adjacent to the park, where their tiny population is largely protected but still vulnerable to human disturbance, especially when people see an owl and keep chasing it into the woods hoping to get a better look. Great Grays live in conifer forests around the edges of large montane meadows, but there are only a handful of these meadows, so once they are disturbed at one location, they do not have many places to retreat.

During the day, they sleep in remote portions of the forest, but in the late afternoon they wake up and move to perches where they can intently scan meadow grasses for voles and gophers. Their movements stir up anxious robins and tanagers that scold the owls, and the alarm calls of these vigilant birds are often the first indication that a Great Gray Owl is in the vicinity.

Although Great Grays look huge, they actually weigh less than smaller Great Horned Owls. They are mostly a bundle of fluffy feathers that keep them well-insulated from frigid mountain winters. In the winter, they probably do not get cold but still move downslope because deep snows make it difficult to find their main food items.

Pairs do not remain together over the winter, but if both sexes return in the spring, they are likely to nest together again. Like other owls, they do not make their own nests but take over abandoned raptor or raven nests, or nest on the tops of broken trees or snags. Both sexes announce their breeding status with deep resonate *hooo* calls, while females begging for food make loud *whoops*.

Their 2–3 eggs are laid in late March, and females incubate for a month while males feed them on the nest. Males continue to bring food after the eggs hatch, but females take the food items and divide them among the nestlings. Young birds leave the nest at 3–4 weeks of age and both parents continue feeding them for another month. At this point, females leave and males continue to provide food and care to the fledglings for another 3 months until they are independent in the late summer.

RANGE "California" Great Gray Owls are mainly found in the Yosemite region, where they were discovered nesting in 1915 (the first record of this species south of Canada). They live and breed around moist montane meadows, from the lower reaches of the Mixed Conifer Zone up through the Upper Montane Zone, from 3000–8500 ft. Many breeding pairs live in red fir and lodgepole pine forests, but some occur in forests of mixed conifers and black oaks. Birds at higher elevations may descend to lower elevations to avoid deep winter snows. **WEST SLOPE:** Found in numerous large meadow systems throughout Yosemite National Park, as well as on adjacent Stanislaus and Sierra National Forest lands. A few birds are occasionally observed on the Eldorado, Tahoe, and Plumas National Forests in the north, and in Sequoia National Forest and Sequoia & Kings Canyon National Park in the south. **EAST SLOPE:** Casual; one October record at a high elevation south of Yosemite National Park was probably a wandering bird.

LONG-EARED OWL *Asio otus*

LIFE HISTORY Surprisingly small and able to compress their bodies into long, narrow shapes, these owls hide during the day in dense willow thickets, where their streaky bodies are hard to see even if you are looking right at them. As a consequence, very little is known about this species in the Sierra Nevada and, unlike other owls, they are rarely heard calling so most are found when someone accidentally spooks one up from its daytime hideout.

These long-winged owls are active nocturnal hunters, leaving their daytime roosts to spend the night hunting in meadows and open forests. Flying 2–6 ft above the ground, they skim back and forth in search of voles, deer mice, and gophers that they detect by sound. They are agile in flight, able to maneuver quickly when flying through branches or pursuing their fast-moving prey.

Very little is known about their breeding season in the Sierra Nevada. Males give their advertising calls in February–March, long *hoo* notes that are evenly spaced 2–4 seconds apart, and both sexes yowl and make other screeching noises. They use the abandoned stick nests of other birds, and unlike other owls, they modify their nests by adding strips of bark, moss, leaves, or feathers. Their 4–5 eggs may be laid sometime in March–May, and females sit on the eggs so tightly that they almost never flush from their nests except in extreme danger. Males and females fiercely defend nests and young birds by hissing loudly then falling to the ground and struggling frantically as a distraction; if these tactics fail, they may savagely attack the face and throat of any intruder.

At 3 weeks of age, young birds lessen the risk of being found by predators by climbing out of their nest and scattering several hundred feet in different directions, hiding in dense foliage. They begin trying to fly at 35 days of age and are fed by males until they are 10–11 weeks old.

RANGE The status and distribution of Long-eared Owls in the Sierra Nevada is poorly understood, with less than half a dozen records for most counties. While it appears that Long-eared Owls are more numerous east of the crest, they are probably just easier to observe in isolated willow thickets along east-side streams. Though they have long been considered a low-elevation species, systematic surveys in Yosemite National Park found that they are fairly common, and perhaps even common, owls in a wide variety of forests to over 8000 ft. It is thought that they descend to the foothills and valley bottoms or leave the area in the winter, but there are very few winter records, and it is not known where birds seen in the winter have come from. **WEST SLOPE:** Other than the surveys in Yosemite, there are few records, making it almost impossible to characterize the status or habitat preferences of Long-eared Owls on the west slope. They might be uncommon and localized breeders in pockets of dense vegetation in the foothills, but they have only been seen or heard a few times. At higher elevations, they are usually found in willow thickets in montane meadows. **EAST SLOPE:** Long-eared Owls are better known east of the crest, where they are uncommon, local breeders below the Mixed Conifer Zone. Their numbers are greatly reduced in winter, when they retreat into dense willow or shrub thickets in valley bottoms, or else leave the area.

Northern Saw-whet Owl *Aegolius acadicus*

LIFE HISTORY Scarcely larger than plump towhees with tiny tails, saw-whets sleep all day in tree cavities, or among branches and leaves where their streaked and spotted plumage blends in among the dappled shadows. They have the most asymmetrical ears of any owl in North America, which gives their heads a somewhat misshapen appearance but also gives them extremely acute hearing abilities. At night they hunt from low perches near forest edges or clearings, and they are very patient hunters who will sit for hours waiting for a prey item to reappear from its hiding place. Most of their diet consists of small mammals like deer mice, but they also grab sleeping birds and there are records of them eating larger birds like Northern Pygmy-Owls, American Robins, and Rock Pigeons. Leftover or surplus food is stored on branches, and if it freezes they thaw it out by sitting on it.

Saw-whets live in a wide variety of forests from foothill oaks to firs in the Upper Montane Zone, but it is not known whether they are year-round residents in all these habitats or if they move upslope to breed and downslope to avoid deep winter snows. Saw-whets can die if snow blankets the ground and keeps them from finding food, so this is one reason why they would move downslope in winter.

In late winter, males start giving advertising calls that may continue into early spring (from January to late April). These calls consist of rapid whistles that can be repeated monotonously for hours. Males may sing from potential nest cavities, attracting females that they feed inside the cavity as an enticement to stay. Saw-whets nest most often in deserted woodpecker holes, especially those left behind by the larger woodpeckers.

Males continue to feed females on the nest throughout the entire nesting season. Females incubate 5–6 eggs for 27–29 days, then stay around to keep the nestlings warm until they are about 18 days old. At this point females leave the nest cavity and may even abandon the nestlings entirely, leaving males to continue caring for them until they fledge a couple weeks later and become independent 1–2 months after that. With their high rate of metabolism, these tiny owls regularly eat double their weight in a single night, so it takes a significant effort to feed their rapidly growing chicks.

RANGE Very little is known about Northern Saw-whet Owls in the Sierra Nevada and their status and distribution is a mystery. **WEST SLOPE:** Occasionally observed and heard calling in the foothills in late winter, where they probably linger to breed in mixed ponderosa pine and oak woodlands. Almost nothing is known about their winter status at higher elevations though large numbers have been found dead along Hwy 80 from 3500–6500 ft in January. Through the summer, they are found from 4500–8500 ft, and there is some evidence that numbers increase at these elevations in October, perhaps as birds migrate south or start moving downslope. **EAST SLOPE:** They are probably uncommon to rare permanent residents in coniferous forests but only a few nests have been found, and their winter status is unknown.

GOATSUCKERS (Caprimulgidae)

COMMON NIGHTHAWK *Chordeiles minor*

LIFE HISTORY With one of the longest migrations of any North American bird, and intolerant of cold temperatures and rainy weather, Common Nighthawks are among the last migrants to arrive in the spring and one of the first to leave in the fall. They are conspicuous as soon as they show up because they hunt at sunrise and sunset, swooping gracefully overhead in search of flying insects, and making strange *peent* calls.

During the day, however, these same birds are rarely observed because they sit lengthwise and are perfectly camouflaged on tree branches or on the ground. Due to their cryptic roosting and nesting habits, and because they apparently fly long distances from their nesting territories to communal feeding areas, their distribution in the Sierra Nevada is poorly understood. It is also thought that their distribution could be limited by competition with bats and Lesser Nighthawks that chase Common Nighthawks away from prime feeding areas. This may be one reason why Common Nighthawks feed in groups, hunt high in the air, and specialize on a rather limited subset of flying insects like queen ants, beetles, and true bugs.

The booming courtship or territorial flights of the males are one peculiar aspect of the lives of these unusual birds. During the height of courtship, males make distinctive booming sounds by flying up to great heights then diving and sending a rush of air through their primary feathers. Booming may be heard through the night or through the day, but is most prevalent at sunrise and sunset when the birds are more active. These diving flights may be directed at a female perched on the ground or at an intruder on the male's territory. Courting males will dive at a female then land next to her, spread his tail, puff out his white throat patch, and croak amorously in hopes of gaining her attention.

Two eggs are laid on bare, open ground and females incubate them for 19 days, tending the eggs closely during the hot summer days but leaving them at night to feed. Once the eggs hatch, males feed the chicks and provide food for females when they are on the nest. Chicks are semi-precocial and begin their first short flights at 23 days of age.

Note: Lesser Nighthawks *are inhabitants of hot barren areas, mostly on desert flats and valley grasslands. They are uncommon in the Owens Valley south of Bishop and in the South Fork Kern River Valley, with a few records from scattered, low-elevation sites along the west side.*

RANGE Though conspicuous during their evening flights over ponds, meadows, marshes, and open slopes, the actual range of Common Nighthawks in the Sierra Nevada is not well known. They are thought to occur in local populations because you can travel long distances without seeing a single nighthawk then encounter many in one area, but this interpretation may be the result of their tendency to gather and feed in groups over certain areas. Hikers and biologists occasionally stumble across one of the well-hidden nests, but these sparse records scarcely improve our understanding of this species' habits in the Sierra Nevada. Common Nighthawks apparently nest in a variety of open areas, including sagebrush flats, clearcuts, burned areas, and alpine fell-fields, from the Mixed Conifer Zone (6000 ft) to as high as 11,000 ft. Spring migrants arrive in late May, with substantial numbers present by the first week of June; then large groups may be observed during August as they gather to feed and move south, and nearly all are gone by the end of August (September sightings are exceptional). **WEST SLOPE:** Observed on an irregular basis anywhere from 1000 ft to the crest. They are locally common breeders some years or absent other years at higher elevations (6000–9000 ft) and also in the foothills from Yuba to Butte County. **EAST SLOPE:** Apparently more abundant on the east side because they are common and predictable in many valleys, especially over sagebrush. At least some of these birds, maybe even most of them, nest on sagebrush flats, but they also nest on mountain slopes nearly to the crest.

Common Poorwill *Phalaenoptilus nuttallii*

LIFE HISTORY There are only two common ways of experiencing these nocturnal sprites: they may be heard giving their low haunting *poor-will* calls just after sunset, or they may be seen sitting on an open trail in a flashlight beam or on a quiet road in car headlights. Slightly smaller than robins, and with softer plumage than owls, poorwills wake up at sunset and perch inconspicuously in openings in brushy areas where they hunt by making quick silent dashes to catch low-flying moths or beetles. Their most common strategy is to leap up vertically to catch a passing insect, then settle immediately back on the ground.

Like nighthawks, poorwills make a shallow scrape on the ground where they lay their two eggs, usually under the protection of a low-hanging plant or rock. Poorwills are astoundingly well camouflaged as they sit on the ground during the day, and this helps hide them from predators. Both parents take turns incubating the eggs for 20–21 days, and the chicks begin flying as soon as they reach 20 days of age. It is thought that most pairs rear two broods each year.

Poorwills are remarkably efficient at surviving extreme hot and cold temperatures. During the summer, they use panting and gular flapping to stay cool. Their claim to fame, however, lies in their ability to enter torpor on a daily basis, or to even stay in torpor for several weeks, to survive cold weather and food shortages. It is not uncommon for them to remain inactive for 10 days, or even up to 25 days, at a stretch. This unique ability to "hibernate" allows poorwills to remain through the winter in some parts of California. Scattered winter records as far north as Mt. Shasta suggest that poorwills may regularly overwinter at low elevations on the west slope.

RANGE Our knowledge of Common Poorwill distribution is mainly limited to records of calling birds, so nonvocal birds (i.e. in midsummer and in winter) are difficult to find. It is unknown whether poorwills overwinter in the Sierra Nevada region, but they are generally first heard calling in May. This can vary by as much as a month depending on weather. Poorwills are present all summer, and there is both an apparent upslope movement and a second peak in calling activity from late summer until they begin migrating south in late September. Poorwills favor a wide variety of semi-arid and open, brushy, or rocky habitats. **WEST SLOPE:** Typically found on south-facing hillsides of manzanita or ceanothus, but they are also possible in open forests or forest clearings. Found on juniper-covered hillsides in the southern Sierra. Regularly observed (or heard) from the low foothills to around

6000 ft. **EAST SLOPE:** Breeds in several types of habitats on the east slope, from sagebrush valleys to rocky hillsides at 8000 ft. There is one intriguing record of a poorwill at Fish Springs, south of Bishop, in early December.

SWIFTS (Apodidae)

BLACK SWIFT *Cypseloides niger*

LIFE HISTORY Black Swifts use some of the most striking nesting habitats of any bird in the Sierra Nevada—soaring cliffs with large, thundering waterfalls—where they build their mossy nests in or near the constant spray of water. So enigmatic are these nesting sites that the first nest was not discovered until 1901. Even more perplexing, these swifts lay only a single, unusually large egg, which is so unlike any other North American swift that it took another 13 years before anyone believed the person who found the nest.

These nests are found in such extreme locations that scientists have observed nest-building behavior on only one occasion. Almost nothing is known of their breeding biology, but they probably begin nesting in June. Both parents take turns incubating their egg for 23–26 days, perched precariously on tiny nesting platforms which are placed in crevices or on ledges hundreds of feet above the ground. The chick takes a very long time to fledge, partly because nests are located in such cold, damp places, and partly because the chick goes without food while adults undertake long foraging expeditions and may only return twice a day with wads of regurgitated insects. Chicks do not make their first flights until 45–50 days after hatching, which is 3–4 times longer than most other similarly-sized birds.

Black Swifts are master aerialists, traveling great distances each day, cruising up and down the length of the Sierra Nevada, dipping down into the foothills or wandering over the crest in their incessant search for clusters of flying ants. Black Swifts generally fly at great heights, so the easiest way to observe them is when they appear briefly near their nesting sites at dawn and dusk. On cold or gloomy days, swifts may feed closer to the ground. They are often seen flying in the company of White-throated Swifts and can be separated at long distances because they are larger and fly with more ponderous wingbeats.

RANGE Although Black Swifts can be found nearly anywhere in California during migration and as they wander great distances each day, their breeding range in the state is limited to a few sites near large waterfalls. The handful of known Sierra Nevada nesting sites are mainly located on the west slope, where foraging birds are most likely observed. They nest in small colonies at single waterfalls so their total Sierra Nevada population is very low, perhaps fewer than 100 birds. Spring migrants show up in the foothills by late April; and small flocks have been seen along the Sierra Nevada crest as they leave the state in early to mid-August. Very small numbers linger in California until October and they could potentially show up in the mountains. **WEST SLOPE:** Uncommon breeders between 3000–7500 ft at scattered locations in Butte, Sierra, Nevada, Placer, Mariposa, Tuolumne, Fresno, and Tulare counties, with the largest population in Yosemite Valley. **EAST SLOPE:** Rare and only known to nest west of Woodfords in Alpine County and at Rainbow Falls in Devils Postpile National Monument.

VAUX'S SWIFT *Chaetura vauxi*

LIFE HISTORY Vaux's Swifts are a flash of quicksilver with furiously beating wings that dart and swoop with amazing speed and dexterity, as they pursue flying insects over mature forests, meadows, and water edges. You may not even notice their aerodynamic, torpedo-shaped bodies, but no other Sierra Nevada birds look like, or fly, like them. Vaux's Swifts observed in the Sierra Nevada are usually in transit to other regions, but some remain to breed.

Very few nests have been found in the Sierra Nevada and little is known of their breeding biology, so their breeding range must be inferred from sightings of birds flying over potential nesting areas during the nesting season. Vaux's Swifts prefer to nest in the hollows formed naturally inside of large, old conifer trees, especially snags. Here they cling to the walls of a cavity and use their sticky saliva to bind small twigs to vertical surfaces and construct tiny nesting platforms. Based on research from other areas, females probably lay 4–6 creamy-white eggs, and both parents share equally in all aspects of incubating the eggs for 18–19 days and rearing their young. Fledglings make their first flights in late July, and they have been observed outside nest trees making clumsy practice flights back into their nesting cavity.

After the breeding season, and in preparation for migrating, Vaux's Swift begin gathering into large flocks that roost together each night at traditional sites. These flocks reach into the hundreds or thousands in some areas, but flocks observed in the Sierra Nevada have been much smaller in size. However, Vaux's Swifts are still quite common during the peak fall migration, from early to mid-September, as migrants from many northern regions pass through the area.

RANGE Vaux's Swifts are mainly observed on the west slope, with the first spring migrants beginning to arrive by mid-April. Single birds or small flocks are seen on an irregular basis nearly anywhere on the west slope from the low foothills up to the Sierra Nevada crest during migration. In June and July, breeding birds are thinly scattered over the landscape though they seem more numerous and can be seen daily over appropriate habitats such as mature conifer forests. In many areas, numbers increase noticeably as migrants pass by in mid-August, continuing at these levels until all the swifts have left by mid-September.

WEST SLOPE: Uncommon breeders, mostly seen over mid-elevation forests between 3000–7000 ft where the largest conifer trees can be found; breed south to Sequoia National Park. **EAST SLOPE:** Uncommon breeders north of Lake Tahoe and rare farther south. Possibly nest in Jeffrey pine forests on the east side.

White-throated Swift *Aeronautes saxatalis*

LIFE HISTORY These sociable swifts frequently mingle with other swifts and smaller Violet-green Swallows, but they always stand out due to their fast, dexterous maneuvers and larger size. Although closely associated with cliffs and rocky canyons, where they nest and roost, White-throated Swifts travel great distances in their daily search for insect swarms, and flocks may be seen over any habitat in the Sierra Nevada, from valley floors to the highest peaks though they prefer crests and ridges where rising air currents entrap flying insects. Every morning they leave their nests and roosts and are largely absent until they return in the evening. The departures and arrivals can be thrilling to watch as dozens or hundreds swirl together, chasing and diving with bold, rattling *scr-e-e-e* calls.

Despite the fact that hundreds nest in Yosemite Valley, and others nest under freeway overpasses in cities and under bridges, very little is known about their nesting habits. Their nests are so deeply tucked in rocky crevices, often on cliffs hundreds of feet above the ground, that early collectors resorted to dynamite in order to learn anything about the nests and eggs. It is known that nests are rounded cups of soft materials fastened to rocks with sticky saliva, and that the birds usually lay 4–5 eggs in May. Incubation is thought to average 24 days, and the chicks are thought to fly when 40–45 days old. Because these birds are unable to take off from the ground, a chick's first attempt to fly is an all-or-nothing proposition (chicks found on the ground have been saved merely by tossing them gently in the air and letting them fly free).

RANGE The distribution and seasonal occurrence of this species in California is complex. White-throated Swifts are present all year and breed locally on cliffs and rocky canyon walls from the foothills to about 9000 ft. In most locations they breed in small numbers, but in some areas, such as Yosemite Valley, they are locally abundant. In the winter, they retreat downslope or head south, but on warmer, sunny days, small groups may show up briefly at lower elevations. These cyclic arrivals make it hard to pinpoint any migratory behavior, but swifts show up in greater numbers in mid- to late March at low elevations, then at higher elevations in mid-April to mid-May; and remain until the end of September. **WEST SLOPE:** Fairly common to locally abundant during the summer. In the winter, they are very scarce in the north and increasingly common towards the south. Christmas Bird Counts in the Kern River Valley have on several occasions recorded more White-throated Swifts than any other count in the nation, including 425 one year. They are also recorded some years on the Yosemite Christmas Bird Count at an elevation of 4000 ft. **EAST SLOPE:** Uncommon to rare, from late March until mid-August; occasionally seen in winter from Inyo County south (where they are probably rare residents). Spring migrants begin moving northward along the east slope in mid- to late March, but do not arrive in the north until early May.

HUMMINGBIRDS (Trochilidae)

BLACK-CHINNED HUMMINGBIRD
Archilochus alexandri

LIFE HISTORY These common summer residents of the arid west originally favored lush, tree-lined canyon bottoms and adjacent drier slopes, but with the destruction of many of these native habitats they have taken up residence in residential neighborhoods and backyards with planted flowers and hummingbird feeders. People who put out feeders look forward to mid-April when male Black-chinned Hummingbirds arrive in great numbers, staking out their territories amid a grand confusion of Anna's, Calliope, and Rufous Hummingbirds.

Female Black-chins arrive soon thereafter and by early May start building tiny cup nests. In their native habitats they use sycamores, willows, oaks, or cottonwoods leaning over or near water, but are now just as likely to locate their nests in various ornamental plants in residential neighborhoods.

For a relatively short period of time, males are a conspicuous presence at flowers and feeders, displaying loudly for passing females by flying in pendulum-like, shallow, U-shaped arcs while making pulsating whirring sounds. But as soon as males get a sense that no new females are showing up and there are no more mating opportunities, they begin departing for Mexico in mid-June and most are gone by mid-July.

Depending on location, females nest from May to June, incubating two eggs on their well-camouflaged nests for about 14 days. By 10 days of age, nestlings are fully feathered and sitting on the rim of the nest waiting to be fed, but they do not leave the nest until they are 21 days old. Females and juveniles abandon their nesting areas in early July, with a fair number wandering upslope, where they are reported as high as 8000 ft in July and August. Their numbers steadily dwindle to a trickle of sightings by mid- to late September.

RANGE The core breeding area of Black-chinned Hummingbirds extends across arid parts of western North America, including all of the Great Basin, with a separate population in the Central Valley and the south coast of California. Unfortunately, knowledge of their breeding distribution and seasonal movements in the Sierra Nevada is confounded by the difficulty of confidently separating females and juveniles from similar hummingbirds. Even the presence of displaying males is not certain proof of their breeding status because they may still be migrating to other breeding locations, and there are not necessarily nesting females in the same area as a displaying male. In general, they are uncommon in the north, and more numerous in the southern Sierra Nevada. **WEST SLOPE:** Generally uncommon and local during the breeding season, almost entirely restricted to suitable habitats on the lowest slopes of the foothills. Upper breeding limits not known but probably around 3000 ft. **EAST SLOPE:** The most common hummingbirds in the Owens Valley, where males arrive in early April and linger until late August. Probably breed locally elsewhere on the east side, but there are few records. In most areas, they are rare to uncommon visitors, but they breed at the base of the Carson Range east of Lake Tahoe and may breed around Markleeville.

Anna's Hummingbird *Calypte anna*

LIFE HISTORY In many parts of the Sierra Nevada, especially on the west slope, these are the default hummingbirds. Extremely common, pugnacious, and aggressive, constantly calling attention to themselves with sharp *tzips* and a scratchy, jumbled warbling, Anna's Hummingbirds are easy to watch and study. At the same time, they have complicated and unique seasonal movements.

Although they are present year round in their prime breeding areas, it is thought that many abandon these sites after breeding and are replaced by other Anna's Hummingbirds, creating the impression of long-term residency. But this has not been studied in the Sierra Nevada and as anyone with a hummingbird feeder realizes, it would be almost impossible to separate out the never-ending parade of Anna's hovering around a feeder.

The prevalent seasonal pattern seems to be that breeding males first arrive on the chaparral-covered hillsides of the lower west slope in November and December. Amid much jostling and chasing, they set up nesting territories and attract females with energetic displays in which males hover near perched females (or intruders they want to chase away) then rise up 100 ft and plummet in spectacular J-shaped dives. At the bottom of each dive, a rush of air through their tail feathers creates an abrupt shriek, then males hover again in front of their intended audience.

They breed early in the year in order to avoid competition from the mad rush of other hummingbirds that start flooding into the foothills in March, but it means that their breeding season overlaps with winter storms, so it is not unusual to see males courageously displaying and flashing their glittering rosy-red head feathers in a December snowstorm. Most females nest from mid-January to mid-April; some fledglings are already flying in mid-February, but nests with chicks have also been reported in June and in early July. Judging from observations at hummingbird feeders, there is a sudden increase in the numbers of adult males in early March, indicating that this is when they abandon their breeding territories.

Females nest in live-oak woodlands near hillsides of manzanita, and while males dominate high perches and large flower patches, females retreat into brushy thickets and are often observed flying quietly back and forth among branches, eating insects and collecting the spiderwebs and plant down they use to make their nests. They spend about 7 days constructing a tight little cup from strands of spiderweb decorated with lichen and bits of leaves. Their two eggs are incubated for 14–19 days, and chicks probably leave the nest in about 23 days though females continue to feed their fledglings another 1–2 weeks.

Although they eat many insects, Anna's Hummingbirds are more easily observed sipping nectar from flowers like manzanitas, currants and gooseberries, monkeyflowers, penstemons, and wild fuchsias (*Epilobium canum*). Like all hummingbirds, they have a strong preference for red flowers because insects do not use these flowers, leaving more nectar for hummingbirds. As foothill flowers dry up in May–June, there is a significant exodus away from the foothills with many heading upslope toward mountain meadows, where they suddenly become common at places like Lake Tahoe and along the east slope.

Note: *Desert-loving* **Costa's Hummingbirds** *barely reach the Sierra Nevada in the arid desert hills south of the Kern River Valley (e.g. Piute Mountains and Kelso Valley Road); they are also common in Inyo County, but mainly in "hot desert" habitats well east of the Sierra Nevada.*

RANGE Anna's Hummingbirds are largely resident on the Pacific slope of the Cascade-Sierra axis though many retreat to Arizona during the hummingbird "winter" when flowers are scarce in California (July–October). **WEST SLOPE:** Common all year below 3000 ft, with a huge influx during the breeding season (November–May). Most breeding occurs in stands of low elevation chaparral and adjacent oak woodlands up to about 4000 ft. After breeding, many wander upslope from June–September, seeking wildflower-strewn montane meadows as high as 10,000 ft. Some remain in the foothills, especially around hummingbird feeders and residential neighborhoods, but it is not clear if these are residents or visitors from elsewhere. **EAST SLOPE:** Primarily occurs as a postbreeding visitor from the west slope, with peak numbers present from June–September, but they are increasingly being found every month of the year with some hummingbirds even lingering all winter in the Owens Valley.

CALLIOPE HUMMINGBIRD *Stellula calliope*

LIFE HISTORY Montane meadows and aspen groves are greatly enlivened by Calliope Hummingbirds during the summer season when flowers carpet entire meadows and hillsides. In fact, Calliopes vary their arrival times in different years and at different locations to match the beginning of the bloom, timing it so that their newly fledged and inexperienced young come off the nest when the peak numbers of flowers are available.

In the Sierra Nevada, they nest in a variety of habitats ranging from willow thickets around wet meadows, to dry montane chaparral slopes, to aspen groves in narrow rocky canyons. Early-arriving birds may linger in the foothills as they work their way north and wait for the snow to melt at higher elevations, but by early April to early May, the spangle-throated males finally reach their breeding grounds and begin to aggressively defend territories by performing their vigorous displays of pendulum-like, U-shaped dives with weak *bzzt* sounds at the bottom of each dive.

There are many gaps in our knowledge of these tiny hummingbirds, but nesting generally gets underway in May with the first eggs and young appearing from late May to mid-June. Females locate their nests under the cover of a branch or a leaf, perhaps to help keep them warm on cold nights. Around montane meadows, they often place their nests on the branches of aspens or in lodgepole pines (where they situate the nest on a broken-off pinecone base so that it looks like a pinecone). Females incubate their two eggs for 15 days and the young fledge at 21 days of age.

Note: *Annual reports of* **Broad-tailed Hummingbirds** *raise the possibility that these lanky hummingbirds of the Rocky Mountains and Great Basin may reach the east slope, or very rarely the west slope, but difficulties in identifying females, and juveniles in the fall, make many records suspect. Unfortunately, the more easily recognized males are seldom observed, but they at least formerly nested in Lundy and Lee Vining Canyons near Mono Lake, and may nest elsewhere.*

RANGE Calliope Hummingbirds breed in the higher mountains of western North America then winter in southern Mexico—making one of the longest migrations relative to body size of any bird. Arrival times on the east side of the Sierra Nevada are slightly delayed due to later flowering times east of the crest, but they typically arrive in early April and start breeding at lower elevations or wait up to a month for access to higher breeding habitats. They are relatively uncommon and thinly scattered in their breeding range, but can be found in nearly every montane meadow with flowers. Males leave by early July, while females and juveniles head further upslope in July, then in August leisurely work their way south along flower-covered mountain ridges and meadows. Few remain in September, or exceptionally into early October in the Owens Valley. **WEST SLOPE:** Spring migrants appear anywhere at lower elevations, becoming briefly numerous in April then quickly departing to breed. Typical breeding limits are probably 4500–7500 ft but more data is needed. **EAST SLOPE:** Breed at higher elevations on the east side. Nesting reported from 7000–10,000 ft in the south, and as low as 5000 ft north of Lake Tahoe.

Rufous Hummingbird *Selasphorus rufus*

LIFE HISTORY Migrating Rufous Hummingbirds storm through the Sierra Nevada twice a year in a blizzard of fiercely whining wings (produced by males), madly chipping notes, and ferocious chases. They are so aggressive and so abundant that their presence, no matter how fleeting, has modified the behavior of other hummingbirds and the evolution of alpine flowers. Anna's Hummingbirds, for example, are thought to breed in the winter so they can avoid having to compete against Rufous Hummingbirds for access to flowers. And a significant majority of subalpine and alpine flowers are more likely pollinated by Rufous Hummingbirds than any other hummingbird.

In the spring, relatively small numbers of Rufous Hummingbirds pass north along the lower foothills, almost entirely on the west slope, briefly mobbing hummingbird feeders from mid-March to late April, but rushing north to their breeding grounds that stretch from southern Oregon to southern Alaska. Males occasionally show off their distinctive courtship displays, towering oval-shaped flights with piercing *dit-dit-dit-deeer* notes at the bottom of each dive, but they always seem to be in a rush and rarely linger.

Males start heading south again in late June, already heading for Mexico when many local birds are still sitting on eggs. Females and juveniles follow a few weeks later, and for about 6 weeks they absolutely overwhelm flower-filled subalpine and alpine meadows with their sheer numbers. They fill every meadow of flowers to capacity, sometimes by the dozens, from mid-July to late August, then head south in such numbers that observers have reported watching them stream past alpine peaks in late August. Some linger at lower elevations through September, and rarely into early October.

Note: *One of the biggest overlooked mysteries in the Sierra Nevada is the status and distribution of* **Allen's Hummingbirds**, *which so closely resemble Rufous Hummingbirds that positive identification requires measuring the width of their outer tail feathers. Even though Allen's are abundant breeders and migrants on the California coast, there are only a few museum specimens or other positive records from the Sierra Nevada.*

RANGE Rufous Humminbirds breed in the Pacific Northwest and winter in Mexico, with those breeding in southern Alaska making the longest migrations relative to body size of any bird. Northbound migrants follow the coast and are uncommon in the Sierra Nevada foot-hills, while southbound migrants occur in great numbers in the Sierra Nevada from 5000–12,000 ft. **WEST SLOPE:** Uncommon migrants though locally common around hummingbird feeders and flower-filled yards from mid-March to mid-April, mostly below 4000 ft, with some lingering into early May. Very rare in the foothills in July–August, and perhaps more likely in September when limited numbers of montane flowers force them downslope in search of food as they migrate south. **EAST SLOPE:** Rare spring transients at low elevations; fall migration conspicuous, mostly at higher elevations where flowers are abundant in late July and early August.

KINGFISHERS (Alcedinidae)

BELTED KINGFISHER *Megaceryle alcyon*

LIFE HISTORY With strident rattling calls and aggressive chases, Belted Kingfishers guard stretches of open, clear water where they make spectacular plunging dives to capture surface-swimming fish. Any river or lakeshore where there are tree branches or other perches over the water may be claimed by kingfishers that sit and stare down into the water waiting for small fish to swim within 2 ft of the surface. In the absence of perches, kingfishers may hover on furiously beating wings to create fleeting mid-air perches. In addition to fish, they oppor-tunistically grab crayfish, amphibians, reptiles, and even small birds or mammals. They live year round in any area where there is open water and some food to eat.

Solitary and highly territorial much of the year, plain-colored males stake out nesting territories in early spring, seeking locations with earthen banks near productive waters. These sites are relatively limited in the Sierra Nevada, creating a clumped distribution in the breeding season. The more colorful females (an unusual sexual re-versal) are soon attracted to males' territories, and after a very brief courtship, in which the male offers the female a fish, pairs defend their territories together and begin excavating burrows in suitable earthen banks. Working in tandem, one bird digging while the other sits out-side vociferously calling, they dig a 3–6 ft upwardly sloping tunnel, kicking out dirt with fused "syndactyl" front toes that act as little scoo-pers and taking up to 7 days to complete their burrows (rarely up to 3 weeks in harder substrates). Burrows are located high on banks to avoid predators and rising waters, but kingfishers nest in a wide variety of substrates and locations if there are no other alternatives available.

Nest building probably peaks in April and May, but kingfishers are surprisingly understudied and there are several locations in the Sierra Nevada where they are present during the breeding season but nesting is not yet confirmed. Both sexes incubate 6–7 eggs in a small chamber at the end of their nesting burrows, with females taking the night shift. Eggs hatch in about 22 days, and chicks leave the burrow in 4 weeks, being lured forth by parents offering them fish outside the burrow.

RANGE One of the most widespread birds in North America, Belted Kingfishers are surprisingly hardy and spend winters as far north as Alaska's Aleutian Islands, or even along high mountain rivers if there is open water. During the nonbreeding season, these year-round residents are widespread but thinly distributed in the Sierra Nevada, using many types of water. In the spring and early summer their distribution becomes centered around prime breeding locations on rivers and lakeshores, where they may become locally common. Large numbers of postbreeding birds wander upslope in July–September, mostly remaining below the treeline (probably because they need trees near water for perches). **WEST SLOPE:** Generally uncommon breeders below 5000 ft, but their breeding limits are poorly known. Southern extent of their breeding range also unknown; they are present as far south as the Kern River but breeding has not been confirmed. **EAST SLOPE:** Generally uncommon breeders, perhaps as high as 8000 ft, but their breeding limits are poorly known. Have bred south to Mammoth Lakes, but they are not known to breed further south though they are present during the breeding season.

WOODPECKERS (Picidae)

LEWIS'S WOODPECKER *Melanerpes lewis*

LIFE HISTORY These remarkable woodpeckers have many enigmatic behaviors and seasonal movements, and because little is known about their lives they are a bit of a mystery. Of all the woodpeckers, they stand out because of their strange flying habits, alternating slow, crow-like wingbeats with long glides and acrobatic, aerial maneuvers as they snatch large flying insects from the air. In the summer, they are the only local woodpeckers that specialize in eating flying adult insects, and then in the winter, they switch to a diet of acorns, conifer seeds, and ripe fruits.

A considerable portion of their time in the winter is devoted to wandering nomadically in search of food crops, then harvesting and defending a significant quantity of acorns or conifer seeds that they store in bark crevices. In the fall and winter, over half of their stomach contents consist of rocky grit to help them eat acorns or other seeds.

During the breeding season, they primarily associate with burned pine forests (87 percent of all nests in one Sierra Nevada study) and nest in large, decaying snags. They use old cavities, but if they have to excavate their own cavities they seek soft, decayed wood because their bones and muscles are not adapted for intensive digging and pounding like other woodpeckers. Because these burned forests occur unpredictably and change on a yearly basis, Lewis's Woodpecker populations are highly irregular, disappearing for years then becoming locally common after a burn. Pairs may remain together several years and reuse old nest sites though this is little studied.

Males have several territorial calls, including a chatter and a churr, and their courtship displays feature wing-up postures and circling flights to show off their flashy red flanks. Both sexes cooperate to incubate 5–9 eggs, males incubating and keeping hatchlings warm at night, females by day. Eggs hatch in two weeks, and chicks leave the nest about a month later. Eggs are typically laid in late May in California, and hatchlings fledge from late June to early August. Even at a single location there can be as much as a one month variation in fledging dates between different nests. Juvenile birds wander nomadically with adults until each adult finds its own winter food supply and starts defending it, singly or in pairs, against all intruders.

RANGE Lewis's Woodpeckers are nomadic and irregular over their patchy range in the western United States, but most populations head west and south for the winter. Seasonal movements in the Sierra Nevada are obscured by their tendency to wander, but in general it seems that the bulk of the population, if not the entire population, moves to the east slope to breed, then back onto the west slope to spend the winter in low-elevation oak (and pine-oak) woodlands. **WEST SLOPE:** Fairly common winter visitors, at least locally, in the oak woodlands of the central Sierra Nevada, mostly in blue oak woodlands below 2000 ft. Their winter limits further north and south are not well documented, but they are rare winter visitors in the Kern River Valley and casual at

Lake Almanor. Transients occasionally show up in the Mixed Conifer Zone, with some fall migrants lingering into early winter and some spring migrants lingering into summer. Lingering summer birds, and records of historical breeding, raise the possibility that they may breed some years. For instance, pairs have been observed defending tree cavities at Foresta (4300 ft) in Yosemite National Park. **EAST SLOPE:** Breeding birds have been recorded in ponderosa and Jeffrey pine forests along the entire east side but mainly in patches of burned forest on relatively flat terrain, where they are sometimes locally common; they may otherwise be absent or transient over large areas. In the northern Sierra Nevada, they are widespread and expected migrants and breeders, and in the south they are erratic migrants and very rare breeders, but it is not clear where their status changes. They are regular in the winter on the northeast fringe of the Sierra Nevada, at least on the east side of the Diamond Mountains near Honey Lake, and east of Sierra Valley, but even here they disappear for a couple months in harsh winters.

Acorn Woodpecker *Melanerpes formicivorus*

LIFE HISTORY Wherever they live, Acorn Woodpeckers are one of the most abundant woodpeckers, and except in rare years when acorn crops fail, or when they eat up all their stored acorns and have to wander in search of food, they are sedentary, year-round residents on their breeding territories. Both their abundance and their year-round presence result from complex social structures that allow them to cooperate in the gathering of food and the raising of young. Acorn Woodpeckers spend their entire lives in vocal, highly gregarious groups that can include over a dozen individual birds.

The busiest time of year occurs around October when acorns ripen and groups of woodpeckers feverishly harvest these highly nutritious nuts while making their loud *wa-ka* calls. Acorns are stored individually in holes drilled into the dead wood or thick bark of special "granary trees" that become densely riddled with holes and acorns. Granary trees are passed down from generation to generation, with an average of 500 new holes added each year. Some trees have had as many as 50,000 holes, which represents at least 100 years of continuous use. In addition to trees, Acorn Woodpeckers also make granaries in fence posts, telephone poles, or the sides of houses; and after filling up all their drilled holes, they begin storing extra acorns in cavities, with 62,000 acorns ending up in the wall of one house in the Sierra Nevada. All this stored food is highly coveted by other acorn-eaters, including jays, titmice, chickadees, nuthatches, squirrels, and mice, so Acorn Woodpeckers spend much of their time guarding their granaries.

Surprisingly, given all this effort, Acorn Woodpeckers prefer to eat flying insects (especially flying ants) and consume as many as they can, even catching and storing extra insects in bark crevices. But acorns are a significant backup that allows them to remain on their territories all year and supplement their diet when insects are scarce. If acorn crops fail or when the woodpeckers have consumed all their stored acorns, they must wander in search of new food supplies, either roaming locally or making large-scale movements and showing up in unexpected habitats.

Breeding strategies in Acorn Woodpeckers are complicated and varied, with each group containing multiple breeding males (up to 7) and one or more breeding females (up to 3). Numerous nonbreeding helpers (up to 10, usually younger birds from previous nesting efforts) assist the main breeding adults in feeding the chicks and defending the territory. Early in the nesting season, there is a lot of squabbling as breeding males disrupt each other's copulation attempts, and females eat each other's first-laid eggs; but once egg-laying is finished, they cooperate to incubate the remaining eggs, and to brood and feed the chicks. It is clearly advantageous to take care of all the eggs equally because eggs are laid in the same cavity, so it is not clear who the parents are.

There can be two peaks in the breeding season, with the primary nesting effort extending from April to late June (cavities may be excavated in March), and they may also attempt a second nesting season in August to late September. Eggs hatch in 11 days, and nestlings fledge a month later. Immature birds occasionally stray locally in the fall but most end up wintering with the main group. The following spring about 80 percent of the immature males and 90 percent of the immature females disperse to new territories, often leaving in separate same-sex sibling groups that stick together for life and form the core of new breeding flocks. Any remaining siblings stay in their natal groups for life.

RANGE Acorn Woodpeckers are residents west of the Cascade-Sierra axis from Oregon to northern Baja California; small numbers rarely stray upslope or east of the crest, especially in August and September, and wandering birds have been recorded as high as 13,990 ft near Mt. Whitney. **WEST SLOPE:** Common and widespread in open oak (and pine-oak) woodlands, mostly below 3000 ft but locally as high as

5500 ft. Prefer valley oaks, blue oaks, and black oaks, alone or in combination with other oaks or other trees. **EAST SLOPE:** Generally very rare transients in the fall. Small isolated populations reportedly reside in the Diamond and Grizzly Mountains east of Quincy; and they are rare but somewhat regular visitors among the scattered oaks west of Independence (particularly at the Mt. Whitney Fish Hatchery) where they may breed.

WILLIAMSON'S SAPSUCKER *Sphyrapicus thyroideus*

LIFE HISTORY Brightly-colored Williamson's Sapsuckers are among the most highly sought birds in the Sierra Nevada. Because they are uncommon, and thinly dispersed, breeding birds in the vast upper montane forests, it takes a bit of luck to find these elusive woodpeckers. They are most easily found when they reveal their presence with odd churring calls or by drumming on distant trees.

During the breeding season, they ascend into higher elevation coniferous forests, with males arriving 1–2 weeks earlier than females and setting up territories around potential nesting sites, often in the same trees or in the same areas as they used the previous year. They announce their territory and their availability by churring, by drumming in a steady roll followed by 3–4 single loud taps, and by calling in the morning until they find a mate (after finding a mate they call in the afternoon). Courting males show off their unique patches of bright color by spreading their wings and fluffing up their throat feathers.

A pair takes 3–4 weeks to excavate a nest cavity, rarely using old cavities, but frequently renesting in the same tree as the year before. Nesting in the Sierra Nevada generally occurs from mid-May to early July, with eggs being laid from late May to mid-June, but these dates are variable from year to year, and nestlings have been seen in late May at lower elevations. Both sexes incubate, and when the 4–6 eggs hatch after 13 days, both adults bring a steady supply of ants to the nestlings until they fledge a month later. Parents disperse almost immediately, but the young are able to feed themselves within a day or two of fledging because they subsist on a diet of ants, which are easy to catch. Except during the breeding season, when they eat ants, Williamson's Sapsuckers specialize in drinking sap and phloem from small holes they drill in the bark of conifer trees (less often in aspens).

RANGE Williamson's Sapsuckers are restricted to very narrow altitudinal limits on both slopes of the Cascade and Sierra Nevada mountains. In the Sierra Nevada, they move upslope to breed at 7000–9000 ft from April to September–October, then descend to around 5000 ft from November to early April, usually remaining all winter at these middle elevations but rarely descending to valley bottoms and lowlands. However, their winter distribution is poorly understood because there are so few records, and needs further study. They prefer to breed in upper montane coniferous forests, especially in lodgepole pines, western white pines, mountain hemlocks, and Jeffrey pines, which reduces conflicts with Red-breasted Sapsuckers that tend to nest in aspens. **WEST SLOPE:** Breed at higher elevations as far south as the Greenhorn Mountains, but there are winter records from the Piute Mountains, and there may even be suitable breeding habitat on nearby Breckenridge Mountain. **EAST SLOPE:** Mostly breed from 7000–9000 ft, but north of Lake Tahoe they regularly nest as low as 5800 ft. In the southern High Sierra, they have been recorded at over 10,000 ft in late June and early July so nesting should be looked for at these elevations. There are also isolated breeding populations in the Sweetwater Mountains north of Bridgeport and the Carson Range east of Lake Tahoe. Very rare on the east side in winter, and it is unknown where the breeding population goes.

RED-BREASTED SAPSUCKER *Sphyrapicus ruber*

LIFE HISTORY In many ways, these sapsuckers are similar to Williamson's Sapsuckers in terms of behavior and seasonal movements, except that the two species generally divide their habitat use: with Williamson's showing a stronger preference for coniferous forests at higher elevations, and Red-breasteds showing a preference for hardwoods at slightly lower elevations. While there is plenty of overlap, they do not seem to exhibit much aggression toward each other, except early in the breeding season.

Although Red-breasted Sapsuckers also use a wide variety of conifers, both for their nest cavities and for their sap wells, they are primarily found among aspens, willows, cottonwoods, and alders. They live around meadow edges where there is a mix of hardwood trees and open areas with flying insects. During the breeding season, they supplement their diet of tree sap with insects, especially ants, and when feeding young they even dip ants in tree sap before taking them to the nest. Their easily-recognized sap wells consist of small holes arranged in straight horizontal rows.

Early in the breeding season, males announce their territories and breeding status with piercing *kee-ah* calls and with a drumming pattern that can be recognized at a great distance—a loud rolling drumming followed by several irregular taps. Pairs are monogamous through the breeding season, and often pair up again the following season if both members survive the winter.

Each year, males excavate new nest cavities, often using the same trees as the year before. Their old, unused nesting cavities become a vital resource for birds like Mountain Bluebirds, and mammals like flying squirrels, that do not excavate their own nesting cavities. Females at first watch from a nearby perch, then increasingly help with the excavation in the final stages, adding a layer of wood chips flaked from the cavity walls. Most nests are built in dead trees or on the dead portions of living trees, and may be one reason why these sapsuckers prefer to nest in older forests. Nest excavation begins as early as mid-April, with eggs being laid anytime from mid-May to mid-June.

Both sexes incubate the 4–5 eggs for 14 days, with young birds leaving the nest in 23–28 days. Young birds start feeding on their own almost immediately after leaving the nest, with the adults sporadically feeding them for a few days but soon splitting up and departing for the winter.

Note: *Until 1983,* **Red-naped Sapsuckers** *were lumped with Red-breasted and Yellow-bellied Sapsuckers as a single species, but Red-napes are now considered the Rocky Mountain equivalent of the west coast Red-breasted Sapsucker. In the Sierra Nevada, Red-naped Sapsuckers are rare but regular winter visitors on both slopes and a very local breeding species on the east slope, with breeding records from the Sweetwater Mountains, Whitney Portal, and a few other east-side locations.*

RANGE Red-breasted Sapsuckers are restricted to the mountains of the Pacific slope from southern Alaska to northern Baja California. They are common breeding and wintering birds on both sides of the Sierra Nevada, moving upslope to breed, then to lower elevations for the winter. After the breeding season, many wander upslope and downslope, but all retreat below the elevation of daytime freezing for the winter. **WEST SLOPE:** From mid-April to mid-September they are fairly common breeders from 4000–8000 ft (rarely as low as 3000 ft), that retreat below 4000 ft from October to early April. **EAST SLOPE:** Breed in mid-elevation forests of the east slope from about 6000–8000 ft, with some regional exceptions at both higher and lower elevations (have bred as high as 10,600 ft near Tioga Pass). Most leave the region or descend to lower elevations after mid-August, with some lingering to late September at higher elevations, or even later at lower elevations.

They are generally rare in the winter, but seem to be locally uncommon in a few low-lying valleys like Sierra Valley and Owens Valley.

NUTTALL'S WOODPECKER *Picoides nuttallii*

LIFE HISTORY Even though these diminutive oak specialists are fairly common, they are scarcely noticed; in fact, they are poorly known and have never been studied in the Sierra Nevada. Much of what we know of their lives comes from scant observations and very limited data; for example, information on their incubation period (an easily documented activity) comes from a single nest. This is even more surprising because they are readily encountered in the foothills where many people live.

Nuttall's Woodpeckers are almost entirely restricted to oak woodlands, especially to areas with blue oaks and interior live oaks. In the southern portions of their range, they venture into riparian woodlands if the more-aggressive Downy Woodpeckers are absent. Unlike many other woodpeckers, these birds pick small invertebrates from surfaces, or while probing in crevices and poking under bark flakes, rather than hammering and drilling into hard wood. They are very active feeders, circling up tree trunks and around branches with quick movements while scanning leaf and bark surfaces. In the fall and winter, they supplement their diet with local fruits and berries, such as the widely available berries of poison oaks.

Mated pairs stay in touch with each other with rattling kingfisher-like calls, as well as sharp *pit* or *pitit* calls. They live year round on the same territory, but in the late summer pairs split up and forage separately. By February, they start spending much of their time together again, and males soon begin excavating a nest cavity in the soft wood of dead tree trunks or limbs. Nest excavation has been recorded from late February to April, but there are few specific records from the Sierra Nevada. Most eggs are laid in late April–early May, but again few of these dates are from the Sierra Nevada. The 4–5 eggs are incubated about two weeks by both parents, with males taking the night shifts. Young birds leave the nest when about 15 days old, and appear to be tended for several more weeks, with begging birds often observed in July. By August, the parents have chased them off.

Note: *Most of the Sierra Nevada is not hot and dry enough for* **Ladder-backed Woodpeckers,** *but they occasionally wander from deserts east of the Sierra Nevada into the Owens Valley, and they are fairly common residents in the low desert hills south of the Kern River Valley. Great care must be made when separating this species from the Nuttall's Woodpeckers.*

RANGE Nuttall's Woodpeckers are mostly found in California, where they are almost entirely restricted to low-elevation oak woodlands west of the Sierra Nevada. **WEST SLOPE:** They are fairly common to common in blue oak and interior live oak woodlands below 2000 ft in the northern Sierra Nevada; up to 3000 ft in the central Sierra; and at least as high as 5700 ft in the southern Sierra (as on the Kern Plateau). Upper altitudinal limits are probably determined by the oaks they favor, but their occasional use of canyon live oaks and black oaks allow them to extend their range upslope, at least seasonally. It is thought that some wander slightly upslope after the breeding season, and they have wintered as high as 4000 ft in Yosemite Valley. **EAST SLOPE:** Expected only in the Owens River Valley, where they are fairly common breeders in riparian habitats along the Owens River and along the lower reaches of creeks draining off the Sierra Nevada. Very rare visitors elsewhere on the east side, mostly in the fall and winter.

DOWNY WOODPECKER *Picoides pubescens*

LIFE HISTORY These tiny woodpeckers take advantage of their size to access feeding niches and foods not used by other woodpeckers. Unlike most woodpeckers that dig into hard wood with their stout, chisel-like bills, Downy Woodpeckers collect insects and arthropods from the surfaces of leaves and small branches, using their bills as probes and delicate forceps that can even pick up insect eggs. Males and females avoid competing with each other by foraging on different substrates—with females foraging on large branches and tree trunks, and males restricting themselves to the smallest branches or even descending to the ground to forage on the stems of weeds and grasses. In the fall and winter, Downy Woodpeckers also feed on berries and fruits (such as poison oak) or seeds and acorns, and they will steal sips of sap from sapsucker wells or nibble on the nutritious cambium layers under tree bark.

Their primary habitats are riparian woodlands or open mixed forests with a large component of oaks and other deciduous trees and shrubs. They are nearly always associated with cottonwoods, willows, aspens, alders, and oaks, but in the winter they are common visitors to backyards and residential areas, where they seek out fruit trees and exotic ornamentals. During the breeding season, they are most closely associated with riparian habitats, but during the nonbreeding season, they freely wander into adjacent oak and mixed oak-conifer forests, even at some distance from water.

Their most common vocalizations are short, sharp *pik* calls, or high-pitched, descending whinnying calls, but in February–March males and females start drumming in short 1–2 second bursts to find each other. Females are attracted to drumming territorial males and pairs forage together until they begin incubating eggs in May or early June (maybe as early as April at low elevations). Courtship is simple, and conspicuously involves males and females chasing each other while flying with slow shallow wingbeats.

Pairs search for potential nest sites together, looking for trees in advanced states of decay because they cannot excavate cavities in hard wood with their small, relatively weak bills. When either sex finds a suitable tree, they call the other over by tapping. Excavation takes 1–3 weeks, with the pair working together.

Both sexes help incubate the 4–6 eggs until they hatch 12 days later, with males incubating at night and both sexes sharing the daytime duties. Nestlings fledge in 18 days but begin conspicuously begging at the nest entrance 2–3 days before they leave the nest. They remain with their parents for another 3 weeks but become increasingly independent and soon leave. Little is known about the lives of immature birds.

If there is a rich supply of food, pairs may be year-round residents on their breeding territories, but it is believed that the more common strategy is that pairs drum together once more in the fall to affirm their pair bond, forage together for several weeks, then females disperse from the male's territory in early winter until the following spring. There may be some seasonal movements by both sexes, upslope and downslope, after the breeding season, but such movements are poorly understood and not well documented.

RANGE Downy Woodpeckers are one of the most widespread woodpeckers in North America; but in California they may be more common in the northern half of the state, where they are year-round residents. In the Sierra Nevada, they are widespread at lower elevations though generally uncommon and patchily distributed because they favor riparian habitats along rivers and streams, especially in the breeding season. Relatively rare away from water though the population seems to spread out and wander through many different habitats in the nonbreeding season. **WEST SLOPE:** Year-round residents up to 4500 ft; numerous higher elevation records after mid-June could represent postbreeding wanderers, but there is a chance that some may breed as high as 6000 ft. Rare fall transients to over 8000 ft. There may be some downslope movement to avoid heavy winter snows, but this is anecdotal information and remains an unanswered question. **EAST SLOPE:** Uncommon year-round residents, nearly always below 7000 ft, with most being found in riparian willow thickets and deciduous woodlands. Although widely distributed, a closer look at their distribution pattern shows distinct clusters of sightings, suggesting they become locally common in prime habitats. For example, many records come from Susanville, Lake Tahoe, Woodfords, Mono Lake, and Bishop.

HAIRY WOODPECKER *Picoides villosus*

LIFE HISTORY Hairy and Downy Woodpeckers present a classic case of convergent evolution, two distantly related species that superficially seem almost identical. Although these two species look alike, they are not closely related and Hairy Woodpeckers differ in several ecologically significant ways. They are not restricted to riparian woodlands but use nearly every type of forested habitat as long as there are large, mature trees for nesting and foraging. In these habitats, the medium-sized nesting cavities left by these common woodpeckers are used by many other cavity-nesting birds and mammals.

Hairy Woodpeckers tend to make a lot of noise as they call and forage on large tree trunks, picking insects from bark surfaces, flaking off bits of loose bark in search of hidden insects, or tapping and listening for the hollow sound of beetle larvae tunnels under the bark. When tunnels are located, they rapidly chip away the bark and wood and may spend up to one hour digging out a single beetle larva.

Because these highly-nutritious beetle larvae are present and accessible year round, Hairy Woodpeckers are permanent residents on their territories, even as high as 10,000 ft, though in particularly hard winters some are thought to temporarily descend to lower elevations. Pairs remain together on these territories and seem to maintain long-term bonds or perhaps even mate for life.

Some of their most common vocalizations are sharp *peek* calls and loud rattles that pairs begin using with increasing frequency from early winter until they start nesting. Short, one-second drumming calls serve to establish territorial boundaries, to summon a distant mate, or for courtship.

Despite all these vocalizations, Hairy Woodpeckers become notably quiet and hard to find while nesting. Beginning in late April, or perhaps a month earlier at lower elevations, pairs spend 1–3 weeks excavating their nest cavities, often building them in aspens or dead conifers. There are few detailed nesting records from the Sierra Nevada, but it seems that chicks hatch in late May at Lake Tahoe and early to mid-June at Yuba Pass just to the north.

Both sexes incubate their 3–7 eggs for about 12 days, with the young appearing at the entrance of the nest hole and begging loudly for food about 3–4 days before they fledge at one month old. Young birds continue to associate with their parents for several more weeks, but nothing is known of their lives after this age.

RANGE Hairy Woodpeckers are widespread in North America, and widespread permanent residents in the Sierra Nevada, where they occupy an extraordinary altitudinal gradient from 3000 ft to treeline. They are most abundant in mid-elevation montane forests of mixed oak and conifer, with a strong preference for stands with mature trees or recently burned forests with large snags, but can be found in nearly all forest types. **WEST SLOPE:** Permanent, fairly common residents from 3000–10,000 ft though probably most common in forests of the Mixed Conifer and Upper Montane Zones from about 4000–8000 ft. **EAST SLOPE:** Permanent, fairly common residents from 6000–10,000 ft but probably most common from 6000–8000 ft. Rarely breed as low as 4000 ft, as in the Owens Valley.

WHITE-HEADED WOODPECKER *Picoides albolarvatus*

LIFE HISTORY White-headed Woodpeckers are specialists of the vast mixed conifer and upper montane forests that dominate middle elevations of the Sierra Nevada from end to end. Closely related to Hairy Woodpeckers, and sharing many of the same habitats, they avoid competing for the same resources by foraging on bark and needle surfaces and by feeding heavily on pine seeds, rather than drilling into wood to find beetle larvae as Hairy and Black-backed Woodpeckers do.

For this reason, White-headed Woodpeckers are restricted to forests with numerous pines, especially areas with two or more species of pines so there is plenty of food available even in years when one species does not produce a crop. Many pine seeds are harvested in late August and September as the cones open, but these dexterous woodpeckers readily drill into unopened cones to pull out unripe seeds, hanging from cone tips to minimize their exposure to sticky sap. They add ants, beetles, and other insects to their diets when they are seasonally available, and in the Sierra Nevada they have been observed making sap wells in the winter. Females forage on incense cedars in the winter, feeding on abundant scale insects (see Brown Creeper account).

These woodpeckers are very sedentary and remain year-round on their territories, with only a few wandering to higher elevations in late summer, and some wandering periodically to lower elevations in winter. It is believed that pairs stay together year round, with an increase in drumming and calling between males and females in March as they establish or reinforce their pair bonds in preparation for the breeding season. Their one- to two-second drumming "calls" help in territorial defense, while *peek-it* or *pee-de-dink* calls and rapid rattling *peek-peek-peek* calls are given by pairs as a way of staying in contact.

Nest holes are excavated fairly close to the ground in large dead trees or even in logs on the ground, and cavities take up to a month to dig, with many false starts and partially excavated holes left behind. Both sexes help excavate cavities in late April or in May, and by the end of May most females lay 4–5 eggs. Males incubate at night, and both parents incubate during the day, trading off every hour or so, and staying in close vocal contact during the entire 14 day incubation period. Young birds leave the nest in late June–early July, about 26 days after hatching, and often stay near their parents through the fall and even into the winter.

RANGE White-headed Woodpeckers are largely restricted to the Cascade-Sierra mountains, where they are fairly common residents in mixed conifer and upper montane forests on mid-elevation slopes. They use a wide range of conifers including Jeffrey, sugar, lodgepole, and western white pines, white and red fir, and Douglas-fir; but ponderosa pine seems to be their preferred tree. Rarely wander upslope after the breeding season, with a few records to treeline. **WEST SLOPE:** Year-round, and sometimes common residents, at 4000–8000 ft, with some moving downslope to the lowest edges of the ponderosa pine forests (around 3000 ft) in mid-winter. **EAST SLOPE:** Distribution varies due to the fragmented nature of their preferred forests on the east side; generally common in the extensive mixed conifer forests from Lake Tahoe north, where they are probably resident above 6000 ft, but they seem to be patchily distributed further south. They are rare to uncommon in Jeffrey pine forests above 7000 ft near Mono Lake and Mammoth Lakes; and rare to uncommon over 8000 ft in pine-fir forests above the Owens Valley. A few show up at lower elevations and valley floors in the winter.

Black-backed Woodpecker *Picoides arcticus*

LIFE HISTORY   Although various woodpeckers are drawn to recently burned conifer forests to feast on wood-boring beetles, none specialize on this niche as much as Black-backed Woodpeckers. Sooty black and perfectly camouflaged on fire-scorched tree trunks, Black-backs actively seek out recently burned forests, sometimes becoming locally common for a few years then moving on. As much as 75 percent of their diet consists of wood-boring beetle larvae (mostly Cerambycidae and some Buprestidae) which are abundant in fire-killed trees. These larvae burrow deep in dead and dying tree trunks, so Black-backed Woodpeckers possess several unique adaptations that make them powerful and efficient hammerers and diggers, including having 3 toes (instead of 4), shortened leg bones, modified ribs, and unique skull structures. The same adaptations that help them grip trees and gain maximum leverage while pounding make them noticeably clumsy when doing simple things like climbing trees.

Another aspect of these fascinating woodpeckers is their notorious tameness. These easily approached birds will not hesitate to build nests in busy campgrounds or along popular trails. In fact, some of their best-known nests are visited and photographed by dozens of birdwatchers each summer and the pairs do not seem to mind at all.

They may be observed foraging on tree trunks, and even on logs, but they are hard to spot because they climb slowly and may circle around behind tree trunks to avoid being seen. Generally quiet, either sex may at times make fast, doubled clicking notes to stay in touch with each other, or complex "scream-rattle-snarl" calls in aggressive encounters. From April–June, they also give short, two-second bursts of drumming to announce their territorial intent or to attract mates. Pairs may remain together all year but this has not been studied.

Males do much of the work of excavating nest cavities in April or May, choosing smaller-diameter trees than other local woodpeckers for their nests, then adding a distinctive, final touch by stripping all the bark away from around the entrance hole. On living trees, this newly exposed wood beads up with sticky sap, creating a protective collar that chipmunks and squirrels (common nest predators) have a hard time crossing.

Eggs are laid in May or even in June, and both parents incubate the 3–4 eggs for 12 days, with males taking the night shift and both sexes sharing the day shifts. Noisy, begging young appear at the nest entrance for several days before they leave the nest at 24 days of age,

sometime in late June to mid-July. The lives of immature birds are unknown, but family groups have been seen together in August.

RANGE Black-backed Woodpeckers are widespread in the boreal forests of Canada and Alaska, and are uncommon residents of montane
forests in the Cascade Mountains and Sierra Nevada as far south as
Tulare County. They live year round among upper montane forests of
lodgepole pines, aspens, and firs, but because they seek burned forests,
they may be found outside of their typical range at any time of year.
After the breeding season, there could be a slight downslope movement
in the fall and winter, but so few birds are observed that it is difficult to
quantify the extent of this seasonal migration. **WEST SLOPE:** Principally known from 6500–9000 ft, but found occasionally at both higher
and lower elevations, especially in the fall. Southern limit of breeding range just east of Johnsondale in southeastern Tulare County, but
they may be found one day as far south as the Piute Mountains. **EAST
SLOPE:** Uncommon to locally common around Lake Tahoe and in
montane forests above 6000 ft to the north. Very few records south of
Lake Tahoe, except in the Jeffrey pine forests from Mono Lake to Mammoth Lakes (including Devils Postpile National Monument).

NORTHERN FLICKER *Colaptes auratus*

LIFE HISTORY No other woodpeckers are as familiar as Northern
Flickers, which not only frequent backyards and neighborhoods, but
also breed in every type of forest from the riparian woodlands of the
lowest valleys to stunted trees at treeline. Due to their abundance,
these common and widespread birds play a major ecological role by
making large nest cavities that many other cavity-using birds and mammals depend on for shelter and raising their young.

Flickers are easy to watch because they spend much of their
time in open woodlands and meadows, conspicuously perching in full
view on tree tops and large branches. They are unique among North
American birds, basing much of their diet on ants that they obtain by
perching on the ground and using their large powerful bills to probe
into anthills. Flickers repeatedly extend their sticky tongues an inch-
and-a-half, lapping up adult and larval ants. In the winter, when ants are
much harder to find, they supplement their diet with various berries,
fruits, and seeds.

In the fall, most move downslope, but their presence at lower elevations and in valley bottoms is episodic because they leave the coldest
areas only when the ground is covered in snow and their food supplies

become limited at higher elevations. In years when large numbers leave parts of the Sierra Nevada, they return to the lowlands in April then quickly move upslope in May, with those remaining in the lowlands beginning to breed right away.

In the mountains, most nests are excavated in May in dead trees or in decaying portions of living trees. This busy month is also a peak time for vocalizations and displays. Their most common vocalizations are rolling *wick-a-wick-a-wick-a* calls given during pair formation and used to announce territories. Both sexes drum with a rapid but evenly-spaced series of taps to help defend their territory; and if tensions escalate, flickers of either sex may face off against intruding flickers of the same sex for a "wicka dance" with the territory-holder and the intruder weaving their bodies back and forth while pointing their bills up, fanning their tails, and loudly calling.

Although males initiate nest excavations, females play a larger role in the final stages. When available, aspens or cottonwoods are their favorite nesting trees, but flickers will use almost any other tree if necessary. There is little data on how many eggs they lay in the Sierra Nevada, but 6–8 eggs have been reported from nests at Lake Tahoe. Incubation lasts 11 days, with males incubating at night and both sexes trading off nesting and foraging during the day. Young birds fledge after 24–27 days with many young birds leaving the nest in mid-June, but what happens after they leave the nest is unknown.

RANGE Northern Flickers are widespread and common in almost every part of North America, and in California they occupy a greater range of habitats and elevations than almost any other bird. From mid-April to mid-September breeding flickers are fairly common in all types of open wooded habitats from valley bottoms to treeline; in the nonbreeding season they use an even wider variety of wooded, brushy, and open habitats, with postbreeding birds wandering high into the Alpine Zone in late summer and fall. Almost all descend below snowline in winter, but even at lower elevations their numbers vary dramatically from year to year, ranging from absent to locally abundant at any given location. **WEST SLOPE:** Breed from the lowest foothills to treeline, and then in the fall and winter they are typically very common below 5000 ft because the foothills have relatively mild temperatures and an abundance of berry and fruit crops. **EAST SLOPE:** Breed from the lowest valley bottoms (3500 ft along the Owens River) to treeline. After the end of the breeding season, there may be a pulse of transients or migrants at higher elevations from late September to early November, but they later descend to lower elevations or leave the region. Distribution in winter is patchy and irregular due to the cold winters on the east side, but they are nowhere common and are generally rare or absent, except in mild winters when small numbers may linger.

PILEATED WOODPECKER *Dryocopus pileatus*

LIFE HISTORY Despite their great size and far-carrying calls, our largest woodpeckers are furtive and difficult to find in the dark, old-growth forests they favor. One way to know they're around is to look for large rectangular excavations where they tear apart decaying logs and dead tree trunks with their powerful bills, leaving slivered shards of wood on the ground. This exposes wood-boring beetles and carpenter ant nests that are these woodpeckers' primary foods. From a distance, the sounds of foraging Pileated Woodpeckers are distinctive because, unlike small woodpeckers that chip away wood with fast strokes, Pileateds make deliberate heavy thuds as they cut deeply and work off inch-long chunks of wood. In the late summer and fall, they also seek out locally available berries and fruits.

In the Sierra Nevada, these giant woodpeckers are mostly restricted to coniferous forests where large-diameter snags and logs are abundant. Tree size is more important than species, so they may also nest in large oaks or cottonwoods and will even use stands of young trees if some large-diameter snags are left standing.

It is thought that pairs mate and defend a single large territory for life. They are so closely linked to these territories that if one mate dies, the other remains and tries to attract a new partner rather than leaving. Due to their sprawling home ranges and affinity for big trees, Pileated Woodpecker populations are somewhat fragmented, and there are vast areas of seemingly suitable habitat where they appear to be absent and other areas where they are locally common.

Beginning in February or March, they signal their growing excitement by drumming or making loud *wuk* calls that may be given singly or run together into a kind of maniacal laughing to convey alarm or territorial intent and to attract mates at a great distance. Courting birds face off and spread their wings, raise their crests, and sway their heads from side to side. Mated pairs spend 3–6 weeks excavating sizable nest cavities in dead, standing trees, finishing them in time to lay 4 eggs sometime in May to mid-June. These cavities are later used by other cavity-nesting birds such as Wood Ducks, mergansers, and small owls, as well as several types of squirrels.

The incubation period is not well documented but eggs probably hatch in 16–18 days, with males taking the night shifts and both sexes trading off every couple hours during the day. Chicks leave the nest at 26–31 days of age, in late May to early July, and stay with their parents until the immature birds depart in the fall and wander all winter in search of their own territories and mates.

RANGE Pileated Woodpeckers in western North America are year-round residents from western British Columbia to central California. They are generally widespread on both slopes of the Sierra Nevada north of Lake Tahoe, but to the south they are more narrowly restricted to a mid-elevation band of mixed conifer and upper montane forests on the west slope. They are scarce residents as low as the lowest edges of the ponderosa pine forests (usually around 3000 ft), and uncommon to locally fairly common in the prime timber belt of black oaks, pines, cedars, and firs. Very few reside or wander upslope into the red fir and lodgepole pine forests of the upper mountains. **WEST SLOPE:** Nearly always found from 3000–7000 ft, though they use pockets of suitable habitat at lower elevations. Those reported from higher elevations are thought to be wandering immature birds, with most being found in late summer. Their southern breeding limit is the Greenhorn Mountains, but they are occasionally reported from Breckenridge Mountain where they could breed. **EAST SLOPE:** Uncommon to fairly common residents around Lake Tahoe and on the forested slopes to the north, but increasingly scarce to the south with a few scattered records as far south as Mono Lake and Mammoth Lakes.

FLYCATCHERS (Tyrannidae)

Olive-sided Flycatcher *Contopus cooperi*

LIFE HISTORY From perches at the tops of towering trees and snags, Olive-sided Flycatchers call loudly and patrol their aerial dominions with strident *pip-pip-pip* calls. Their diagnostic songs, *what-PEEVES-you*, are far-carrying, giving the impression that these large flycatchers are abundant and widespread, when in fact their numbers have decreased alarmingly in recent decades.

While other flycatchers catch insects closer to the ground, Olive-sided Flycatchers hunt exclusively by darting out from the forest's highest perches ("sallying") and chasing high-flying insects in mid-air. These powerful fliers prefer tall old-growth trees overlooking wide open spaces and use deep wingbeats and sharp turns to hunt down the large bees, wasps, and flying ants that form the bulk of their diet.

Pairs of Olive-sided Flycatchers are famously aggressive towards other birds, perhaps more than any other flycatcher in the Sierra Nevada. Possessing strong pair bonds, they are able to defend territories of about 100 acres. By late June, females construct nests that are placed far out on horizontal branches anywhere from 5–70 ft above the ground (over 100 ft is exceptional). The nests are protected by branches above and usually have broad views of the surrounding area.

Because they nest at such lofty heights, little is known of their nesting behavior, but it is thought that females incubate 3 eggs for 14–16 days, and that young remain on the nest for 15–20 days. Males will bring food to females during the early days of incubation, and both parents feed the young birds. Fledgling departure from the nest is drawn out because young birds spend time on nearby branches or return to the nest after their first flights. Family groups may stay together until migration but this is not known for certain.

RANGE Olive-sided Flycatchers are summer residents of montane coniferous forests the full length of the Sierra Nevada. Their long flights from South America each spring—one of the longest migrations of any North American bird—means that Olive-sided Flycatchers do not arrive in southern California until mid-April, later than many other migrating passerines. By mid-May they have advanced to the northern reaches of the Sierra Nevada, primarily along the foothills of the west slope, and have begun ascending into the mountains, where they breed in all coniferous forests except the upper reaches of the Subalpine Zone. **WEST SLOPE:** Fairly common in the foothills during spring migration, first arriving in the southern Sierra Nevada the last week of April and reaching the central Sierra Nevada the first week of May. Peak numbers arrive 1–2 weeks later, when the entire population moves upslope to breed in tall conifers at all elevations. In Sequoia & Kings Canyon National Parks, they can be surprisingly common over 9000 ft in early August, but it is not clear whether these are nesting birds or family groups roaming upslope after the young have left the nests. Most vacate the region in mid-August though scattered birds remain until mid-September. **EAST SLOPE:** Timing as on west slope but spring migration notably subdued on east slope, with migrants uncommon south of Mono County. Most nest in the forests of higher canyons and slopes where large conifers tower over wide open spaces.

WESTERN WOOD-PEWEE *Contopus sordidulus*

LIFE HISTORY From dawn to dusk, and sometimes at night, the downslurred *pee-ur* calls of Western Wood-Pewees provide the sound track of summer. There is hardly a forest they do not like and they are especially abundant around forest edges, clearings, riparian zones, and wet meadows. At times they seem like one of the most abundant birds, but surveys in Yosemite and Sequoia & Kings Canyon National Parks suggest that the inconspicuous and relatively quiet Dusky Flycatchers are considerably more common and widespread than wood-pewees in all areas surveyed.

Wood-pewees are particularly visible because they perch and call repeatedly from bare branches around open areas. Several times each minute, these fast, powerful fliers swoop out dramatically to snatch passing flies, bees, wasps, or moths. At the moment they close in on a flying insect, they characteristically use an odd, floating glide as they prepare for the abrupt aerial maneuvers that some insects use to evade predators.

Second only to Olive-sided Flycatchers, wood-pewees winter further south than any other flycatcher in the Sierra Nevada and travel a tremendous distance on migration. A hardy few show up during the last week of April, but most show up the second week of May. For example, over 350 were counted at Butterbredt Spring, a popular migration hotspot in the southern Sierra Nevada, on the morning of May 19. Many wood-pewees observed in May are migrating north but some are also beginning to nest at this time.

Females construct cup nests of tightly bound spiderwebs and silvery plant fibers that straddle forked twigs near branch tips 15–30 ft above the ground. Both deciduous and coniferous trees are used, but aspens, cottonwoods, and pines seem to be favored. Once learned, these distinctive nests are easily found. Females lay 3 eggs that hatch after 12 days. Both parents care for the nestlings until they leave the nest at 14–18 days of age. Wood-pewees may be observed nesting or caring for young in early August, suggesting an extended breeding season.

RANGE Western Wood-Pewees are common to abundant summer residents in every type of forest, except the densest stands of trees or arid pinyon-juniper woodlands, from the base of foothill slopes to subalpine forest. They can be found from late April to early October, but are particularly common from mid-May to mid-August. **WEST SLOPE:** Widespread, but especially abundant in riparian areas, ponderosa pine forests, interior live oak and black oak woodlands, and in sites that have recently burned. **EAST SLOPE:** Despite a general absence of suitable habitats for this forest-loving flycatcher, arrival and departure dates seem to mirror those on the west slope. Some remain to breed along the many streams and canyons draining the east slope.

WILLOW FLYCATCHER *Empidonax traillii*

LIFE HISTORY Soon after arriving in the spring, Willow Flycatchers take up residence in thickets of willows and shrubs in riparian corridors and meadows. Though difficult to identify, and easy to overlook among dense branches, they are conspicuous when males (and females) perch on high, dead branches and broadcast their snappy *fitz-bew* songs. Their brief, intense nesting season is fueled by the abundant insects found around water: mainly wasps, bees, beetles, and flies.

Females build compact cup nests in vertical forks 5–30 ft high, where they lay 3–4 eggs. In addition to parasitism by cowbirds, Willow Flycatcher nests may fail when grazing cows knock nests and eggs down or expose the nests to predators by eating away protective leaves. Eggs in successful nests hatch in 12–13 days, and nestlings remain in the nest 12–15 days while being fed by females. Young birds leave their nests between early July and mid-August.

Formerly common along waterways throughout California and the Sierra Nevada, Willow Flycatchers are now almost entirely extirpated from the state except for a handful (around 150) that persist in the Sierra Nevada. The decline in Willow Flycatcher populations is cause for great concern because it indicates how the health of fragile meadows and streamsides has been severely impacted by humans and livestock.

RANGE Willow Flycatchers survive in perilously low numbers in the Sierra Nevada in widely scattered riparian and wet meadow habitats. These late-arriving summer residents begin to show up on their nesting territories from late April (South Fork Kern River) to early June (montane meadows). Most leave their nesting territories by early August, with a few stragglers still nesting until mid-August. Migrating birds can be found until late September. **WEST SLOPE:** One large breeding population of several dozen pairs (of the "Southwestern" subspecies *E. t. extimus*) is found along the South Fork Kern River. Another subspecies (the "Little" Willow Flycatcher, *E. t. brewsteri*) breeds in extremely small numbers in montane meadows near Shaver Lake, Donner Pass, and Lake Almanor. **EAST SLOPE:** "Little" Willow Flycatchers breed at a handful of montane meadows, including a small population along the Little Truckee River in Nevada County, and a newly discovered population at Red Lake in Alpine County. Small numbers nest among sagebrush and wild rose thickets along the lower reaches of east-slope creeks from Mono Lake to Owens Valley.

HAMMOND'S FLYCATCHER *Empidonax hammondii*

LIFE HISTORY These common summer residents are usually the first *Empidonax* flycatchers to arrive each spring, but they are easily overlooked in favor of vocal Pacific-slope Flycatchers that fill the woods with such gusto. Hammond's Flycatchers are secretive birds, staying well-hidden in the interiors of deeply shaded conifer forests. They breed in a wide variety of conifer forests, and have been described as red fir specialists, but recent surveys in Yosemite and Sequoia & Kings Canyon National Parks found them far more abundant in giant sequoia and white fir habitats than in red fir.

Here, with effort, they may be observed among the dark foliage, repeatedly flicking their wings and making very short flights to catch passing moths, flies, or beetles. On occasion, especially early in the breeding season, Hammond's Flycatchers perch on low branches and catch prey on the ground or on the undersides of leaves. During the peak of the breeding season, however, males spend much of their time in the upper two-thirds of tall conifers, perched on thin, dead branches and vocalizing repeatedly in the forest gloom.

Given their high stations in tall, shaded forests, it is not surprising that little is known about the life history of these small, plainly-attired flycatchers. In fact, they are best known for being extremely difficult to distinguish from Gray and Dusky Flycatchers, and during migration it is nearly impossible to separate these 3 species when they are silent and found in uncharacteristic habitats. On the other hand, breeding Hammond's Flycatchers can be confidently identified through careful study of their songs and calls, and by their use of well-developed conifer stands.

Females build cup nests of bark strips and grass stems in the forks of conifer branches 6–60 ft above the ground as males maintain close guard. Females incubate the 3–4 eggs alone for 15 days, but both parents care for the nestlings for 17–18 days and for another 20 days after the young leave the nest.

RANGE Hammond's Flycatchers are common and widespread breeders in the mountains and conifer forests of western North America. **WEST SLOPE:** Arrive in the foothills of the Sierra Nevada from mid- to late April though they do not show up at higher elevations for another month. Migrants are found at low elevations and in a wide variety of habitats but breed in dense conifer forests from 4500–7000 ft (rarely down to 3000 ft or up to 8000 ft). Wander to even higher elevations after nesting, and in August have been found over 12,000 ft. They linger and molt before fall migration, so freshly plumaged Hammond's Flycatchers are the last *Empidonax* flycatchers to leave the Sierra Nevada. Any "empid" found in September or October is most likely this species, and they have been found as late as mid-October. **EAST SLOPE:** Rare spring (mid-April to early June) and fall (early August to mid-October) migrants.

GRAY FLYCATCHER *Empidonax wrightii*

LIFE HISTORY Like silver ghosts haunting the sagebrush flats and pinyon-juniper woodlands they call home, Gray Flycatchers largely escaped scientific attention until an ornithologist in the 1940s discovered they could be identified by their unique way of wagging their tails down (other *Empidonax* first flick their tails up then drop them). This discovery, and the ability to readily identify this cryptic species, opened the door to new insights about the bird's life history and distribution though much remains to be learned.

Gray Flycatchers can be found perching on the lowest branches of large conifers or the top of shrubs, from which they sally out to catch passing insects or hover to glean insects from twigs and leaves. They feed at low levels and are often seen snatching insects from the ground. No other details about their diets have been published.

Gray Flycatchers breed on hillsides of tall, well-developed desert shrubs or on rocky slopes among open conifers. Of 17 nests reported in the northern Sierra Nevada, for example, 15 were in Jeffrey pines and two were in junipers, but in other areas they nest in sagebrush and dense shrubs such as bitterbrush (though they avoid montane chaparral). The breeding season begins in late May to early June, but mated pairs have been observed in mid-May. Unlike other flycatchers, they have an extended breeding season that includes a second clutch of eggs laid in late June to early July.

Females, occasionally with help from males, build bulky cup nests of bark strips lined with wool or fine plant fibers. The nests are often located on branches against the main trunks of trees or shrubs. Females incubate 3–4 eggs for 14 days, then both parents tend the young for 16 days on the nest, and another 14 days after the young have fledged.

RANGE Gray Flycatchers are locally common summer residents in dry, open areas east of the Sierra Nevada though patchily distributed and often absent from large areas of suitable habitat. **WEST SLOPE:** Migrating or wandering birds rarely observed from late April to September, with very few records of fall migrants. Most sightings are from low-elevation chaparral habitats but occasionally at higher elevations. **EAST SLOPE:** The majority of the population is present from mid-May to mid-August, but observed as early as the first week in April. Most leave by third week in August though some remain until late September. Locally common summer residents below 8000 ft but may breed as high as 11,000 ft.

Dusky Flycatcher *Empidonax oberholseri*

LIFE HISTORY These little flycatchers favor clearings with shrubs and scattered trees, including openings in forests otherwise occupied by nesting Hammond's. These two very similar species generally breed at different elevations (Hammond's mostly at 4500–7000 ft, and Dusky at 6500–8500 ft), but in the occasional areas where they overlap their use of different habitats helps keeps them separate. Dusky Flycatchers favor any open area from ponderosa pine stands in the foothills to patches of gnarled whitebark pines at treeline, but they are particularly abundant in montane chaparral where manzanita and ceanothus grow densely under isolated pines. One study in Sequoia & Kings Canyon National Parks found Dusky Flycatchers in 24 of 28 surveyed habitats, making them one of the most abundant flycatchers in the parks. In this study, Duskys were twice as widespread and 8 times more abundant than Hammond's Flycatchers.

Mirroring their preference for shrubs and small trees, Dusky Flycatchers perch on low branches where they sing and hunt for flying insects. They occasionally pounce on prey items on the ground or hover while picking insects from twigs and leaves.

Nesting activity begins in late May or early June with females building tight cup nests in the forks of branches on small trees or shrubs an average of 6 ft above the ground. Females incubate 3–4 eggs for 15–16 days. Both parents raise the young until they leave the nest at 18 days of age, at which point individual birds may wander upslope before heading south. Dusky Flycatchers leave the Sierra Nevada at a fairly early date, wearing a dull, worn plumage that is molted on their wintering grounds.

RANGE Dusky Flycatchers breed in mountainous areas throughout

California and are particularly abundant on both slopes of the Sierra Nevada. Most of the population arrives in mid-May and begins leaving their nesting grounds in mid-August, but records span from the first week of April to late September. **WEST SLOPE:** Common and widespread summer residents of open forests and montane chaparral habitats from 4000 ft to over 11,000 ft though mainly found above 6000 ft. **EAST SLOPE:** Breed in open forests and shrub habitats from Jeffrey pine woodlands to the crest, including willow thickets in both wet meadows and dry sagebrush flats.

PACIFIC-SLOPE FLYCATCHER *Empidonax difficilis*

LIFE HISTORY In 1989, "Western Flycatchers" were split into Pacific-slope and Cordilleran Flycatchers on the basis of genetic evidence and differences in their call notes. In general the sole field mark for separating these species is the single upslurred *su-wheet* call note given by Pacific-slope Flycatchers, versus the sharply, two-syllabled *pit-PEET!* given by Cordilleran Flycatchers. Unfortunately for biologists and birdwatchers, some males are bilingual and freely use both vocalizations, making field identification dubious until more is learned about these species.

Breeding only on the west slope of the Sierra Nevada, Pacific-slope Flycatchers inhabit well-shaded riparian forests of alders, maples, and cottonwoods, often mixed with oaks and conifers. From perches at low to moderate heights, Pacific-slope Flycatchers make quick, ascending flights to snatch wasps, bees, or flies from the air or from the surfaces of leaves and branches. They spend their days sitting on such perches, swiveling their heads from side to side watching for prey, while incessantly calling.

Females build cup nests of green mosses, dry grasses, and bark strips lined with finer materials. Nests are located in a wide variety of sites including mid-sized trees or shrubs, the tangled roots of toppled trees, tree or rock cavities, and even on porch rafters or under the eaves of houses. Females incubate 4 eggs for 14–15 days. Both parents tend the nestlings for 13–15 days, and continue feeding the fledglings for another 10–15 days off the nest.

RANGE Pacific-slope Flycatchers are summer visitors in moist woodlands west of the Sierra Nevada. Migrants can appear surprisingly early, from mid-March to mid-April depending on weather. After the breeding season some individuals wander upslope to as high as 11,000 ft. Most leave mid-August to September, but they have been seen in early

October. **WEST SLOPE:** Locally uncommon breeders in a fairly narrow altitudinal band from about 2000–5000 ft, where they are primarily confined to deciduous vegetation along streams and moist ravines in well-shaded ponderosa pine and oak-conifer forests. **EAST SLOPE:** Thought to be uncommon migrants at lower elevations, observed from mid-April to early October (with one seen near Bishop in late November). See the Cordilleran Flycatcher account for uncertainties in confirming the identity of east-slope birds.

CORDILLERAN FLYCATCHER *Empidonax occidentalis*

LIFE HISTORY Very little is known about the life history, identification, and behavior of Cordilleran Flycatchers because nearly all studies on the "Western Flycatcher" complex have been conducted on populations of Pacific-slope Flycatchers. These birds remain an enigma, but their life history is thought to be very similar to Pacific-slope Flycatchers.

RANGE Cordilleran Flycatchers are primarily birds of the Rocky Mountain region, and their status in the Sierra Nevada remains a point of conjecture. **WEST SLOPE:** No known records. **EAST SLOPE:** Birds giving Cordilleran Flycatcher-type calls have been found vocalizing and nesting in various canyons between Mammoth Lakes and Leavitt Meadows (on Hwy 108 below Sonora Pass), where they occur in aspen and conifer forests near streams. The identity of these birds has yet to be confidently established. Careful studies are needed to survey these populations and determine the taxonomic status of both breeding and migrating birds.

BLACK PHOEBE *Sayornis nigricans*

LIFE HISTORY When other flycatchers depart at summer's end, Black Phoebes remain at lower elevations, adding a note of cheer with their upslurred whistles and a sense of formality with their tuxedo-like, black-and-white plumages. Found near bridges, homesteads, and farms, and showing little fear of humans, they are always a friendly and welcome presence. At all seasons Black Phoebes live near water, where they find a steady supply of insects and, in the breeding season, a source of mud for their nests.

Black Phoebes are often observed perching on boulders along foothill streams and rivers; or on bare twigs and fences near any source of water, even small stock ponds or irrigation ditches. Using low perches (often under 6 ft high), and occasionally while sitting on the ground, Black Phoebes fly out to catching passing wasps, bees, flies, and dragonflies. Their diet also includes small berries.

Although Black Phoebes formerly nested on the vertical faces of cliffs and boulders, they are one of few birds that now nest almost exclusively around farms and human structures. Their mud nests (like those of Barn and Cliff Swallows but smaller) have become a familiar sight under eaves or bridges. Because they are year-round residents and do not have to migrate first, pair formation begins in early January and continues through February, with males signaling their interest by hovering enthusiastically around perched females.

Females construct nests (starting in March) by hovering and flinging mud pellets against vertical surfaces then building out with a mixture of mud and plant fibers or hairs. The semicircular nests are located near or over water and are built close to some kind of ceiling that helps keep out predators. Females incubate 4–5 eggs for 15–18 days. It is not known if males assist with incubation duties, but once the eggs hatch both parents tend the nestlings for 21 days. Then, while males continue feeding the first batch of fledglings, females begin a second nesting effort.

RANGE In California, Black Phoebes are year-round residents that breed at low elevations west of the Sierra Nevada; after nesting (early July–early August) they frequently wander into the mountains up to 10,000 ft, where they can be found until mid-September. **WEST SLOPE:** Fairly common, with the bulk of the population residing below 3000 ft, but uncommon up to 5000 ft at all seasons. Some downslope movement in winter results in increased numbers in the foothills. Nearly always found close to water, but may be observed passing through dry forests and open areas, apparently wandering in search of new territories. **EAST SLOPE:** Rare migrants and post-breeding wanderers from early March to mid-May, and from mid-July to mid-September. One small population breeds in parts of Inyo and Mono counties, where they are also a regular presence through winter. Elsewhere on the east slope they are very rare in winter (seen once every 6–7 years on most Christmas Bird Counts).

Say's Phoebe *Sayornis saya*

LIFE HISTORY The sad, but sweet *pee-ur* calls of Say's Phoebes can be heard in open, arid, low-elevation habitats from sagebrush flats to dusty farmyards. At all times these pale, earth-colored flycatchers perch near the ground, usually on bushes or solitary fence posts, swooping out to catch passing insects or darting down to pluck insects and spiders from the dirt.

Say's Phoebes restrict themselves to the warmest regions of California, but at the same time they are one of the hardiest flycatchers, remaining in fair numbers through the winter at low elevations (though in far smaller numbers than Black Phoebes). It is believed that they survive cold temperatures because most of the insects they eat are captured on or near the ground, where temperatures remain higher and insects stay more active.

In April, Say's Phoebes build bulky cup nests of dry grasses, hairs, and spider webs on various rocky or dirt embankments, and sometimes in or around buildings. Females incubate the 4–5 eggs for 12–14 days, with both parents feeding the nestlings another 14–16 days. Males continue caring for the fledglings while females lay a second clutch of eggs.

RANGE Say's Phoebes are found in open deserts east of the Sierra Nevada, and in the hottest portions of the Central Valley west of the Sierra Nevada. Uncommon in desert portions of the southern Sierra Nevada. Many individuals breed in the Great Basin and winter in the Central Valley, apparently migrating along routes that take them eastward over Sierra Nevada passes in early spring and westward in late summer. **WEST SLOPE:** Rare migrants at any elevation (observed up to 12,000 ft) from early March to mid-April, and from early August to mid-September. Uncommon breeders in the South Fork Kern River Valley and desert mountain ranges and slopes to the south (i.e. Scodie and Piute Mountains). May breed as far north as El Dorado County on the west slope but foothill records are lacking north of the Kern River. Disperse from the valley floor into the foothills in winter, where they are fairly common at low elevations (numerous individuals observed on every Christmas Bird Count at Lake Oroville and the Kern River), and uncommon to rare at higher elevations (single birds observed once every 4 years on the Grass Valley Christmas Bird Count, and once on the Yosemite count). **EAST SLOPE:** Observed all winter at low elevations, with the highest numbers found around Bishop and Owens Valley. Also found every couple winters at Honey Lake but very rarely at other eastside locations. Rare breeding birds north of Sierra Valley, and uncommon south of Mono Lake, but their breeding status in the central Sierra Nevada is poorly documented.

ASH-THROATED FLYCATCHER *Myiarchus cinerascens*

LIFE HISTORY Alone among flycatchers, Ash-throated Flycatchers hold reign over arid, brush-covered slopes where their "referee whistle" calls are a distinctive summer sound. Look closely and you will spot these elegant flycatchers perching in their characteristic upright postures on the low branches of oaks and pines or the tops of manzanita and ceanothus. Because they are tolerant of high temperatures and do not need to drink, they are not dependent on sources of water or lush vegetation, and so are the only flycatchers in many foothill woodlands and chaparral-covered hillsides.

Ash-throated Flycatchers are active predators. In open habitats, they sally out to snatch prey from leaves or the ground, very rarely chasing insects in mid-air; and while in dense foliage they stalk their prey with quick, short flights among the branches, moving from branch to branch and covering wide areas. Their diets are surprisingly broad, including not only many types of bees, wasps, beetles, caterpillars, and grasshoppers, but also a small selection of fruits, berries, small reptiles and rodents. Within their preferred habitats, they have very little competition from other flycatchers for food or nest sites.

Although Ash-throated Flycatchers reside in brushy habitats, they require the presence of cavity-filled trees on their breeding territories. Because they can only nest in these cavities, Ash-throated Flycatchers chase away other cavity-nesting birds such as titmice, swallows, bluebirds, and woodpeckers as large as flickers. They also use nest boxes put out by humans, which has helped them expand their range in the foothills.

Females collect bits of cow dung, dried grass stems, and various hairs (mainly from rabbits) and use these to fill the nest cavity. It is unknown whether males assist in nest-building, one indication of how little is known about the life history of these common birds, but females incubate the 4–5 eggs. Active nests have been observed from late April to early July. Eggs hatch after 15 days and both parents tend the nestlings for another 16–17 days.

RANGE Ash-throated Flycatchers are widespread summer residents in arid, low-elevation habitats with a mix of brushy thickets and scattered trees throughout the western United States and Mexico. Some arrive during the first week of April in the central and southern Sierra Nevada, but most show up in late April into early May, with sizable numbers continuing to migrate through the region in late May. Small numbers of post-breeding individuals drift briefly upslope, and it is somewhat of a mystery whether birds observed in mixed conifer forests in mid-summer are breeders or transients. A few are observed at low elevations as late as the end of September. **WEST SLOPE:** Fairly common migrants and breeders below 3000 ft, but possible as high as 4500–5500 ft wherever dry, south-facing hillsides approximate their preferred habitats. **EAST SLOPE:** Rare spring migrants at low elevations from late March–May; then as fall migrants, often at higher elevations, in late July–August. Breed in juniper woodlands of the Great Basin, but their status as breeders on the east slope of the Sierra Nevada is not clear.

WESTERN KINGBIRD *Tyrannus verticalis*

LIFE HISTORY Western Kingbirds are conspicuous members of the foothill bird community on the west slope, where their loud bickering calls and flamboyant flights are an ever-present element of open ranchlands and woodlands. It is hard to miss the kingbird's acrobatic chase of passing bees, wasps, and flies, and if you are close enough you may hear an audible snap of the kingbird's bill as it clamps down on its prey and swoops back to its original perch. Ranchers in some areas use the wonderful old nickname "bee martin" to describe this bird's agile flight and diet of bees.

More than anything else, kingbirds are noted for their pugnacious territory defense, which may be leveled at any winged intruders except members of their own species. Swooping back and forth with great clamor and fury, a pair of Western Kingbirds, sometimes accompanied by a few of their closest neighbors, showers intruders with a torrent of protest while hovering on fiercely beating wings. So fearless are kingbirds that they may cling to the back of larger birds, up to the size of Red-tailed Hawks, pecking at them as they fly away, and they will not hesitate to scold humans who approach too closely.

Commencing in May, both parents select a horizontal surface on places like tree branches, telephone poles, fences, or building ledges. They spend 4–8 days building large, untidy nests of stems, twigs, and plants fibers that they line with finer materials felted together into a tight cup. Females then incubate 3–5 eggs and chicks hatch about two weeks later. Chicks are tended on the nest by both parents for another two weeks, at which point they clamber out of the nest and make their first flights a few days later.

RANGE Western Kingbirds breed in open habitats below 5000 ft nearly everywhere in California. **WEST SLOPE:** Arrive anytime after mid-March, and by mid-April are common in foothill grasslands and open woodlands below 2000 ft, with small numbers occurring locally up to 3000 ft. Numbers remain high until the bulk of the population begins migrating south in mid-August. Postbreeding birds regularly wander upslope where they may be observed up to 8600 ft from mid-July to late August. A few remain in the region until the end of September. **EAST SLOPE:** Uncommon spring migrants in April, with small numbers remaining to breed below 7500 ft. Uncommon fall migrants in August, and a few linger until mid-September.

VIREOS (Vireonidae)

Plumbeous Vireo *Vireo plumbeus*

LIFE HISTORY See Cassin's Vireo account below.

RANGE [*Note: Due to the difficulties in properly identifying Plumbeous and Cassin's Vireos, and lack of sytematic surveys, very little is known about the distributional limits of these two species in the Sierra Nevada.*] Plumbeous Vireos breed in low-elevation mountain forests throughout the arid Intermountain West, ranging as far west as the east slope of the Sierra Nevada where they nest in pinyon-juniper woodlands and Jeffrey pine forests. Spring migrants probably arrive in mid- to late April and remain through September or October. Scattered individuals overwinter in California and are sometimes found at low elevations in the southern Sierra Nevada. **WEST SLOPE:** Uncommon in pinyon-juniper woodlands throughout southeastern Tulare County (eastern portions of Dome Land Wilderness, Troy Meadows, Kennedy Meadows, Chimney Creek Campground, Sacatar Trail Wilderness, Owen's Peak Wilderness) and northern Kern County (Piute and Tehachapi Mountains, Scodie Mountains). In the Piute Mountains, and perhaps at other locations, they breed to the upper limits of pinyon-juniper woodlands, where they are replaced by Cassin's Vireos at higher elevations. **EAST SLOPE:** Breeding birds expected in pinyon-juniper woodlands on the east slope as far north as Alpine County though they are also reported from Jeffrey pine forests on the south side of Mono Lake. Their status in the Carson Range on the east side of the Tahoe Basin is unclear.

Cassin's Vireo *Vireo cassinii*

LIFE HISTORY Formerly lumped together as "Solitary Vireos," Cassin's and Plumbeous Vireos were recognized as separate species in

1997. Although they breed in different habitats, they apparently have very similar life histories and are covered here in one account.

These slow, deliberate birds are often observed moving among the outermost twigs and leaves of trees, pausing and scanning for insects that they grab with quick thrusts of their stout bills. Occasionally they hover briefly to gain access to insects, but they would otherwise be inconspicuous if not for their loud, persistent songs, which have the easily recognized cadence *Question? Answer. So what!* These vireos also make harsh scolding calls, as do other vireo species.

Cassin's Vireos breed in a wide variety of open forests though they favor a mix of conifer and deciduous trees at mid-elevations. They have no particular affinity for water, choosing dry upland forests or ribbons of alders and cottonwoods along streams with equal enthusiasm. Males establish their territories and begin singing as soon as they arrive. In preparation for the arrival of females, they pick potential nest sites and construct the crude beginnings of a suggested nest that females might accept or reject in favor of ones they make themselves.

Complete nests are woven from dried grasses and leaves, and suspended from forked twigs near the ends of branches, often in incense cedar, black oak, and canyon live oak. Both sexes incubate the 4 eggs for 13 days, and males frequently sing while they are sitting on eggs or perched nearby. They are tight sitters, remaining on the nest even when an intruder gets really close, or scolding loudly if a human or jay gets anywhere near their nest. When young birds leave the nest at 14 days of age, parents divide the chicks and depart from their breeding territory with their separate half of the brood.

RANGE Cassin's Vireos are common and characteristic breeding birds of mid-elevation forests from the west slope of the Sierra Nevada to the Coast Ranges. **WEST SLOPE:** Cassin's Vireos are common breeding birds in many types of fairly open mixed conifer and oak forests, both on dry sites and near streams, from 3000 ft to nearly 8000 ft. Spring migrants start arriving in early April, but numbers reach their peak late April to mid-May and remain high until the end of August. Some individuals wander as high as 10,000 ft after the breeding season. Males may be heard singing on their territories before heading south in early September, and a few remain in the region until mid-October or even through the winter. **EAST SLOPE:** Uncommon migrant with peak numbers occurring from mid-April to mid-May, and in August, with a few lingering into September. Small numbers breed in the Carson Range on the east side of Lake Tahoe, and it is possible that additional pairs breed at other scattered locations on the east side.

HUTTON'S VIREO *Vireo huttoni*

LIFE HISTORY Although unremarkable in color and behavior, these small vireos of live oak woodland are an unmistakably cheery presence when they start singing on sunny warm days in early February. Their loud and earnest songs are constantly repeated *zu-whee* notes, which can be given in a leisurely or rapid-fire sequence, and sometimes mixed with raspy, scolding *rheee* calls. Their close affiliation with live oaks, which keep their leaves and have insects year round, allows Hutton's Vireo to be the only North American vireos that stay on their breeding territories year-round. Shortly after they begin singing in late winter, Hutton's Vireos establish pair bonds although some may remain paired all year.

More than any other species, Hutton's Vireos are affiliated with live oaks, but they can also be found in mixed forests that include black oaks, ponderosa pines, and a shrubby understory. Despite their relative abundance, Hutton's Vireos have been mostly overlooked because they nest early and are largely silent in the months when biologists typically start their fieldwork. Fairly reclusive and well-hidden among dense oak leaves, Hutton's Vireos spend the day quietly gleaning small insects from leaves and twigs, and occasionally snacking on elderberries, poison oak, and coffeeberries. In the winter, they join flocks with other small birds like kinglets, chickadees, titmice, bushtits, and nuthatches that move noisily through the foothill forests.

Nesting dates are not well-documented in the Sierra Nevada, but nest-building begins in early February in southern California with fledglings possible by late February. Both sexes help construct small, hanging cups that are suspended from forked twigs near the ends of horizontal branches. Nests are further camouflaged with bits of lichens and mosses on the outer surface. Both parents incubate the 4 eggs for 14–16 days, sitting deep inside the nest with only their eyes visible over the rim. Young birds leave the nest at 14 days old but remain with their parents, being fed for another 3 weeks. The presence of nesting pairs in July–August suggests that they may raise two broods, but this has not been documented.

RANGE Hutton's Vireos are residents of live oak woodlands in coastal and foothill regions west of the Sierra Nevada crest. **WEST**

SLOPE: Fairly common in a narrow altitudinal band of live oak woodlands below 3500 ft. Occasionally found breeding in pockets of suitable habitat as high as 5000 ft, and rarely wander to the upper limit of black oak woodlands (around 6000 ft) after breeding. There appears to be substantial downslope movement to the low foothills or even to the Central Valley floor during winter. **EAST SLOPE:** Rare transients, mostly in the fall, with scattered records along the east side.

WARBLING VIREO *Vireo gilvus*

LIFE HISTORY Almost anywhere there are tall deciduous trees near water or wet meadows in the Sierra Nevada, you may see Warbling Vireos foraging among dense canopy leaves, but you are far more likely to hear their loud, sweet warbling songs. These two-parted songs are so common that they are surprisingly easy to overlook until you learn the way the first phrase ends on an up note, and the second phrase ends on a down note, in a characteristic alternating cadence that no other birds follow.

Warbling Vireos favor riparian woodlands at mid-elevations, but they follow these woodlands downslope to about 3000 ft, and upslope as high as 8500 ft. They may also be found in coniferous forests wherever there are some dogwoods, maples, or oaks in the mix. Where their breeding habitats overlap with Cassin's Vireo, Warbling Vireos favor streamside forests while Cassin's tend toward drier forests on nearby hillsides.

Foraging on the outer ends of branches, Warbling Vireos spend more time in individual trees rather than moving from tree to tree like other vireos. Much of their diet (40–80 percent) consists of caterpillars that they glean from twigs while moving slowly through the canopy. In August and September, they add elderberries and poison oak berries to their diet.

Warbling Vireos build their nests in the outer branches of tall deciduous trees like aspens or cottonwoods, and in the Sierra Nevada they may use lodgepole pines as well. Even though males often sing while incubating eggs, their nests are so well hidden that they are very hard to find. Females weave together bark strips, plant fibers, and grass stems to create a tightly-made, but frazzled-looking cup suspended from the forks of several twigs. Both sexes incubate the 4 eggs for 14 days, and although the male's contribution to incubation is variable, both parents equally feed the nestlings until they leave the nest when 14 days old.

Note: *Very similar in appearance and easily overlooked,* **Red-eyed Vireos** *are rare but regular migrants in the Kern River Valley and along the east side.*

RANGE Warbling Vireos are widespread and common breeders in mid-elevation riparian woodlands over much of California. **WEST SLOPE:** A few migrants make an early appearance in April, but during the first half of May migrating birds can be very common to abundant (up to 1400 have been observed in a single mid-May morning at Butterbredt Springs in Kern County). The bulk of the breeding population begins showing up in early May and remains until mid-August, with nesting commonly observed the first half of June. Very few wander upslope after the breeding season, but those that do can be seen up to 10,000 ft. Numbers decrease gradually from mid-August to mid-September. **EAST SLOPE:** Timing as on west slope, though much easier to find because they are one of the most common birds found in the lush riparian corridors and aspen groves of the east slope.

CORVIDS (Corvidae)

PINYON JAY *Gymnorhinus cyanocephalus*

LIFE HISTORY These large jays of pinyon-juniper woodlands have extremely complex lives built around highly social flocks that coordinate every activity through diverse calls and behaviors. Most individuals form lifelong pair bonds and spend their entire lives in the same permanent flocks they were born into. These flocks may number over 500 birds that defend traditional nesting locations and traditional caching areas.

Pinyon Jays have evolved for one highly specialized activity— locating, harvesting, storing, and recovering huge numbers of pinyon pine seeds. They have long, strong bills and unique jaw structures adapted for hammering open green cones and extracting pine seeds; they have long wings so they can commute long distances to find and harvest widely dispersed cone crops; their throats are expandable so they can carry many seeds at once; and they have extraordinary spatial memories that allow them to relocate buried caches of seeds many months later, even when the caches are covered in snow. A flock of 250 jays is estimated to harvest and bury 4.5 million seeds each fall, and a successful harvest allows them to begin nesting in mid-winter, while a crop failure forces them to travel great distances in search of alternate food sources like juniper berries, acorns, large insects, or small vertebrates. So close is the evolutionary relationship between jays and pinyon pines that pine seeds can only germinate if collected and buried by jays.

Because they mate for life, these jays are highly selective when choosing a mate and the process can take over 6 months. Even worse is trying to arrange a private courtship in the midst of 500 nosy neighbors, so they have developed a subtle and complex courtship that involves prospective mates furtively feeding each other or sneaking off so they can sit silently side by side and not be noticed. A male may pick up a twig and sit silently before a female, but if she does not respond, he will drop the twig and perch at her side again; later in the process she may follow him while he carries the twig into some trees.

From August–October the flock's primary activity is finding and harvesting pine seeds, with mates sharing their secret hiding places with each other. Then in December–March, they eat stored seeds and begin nesting. However, the exact timing of their nesting season varies greatly depending on how many seeds they harvested the preceding fall and how deep the snow has accumulated. As with every other activity the nesting effort is highly coordinated: each morning the entire flock flies to its traditional nesting location and each pair starts constructing their bulky, well-insulated nests at the same time, building them on the sunny sides of pinyon pines, juniper trees, or Jeffrey pines.

Egg-laying is also highly synchronized, with all the females flying to their nests and laying at the same time while males stand guard on nearby treetops. The 3–5 eggs take 17 days to hatch and females sit almost continuously while males fly off in large flocks to find food and bring it back to feed their mates all at the same time. Chicks leave their nests at 3 weeks old, joining crèches (a kind of avian daycare center) with hundreds of other fledglings that will all be fed by their parents for another 6–8 weeks. At 3 months of age they join the main flock, staying with them through the fall harvest season then splitting off as separate flocks of immature birds that roam the home territory when the adults begin breeding the following winter.

RANGE Pinyon Jays are restricted to arid pine woodlands throughout the interior West, where they are permanent residents except when seed crops fail and they wander in huge numbers far outside their normal range; roaming birds are usually reported August–January and they may be seen at any elevation. **WEST SLOPE:** Wandering birds are rarely observed on the west side, mostly in transit and at any elevation. Rare but regular in the Kern River Valley; observed at all seasons at Kennedy Meadows on the Kern Plateau and on the east side of the Piute Mountains so these are probably local breeding areas. **EAST SLOPE:** Although many parts of the east slope and adjoining desert flats are ideal Pinyon Jay habitat, their distribution and numbers shift irregularly from year to year and they are seldom predictable. However, a broad look at recorded observations shows several distinct clusters of sightings that likely correspond to traditional breeding areas. They are regularly reported around Bishop and Lake Crowley. There are many records from around Mono Lake, especially in the Jeffrey pine forests east of Mono Craters, and there are small clusters of sightings around Bridgeport Reservoir and Indian Creek Reservoir. They are only rarely reported further north in the Sierra Nevada though they may be regular breeders in Great Basin hills just to the east.

STELLER'S JAY *Cyanocitta stelleri*

LIFE HISTORY If there is one bird that every visitor to the Sierra Nevada will experience, it would be ubiquitous Steller's Jays with their jaunty crests and iridescent blue feathers. These noisy, boisterous birds mill around every picnic area, campground, trailhead, and viewpoint in the mountains, not just waiting for handouts but apparently enjoying being the center of attention. In fact, they have become so accustomed to the human presence that they have extended their native range upslope to 10,000 ft (as at Tioga Pass) and downslope into foothill towns and backyards to take advantage of human activity. This proclivity to humans makes it hard to tell how common these birds really are because they seem abundant everywhere you go, but in remote forests they are actually more thinly dispersed.

Steller's Jays are intelligent, social corvids of montane conifer forests, but they are so adaptable and can eat so many different types of food that their habitat choices are almost unlimited. They are year-round residents in many types of wooded habitats, but their preference is for coniferous forests or forests of oaks and mixed conifers. After the breeding season there is a significant downslope movement by higher elevation adults, as well as roving gangs of carefree young birds, that wander freely through all types of atypical habitats. At all times these jays have various social dynamics which they demonstrate through a range of complex vocalizations and body postures. For instance, rather than defending territories, breeding pairs are dominant over all other individuals near their nest, but their dominance decreases as they move away from their nest while the dominance of other pairs increases, creating extremely complicated mosaics of social dominance. Aggression may be signaled when two birds sidle up against each other with their crests raised, but this same gesture made with their crests down is an overture toward courtship.

Pairs have long-term bonds and are monogamous, rarely spending time apart, even when building their nest and raising young birds. During the early stages of courtship, which can begin in December, females may fly to their intended future nest sites and spread their wings, inviting their mates to fly over and feed them. Bulky nests are built in early May, being placed about 10–15 ft high on horizontal branches close to tree trunks and crafted from a mix of sticks, rootlets, pine needles, moss, and mud. Females do most of the nest-building and all the incubation, but their mates fly with them as they find items for the nest. Males also continue to feed females as they lay 4–5 eggs in late May and then incubate them for about 16 days.

Given how noisy jays can be, adults are surprisingly quiet and secretive around their own nests, but their growing chicks become very loud as they prepare to leave the nest at 16 days of age and as they follow the parents begging for food for another month. Young birds may even remain with their parents as a family group into the fall or winter, but many leave in September or October, joining raucous packs of roving juveniles that wander all winter.

Steller's Jay are the ultimate omnivores, willingly tasting and eating just about any food. They forage among tree branches, and on the ground they may be observed tossing aside leaves with their bills then taking food items up to safe branches there they hammer at the food with their bills. Their diet includes berries, fruits, and insects; as well as acorns and pine seeds, which are their staple foods. Surplus acorns and seeds are buried singly in the ground or stashed in bark crevices for later retrieval. During the nesting season, they eat a fair number of the eggs and nestlings of small birds.

RANGE Steller's Jays are one of the most characteristic birds of montane coniferous forests in western North America. They are year-round residents almost everywhere they breed in the Sierra Nevada, but some postbreeding adults and most juveniles wander widely and large flocks are readily seen from September to early spring, mostly in the foothills and valley bottoms. Some high-elevation breeders periodically wander downslope in the winter as well. **WEST SLOPE:** Common residents in conifer and mixed conifer habitats from around 2000–8000 ft, occasionally breeding as high as 10,000 ft. Mostly absent from foothill oak woodlands and ponderosa pine forests during spring and summer, but common to abundant during the fall and winter. **EAST SLOPE:** Common to abundant, especially during the breeding season from April–October, but numbers may decrease slightly or dramatically in the winter depending on the severity of winter conditions. Breed from pinyon-juniper and riparian woodlands at the lowest elevations into the upper limits of well-developed conifer forests around 8000 ft, usually near water because they require mud to make their nests.

WESTERN SCRUB-JAY *Aphelocoma californica*

LIFE HISTORY Although these jays have a more limited range than Steller's Jay, they are better known in foothills towns and neighborhoods where they are noisy and conspicuous year-round residents. Scrub-jays reside in dry shrubby woodlands, but there are two distinct populations in the Sierra Nevada: a west-slope "California" subspecies found in oak woodlands with an understory of chaparral shrubs, and an east-slope "Woodhouse's" subspecies found in pinyon-juniper woodlands with an understory of sagebrush and other desert shrubs. The California race is recognized by its sharply offset white throat and clean blue color, and the Woodhouse's by its streaked, dusky gray throat and dull blue color.

Like their corvid relatives, scrub-jays are intelligent, socially complex birds with wide-ranging appetites. They eat many types of insects and small animals during the spring and summer, employing a diversity of feeding techniques like catching small birds in mid-air, pulling eggs and nestlings of other birds from their nests, bashing small snakes on the ground, rubbing hairy caterpillars on branches to remove their hairs, picking ticks off deer, and flycatching aerial insects. They also eat whichever fruits are in season, and then in the fall and autumn they switch to harvesting masting acorns (on the west side) or pinyon pine seeds (on the east side). From September–November each bird collects and hides as many as 5000 acorns or 6000 pine seeds in separate caches in the soil (1 seed per cache). The location of each seed can be remembered for up to 250 days, but nearly the entire crop is dug up and eaten in January–April, and then they switch over to a diet of protein-rich animals in preparation for their breeding effort.

Pairs are monogamous and defend permanent, life-long territories, on which they maintain constant visual or vocal contact with each other. Young birds may "float" around for 2–3 years while waiting for a chance to establish their own territories, a chance that almost always happens when a territorial bird dies and its mate takes on a new partner. Floaters wander freely and are tolerated on strangers' territories until breeding gets underway in April, when they are chased away. Perhaps not coincidentally, this is the time of year when scrub-jays show up at mountain sites where they do not otherwise breed (like Lake Tahoe).

Pairs begin making false nests in February but do not complete a final functional nest until March, just in time for the 2–5 eggs that females lay in late March–early April. The entire period of courtship, territorial defense, and nest-building is a very noisy time, with scrub-jays showcasing their extensive repertoire of complex vocalizations and stylized behaviors.

Nests are built in the dense foliage of trees or shrubs, usually within 12 ft of the ground. Both sexes help construct a bulky cup of twigs lined with small rootlets, plant fibers, and animal hairs that takes about 12 days to finish, with either bird standing lookout while the other adds material to the nest. Females incubate for 18 days and may be fed by their mates. Young birds leave the nest 3 weeks after hatching but follow their parents and are fed for up to 3 months.

RANGE Western Scrub-Jays are widespread in scrubby dry woodlands throughout the western United States, and found at low elevations all around the Sierra Nevada. **WEST SLOPE:** Common to abundant year-round residents in a variety of brushy oak woodlands, preferring sites with a mix of grassland, chaparral shrubs, and oak trees in close proximity. Found as high as 4000 ft in the northern and central Sierra Nevada, but occurs over 6000 ft on the Kern Plateau and other southern slopes. **EAST SLOPE:** Uncommon year-round residents with a complex status; the "California" subspecies has a patchy distribution from Carson City north and is mostly found at lower elevations away from the Sierra Nevada crest, though it appears at Lake Tahoe briefly from mid-April to mid-May and from mid-September through late October; the "Woodhouse's" subspecies occurs on desert slopes south of Carson City, where it breeds in pinyon-juniper woodlands then wanders into sagebrush and riparian woodlands during the nonbreeding season. East slope birds of both subspecies occasionally wander to treeline or to the Sierra Nevada crest in late summer and fall.

CLARK'S NUTCRACKER *Nucifraga columbiana*

LIFE HISTORY Every high-mountain visitor is soon greeted by the raucous *kraaa* calls of these large, flashy corvids, and there is hardly a subalpine trail, campground, or slope where you can escape their constant presence. Fortunately these intelligent, dynamic birds are fun to watch, and even more fascinating when you understand what they are up to.

The Sierra Nevada's entire population of Clark's Nutcrackers seems to nest in coniferous forests on the lower east slope, where they subsist on stored pine seeds and begin nesting in frigid wintery conditions as early as March. Pairs spend about a week constructing heavily insulated nests made with hundreds of twigs and densely lined with fine materials, then tightly woven onto stout branches on the leeward side of trees so they will not be blown away by winter storms. Both parents cooperate to keep their 2–3 eggs constantly protected from freezing temperatures, the males being one of few songbirds in North America that have brood patches. When chicks hatch in 18 days, their parents keep them constantly warm, feeding them pieces of pine seeds until they can leave the nest in about 3 weeks. Young birds begin flying by early May (at lower elevations) to mid-June (at higher elevations), but nesting dates are highly variable based on food supplies and snow depths.

As soon as snows start to melt in the Subalpine Zone, family groups move upslope, either singly or in loose flocks, to feed on pine seeds that they harvested and buried the previous fall. By the time most hikers, campers, and tourists arrive in early June, nutcrackers are already abundant and acting as if they had been there all winter. Nutcrackers spend the summer ruling their subalpine and alpine domains, eating the last of their stored seeds and snacking on whatever insects, voles, chipmunks, ground squirrels, nesting birds, and dead animals they can find or catch. Their ability to relocate stored seed caches across miles of complex mountain terrain, even when caches are buried under snow, verges on miraculous and is a testament to their extraordinary spatial memory.

In late July they begin to tear apart the still-green cones of whitebark and limber pines to eat unripe seeds; then in late August and early September the cones ripen in great numbers and nutcrackers harvest uncounted millions of seeds from one end of the Sierra Nevada to the other. Nutcrackers and whitebark pines have coevolved to the point where they are utterly dependent on each other for survival, nutcrackers for a supply of highly nutritious seeds, and pines for the long-range dispersal of their seeds. Everywhere you look in the Subalpine Zone you see whitebark pines growing in clumps where 1–15 seeds at a time were buried by nutcrackers then forgotten; in fact, scientists think that all the subalpine forests of the Sierra Nevada were "planted" by nutcrackers because whitebark pine seeds cannot germinate unless buried by birds.

Each nutcracker harvests as many as 90,000 seeds each fall, chiseling seeds out of cones, then carrying over 100 at a time in special pouches under their tongues, and burying them in thousands of separate, small caches over many miles and several thousand feet of elevation (thus ensuring that they can find caches at every season). In late July, juvenile birds begin to imitate their parents' foraging techniques though they are terribly clumsy at first, getting easily distracted, dropping seeds, and losing their balance while trying to pry seeds from cones.

In the fall, groups of nutcrackers may be seen wandering at any elevation, either because the seed crop failed and they must find other food sources, or because they finished their high elevation harvest and have set out to supplement their seed storage with some low-elevation Jeffrey and ponderosa pine seeds. It is thought that most overwinter at lower elevations but their winter movements are poorly known.

RANGE Clark's Nutcrackers are widespread and common in the high mountains of the interior West. Their status and distribution in the Sierra Nevada is hard to sort out because they can be found at any elevation at any time of year and because vast stretches of the high mountains have never been surveyed in the winter. It is generally assumed that the entire population breeds on the east slope and that in early June they wander upslope and disperse throughout the Upper Montane, Subalpine, and even Alpine Zones, where they remain through the summer. Most stick around for the late summer seed harvest, but late summer and early fall is also when small flocks appear at many unexpected locations further downslope. **WEST SLOPE:** Common in montane forests above 6000 ft through summer and fall, and occasionally reported at lower elevations. Suspected of breeding around Lake Almanor, and there are many April and May sightings on the Kern Plateau at a season when they could be breeding. **EAST SLOPE:** Breed widely in coniferous forests above 7000 ft, and rarely as high as 10,000 ft. After breeding they move upslope to spend the summer in the high country; but in some areas (as at Lake Tahoe) they instead move downslope. Sometime around October they retreat downslope for the winter. Their range north of Lake Tahoe, and south of Olancha Peak, may be limited by the scarcity of their favorite food trees.

BLACK-BILLED MAGPIE *Pica hudsonia*

LIFE HISTORY The dry desert slopes of the eastern Sierra Nevada are much brightened by these lively, flashy corvids with their long tails, bright white patches, and iridescent black plumage. Even at great distances they are distinctive and easily recognized, and at close range you cannot miss their raucous *skaa skaa ka ka ka ka* calls.

Like their corvid relatives, these are intelligent and curious birds. And when it comes to food, magpies are extraordinarily resourceful, watching each other and watching predators to learn about the status of local food supplies. One of their primary foods is carrion, and they will as eagerly steal morsels from a carnivore's kill as they will scoop up dead animals along a highway. In the summer they supplement their diet with ground beetles, caterpillars, and grasshoppers, but they also keep their eyes open for berries, fruits, and grains, with an emphasis on tasting and eating whatever is locally abundant. Many of their foods are perishable, but they still readily cache food in scattered locations for 1–2 days, and they can find buried food by smell.

Entire books have been written about the many interesting behaviors exhibited by magpies, and they do fascinating things like hold "funerals" when a dead magpie is discovered, with all the local birds gathering to walk around the body while calling loudly and touching it. Individual birds and family members can apparently recognize each other by their facial skin and the shape of their white wing patches.

Many pairs probably mate for life, with pairs working closely together to build bulky, thorny nests of fairly substantial dimensions with mud floors and domed roofs. Nests take about 40 days to build with males collecting bigger thorny sticks for the structure and females providing a mud interior and lining of fine grasses. Nests may be reused year after year and can become several feet tall. Most nests are located in riparian thickets close to water with open grasslands or sagebrush flats nearby where they forage for food. The 4–9 eggs are laid by mid-April with females incubating alone. Males feed their mates and then feed the chicks that hatch 18 days later. Chicks fledge in early June at 24–30 days of age, but there is such fierce fighting amongst themselves that many die in the nest. These fights result in rigid pecking orders that are maintained during the entire 6–8 week period that parents feed the fledglings. After the nesting season, many birds wander locally or slightly upslope but return to valley bottoms and flock together through much of the fall and winter.

Note: *Differing only in the color of their bills,* Yellow-billed Magpies *are residents of the Central Valley that may wander onto or locally breed on the very lowest slopes of the mountains. They are best known in open oak woodlands and grasslands of the central Sierra Nevada.*

RANGE Black-billed Magpies are widespread, common, and conspicuous in scrubby arid areas throughout the interior West. Found all along the east base of the Sierra Nevada, where they favor well-watered valleys during the breeding season, then wander more widely into the mouths of mountains canyons or onto sagebrush flats in the fall and winter. **WEST SLOPE:** Very rarely wander onto the west slope, mostly in the late summer or early fall, where they have been reported at almost every elevation. **EAST SLOPE:** Despite their abundance in the nearby Great Basin, magpies have a somewhat limited distribution on the east side of the Sierra Nevada. Scattered records have come from many diverse locations, but the vast majority of sightings fall into discrete clusters centered around Quincy, Sierra Valley, South Lake Tahoe, Woodfords, Bridgeport, Mono Lake, Crowley Lake, and Bishop. In these locations they are fairly common year-round residents, with most breeding from 4000–7000 ft. They rarely range as far south as Lone Pine in the Owens Valley, where they are thought to have arrived after the area was settled and cultivated.

AMERICAN CROW *Corvus brachyrhynchos*

LIFE HISTORY Despite being one of North America's most familiar and widespread birds, American Crows are surprisingly little known and studied in the Sierra Nevada. It is not even entirely clear if they are rare, very local, or simply overlooked in favor of larger and much more conspicuous Common Ravens, but it has been said that ravens are birds of the wilderness while crows are residents around small towns and agricultural areas, and this goes some distance towards explaining their distribution in the Sierra Nevada as well.

Crows are exceptionally intelligent and highly social birds, spending much of their lives in groups that change in composition on a seasonal and daily basis, probably reflecting subtle details like the birds' moods and individual personalities. During the winter, hundreds of birds may roost together at night in traditional locations, with local breeding pairs splitting off to sleep on their nesting territories or rejoining the larger flocks on different days.

Even the concept of territory has many interpretations in the world of crows; pairs may only defend their nest sites and happily feed side by side with neighbors, or else defend large, non-overlapping territories. Breeding pairs are generally joined by up to ten "auxiliaries" to create cooperative breeding groups that include up to 4 generations of their previous offspring, as well as miscellaneous adults that join the breeding group. These auxiliaries are often called "helpers," but they do not always help breeding pairs, or they may be chased away during the early stages of nesting then come back later to help feed newly hatched chicks.

Crows breed in many types of habitats but usually favor scattered trees or forest edges where they rest and nest, as well as open areas where they feed on the ground (eating almost any kind of edible plant or animal that they can find). There is almost no published information on their nesting dates or breeding distribution in the Sierra Nevada, but they are likely to begin nesting in April. Pairs spend about two weeks constructing bulky, well-hidden stick nests, and then females incubate their 3–6 eggs for about 17 days while being fed by their mates and some of the auxiliary birds. Young birds fledge at about one month of age and either join groups of young crows or stay with their family groups for up to 4 years; or more likely, they switch back and forth on a regular basis as many teenagers do.

RANGE American Crows are common all over North America except in the arctic and southwestern deserts. They are absent in much of southern California, and scarce in the southern Sierra Nevada, but their overall status in the Sierra Nevada is complex and poorly documented. They are clearly local residents in some rural neighborhoods and agricultural areas, but there may also be an increase in numbers as migrants move through the area in mid-February to May and late August to October, and there appears to be a large influx of crows in the winter at low elevations. The status of some local populations is probably changing in response to the relatively recent arrival of Common Ravens in the Sierra Nevada because the two species co-exist uneasily with each other. **WEST SLOPE:** Typically found near towns and agricultural areas at lower elevations, where some might be local year-round residents, but most are probably only migrants or winter visitors. Hundreds are counted on each of the Christmas Bird Counts in the northern and central Sierra Nevada, but numbers drop off to the low dozens south of Calaveras County and they are even rarer in Tulare and Kern counties. There is no information on how many remain after migrants leave in March or where they might breed. **EAST SLOPE:** Their distribution and numbers vary locally, but they seem to be fairly common migrants and winter visitors with only a few local populations remaining to breed. At Lake Tahoe and Sierra Valley they are fairly common spring and fall migrants, but rare winter visitors. They are year-round residents at Honey Lake and Carson Valley, and they might be resident around other agricultural areas. Since 2000 there has been a big jump in wintering numbers in the northern Owens Valley, and many now breed in the area.

COMMON RAVEN *Corvus corax*

LIFE HISTORY It is not surprising that ravens have made an indelible stamp on human culture and have been portrayed in myth, symbol, and story. Their dark, looming presence seems intimidating but they are actually one of the world's most intriguing birds, and when you watch them closely you quickly see their intelligence, creativity, and personality. For an entertaining glimpse into the incredibly complex lives of these amazing creatures read Bernd Heinrich's *Mind of the Raven*.

Ravens are best known as scavengers, and in fact most sightings in the Sierra Nevada are of pairs flying along mountain roads looking for road-killed animals. But they are opportunistic and omnivorous, eating whatever is locally available. As soon as young ravens leave the nest, they begin examining and touching every object with their bills, willing to taste anything at first but gradually learning how to distinguish between what is edible or inedible. Ravens consume lots of insects, especially grasshoppers, and many seeds and grains, but ultimately they eat everything from scorpions to baby birds. It is true that one of their favorite foods is meat from carcasses, but they are limited to carcasses that have already been torn open because their bills are not strong enough to tear skin.

Unlike many of their close relatives, ravens generally live in pairs or remain solitary until they find a mate. Young birds probably wait 2–4 years before they begin nesting and may hang out in thuggish groups with other young ravens that band together so they can overwhelm territorial pairs that attempt to defend prized food items. These groups of youngsters roost together at night, with numerous birds gathering to share information and directions to local food supplies. Their most common call is a raspy *rrrock*, distinctly different than the clear caw of a crow, but ravens have a rich vocabulary with many unusual vocalizations, including an eerie *clocking* call. Additional social information is conveyed through postures and behaviors, and they often raise their shaggy throat feathers to signal aggression. Ravens have a complex relationship with crows, and they seem to avoid each other by using different areas.

Surprisingly little is known about their nesting behavior, perhaps because nesting ravens are very secretive. Pairs remain together throughout the year, but it is not known if they mate for life. They often build large stick nests on cliffs and rocky ledges where they can watch for approaching danger and scan the landscape, but will nest in remote forests if food is nearby. Nests may be used for years, and it is thought that females do much of the actual construction while males find nesting materials. The 3–7 eggs are laid in March to mid-May, and females incubate while males stand guard and feed females until the eggs hatch 20–25 days later, in mid-April to mid-June. After 4–7 weeks, young birds are ready to leave the nest and join up with other young birds that gather at communal roosts starting in July or August.

RANGE Common Ravens are one of the most ecologically diverse and widespread birds in the world, and in the Sierra Nevada they freely use all habitats from valley bottoms to the highest peaks, though most seem to breed well below treeline. In the fall, many probably wander downslope in search of food, but it would not be hard for them to wander upslope and downslope on an almost daily basis. Despite their widespread abundance they appear to be recent arrivals in the Sierra Nevada, having followed highways and campgrounds into the mountains. For example, the first record of one on a Yosemite Christmas Bird Count was in 1966, and only since 1982 have they been reported annually on every count. Single birds were first reported on the South Lake Tahoe Christmas Bird Count in 1990, and since 2000 more than 50 birds have been seen on almost every count. Little long-term data exists for other locations, but in nearly every case the numbers of ravens observed have increased year after year. **WEST SLOPE:** Generally common residents from the edge of the Central Valley nearly to treeline, with nonbreeding birds wandering everywhere, including to the highest peaks. But there are some interesting exceptions; for example, ravens are very rarely reported on the Folsom Christmas Bird Count, which does not make sense until you discover that this same count regularly reports over 500 crows and you realize that the two species seldom overlap with each other. **EAST SLOPE:** Same general pattern as on the west slope.

LARKS (Alaudidae)

HORNED LARK *Eremophila alpestris*

LIFE HISTORY Horned Larks are a delightful presence in those desolate wastelands where birds would be least expected. Whether heavily grazed meadows, barren sagebrush flats, or agricultural fields, Horned Larks gather by the hundreds or thousands. They are surprisingly well camouflaged in these sites, but they give themselves away with high-pitched, sputtering calls as they zigzag back and forth eagerly searching for small seeds and insects. When flushed, an entire flock swirls up in a chaotic but somehow beautifully orchestrated movement that takes them in a loose circle and back down to the ground.

The only time of year they are not found in flocks is during the breeding season, which starts as early as January at low elevations, when males start establishing and defending territories with chases and songs delivered from the ground. By March, nest-building is underway and males switch over to giving spectacular flight songs that begin with steep stair-stepping flights to as high as 750 ft. From these heights, males turn to face the wind, spread their wings and tails, and while gliding in place sing jumbled, twittering songs that last up to eight minutes long.

Meanwhile, females scoop out small depressions on the ground in the shelter of plant tufts or stones then line them with a mix of fine plant and animals materials. Small ramparts or pavements of pebbles are often built on one side of their nests. Females incubate 4 dingy gray eggs for about 11 days then both parents tend the young on the nest another 9–12 days. Nestlings leave the nest and make their first flights 3–5 days later. After taking a break for a week or so, adults start a second nesting effort.

RANGE The taxonomy and distribution of Horned Larks in California is complicated, with at least 5 subspecies in the Sierra Nevada region alone. Most are year-round residents at low elevations, but others nest above treeline. They are occasionally observed in transit at mid-elevations but a lack of open areas means they are scarce visitors here. In the nonbreeding season, they occur in large flocks that roam widely and unpredictably; in different years they may be extremely abundant or absent at any given location. **WEST SLOPE:** Year-round residents in low-elevation grasslands and agricultural areas. Particularly abundant during the winter with numbers highest on valley floors and diminishing at higher elevations. Regularly observed on Christmas Bird Counts below 1500 ft but they also occasionally show up on the Lake Almanor Count at 4500 ft. Transients are very rarely observed at mid-elevations, most notably in April when they are on route to high-elevation breeding sites. Uncommon breeders above treeline from early May to late October. **EAST SLOPE:** Abundant year-round residents at low elevations, but they are unpredictable in December and January in areas where snow levels get too deep. Highest winter numbers are reported from Honey Lake, where Horned Larks frequently mix with longspurs in large flocks. Breed in dry open areas both below and above the main forested belt.

SWALLOWS (Hirundinidae)

PURPLE MARTIN *Progne subis*

LIFE HISTORY These large, long-lived swallows are like glittering purple fighter jets. Seldom seen due to their habit of flying at great heights, Purple Martins may be easily confused with Merlins or European Starlings at a distance due to their direct, powerful flight. Despite being extremely popular backyard birds in the eastern United States, Purple Martins are poorly known in California, with their populations declining significantly after European Starlings appeared in the 1950s, and took over many of the nesting cavities that martins might otherwise use. In California, martins breed in small local populations and nest in natural cavities rather than using nestboxes, so most observers will not encounter this bird except by chance or when looking for them at known locations.

Eating only flying insects and being particularly vulnerable to cold weather and rain, Purple Martins arrive at the fairly late date of May or even early June. Males arrive up to three weeks earlier than females and seek out large isolated trees near open areas, often finding them in places where forests have burned. Males attempt to attract passing females by making dramatic arcing flights and singing from the nest holes they have staked out. As part of their courtship, pairs may check out a number of woodpecker holes and other natural tree cavities before filling one with a loose assortment of grasses, leaves, and twigs. The 3–6 white eggs are incubated for 15–17 days, primarily by females though males spend a considerable amount of time in the cavity as well. Both parents tend young on the nest for 26–30 days (a substantial amount of time).

RANGE Purple Martins are uncommon and spottily distributed in California, breeding primarily in a narrow strip along the northern coast and at a handful of scattered locations on the west slope of the Sierra-Cascade axis. **WEST SLOPE:** Known at a few breeding sites from the upper edges of blue oak savanna to as high as the lower edges of ponderosa pine forest. Nests have been found in western Yuba, Nevada, Placer, and Mariposa counties, with a high likelihood of being discovered in other counties. Outside of known locations, transients are very rarely encountered, and usually detected by their distinctive, low *churr* flight calls. Present from May–August, sometimes also in April or September. **EAST SLOPE:** Rarely observed at low elevations, and several times at Lake Tahoe. Perhaps less than two dozen fall sightings, and fewer than half a dozen spring sightings from the east slope.

TREE SWALLOW *Tachycineta bicolor*

LIFE HISTORY During spring and summer, Tree Swallows are commonly observed gliding dexterously over wet meadows, marshes, and lakes, especially in areas where dead trees are surrounded by water such as around beaver ponds. When other species start moving through the area in huge numbers in April, competition for nest sites between Tree Swallows—and between swallows and other cavity-nesting birds such as chickadees and bluebirds—becomes so fierce that their battles may result in injury or death. Among swallows, birds of the same sex battle each other, with winners killing nestlings in the nests of losers and taking over their nest sites. Once they establish ownership, anytime between February and April, Tree Swallows aggressively guard their nest sites until they begin breeding in May–June. At the same time, Tree Swallows also engage in playful behaviors, such as flying up and releasing feathers that many swallows chase at once.

In the high mountains and on the east side, they commonly nest in aspen groves. Females fill up natural cavities or woodpecker holes with dry grasses and pine needles to form cups that they line with feathers. Females incubate 4–6 eggs for 13-16 days, then continue to brood the nestlings for 16–24 days while males help feed the chicks on the nest. In August, Tree Swallows (especially juveniles) start gathering in preparation for migration, lining up by the hundreds or thousands on fence wires and dead tree branches.

While most swallows leave California in late summer, Tree

Swallows can supplement their diet with berries and seeds due to their unique ability to digest wax, so some linger over the winter. Both over-wintering birds and very early migrants show up on their breeding grounds as early as February (rarely in January). These early-arriving birds run a tremendous risk of starving to death during cold storms, but those that survive can claim ownership of the very scarce nesting cavities found in trees and snags near water.

RANGE Tree Swallows are widespread in California though absent or rare as breeders in desert regions. **WEST SLOPE:** Possible during winter in small to moderate numbers from the Central Valley to the lowest edges of blue oak savanna. Migrating birds arrive as early as February but reach their peak numbers in April when migrating birds can be very common. Breed in open habitats with snags and nesting cavities near water or around wet meadows from the Central Valley to 9000 ft. Huge numbers gather in August for their migration south, and migrating Tree Swallows continue to be observed in the mountains through September. **EAST SLOPE:** Arrival and departure dates as on the west slope, except that most Tree Swallows leave by the end of September (single birds only rarely linger into the winter, particularly in the Owens Valley); the first hardy migrants trickling north again in late January or February. Breed almost anywhere there is a combination of trees and water or aspen groves.

Violet-green Swallow *Tachycineta thalassina*

LIFE HISTORY Given their beautiful colors and confiding manners, including their use of nest boxes and nest sites around houses and barns, it is surprising that the biology and behavior of Violet-green Swallows is so poorly understood. Even relatively accessible information like the roles of males and females while nesting has not been well documented.

Violet-green Swallows are ubiquitous in the Sierra Nevada, with their wonderful aerial antics being observed almost anywhere from soaring cliffs to woodlands along desert streams. Unlike Tree Swallows, Violet-green Swallows are not closely wedded to water, instead roaming widely over the landscape and congregating wherever they find suitable nest sites in tree cavities and rock crevices. The only habitats they seem to avoid are dense forests, but even there they nest around meadow margins, feeding freely over the forest canopy. At Mono Lake, they nest in crevices among tufa towers. In the breeding season, it is common to see Violet-green Swallows flying with White-throated Swifts, or with Vaux's Swifts during migration, but they compete fiercely with Mountain Chickadees, bluebirds, other swallows, and other cavity-nesting birds for nest sites.

Based on scant observations, it is thought that both sexes cooperate in selecting and building nests of dry grasses and feathers sometime in May–July, with females doing most of the work. Females incubate 4–5 eggs for 13–15 days then both parents, or mostly females, tend the young on the nest for 23–25 days. Fledglings stick around the nest for a few more days, and continue to be feed on the wing after they start flying.

RANGE Violet-green Swallows are widespread breeding birds in California, with small numbers wintering along the coast or in lowlands west of the Sierra Nevada. **WEST SLOPE:** Occasionally observed at the lowest edges of the western foothills throughout the winter, with the first spring migrants arriving in mid-February. By April they are common everywhere they breed, from the lowest edges of the foothills to treeline though their population levels are highest at mid-elevations from 3000–7000 ft. From late August through mid-October, Violet-green Swallows are one of the most conspicuous migrants in the Sierra Nevada, flying past lookout points almost continuously for days at a stretch. Observers have also reported them flying east to west over the Sierra Nevada in the spring, and flying west to east in the fall, hinting at the presence of a trans-Sierra migration route. **EAST SLOPE:** Arrival and departure dates as on the west slope, but they are not present in the winter. Breeding birds most common above 6500 feet.

Northern Rough-winged Swallow
Stelgidopteryx serripennis

LIFE HISTORY Dusty brown like the sandbanks where they nest, Northern Rough-winged Swallows are easily overlooked or misidentified as dull versions of other common swallows. Not surprisingly, their life history in California is little known, with much of our knowledge of this species coming from studies on east-coast populations. Close observation reveals that, more than other swallows, Rough-wingeds skim the ground around bushes and irregular terrain with great ease and dexterity. They habitually feed just above water, snatching insects from the water's surface. Their name comes from a row of odd, recurved spines along the leading edge of their wings, but these have no known function.

Rough-wingeds nest in steep sand, earth, or gravel banks, where they dig burrows or use former kingfisher nests. These sites are limited so these swallows occur locally and are primarily restricted to lower elevations where river sediments accumulate. At mid-elevations on the west slope, they frequently nest on gravelly bluffs around hydraulic mining pits. On rare occasions, they nest on rock ledges, in buildings, or inside small drainpipes.

Arriving in the foothills by March, pairs immediately search out potential nest sites while the otherwise drab males fly around flashing their white undertail coverts. Most pairs nest alone, but the limited nature of their nesting habitats means that several pairs may nest near each other or around the periphery of large Bank Swallow colonies. Over the course of 3–20 days, females (with limited help from males) fill burrows with grasses and miscellaneous plant materials that they collect from the ground. Amazingly, these swallows fly straight into their burrows without first landing on the outside, but if females cannot enter nesting burrows with awkward pieces of nesting materials, they will drop them to the ground, creating distinctive trash heaps under their burrow entrances.

Nest burrows can be up to 6ft deep, but nests are usually built close enough to the entrance that they are visible from the outside. Females lay 4–8 eggs in May or June. They incubate eggs for 16 days, and both parents tend young on the nest until they fly at around 20 days of age. It is unknown whether parents continue to feed young after they leave the nest.

RANGE Northern Rough-winged Swallows breed at low elevations everywhere in California, and are absent only in areas that lack suitable nesting habitat. Small numbers winter in the deserts of southeastern California, and occasionally wander northward along the coast. WEST SLOPE: First arrive in late March, with migrants continuing to move through the region in April. Breeding birds are uncommon and local in open habitats below 5000 ft. Fall migration begins in late July with most of the population vacating the region by the end of August. Migrants are occasionally observed as high as 10,000 ft and sometimes as late as mid-October. EAST SLOPE: Similar to west slope, except that breeding occurs from around 4000 ft up to 7000 ft.

Bank Swallow *Riparia riparia*

LIFE HISTORY Bank Swallows are slim, exuberant swallows that move energetically in three dimensions on quick, fluttery wingbeats, seldom pausing to glide in the manner of other flying swallows. Unlike their larger cousins, Northern Rough-winged Swallows, Bank Swallows are remarkably social creatures, seeking each other's company wherever they fly and nesting in colonies that can include over 1000 pairs.

Despite being one of the most widely distributed songbirds in the world, Bank Swallow populations are scarce and declining in California. They nest almost exclusively (95 percent of known nest sites in California) in steep banks of soft alluvial soils along rivers or lakes, but these habitats have been severely impacted by livestock, dams, and various water projects. Even under the best conditions, eroding river banks may mean that colonies must move and find new sites every few years.

Biologists have a difficult time tracking down and researching these ephemeral colonies, so witnessing a colony in full breeding activity is a rare pleasure. There is a fantastic energy as hundreds of swallows swirl around in constant motion, chirping with their odd, electrical-sounding, buzzy calls, darting in and out of nesting burrows, scolding and chasing each other.

Bank Swallows arrive in mid-April, typically in the company of mixed swallow flocks, scoping out previous colony sites then choosing one for the new season. Males immediately begin the work of scraping out new burrows, or refurbishing pre-existing burrows, with their bills, feet, and wings. After making a good start, males advertise their burrows by flying in tight excited circles and perching at their burrow entrances while flashing their sparkling white throat feathers. A female may signal her acceptance of the male by joining him in the 4–5 day effort of finishing the one- to three-ft-long burrows, while unsuccessful males abandon their burrows and start building new ones (burrows located higher on the bank are considered dominant).

Both sexes collect various plant materials from the ground for their nests, with males initiating the effort and females adding the final touches. Pairs share all nesting duties including incubating the 4–5 eggs for 12-16 days, and feeding the young until they leave the nest at 19 days of age. Fledglings return to the nest each night for several days and stay around the colony for up to a week while flying increasingly wider circles to familiarize themselves with the local terrain, but they soon join the huge flocks of swallows that gather in lowland areas in late August in preparation for migration.

RANGE Formerly fairly widespread in lowland areas of California, but no longer found in southern California and increasingly rare in the north where the majority of California's Bank Swallows nest along the Sacramento and Feather Rivers in the Central Valley. **WEST SLOPE:** Perhaps a former breeding species but at best probably a rare migrant these days. Look for them in mixed swallow flocks in April and May, and they might be observed in August or early September. **EAST SLOPE:** The widespread presence of soft alluvial soils along the eastern base of the Sierra Nevada creates substantial suitable habitat for this species, and at present there are known colonies at Honey Lake, Bridgeport Reservoir, Lake Crowley, and Bishop. Long-abandoned colonies along the Owens River may become reestablished now that water has been returned to the streambed. Abundant around known colonies from early April to early September but rare elsewhere on east slope, including locations as high as Lake Tahoe.

Cliff Swallow *Petrochelidon pyrrhonota*

LIFE HISTORY Highly social Cliff Swallows have some of the most dynamic breeding behaviors of any Sierra Nevada bird. Always seeking the company of their own kind, Cliff Swallows feed, gather nest material, and breed in large, noisy congregations, with some colonies including as many as 3500 nests. The benefit of living in such large colonies is that Cliff Swallows watch each other closely and follow successful foragers to see where they are finding food. Much of their diet consists of swarming insects that occur in ephemeral patches, so a steady parade of swallows chasing an insect swarm and keeping track of it helps every individual colony member.

Equally interesting are the negative aspects of living in a colony, including excessive bickering and feuding, not to mention neighbors who steal nesting materials as soon as pairs add them to their nests. One bird must always stay behind to guard the nest, but this creates another problem: females left alone at the nest or off gathering nesting materials are attacked by males who chase them or pounce on them, forcing copulation. This attack strategy is so common that Cliff Swallows of both sexes flutter their wings over their backs as they sit on the ground and gather mud because it's the only way to keep marauding males from pouncing on them. Not only are there rogue copulations, but many females in a colony sneak into other nests and lay eggs among their neighbor's eggs, with the end result that up to 50 percent of all the nests in a colony contain nestlings that are not related to both parents.

Colonies are located on the vertical walls of buildings, bridges, and cliffs wherever there is an overhang to protect the nests from rain. As soon as they arrive in March or April, pairs build or refurbish gourd-shaped nests made entirely of mud pellets gathered from nearby mud puddles and lake margins. Nest are formed of 900–1200 mud pellets, and take about 24 total hours to complete (spaced over 1–2 weeks so that layers of wet pellets have time to dry).

In the very early stages of nest construction, pairs wander widely and memorize the locations of backup colony sites in case a disaster befalls their first choice. Assuming things go well, the sides of the nest are built up and domed over to create a cozy chamber lined with grasses and feathers. They lay 4–5 eggs in May or June (after insects become abundant enough to feed nestlings), and both parents incubate the eggs for about 13 days, sharing all parenting duties until their young leave the nest at 23 days of age. Fledglings gather by day on wires and branches in a crèche (a gathering of up to 1000 youngsters), where they are fed by their parents, but they still return each night to sleep in their nests for another 3–5 days.

RANGE Formerly restricted to mountains of the western United States, Cliff Swallows have expanded their range across nearly all of North America over the past 100 years due to their use of human structures like buildings and bridges. They are common and widespread breeding birds in California, and still even nest on their original habitat of steep canyon walls in the Sierra Nevada. **WEST SLOPE:** First arriving in mid-February, and reaching their peak numbers by early April, Cliff Swallows wander widely then nest abundantly wherever they find appropriate nesting sites. Every west-slope river canyon and bridge below 5000 ft is guaranteed to have at least one small colony, often many colonies. They also nest under the eaves of countless houses, barns, and other human structures. Departure is rapid after late August, with decreasing numbers found in September. Virtually the entire population gathers in valley bottoms prior to migration though a few may be found exceptionally up to 12,000 ft. Migrating Cliff Swallows are seldom observed from mid-elevation viewpoints in the fall, unlike Tree and Violet-green Swallows which are abundant. **EAST SLOPE:** Arrival and departure as on west slope, but they regularly nest at higher elevations (over 8000 ft).

Barn Swallow *Hirundo rustica*

LIFE HISTORY The world's most abundant and widely distributed swallows were rare in the Sierra Nevada until modern times, when they stopped nesting on the rocky walls of caves and began nesting on an ever-growing number of buildings and bridges. Following humans into the mountains, Barn Swallows are now common everywhere at low to mid-elevations, and their close associations with humans make them the most familiar of our swallows.

Barn Swallows are easy and fun to observe as they skim back and forth over the tops of grasses in fields, pastures, and meadows. They hold their elegant forked tails closed in flight, but spread them as they turn abruptly or come to a landing. Males with the longest outer tail feathers have the greatest success attracting mates, but longer tail feathers are also tiring to carry around and get in the way when trying to avoid predators.

Barn Swallows begin returning from their South American wintering grounds in March, with most of the early arrivals continuing north to breed. Local breeding birds tend to arrive in April and immediately pair up. After scouting around for suitable nesting sites, they narrow their list of options then pick one that seems suitable or else refurbish a nest from the previous year. Nests are typically located on vertical walls or atop beams, either singly or in small colonies at favored locations, and sometimes on the edges of Cliff Swallow colonies. Nests are constructed from a mix of mud pellets and grass stems, with a mud ledge built first so the pair can stand and build up the sides to form a shallow cup (much like Black Phoebe nests, but unlike the gourd-shaped nests of Cliff Swallows).

Peak nesting activity occurs in June or July (perhaps earlier at low elevations), with both parents incubating the 3–7 brown-spotted eggs for 14–16 days then caring for the nestlings another 17–24 days. An additional unmated adult may assist in protecting the nest and sitting on eggs or nestlings; the nesting pair tolerates this, and if one of the pair dies, the unmated adult steps in as a replacement mate. But in some areas, a large percentage of unmated males instead seek out active nests and kill the newly hatched nestlings in an attempt to initiate divorce in the nesting pair so that the unmated male can establish a pair bond with the newly available female. If all this seems sinister and antisocial then consider late summer—when Barn Swallows gather by the thousands in busy, merrily twittering flocks—to see that all is forgiven.

RANGE Barn Swallows are common and widespread as migrants and breeding birds everywhere in California except at high elevations and in densely forested areas. **WEST SLOPE:** Migrants first appear at low elevations in late March then increase dramatically in numbers as the main pulse of breeding birds arrive between mid-April and early May. Especially common below 5000 ft, but breeding birds are occasionally found at higher elevations (up to 7000 ft). Some fall migrants trickle through in late July, but by August there is a significant buildup as thousands of Barn Swallows flock around fields and pastures. Nearly all these migrants gather in lowland areas, but very rarely some are seen in the high mountains. They all depart by mid-October, but a few sometimes linger at low elevations through the winter. **EAST SLOPE:** Arrive in early March and breed locally between 4000–8000 ft though they are generally uncommon above 6000 ft. Numbers then pick up in mid-August to late September when Barn Swallows could be classified as abundant around lowland valleys and farms. During the winter, a few individuals or pairs are occasionally observed from Mono Lake south.

CHICKADEES and TITMICE (Paridae)

MOUNTAIN CHICKADEE *Poecile gambeli*

LIFE HISTORY Ever-popular Mountain Chickadees are familiar and widespread birds in coniferous forests of the Sierra Nevada. Fearless and curious, their cheery *phee-bee-bee* songs (easily translated as "cheese bur-ger" or "hey swee-tie!") provide an incessant soundtrack for summer backpacking and camping trips. In the winter, their bold *chick-a-dee-dee* calls are a delightful addition to the snow-covered landscape, especially because chickadees frequently mingle with other small birds in mixed-species flocks.

Chickadees survive winter snows and freezing temperatures by eating various seeds, and foraging for the adults and eggs of hidden insects and spiders among the needles of incense cedars and other conifers. Every other year in Yosemite National Park, these acrobatic and agile foragers switch to a diet of lodgepole needle miner moths, whose larvae burrow into lodgepole pine needles in vast numbers on a 2-year cycle; chickadees expose the larvae by peeling back the sides of pine needles like bananas. Around March chickadees start searching for food among white fir needles; in the late summer they forage mostly in sugar pines, and then in the autumn they shift to black oaks.

Although their calls sound deceptively simple, chickadee vocalizations are surprisingly complex and encode a wide range of social signals used to shape group dynamics. Except for a brief period during the breeding season, Mountain Chickadees live in stable, highly social groups whose membership and territorial boundaries remain consistent from year to year. This long-term social cohesion creates a context in which sophisticated vocabularies can develop.

On warm, late-winter days, pairs begin to establish smaller territories within the group's larger territory, and by late April pairs split off from the group for the summer breeding season (reassembling as a group again in late summer). Nests are located in woodpecker holes or natural cavities, mainly in conifers or aspens. Males find and investigate potential nest sites, while females make the final choice, building a soft felted cup over a foundation of wood chips and laying 6–12 white eggs. Eggs are incubated by females for 12 days while males feed them at the nest. Females boldly defend their nests from potential predators, sitting tightly on the eggs and snapping at anything that comes close, or hissing loudly in the dark cavity and swaying like snakes if threatened. Both actions are likely useful defenses against ubiquitous egg-predators, such as the chipmunks that scamper up and down tree trunks all summer long.

On successful nests, parents tend their nestlings for up to 21 days then either split the brood and raise fledglings separately or else rear them as a family. Juveniles soon leave their parents and join new groups elsewhere. It is unknown whether pairs raise second broods later in the summer, but the presence of numerous nesting pairs at Tuolumne Meadows (8600 ft) in late July suggests that two broods may be more common than previously reported.

RANGE Mountain Chickadees are common residents in all types of conifer forests on both slopes of the Sierra Nevada (avoiding only gray pines on the west slope). Common from 4000–9000 ft, but found at higher elevations if tall conifers are present. On the west slope they are scarce residents in forests as low as 3000 ft. Some juveniles descend into the lower foothills in winter, occurring in oak woodlands or sagebrush flats.

CHESTNUT-BACKED CHICKADEE *Poecile rufescens*

LIFE HISTORY These tiny denizens of damp and well-shaded coniferous forests are recent arrivals from the Cascade Mountains of Oregon. One was found on the North Fork of the Feather River in 1939, and by 1951 they were being regularly reported in the northern Sierra Nevada. In the 1960s they extended their range to the southern borders of Yosemite National Park, where they reached the southernmost extent of Douglas-firs, their preferred trees. There is now considerable mingling of Chestnut-backed Chickadees and Mountain Chickadees, especially in winter, when flocks of the two species form the nucleus around which other species gather. However, Chestnut-backed Chickadees have a decided preference for dense, shaded stands of conifers while Mountain Chickadees choose more open parklike stands. Chestnut-backed Chickadees do not appear to compete with Mountain Chickadees, who are far more widespread and up to 10 times more numerous.

Both species feed heavily on insects, spiders, butterfly and moth larvae, plus a variety of berries and conifer seeds. In winter, both spend a lot of time feeding in incense cedars where there is an abundant supply of the scale insects (*Xylococculus macrocarpae*). The most common foraging strategy of Chestnut-backed Chickadees is to pick their way methodically upwards through a tree's foliage, then fly from the top of a tree to the base of the next tree's canopy and begin working upwards again.

By early April, pairs begin searching for suitable tree cavities or places where decayed wood is soft enough for them to excavate their own cavities. Males lead the way in finding and selecting cavities, and females build the nests over 7–8 days with no help. Unlike Mountain Chickadees, female Chestnut-backed Chickadees first prepare a mossy foundation then add a cup woven of animal fur and thin bark strips. In the Sierra Nevada, clutches of 6–7 finely red-spotted eggs are laid between mid-April and mid-May, with females incubating for 12–14 days while males bring food to the nest entrance. Females also take charge of keeping the nestlings warm and covered but both parents share feeding duties. Young birds may leave the nest at 14 days of age if threatened by predators, but usually require 23 days before they are ready to leave the nest; they then spend 2-3 weeks feeding with their parents until they become independent.

RANGE Chestnut-backed Chickadees are found only on the west slope, almost entirely in conifer forests between 2500–5000 ft. They are year-round residents of mixed conifer forests where Douglas-firs, white firs, incense cedars, ponderosa pines, bigleaf maples and black oaks predominate. Some may wander downslope in response to deep snows. One exceptional east slope record of a bird on the southwest shore of Lake Tahoe in November.

Oak Titmouse *Baeolophus inornatus*

LIFE HISTORY In 1998 the Plain Titmice of western North America were split into two species based on differences in their vocalizations, plumages, and distribution. Those on the west slope of the Sierra Nevada were renamed Oak Titmouse and those on the east slope are now called Juniper Titmouse, with these two sedentary species clearly separated by the dense conifer forests and high elevations of the Sierra Nevada. Little is known of the life history of Juniper Titmice, but the two species are generally considered to have many similar behaviors.

True to their name, Oak Titmice are residents of oak woodlands at low elevations on the west slope. Their bold and scratchy *tsicka-dee-dee* calls and ceaseless activity are a conspicuous presence wherever oaks grow, even around houses and small towns. Pairs mate for life and maintain stable territories year after year, not joining mixed-species flocks in the wintertime in the manner of chickadees.

Titmice use their stout little bills to hammer and pry open acorns (Oak Titmice) or pinyon pine nuts (Juniper Titmice), which are food items that other small birds cannot access. The rest of the time they can be seen vigorously flaking off bits of bark, or investigating leaves, flowers, and twigs in search of arthropods. In the fall and winter, their diet consists primarily of seeds and berries (including poison oak).

In February, pairs begin earnestly searching for potential nest sites. Females select a suitable natural cavity in a tree trunk or large branch (less often in an abandoned woodpecker cavity) while males accompany them and provide food as they alter cavities and build nests in March. Females lay 6–8 white eggs on a bed of moss, bark, and grass, lined with soft fur and feathers. They incubate eggs for 14–16 days then both parents tend the nestlings until they fly at around 17 days of age. Young birds remain with their parents for 3–4 weeks, then strike off to establish their own territories.

RANGE Oak Titmice are common residents in oak woodlands from the Central Valley to about 4000 ft on the west slope, and perhaps rarely as high as 5000 ft. Exceptions occur at the southern end of their range, where they use juniper-Joshua tree woodlands (e.g. west side of the Scodie Mountains) and breed up to 6700 ft (Piute Mountains). **WEST SLOPE:** Individual birds are occasionally found over 7000 ft from mid- to late summer. **EAST SLOPE:** Although west-slope birds may very rarely ascend nearly to the Sierra Nevada crest on the west side, it is believed the only east slope records come from breeding birds on the east side of Walker Pass (eastern Scodie Mountains) and from Walker Creek southwest of Olancha.

Juniper Titmouse *Baeolophus ridgwayi*

LIFE HISTORY Little known. See account above for behavior of the similar Oak Titmouse.

RANGE Juniper Titmice are inhabitants of arid, open pinyon-juniper pine woodlands on the lower slopes of Great Basin mountain ranges east of the Sierra Nevada, but their exact range in the Sierra Nevada is poorly known. In the southern Sierra Nevada, Juniper Titmice are likely separated from the Sierra Nevada by the inhospitable Owens Valley, but north of Bishop suitable habitat mingles with hilly terrain adjacent to the Sierra Nevada foothills and their distribution needs further study. Juniper Titmice are relatively common east of Mono Lake and may occur in the Bodie Hills north of Mono Lake. They are thought to be sparse breeders in the Carson Range on the east side of Lake Tahoe, and should be looked for in the arid hills east of Markleeville (the southern end of the Pine Nut Mountains). They have also been found in the Bald Mountain Range northwest of Reno, and could show up on the east slopes of the Diamond Mountains just to the north. Nonbreeding birds may wander, as evidenced by a handful of winter sightings in Bishop, where they are not known to breed. A titmouse observed on the north shore of Lake Tahoe in September is interesting because it could have been either species.

BUSHTITS (Aegithalidae)

BUSHTIT *Psaltriparus minimus*

LIFE HISTORY Despite being one of the smallest birds in North America and weighing only as much as 3–4 paper clips, Bushtits have an outsized, conspicuous presence. Except for a brief spell while nesting, they spend all their time in constantly chattering flocks of 10–25 birds flitting from tree to tree. Because they are so small, Bushtits must spend their entire day foraging. They eat up to 80 percent of their body weight in food as they acrobatically maneuver and hang upside down while inspecting branches and prying open leafy tangles in their ceaseless search for small insects and spiders. Although they maintain large, poorly defined territories, these flocks wander so widely that at times they appear semi-nomadic. In the winter, they mingle freely and peacefully with mixed flocks of nuthatches, chickadees, and kinglets, but if they encounter another Bushtit flock there is likely to be a bit of territorial squabbling.

While much of their complex social system is not fully understood, it appears that Bushtit flocks are remarkably stable, with membership and flock territories remaining constant from year to year.

Even during the breeding season, when other species pair up and defend nesting territories, nesting Bushtits continue to mingle freely with flock mates, checking out each other's nests, roosting together at night in the early part of the nesting season, and often cooperating to help raise each other's young. This cooperative breeding strategy has drawn the attention of biologists because the helpers are not directly related to the nesting pair, but instead help out on the chance that they can contribute eggs (if helpers are female) or sperm (if male) during subsequent nesting efforts.

Pairs begin searching for suitable nest sites in late March or early April, eventually selecting well-hidden spots within the branches of trees or shrubs about 10 ft off the ground (sometimes 4–50 ft). Nests are pendulous and sock-like, about 10–12 inches long, and take anywhere from two weeks to two months to construct from bits of twigs, grass, moss, and lichens, all held together with spider webs. A small entrance hole at the top allows the pair to fill the interior with a rich lining of feathers and fur. Both parents incubate 5–7 white eggs for 12 days then tend the nestlings until they leave the nest at 18 days of age. Other Bushtits may help raise the first clutch of chicks but play an undetermined role when the pair starts a second brood of eggs several days later. Newly fledged chicks join chicks raised by other flock members then join the main flock at the end of the breeding season, when they may all wander upslope until cold weather forces them back downslope sometime in October.

RANGE Two distinct subspecies of Bushtits occur in the Sierra Nevada, with the brown-capped race of western California occurring in oak woodlands and mixed chaparral of the lower west slope, and the gray-capped race of the interior West roaming pinyon-juniper woodlands and sagebrush thickets on the east slope. It is unclear if these races meet or overlap north of Lake Tahoe, or whether they cross the Sierra Nevada crest in the south. **WEST SLOPE:** Common up to 3000 ft, and locally uncommon at higher elevations (up to 4000 ft in Yosemite National Park and 6500 ft in Sequoia National Park). The west-slope subspecies ranges upslope along the South Fork Kern River, crosses the Sierra Nevada at Walker Pass and is found along the east slope as far north as Walker Creek just west of Owens Lake (at 7500 ft). **EAST SLOPE:** Widely distributed breeding species on the east side, where they nest from 6000–8000 ft in brushy riparian habitats. May appear scarce due to the relative inaccessibility of their nesting habitat, but far more conspicuous in winter when noisy groups wander through various habitats

NUTHATCHES (Sittidae)

RED-BREASTED NUTHATCH *Sitta canadensis*

LIFE HISTORY Red-breasted Nuthatches are common residents of mid-elevation coniferous forests, where they frequent shaded stands of mature white and red firs, Douglas-firs, incense cedars, and other conifers. In the mountains, Red-breasted Nuthatches only seem to avoid lodgepole pine forests at high elevations. They primarily require snags or large dead limbs in an advanced state of decay that they can readily excavate for nest cavities. Surveys in Sequoia & Kings Canyon National Parks found that Red-breasted Nuthatches occur in twice as many habitats and are many times more numerous than White-breasted Nuthatches (which are found more often in low-elevation oak woodlands).

Although prone to wandering, especially in winter, Red-breasted Nuthatches are generally year-round residents in most localities. Their loud, far-carrying *yank-yank-yank* calls are characteristic sounds in montane conifer forests at all seasons, and when intruders are spotted, nuthatches are often the first to raise the alarm for all the forest's birds. In the winter, over half of the population joins large, noisy foraging flocks along with chickadees, kinglets, various woodpeckers, and other small birds.

Red-breasted Nuthatches forage on the bark and upper branches of large trees. Here they probe under bark flakes and in crevices in search of insects (including their eggs and larvae) and spiders. In the fall and winter, they switch to a diet of conifer seeds and begin caching seeds and insects in small crevices in preparation for cold days and dwindling food supplies. They have been observed caching food in rock crevices hundreds of feet off the ground, and it has been speculated that many cliffside conifer trees in Yosemite Valley might have been planted by nuthatches.

In late April and early May, pairs begin excavating nest cavities in soft decayed wood, typically choosing firs or aspens. Several preliminary cavities may be excavated, with females doing much of the digging and males bringing food, before one is chosen. Females incubate 5–6 eggs, while males continue to bring them food until the eggs hatch 12 days later.

Red-breasted Nuthatches protect their nests by gathering pitch and thickly smearing it around the nest entrances, a strategy that keeps away predators and competitors but requires that parents fly headfirst into nest holes rather than landing and walking in. When threatened inside their nest cavities, females may spread their wings and sway slowly back and forth, a strategy that is surprisingly effective at scaring squirrels away. Both parents feed nestlings until they begin flying at 18–21 days; fledglings stay with the parents another two weeks, and families sometimes remain together over the winter.

RANGE Red-breasted Nuthatches are widespread in conifer forests throughout California, mainly nesting at mid-elevations but wandering widely in winter and some years moving to lowlands in huge numbers. Christmas Bird Count numbers from different Sierra Nevada locations fluctuate dramatically from year to year, ranging from zero to several hundred birds. **WEST SLOPE:** Common residents of the prime conifer belt between 3000–8000 ft, sometimes to 10,000 ft in the southern Sierra Nevada. Breeding birds may also use densely shaded forests at lower elevations in canyons and on north-facing slopes. After breeding, they readily wander from foothills to treeline; sometimes overwintering in conifer forests at higher elevations though large numbers are pushed downslope in years with little food. **EAST SLOPE:** Fairly common breeder from 7000–8000 ft. In the winter, they are irregular in conifer forests at any elevation, common some years and absent in others.

WHITE-BREASTED NUTHATCH *Sitta carolinensis*

LIFE HISTORY White-breasted Nuthatches are a delight to watch as they make soft *quank* calls and scuttle about the bark of oak trees and on lower branches. Unlike other nuthatches, this species spends much of its time foraging on tree trunks near, or sometimes on, the ground. They creep effortlessly on all sides of branches, even clinging upside down as they chip away flakes of bark and probe for insects and larvae. Upon seizing a food item they eagerly wedge it into a bark crevice and hammer it to pieces. During the fall and winter, they harvest large numbers of acorns (or pine seeds in some habitats), pounding some open to eat right away and caching the rest for consumption during colder months.

Little is known about the basic biology of White-breasted Nuthatches even though they are common, easily approached birds. They are mostly year-round residents, with little of the upslope and downslope movements seen in other nuthatches. Resident pairs briefly join mixed flocks of foraging birds moving through their territories but then drop out as the flocks cross over their territorial boundaries. Pairs begin courting in winter and start looking for old woodpecker holes or tree cavities even though they do not nest until several months later. Females add bits of bark and make cup nests of shredded bark and grasses lined with soft hairs and feathers while males bring them food. There is some evidence that White-breasted Nuthatches gather beetles that secrete noxious oils and smear them around the entrances of their nests to deter predators.

Egg-laying dates range from late March (in the western foothills), to May (in montane forests), to June (at Lake Tahoe). The 5–6 eggs are incubated by females for 12–14 days as males bring food to the nest. Both parents feed nestlings for 14–16 days on the nest, and then for another two weeks after young abandon the nest. Juveniles leave their parent's territories soon thereafter.

RANGE Two distinct races of White-breasted Nuthatches occupy the Sierra Nevada, both found in open woodlands with many large trees. These may be split into separate species so it is worth learning their distinctive calls and range differences. The west-side race (*S. c. aculeata*) resides in low-elevation oak woodlands and gives 1–2 nasal *keer* calls; while the east-side race (*S. c. tenuissima*) ranges widely among pines on the east slope, crossing over the crest and descending to about 8000 ft on the upper west slope, its high-pitched calls are given in rapid series. The range limits of these two subspecies have not been fully determined and present a fascinating question for curious birdwatchers. **WEST SLOPE:** Common in oak woodlands below 3000 ft, usually in blue or black oaks, often with a mix of gray or ponderosa pines. Rare at higher elevations, where it becomes important to carefully distinguish them from possible east-side nuthatches. Records above 8000 ft almost certainly pertain to the *tenuissima* race, but this needs to be confirmed. **EAST SLOPE:** An uncommon resident in forested areas on the east slope as high as treeline. Found in pinyon pine woodlands at lower elevations, and in mixed conifer forests at higher elevations but also ranges freely into nearby cottonwood and aspen stands, especially to nest.

PYGMY NUTHATCH *Sitta pygmaea*

LIFE HISTORY These small but energetic nuthatches would be difficult to spot among the needle clusters and treetops where they forage if they were not so noisy. Always occurring in pairs, family groups, or small flocks, these extremely social birds give sharp *peep* calls that accompany their every activity. When they join mixed-species foraging flocks in winter, other species coalesce around and follow these persistently calling nuthatches.

There are numerous advantages to this flocking behavior, including increased foraging efficiency and predator defense, but one of the Pygmy Nuthatch's most remarkable behaviors is flock roosting in winter as a way of staying warm. At all seasons these nuthatches sleep in tree cavities, but on cold fall and winter nights multiple flocks may sleep together, with up to 100 birds recorded in a single cavity.

Pygmy Nuthatches capitalize on their diminutive size by scampering effortlessly among clusters of pine needles and smaller twigs that other nuthatches rarely use. Competition is further reduced because Pygmy's restrict themselves to the uppermost portions of large ponderosa and Jeffrey pines, and seldom wander into mixed conifer or oak forests used by the other two nuthatches in the Sierra Nevada. Like other nuthatches, however, they feed heavily on insects, especially beetles, and in winter switch to a diet of conifer seeds, some of which they cache in the fall.

After wintering in small flocks, which are often family groups that stay together in the fall, pairs begin searching for well-decayed snags, stumps, or large branches where they excavate nesting cavities in April or May. Breeding pairs are frequently joined by 1–3 yearling males who assist in part or all of the nesting effort, including helping build and defend nests, and feeding incubating females and nestlings. Very few songbirds in North America practice this remarkable behavior.

Pygmy Nuthatches may take up to 6 weeks to dig a nesting cavity in soft wood, lining it with jumbles of feathers, bark fragments, mosses, hairs, and snakeskins. In May or June, females lay and incubate 5–6 reddish-brown eggs while males and any helpers bring them food. When threatened, females will defend their nests by spreading their wings and swaying back and forth. Nestlings are fed on the nest for about 20 days then fed another month after leaving the nest. Juvenile birds may depart and join a different group for the winter or stay with their family until the following spring.

RANGE Pygmy Nuthatches are mainly restricted to mature ponderosa and Jeffrey pine forests that have been little disturbed by logging or snag removal, but they are occasionally found in other conifer forests and will also nest in aspens and cottonwoods. **WEST SLOPE:** Reported as locally uncommon in ponderosa pine forests from 3000–7000 ft, and wandering up to treeline, but distribution is so spotty and poorly understood that it is noteworthy to find this species anywhere on the west slope south of Lake Almanor. Peak numbers seem to occur from May–August, and they are seldom observed over the winter. Of 13 west slope Christmas Bird Counts, only the Lake Almanor count regularly records Pygmy Nuthatches, and they are largely absent on all other counts except in Yosemite National Park. **EAST SLOPE:** Fairly common and found year round in Jeffrey pine forests below 8000 ft, with some wandering up to treeline in late summer. Regularly found on east slope Christmas Bird Counts, especially in the northern Sierra Nevada.

CREEPERS (Certhiidae)

Brown Creeper *Certhia americana*

LIFE HISTORY Exquisitely colored to look like pieces of bark, Brown Creepers are so well camouflaged that they would be easily missed except for their frequently uttered, pure-toned *tsee* calls. Once learned, these calls, along with the creeper's cascading *see-see-se-teetle-te-see* songs (cleverly translated as "trees, trees, beautiful trees"), will be heard in nearly every forested area in the Sierra Nevada, revealing the full abundance of these otherwise overlooked forest birds.

Creepers feed almost exclusively on arthropods hiding in bark crevices and under flakes of bark. A creeper's typical foraging strategy is to hitch upward on a tree trunk, using its long claws and stiff tail like a small woodpecker, to a height of about 30 ft, then flying down to the base of a new tree and starting upward again. Creepers use less energy if they forage on single large trees rather than many smaller trees, so they tend to be more abundant in stands of mature conifers. In the winter, over 70 percent of their time is spent foraging on incense cedar bark in search of abundant scale insects (*Xylococculus macrocarpae*).

Creepers are generally loners, but little is known about their life history, including how long pairs stay together. Pairs are often observed searching for nest cavities or building nests in May, and active nests are commonly found in June or even July. Nearly all nests are located relatively close to the ground behind loose sections of bark on dead or dying (occasionally living) trees.

Females construct nests while males sing and occasionally contribute bits of bark, grasses, and mosses. The foundation of the nest is lined with finer materials and attached to the inner bark with strands of spider webs, forming hanging hammock-shaped structures that look like narrow gravy dishes. Females incubate the 5–6 white eggs while males feed them. Eggs hatch in 14 days, and both parents feed the nestlings until they begin flying at 14–17 days of age. Young are tended for another 20 days after they leave the nest, but the dynamics of family groups after this point are not known.

RANGE Primarily found in conifer forests, Brown Creepers freely range into mixed forests or deciduous woodlands, especially in winter when large numbers may even move downslope into adjacent lowlands. **WEST SLOPE:** Fairly common residents of the conifer belt from 3000–8000 ft, where they seemingly use all types of conifers; less common to treeline where they are irregular breeders among lodgepole pine forests. **EAST SLOPE:** Fairly common residents of conifer belt up to 8000 ft, rarely to 10,000 ft.

WRENS (Troglodytidae)

ROCK WREN *Salpinctes obsoletus*

LIFE HISTORY Easily detected by their ringing *tick-ear* calls, Rock Wrens are far more difficult to spot as they duck in and out of rock crevices, picking their way among boulders in search of insects and spiders. Smudgy gray at a distance, Rock Wrens examined at close hand reveal fine patterns of dots and bars that mimic the appearance of textured rocks. Despite their camouflage, these birds are readily observed, so it is surprising that almost nothing is known of their basic biology. In fact, published information on this bird's breeding biology in California is mostly limited to observations made on a single nest for one day.

Males are prodigious songsters and will sing over 100 different loud trilling songs. Pairs cooperate in building nests in rocky crevices or rodent burrows, first laying down foundations of small pebbles that may extend beyond nest entrances as "paved" entryways. On top of these foundations, females do most of the work constructing a cup of dry grasses lined with soft hairs. Records of nesting pairs indicate that eggs are laid in early May at low elevations though they likely nest in June at higher elevations. Information from other regions suggests that Rock Wrens may have 2–3 broods, but it is not known if this is true for the Sierra Nevada. Females incubate 5–6 white eggs for about 13 days. Both parents tend the nestlings for 14–16 days, and it is thought the family may stay together for another month.

RANGE Rock Wrens occupy the broadest altitudinal gradient of any bird in North America, ranging from below sea level in Death Valley to 14,000 ft on the highest Sierra Nevada peaks. During the breeding season they are nearly always associated with rocky hillsides, talus slopes, and earthen cuts. They are largely absent from forested areas, but may show up on rock outcroppings, cliffs, or rocky river banks in the middle of otherwise unsuitable habitat. In the winter, most descend to the lower portions of foothill slopes or into adjacent valleys. **WEST SLOPE:** Uncommon below 3000 ft and above 9000 ft, but surprisingly rare at mid-elevations. In one study in the Yosemite region, this species was 6 times more abundant in gray pine habitats at low elevations than at any higher elevation habitat. In the winter, relatively common below 2000 ft, and rare up to about 4000 ft. **EAST SLOPE:** Widely, but perhaps thinly dispersed everywhere on the east slope from mid-March to mid-October. They apparently descend to warm valley bottoms for the winter, but populations are somewhat localized. For instance, they are uncommon on the Honey Lake Christmas Bird Count but absent on the nearby Sierra Valley count; regular on the Carson City count but absent on the adjacent Reno count; and fairly common on the Bishop count but essentially absent on the nearby Mammoth Lakes count.

Canyon Wren *Catherpes mexicanus*

LIFE HISTORY Canyon wrens are found on rock walls, boulder fields, and even on sheer cliffs in shaded moist river canyons, where they forage among rock crevices and under boulders. Their flattened heads, short legs, and long sharp claws help them cling to rock faces and poke into rocky cracks. It is thought that their brilliant white throats reflect light into dark crevices as they search for hidden insects and spiders. Both Rock Wrens and Canyon Wrens constantly bob up and down and swivel back-and-forth as they forage, but the smaller Canyon Wrens are easily distinguished by their sweet cascading songs that ring out in rocky canyons like celestial waterfalls of sound, *tsee tsee tsee teeyou teyou tyou tyou tyou*, falling in pitch and slowing from fast trills into echoes of themselves.

Also like Rock Wrens, Canyon Wrens are very little studied and poorly known. They typically nest on ledges in caves or other rock recesses, where pairs cooperate in laying down foundations of twigs and other coarse materials that are built up with feathers, plant down, and a great variety of miscellaneous items. Females incubate 5–6 white eggs for 12–18 days as males provide food. In the Sierra Nevada, it appears that nesting activity peaks from May–June, but if they lay two clutches of eggs, as they do in some other areas, then active nests might be found later in the summer as well. Both parents tend nestlings for about 15 days, and it is thought that family groups stay together for weeks or months after young leave the nests.

RANGE Long thought to be sedentary residents of steep-walled gorges at low to mid-elevations along major rivers and streams, where they frequent cliff faces and jumbles of large boulders; however, Christmas Bird Count data and other records suggest that many Canyon Wrens retreat to the southern Sierra Nevada in winter (south of Yosemite National Park and Mono Lake), at least from October–February. **WEST SLOPE:** Fairly common during the breeding season in appropriate habitats up to 5000 ft; rarely wandering to higher elevations, mostly in late summer. **EAST SLOPE:** Uncommon breeders in appropriate habitats up to 8000 ft; with a handful of late summer records as high as 12,000 ft.

BEWICK'S WREN *Thryomanes bewickii*

LIFE HISTORY Although thinly distributed among foothill brush fields, Bewick's Wrens give the impression of being common by drawing outsized attention to themselves with loud trilling songs. Gray-brown and finely patterned, Bewick's Wrens otherwise blend into the shadows of dense shrubs where they spend their time probing energetically among leaves and debris for the adults and larvae of various arthropods. Foraging Bewick's Wrens rarely feed higher than 10 ft from the ground and generally remain in or near shrubs and brushy tangles, only rarely feeding on the ground in open areas.

In behavior and habitat they overlap with House Wrens, an aggressive, egg-killing species that in some areas is thought to be gradually displacing increasingly uncommon Bewick's Wrens. In the Sierra Nevada the two species avoid conflict, to a degree, by utilizing different habitats, with Bewick's more often found in dry, open, brushy areas and House Wrens favoring oak groves and woodlands.

Solitary in the nonbreeding season, Bewick's Wrens pair up in March and search for cavities in trees, rocks, or old buildings. Males initiate nest building, but the pair works together to build large irregular cup nests of various materials like twigs, grasses, feathers, mosses, leaves, and hairs. A few shed snakeskins are often woven into nests, a behavior shared with House Wrens. The first clutches of eggs are laid by early April, and they probably raise two broods each summer. Females incubate 5–7 eggs for 14 days while being partly or wholly fed by males.

Both parents tend chicks 14 days on the nest, and another 14 days after they leave the nest. Young males acquire their own territories about two months later and soon master the 9–22 songs they sing for the rest of their lives.

RANGE Bewick's Wrens are largely restricted to brushy slopes, open oak woodlands, and riparian thickets at low elevations on both slopes; they prefer a combination of brushy thickets, openings and scattered taller trees. Resident throughout their range, but some wander upslope in late summer and a few may even remain to winter at elevations above their breeding range. **WEST SLOPE:** Fairly common below 2000 ft, and locally uncommon to at least 4000 ft. They rarely wander upslope into the Upper Montane Zone and occasionally winter there. **EAST SLOPE:** Locally uncommon below 8000 ft. Breed in patches of dense shrubs among sagebrush or along creeks but also among junipers. At least in winter, appear to be most common from 4000–6500 ft.

House Wren *Troglodytes aedon*

LIFE HISTORY House Wrens are noisy and rather pugnacious little creatures whose rich bubbling songs provide a wonderful backdrop around overgrown woodlands and forest edges, usually far from human habitation but occasionally near rural houses and ranches. Here they jauntily and actively probe leafy tangles and branches in search of larval and adult insects or spiders, and between bouts of loud singing they investigate and scold approaching intruders. They have an unpleasant reputation for killing the eggs and nestlings of other birds on their territories, but at the same time males have been observed feeding baby birds at nests of other species or even bringing food to the parents to help them out.

Migrants show up as early as late March but most wrens, both migrating birds that continue north as well as breeding birds that remain to nest, arrive in April. Males claim territories (possibly booting out Bewick's Wrens that have expanded their habitat use during the House Wrens' winter absence) and immediately scout out potential nest cavities that they begin cramming full of hundreds of small sticks. Females likely find mates within hours of their arrival, choosing males on the basis of the multiple nests they have prepared and signaling their acceptance by adding the finishing touches to one of the preparatory nests. Males usually sing within a few feet of their nests, and seem to direct their exuberant songs almost exclusively at their mates. Females sing as well though they probably do not use the 20–50 different songs that a male typically sings.

Sometime in May or June, females begin incubating 6–8 eggs for about 14 days. Both parents tend the nestlings for 12–18 days then males continue feeding fledglings for another two weeks while females start new clutches of eggs. However, there is a constant threat that other males will challenge territorial males to bouts of circular chases and loud singing that may last hours at a time. About 50 percent of these challengers are successful and take over the territory, promptly killing the eggs or nestlings of previous males to ensure that resident females will be ready to start new nests within a couple days.

RANGE House Wrens are common breeding birds of foothill woodlands and thickets, especially in the vicinity of streams. Their altitudinal range overlaps significantly with the very similar Bewick's Wren, but the two species avoid competition by breeding in slightly different habitats (see above account). **WEST SLOPE:** Arrive on their nesting grounds, mostly in blue and live oak woodlands, in mid-April and leave by the end of September or early October. Most abundant below 5000 ft, but have bred as high as 7000 ft and possibly higher. Significant upslope movement of juveniles to treeline has been reported, with the bulk of the population leaving the mountains in late August. Uncommon in winter at the lowest elevations with a handful of records below 4000 ft. **EAST SLOPE:** Breed as high as 8000 ft, often in aspen groves and in riparian woodlands on desert slopes. Very rare in winter in warm desert valleys as far north as Lone Pine.

PACIFIC WREN *Troglodytes pacificus*

LIFE HISTORY Creeping along like mice cloaked in chocolate-brown feathers, Pacific Wrens are nearly invisible among dank shaded roots, fallen logs, and tangled vegetation, revealing themselves only with their sharp scolding *timp* notes and outbursts of song. Formerly known as Winter Wrens, these diminutive birds are famous for their outstanding songs—overflowing cascades of penetrating notes pouring out at around 36 notes per second. Territorial males often ascend from out of the forest gloom onto a favorite singing perch, belting out a song that for the wren's body weight has 10 times the power of a crowing rooster.

Pacific Wrens are the only North America wrens found in association with old growth and mature conifer forest, and they are further restricted to deep, moist shade among tangles of uprooted trees, dead logs, and clumps of ferns and mosses. They are clearly impacted by logging and fragmentation of conifer forests though some also utilize woodlands in moist canyons and on north-facing hillsides. Foraging Pacific Wrens methodically search substrates near the ground while hopping along slowly, examining crevices and unhesitatingly entering dark, confined spaces in search of hidden spiders and insects.

Although solitary over the winter, Pacific Wrens are known to roost communally on cold nights (with 31 recorded sleeping together on a cold night in Washington). Males begin building a number of nests on their territories starting in March (unfortunately, very little is known about their life history in California). These stout, domed structures are about 7 inches across and constructed of various leaves, mosses, and grasses placed in any kind of recess or hole.

When prospective females approach, males sing softly and guide them to each of their sample nests. If the quality and density of nests suggests a male has a high-quality territory then a female chooses one nest and lines it with feathers in preparation for laying 5–8 white eggs in late April or early May. Each highly attentive male remains within several feet of his mate from the moment she first appears on his territory until she starts incubating eggs, at which point he may begin building a new set of nests and trying to attract another mate (not all males do this). Eggs hatch in 14–17 days and both parents tend the nestlings until they leave the nest at 15–20 days of age. It is not known how long the fledglings remain with their parents, and it is thought that pairs nest twice each summer in California.

RANGE Pacific Wrens seem to be locally uncommon residents in moist conifer forests at mid-elevations on the west slope, but much remains to be learned about the status and distribution of this reclusive species in the Sierra Nevada. Numbers increase everywhere from October–March, probably due to the arrival of migrants, when Pacific Wrens are found in many areas where they do not breed. WEST SLOPE: Breeds in a variety of mixed conifer forests below 5000 ft. In Yosemite and Sequoia & Kings Canyon National Parks, they occur at substantially higher densities in giant sequoia habitats. In late summer a few move upslope into fairly dense stands of Jeffrey pines, lodgepole pines, or red firs, but it is possible that some pairs breed as high as 8000 ft anyway. Very scarce south of Sequoia & Kings Canyon National Parks. Southern breeding limit is at Alta Sierra in the Greenhorn Mountains, but one day they might be found breeding in the Piute Mountains. EAST SLOPE: Rare in dense, damp forests during the winter, with many scattered records. Not known to breed on the east slope until recently discovered breeding in the Carson Range east of Lake Tahoe. One or more singing males at 7500 ft on Pine Creek, north of Bishop, suggests the possibility that other east-slope breeding locations may be discovered one day.

MARSH WREN *Cistothorus palustris*

LIFE HISTORY Marsh Wrens are common residents of marshes, where their bold songs are an ever-present backdrop to the whine of midges and splash of lurking swamp creatures. These fierce little wrens perch prominently atop towering cattails, squabbling endlessly with each other, and foraging for insects and spiders on plant stems or on the surface of water. In the winter, they turn secretive and hide easily among the stems of cattails and dense marsh plants.

Listening to the harsh scolding vocalizations of Marsh Wrens, you would hardly know these are one of the impressive songbirds in North America. Driven by intense competition for resources in the marshes where they breed, males sing as many as 200 types of song, each song lasting only one to two seconds but given in rapid volleys that overwhelm the listener. Following predetermined sequences of songs, all the males in a given population hurl songs back and forth at each other, sometimes skipping ahead in the sequence to convey different messages. Intense competition also drives Marsh Wrens, males and females of all ages, to seek out and destroy eggs and nestlings in every bird nest they can find, a behavior that forces other marsh birds like blackbirds to nest in groups. In one study, up to 50 percent of Red-winged Blackbird nests failed due to Marsh Wrens.

On the other hand, aggressive Yellow-headed Blackbirds prevent Marsh Wrens from entering their own nests by standing in front of the wren's nest holes, and then if this fails, blackbirds hop up and down on top of the wren nests to flatten them. Many Marsh Wren nest failures are due to Yellow-headed Blackbirds, and they wisely retreat when Yellow-headeds show up to breed.

Perhaps in response to this pressure, male Marsh Wrens build an average of 20 nests for each female they attract. Extra nests likely serve as decoys but may also indicate a male's vigor to prospective mates. Highly successful males lead visiting females to their courting areas, where they have constructed multiple "dummy" nests. A female signals her acceptance of the male by adding an inner doorstep to one of his bulky domed nests and lining it with soft cattail fluff and feathers. Early in the season, when prospective females are still arriving in the marsh, males may build new sets of dummy nests and start the process over again. Females may raise two broods per summer, each consisting of 4–6 dark-brown eggs. These are incubated by females for 14–16 days, with nestlings needing about 14 days after they hatch before they are ready to fly. Males usually help feed older chicks, giving females time to nest again.

RANGE Marsh Wrens are nearly always found around low-elevation marshes with tall abundant marsh vegetation, but these habitats are limited in the Sierra Nevada and the geographic and seasonal distribution of Marsh Wrens is complex. **WEST SLOPE:** Marsh Wrens are common residents in the Central Valley that range locally into the Sierra Nevada in some foothill marshes. Breed to nearly 3000 ft along the South Fork Kern River Valley, but elsewhere they may only nest below 500 feet. Migrants or postbreeding birds occur in a wide variety of habitats up to 10,000 ft from mid-August to mid-September. Uncommon below 3000 ft in winter and very rare up to 4500 ft. **EAST SLOPE:** A locally common to rare breeder below 7000 ft at scattered marshes along the east side, with numbers increasing during fall migration from late August into October. A few wintering birds may linger at lower elevations or around hot springs. Spring migrants arrive in early April at sites where they do not winter. Formerly bred at South Lake Tahoe and the occasional presence of singing males indicates that they may nest there again.

GNATCATCHERS (Polioptilidae)

BLUE-GRAY GNATCATCHER *Polioptila caerulea*

LIFE HISTORY Closely resembling kinglets in foraging beat and manner, Blue-gray Gnatcatchers avoid competition with their near-relatives by occupying hotter, low-elevation habitats during the breeding season. Here, among tangles of foothill shrubs and small trees, these energetic little birds use their long, slender bills to probe for tiny insects and spiders among clusters of leaves or under bits of bark. In manner, they are fidgety, moving constantly, peering every which way and swishing their tails from side to side. At the same time gnatcatchers are garrulous and frequently utter sharp wheezing calls. During the breeding season, pairs remain close together and seldom stray more than 100 ft from their nest. From April to July, males may be heard giving rambling songs that include chips, wheezes, and various twitterings.

From early May to early June, both sexes participate in building compact nests that straddle branches so tightly that they resemble clumps of debris or mere branch deformities, a perfect camouflage against raiding Western Scrub-Jays. Built of plant fibers and bark strips woven together with spider silk, their nests look much like large hummingbird nests. Only females possess brood patches, yet both sexes incubate the 4–5 pale blue eggs for 11–15 days. Young gnatcatchers remain on the nest for up to 15 days and are fed by the parents for another 3 weeks. Males then tear apart old nests and reuse the material to build new nests, with second clutches of eggs laid sometime around early July.

RANGE Blue-gray Gnatcatchers are restricted to dry and shrubby forested habitats throughout the United States. **WEST SLOPE:** Generally uncommon, though sometimes locally abundant, during the breeding season. First arrive in mid-March and linger into early October, but the bulk of the breeding population present from mid- to late April through late August. Breed in dry habitats with a mix of shrubs and trees, particularly blue oaks, from the Foothill Oak Zone up to the lower Mixed Conifer Zone around 5000 ft. In late summer, a few wander upslope into montane chaparral as high as 8000–10,000 ft. Occasionally winters on sunny slopes below 4000 ft. **EAST SLOPE:** Seasonal abundance closely matches west slope populations except that in the winter gnatcatchers are very rare in the southern Sierra Nevada and unexpected anywhere north of Mono Lake. Breed along the entire east side between 6000–8000 ft, mostly in pinyon-juniper woodlands with an understory of various desert shrubs like mountain mahogany, sagebrush, or bitterbrush.

DIPPERS (Cinclidae)

AMERICAN DIPPER *Cinclus mexicanus*

LIFE HISTORY Thanks to John Muir, who cherished these birds and immortalized them in his writings, American Dippers are the Sierra Nevada's most famous birds. And anyone who sees them will understand why. Dippers are the animated spirits of rushing mountain streams, overflowing with lively energy and enchanting bubbling song. They are so closely linked to the water that when they fly along a stream, they devotedly follow every twist and turn rather than flying overland. They are absolutely fearless on the edge of furious rapids and plunging waterfalls, diving effortlessly to feed and popping to the surface like a buoyant cork. One naturalist watched a dipper being swept over the brink of Yosemite Falls, but it simply flew out of the plummeting foam and flew back upstream, continuing to feed as if nothing had happened.

Pairs live year round at almost any elevation where they find fast-moving, unpolluted waters and abundant aquatic invertebrates, moving downslope in the winter only if things get too icy. They feed by making short underwater dives or by walking along the shore peering underwater; their dives last up to 15 seconds and they stay underwater by angling their open wings so that the water's current pushes them against the bottom. As North America's only aquatic songbird, they have many specialized adaptations for surviving these demanding conditions, including low metabolic rates, added oxygen-carrying capacity in their blood cells, and twice as many feathers as similar-sized songbirds. In fact, all of their skin is covered with thick downy feathers, and even their eyelids are feathered.

Surrounded by loud roaring streams, dippers may use their namesake dipping behavior as long-distance social signals; in addition, the complex bell-like songs of both males and females are so loud they can be heard nearly a mile away. Pairs defend long linear territories that extend one quarter to two-and-a-half miles along streams or rivers, and if they have to leave these territories in the winter, they usually return to the same location the following spring.

Pairs construct their large ball-like nests of woven mosses, grasses, and leaves behind waterfalls, on rocky ledges, or under bridges and culverts where the babies will be safe from high waters and predators. Their nesting season may start early or be delayed by a late runoff of high waters, and whenever possible many pairs apparently raise two broods in quick succession, meaning that pairs may be found nesting anytime from April to late July.

Females incubate 4–5 eggs for 16 days, with males bringing most of their food; both sexes help raise the nestlings. Young birds fledge at 24–26 days and within a few days or a few weeks they are independent and take care of themselves, leaving their parents to immediately tear out the nest lining, reline their nest with fresh material, and start a second brood. The parents typically split the broods in half and divide up their territory so they do not compete with each other while feeding dependent fledglings. In August, adult dippers molt their flight feathers and are flightless from 4 days to two weeks, a period in which they are very secretive and nervous.

RANGE American Dippers are found along fast, rushing waters throughout western North America, using habitats from the bottom of the Grand Canyon to ocean shores. Fairly common during the breeding season in the Sierra Nevada and found along rivers and streams from valley bottoms to about 9000 ft. Some young birds wander to over 11,000 ft from mid- to late summer, and can be found feeding along the edges of glacial lakes in the high country. The entire population moves downstream to avoid frozen water but remain wherever water stays open. **WEST SLOPE:** Found along the entire west side and reported to nest as low as 1500 ft, but probably more limited by lack of suitable habitat than elevation. **EAST SLOPE:** Breed in many east-side canyons and along mountain creeks where there is fast-flowing water and potential nest sites. The southernmost clusters of well-reported sightings are from Big Pine Creek above Big Pine.

KINGLETS (Regulidae)

GOLDEN-CROWNED KINGLET *Regulus satrapa*

LIFE HISTORY Despite being one of the most abundant birds in mid-elevation coniferous forests, Golden-crowned Kinglets are difficult to observe and their behavior during the breeding season remains virtually unstudied in California.

Equipped with unusually dense plumage, many of these kinglets remain year round on their breeding grounds even in frigid winter temperatures. During the winter, they occasionally mingle with chickadees and creepers but typically remain in small flocks of their own kind, often ranging into a wider range of habitats than they use during the breeding season. These agile birds have been called branch-tip specialists because they are so lightweight they can cling to tiny branch tips that would bend under the weight of heavier-bodied birds. Moving constantly, they scan branch tips and tree bark in search of adult insects, spiders, and mites, as well as their eggs, which are a plentiful food source in the winter.

Both sexes begin building deep, well-insulated cup nests in May, weaving needles and grasses together with spider webs and bits of moss and lichens for camouflage then adding a lining of feathers and hair. These nests are well hidden amid dense clusters of needles and rarely found. Males bring food to females as they incubate 5–10 eggs for 14–16 days. Both sexes then tend the young on the nest for 16–19 days, but while females almost immediately begin incubating another clutch of eggs, males care for the first batch of fledglings until they reach independence at 17 days of age. Fledglings recorded as late as September.

RANGE Golden-crowned Kinglets are common residents in mid-elevation coniferous forests, but they will also range to both higher and lower elevations to nest in isolated groves of conifers away from the main belt of trees. A few wander to treeline in late summer, and may rarely nest as high as 10,000 ft. Some years, large numbers descend into the foothills, where they are possible in a wide variety of deciduous and coniferous forests. **WEST SLOPE:** Primarily breed in stands dominated by mature giant sequoia, red and white fir, and Douglas fir between 3000–8000 ft, where they are common to abundant from April–September. Golden-crowneds are surprisingly widespread, as shown by one Yosemite National Park study where they were detected in 22 different habitat types during the breeding season (compared to 5 habitat types for Ruby-crowneds). Also found in a wide range of forested habitats from the low foothills to 8000 ft in winter, but numbers are unpredictable at that season. **EAST SLOPE:** Locally uncommon resident in scattered pockets of firs and pines, but common at some locations (for instance, they are one of the 10 most common birds at Devils Postpile National Monument). Found the full length of the Sierra Nevada, though increasingly scarce and localized at the arid southern end of the range. Small numbers occasionally descend to valley bottoms and desert slopes in winter.

Ruby-crowned Kinglet *Regulus calendula*

LIFE HISTORY One of the joys of birding in the western foothills during winter is the ubiquitous presence of these abundant, noisily chattering kinglets. Their primary winter vocalizations are best compared to bursts of clacking typewriter keys though by the end of February males begin practicing songs that start as a series of high notes that build into a gallop of exuberant warbles. Grinnell and Storer, in their classic *Animal Life of Yosemite*, describe the song as *see, see, see, oh, oh, oh, property, property, property*. A month later, males depart to breed in montane coniferous forests, followed soon thereafter by females.

Much of their breeding biology remains poorly known, in part because pairs build their well-insulated nests deep within dense needle clusters as high as 100 ft above the ground. Males attract females and challenge rivals by raising their otherwise hidden red crowns, sometimes stretching their bodies into exaggerated postures to highlight these colorful displays. By late May, females spend about 5 days constructing thick nests of mosses, lichens, and bits of plants, woven together with spider webs and thickly lined with feathers. Females incubate 7–8 white eggs for 12–14 days while males bring food. Clutches of 12 eggs are possible, the highest number of eggs relative to a bird's size for any songbird in North America. Both parents tend the nestlings until they leave the nest around 16 days of age, and it is thought that families break up as soon as fledglings become independent.

Ruby-crowned Kinglets seem to enjoy the company of other birds, especially in winter when they are nearly always found in the company of mixed-species flocks with warblers, nuthatches, chickadees, and other songbirds. They forage almost exclusively on the outermost foliage and often hover in mid-air to snatch small insects and spiders at the slender tips of branches.

RANGE Ruby-crowned Kinglets breed in montane conifer forests with a strong preference for lodgepole pine forests, especially near water or the margins of meadow. They sometimes appear in great numbers at low elevations during migration or winter. **WEST SLOPE:** An abundant migrant and winter resident in many types of forested and shrubby habitats below 4000 ft from late September to mid-April. During the summer, most apparently head north because they are uncommon breeders at higher elevations between May–July, when they are found mostly in lodgepole pine or mountain hemlock forests of the Subalpine Zone. Rarely breed as low as 4000 ft or up to 10,000 ft, and primarily found between 6000–8000 ft. **EAST SLOPE:** While huge numbers of migrants briefly show up in valleys and on foothill slopes in April, and a smaller number of migrants appear in late September to mid-October, numbers of wintering birds range from rare to fairly common. Though considered a common breeder in some locations, they are likely generally rare on their breeding grounds (6000–10,000 ft) from late April to late October.

SYLVIID WARBLERS (Sylviidae)

WRENTIT *Chamaea fasciata*

LIFE HISTORY Scientists have long debated the taxonomic status of these tiny, fluffy birds. They are currently thought to be the only Old World warblers found in North America, and many aspects of their lives are very unusual. Young birds move an average of 1300 ft from their birthplace, form life-long pair bonds when they are only 30–40 days old, and live on the same one- to two-acre territory with the same mate for their whole lives, up to 12 years. They are the most sedentary birds in North America, and pairs spend the day puttering around together on their territories making soft contact calls and foraging among branches and leaves for insects, caterpillars, fruits, and seeds. Poison oak berries form a significant portion of their winter diets. Because of their life-long loyalty to the same patch of bushes, pairs lose everything when chaparral thickets are cleared for fire prevention.

Both sexes sing year round from dense shrublands, using loud vo-calizations to stay in touch and announce their territorial boundaries. Males have a distinctive "bouncing ball" song, *pit-pit-pit-pit-pit-tr-r-r-r*, while females make a series of evenly spaced *pit* notes. The affection of pairs is constant; they not only preen each other but at night they lean against each other and interweave their feathers to make one big puffy ball before going to sleep. Both help in every aspect of making their tidy little nests and raising 3–4 young. Unfortunately, Wrentits have not been studied in the Sierra Nevada so everything we know about them comes from well-studied populations around the Bay Area, but it is thought that their nesting season begins in March and can last until July. Nests are located less than 3 ft high and are well hidden in dense foliage, being made of cobweb frameworks that are shaped into cups with bark strips then lined with fine materials.

Males and females both have brood patches and incubate their eggs for 15 days, with females taking the night shifts and both sexes sharing the day shifts. Young birds leave the nest at 15 days of age, still not able to fly but able to move through the vegetation with ease. Fami-lies stay together for at least 30 days and a small percentage of pairs try to raise two broods each summer.

RANGE Wrentits are entirely limited to shrubby habitats west of the Cascades-Sierra axis from Oregon to Baja California. In the Sierra Nevada, they are mainly associated with extensive thickets of chamise, ceanothus, manzanita, and scrub oaks, and have an astonishing ability to colonize isolated patches of bushes as small as one acre in the middle of other habitats. **WEST SLOPE:** Common residents on nearly every low-elevation chaparral-covered hillside and canyon wall from Quincy to the Greenhorn Mountains, often extending far into the heart of the Sierra Nevada along south-facing canyon walls. Most abundant below 3000 ft, but locally common to at least 5000 ft, and rarely to about 6000 ft. Records above 3000–4000 ft need to be carefully evaluated because postbreeding birds occasionally wander upslope and it is telling that most higher elevation records are from June–August and may not represent breeding locations. **EAST SLOPE:** Because of this species' notoriously sedentary nature, it comes as a bit of a shock that there are records from several east-slope locations including Truckee; most notably there have been a cluster of sightings between Bishop and Lone Pine since 1992 that may represent a new breeding locality. East-side birds have been found in willow and wild rose thickets.

THRUSHES (Turdidae)

Western Bluebird *Sialia mexicana*

LIFE HISTORY These lovely residents of foothill oak woodlands are a charming presence with their soft *few* calls and bright blue colors. They can be easily overlooked, but in backyards with bird baths and nest boxes they become regular visitors. Nest boxes may be used during the spring for nesting, or in the middle of winter when groups of bluebirds pile in at night to keep warm.

Western Bluebirds verge on common in the fall and winter when small flocks descend into the foothills to feast on abundant crops of berries, especially crops of mistletoes and toyons, which they find among chaparral thickets and oak woodlands. They become less noticeable in the spring as they spread out or migrate to open woodlands, wooded edges, or burned forests where they search for rotted tree cavities or old woodpecker holes to nest in. Cavities are a limited resource and there can be fierce competition between bluebirds, swallows, nuthatches, chickadees, woodpeckers, starlings, and wrens for these sites, so bluebirds like to arrive as early as April to claim a hole.

Once pairs claim their nest sites, females begin collecting bits of grasses, mosses, hairs, and soft fibers to make tidy little nests while males stand guard. The same pair bonds may be reestablished for several years in a row, but both sexes seek additional copulations with other bluebirds during the nesting season, leading to mixed paternity for the eggs. Depending on elevation, nest-building starts from early April to mid-May, but because pairs may lay 2–3 successive clutches of eggs some will still be nesting in August. During the breeding season both adults and young birds eat a steady diet of insects, which they catch by dropping to the ground from low perches.

Clutches contain an average of 5 eggs, which are incubated by females and take two weeks to hatch. Young birds start flying when they are 3 weeks old, and siblings typically stay together for about two weeks before dispersing; however, some remain with the family group, helping their parents raise the next brood. Some family groups even stick together into the winter.

RANGE Western Bluebirds have a fairly complex distribution in the Sierra Nevada with a mix of winter arrivals, local residents, and transients moving fluidly over the landscape in unpredictable patterns. It is not known if some arrive from other regions or if local populations simply move up and down slope with the seasons, creating the sense of large-scale migrations. **WEST SLOPE:** Generally common, though probably somewhat nomadic, in foothill oak woodlands in the fall and winter, with numbers increasing in late summer and noticeably decreasing in March. Wintering birds common in various oak woodlands below the Mixed Conifer Zone; numbers drop off above 3000 ft but small flocks are regularly found in snow-free open areas as high as 6600 ft in Yosemite National Park. Nest from the edges of the Central Valley to mid-elevations, at least as high as 5000 ft, and sometimes higher where there are open meadows and oaks, or burned stands of trees, among conifer forests. Flocks of postbreeding birds wander upslope to over 11,000 ft in mid- to late summer. **EAST SLOPE:** Generally uncommon anywhere east of the crest, though locally common in small numbers at a few locations. Regular breeders around Sierra Valley, Truckee and Lake Tahoe, Carson Valley, and Bridgeport in the northern Sierra Nevada; but only nesting in very small numbers anywhere to the south, as in Lee Vining Canyon and a few sites along Independence Creek west of Independence. There is often a significant increase in numbers in September and October, but most soon head to the west slope. Irregular and local in early winter, becoming extremely scarce or absent from late December–March.

MOUNTAIN BLUEBIRD *Sialia currucoides*

LIFE HISTORY Mountain meadows with scattered trees are the favorite haunts of Mountain Bluebirds that dash around like glowing dots of cerulean blue, using their long wings to hover while scanning the ground for grasshoppers and insects that they dive down to catch. This is an energetically costly way of hunting, using 4–8 times more energy than sitting on a perch and scanning the ground, but if food is scarce males fall back on this additional strategy to help them find extra food for their hungry nestlings.

In some ways, these opportunistic birds have benefited from human activities like forest clearing and programs to put out nest boxes, but in the absence of these factors Mountain Bluebirds seek out open habitats with short-grass meadows, including recently burned forests, sagebrush flats, and alpine hillsides where they forage, and nearby trees where they use rotted cavities and old woodpecker holes for nesting. Here you can hear their soft nasal *tew* calls as soon as males begin arriving in March to stake out large territories that include several potential nest sites. Females arrive 1–2 weeks later and pick mates on the basis of the nesting cavities they like rather than on any qualities of the males themselves. As soon as they have attracted mates, males guard much smaller territories around cavities chosen by females and spend all their time very closely guarding females, so close in fact that females sometimes scold males to get a little space.

Competitors for these holes include Mountain Chickadees, Northern Flickers, European Starlings, and Tree Swallows. Swallows are such significant competitors that bluebirds are forced to arrive on their breeding grounds as early as possible, and bluebirds will even kill swallows they find in their nests.

Females fill the bottoms of their nest cavities with dry grasses then lay 5–6 eggs that they incubate for 13 days while males bring them food. A female signals her hunger by flicking her wing open, and the male immediately flies off to find her some food. As soon as the chicks hatch, males try to feed them too, but females intercept all the deliveries and make decisions about how much they want to eat themselves and how much to feed the chicks.

Young birds leave the nest at 18–21 days, and are dependent on their parents for a week (in a good food year) to several months (when food supplies are low). About 50 percent of the adults raise a second brood so nesting activity can be observed from April to late July in the Sierra Nevada. Young birds and family groups begin forming postbreeding flocks that wander widely in search of insects and berries in late summer then work their way southward and downslope throughout the fall.

RANGE Mountain Bluebirds breed in open subalpine forests on the upper west slope, then over the crest and down the east side from aspen-edged meadows out into pinyon-juniper woodlands on arid hillsides. Postbreeding flocks are commonly seen at upper elevations until mid-October, but by early November nearly all have retreated to wintering grounds throughout the Central Valley and southern California. Rare in winter, but return to low elevations around the Sierra Nevada in early March and begin breeding or moving to higher elevation breeding locations as soon as the snow melts, usually by mid-April. **WEST SLOPE:** Varying numbers winter in open fields and oak woodlands at the lower edge of the foothills, usually numbering in the single digits in the central Sierra Nevada but seen by the dozens in the Kern River Valley and southern locations. Transients are occasionally observed around low to mid-elevation meadows from mid-February to mid-May, and from mid-October to mid-November, but they primarily breed above 8000 ft. **EAST SLOPE:** Fairly rare in winter with most records coming from Sierra Valley and Bishop (where several hundred may linger in mild winters). In early March, they become common in valley bottoms all along the east side, where they remain until they start moving upslope in late March–April. Most breed from about 6000 ft to tree line, but they have been reported breeding as high as 12,000 ft. Common everywhere until they suddenly leave or retreat to valley bottoms by late October.

Townsend's Solitaire *Myadestes townsendi*

LIFE HISTORY It is a rare and special treat to hear the loud warbling songs of Townsend's Solitaires in the high mountains. These somber, gray thrushes will sing briefly from high treetops on forested rocky ridges then drop down into the understory to feed quietly with their mates, leaving you wondering which species sang such sweet, cascading songs. Solitaires may be observed flycatching for aerial insects from exposed branches, or flitting silently through the open understory in search of insects on the ground or on the surfaces of leaves and bark.

They linger at lower elevations in the spring until snow melts at higher elevations because many of them nest on or near the ground, but as soon as possible they move upslope to breed in montane coniferous forests. Pair bonds are formed in April, when most of them are still waiting at lower elevations, but within a month pairs arrive on their breeding grounds and begin nesting. For their nests females may scoop out a little dirt shelf among a snarl of exposed roots or on a dirt bank where they place their simple cup nests of loosely woven twigs, rootlets, pine needles, and fine grasses. They incubate 3–5 eggs for 12 days, with males feeding them the whole time. Young birds fledge in 10–12 days, and are fed by the parents for two weeks, with the broods being divided in half and cared for by individual parents. Because many ground nests are discovered by predators, solitaires rear at least two broods each summer and some are still nesting in July. In August, adults and immatures wander together in loose groups but by September they head downslope and start defending winter territories.

Other than breeding, the central aspect of the solitaire's year is the acquisition and defense of winter feeding territories from September to March. Their primary foods at this season are juniper berries (sometimes 100 percent of their diet) on the east slope, or miscellaneous berries of foothill chaparral and oak woodlands (such as toyon, madrone, and mistletoe) on the west slope. Finding a rich patch of berries can mean the difference between life and death, so each bird fiercely defends an individual territory, singing loudly and sitting on prominent perches so they can advertise their presence and chase away intruders. By late March they stop defending these territories and start looking for mates.

RANGE Townsend's Solitaires are primarily restricted to the arid West, where their range mostly overlaps the range of junipers. In the Sierra Nevada they breed on both slopes in montane and subalpine forests, and occasionally in the Alpine Zone, from 5000–10,000 ft. Nearly all descend to the foothills or adjacent valley bottoms in winter, with most west-slope breeders crossing over the crest to winter in juniper woodlands with birds that bred on the east side. **WEST SLOPE:** Generally uncommon and sparsely distributed at all seasons. Winter in small numbers in oak woodlands and chaparral-lined canyons at low elevations, with a few lingering as high as 9000 ft (where they eat Sierra juniper berries); slightly more common in the desert foothills of the southern Sierra Nevada. **EAST SLOPE:** Widespread wintering birds among junipers on arid slopes and flats where they are fairly common; uncommon to rare in other forested habitats as high as 9000 ft. Breed at higher elevations. An excellent example of their local distribution patterns can be shown by comparing their reversed status at Lake Tahoe and at nearby Sierra Valley; wintering solitaires are fairly common in the lower elevation Sierra Valley from late summer through March, then in April solitaires show up to breed at the higher elevations around Lake Tahoe, where they remain fairly common until late summer.

HERMIT THRUSH *Catharus guttatus*

LIFE HISTORY These denizens of dark, shaded forests have an intriguing life history in the Sierra Nevada. Paler, grayish-backed birds start arriving from Mexico in late April and become widespread breeders in the mountains by May, foraging and nesting in all types of coniferous forest from above the foothills to treeline. These birds quickly depart in mid- to late August, and after a brief lull in early September, an entirely different population of darker, brownish-backed birds start arriving from the north in mid-September, then spend the winter foraging in the moist, brushy thickets of the foothills, and head back north in early April. Hermit Thrushes are found in their lowest numbers in April and September, when stragglers from the two populations briefly overlap each other.

Breeding males arrive a few weeks early to establish territories amid the brushy understories of conifer forests; they can be found in a wide variety of habitats from dark stands of giant sugar pines and firs at lower elevations to open and scattered pockets of lodgepole and white-bark pines at higher elevations. True to their nature, Hermit Thrushes prefer shaded forest interiors, but within these habitats they seek out edges where they glean insects from bushes, or from the ground where they hop along, silently scanning and flicking leaves aside with their bills.

Hermit Thrushes are difficult to see because they stay behind screens of tangled branches, but you will often hear their clucking *tchup chup chup* calls; and in the spring males sing ethereal songs that are one of the most diagnostic sounds of summer afternoons in the mountains. These serene flutelike songs have been described as *Oh holy holy, ah, purity purity, eeh, sweetly sweetly.*

When they arrive, females intentionally invade male territories then signal their acceptance of a male by not fleeing his hostile respons-es. After several days of chasing the female in circles, a male will gradu-ally come to accept her presence on his territory by the third or fourth day, and she can begin to build a small bulky nest on the ground or as high as 6 ft on the branches of small conifers or bushes. Females incu-bate 3–6 eggs for 12 days; males stand constant guard and warn them of approaching danger while bringing them food and bits of new nesting material. Young birds fledge at 12 days of age, but nothing is known of their lives after they leave the nest.

Migrating and wintering thrushes are rare to fairly common in the brushy thickets and chaparral stands of the foothills, where they stay in shaded interior reaches searching for berries such as toyon, ma-drone, manzanita, or poison oak, and whatever insects they find.

Note: *The elusive* **Swainson's Thrush** *was, until the 1920s, a fairly com-mon breeder in the Sierra Nevada, at least in areas where there are good records such as Yosemite National Park and Lake Tahoe. Then the breeding population seemed to completely disappear until around 1990, when singing males once again began to be reported from scattered loca-tions; however, it is hard to tell if they reappeared or if more intensive* *surveys simply found them in remote sites. They nest in willow thickets near streams, lakes, and wet meadows in the Mixed Conifer and Upper Montane Zones on both slopes. Currently known to breed at a few montane sites along the east side from west of Bishop to Plumas County, being found most dependably around Bassetts Station and Gold Lakes Basin, but quickly departing by early August. Spring migrants are fairly common in the Kern River Valley and along the east side.*

RANGE Hermit Thrushes are widespread breeders in western and northern North America with the entire population shifting south in winter. Summer visitors are fairly common in coniferous forests from above the foothills to treeline throughout the Sierra Nevada. Migrating birds are found at lower elevations of both slopes in the fall, and by December those that remain are almost entirely restricted to the lower foothills of the west slope. **WEST SLOPE:** Widespread winter residents below snowline, usually below 3000 ft. Widespread summer residents from lower limits of the Mixed Conifer Zone to the Subalpine Zone, approximately 4000–10,000 ft. **EAST SLOPE:** Widespread breeders from 6000–10,000 ft, nesting in conifer forests, occasionally in aspen groves and mountain mahogany thickets. Breeding birds leave by the end of August but migrants from the north linger in small numbers on the east slope until late November with a few records around Bishop through the winter.

AMERICAN ROBIN *Turdus migratorius*

LIFE HISTORY Few sounds in the Sierra Nevada are as enchanting and uplifting as the lively, musical songs of American Robins ringing through mountain forests and canyons. Even when the ground is still covered in snow and ice, their lilting *cheerily cheerily cheer up cheer up* songs signal the coming spring, then during the warmer months they rival, and perhaps even surpass, Hermit Thrushes as the characteristic sound of summer in the mountains.

Huge numbers of robins nest in every forested habitat from low-elevation woodlands to scattered patches of trees near the Sierra Nevada crest. They first establish territories with a flourish of song and squabbling in April, and by May have launched into a busy nesting season that extends through July and may entail raising 2–3 broods. Nesting robins favor a combination of trees for perching and nesting, and moist open ground where they find ground-dwelling insects and worms as well as a supply of mud for their nests. They nest from the ground to the tops of any type of tree, but most nests are located just under the bulk of a tree's foliage for some protection from sun and rain.

Females spend about a week constructing deep cup nests with outer walls of dry grasses and twigs, and inner foundations of mud that they mold to their body shape by sitting in the nest and rotating around. Long after the nesting season is over you may spot one of these durable nests sitting on a tree branch. Females incubate their 3–4 eggs for 13 days, and although males rarely feed females on the nest, males play a larger role in feeding the nestlings both on the nest and for about 3 weeks after they leave the nest.

Adults molt as soon as they are done breeding, then in September join growing flocks of adults and immatures that migrate south or wander together in the winter. Flocks play a major role in robins' lives, mostly during the nonbreeding season but even in the breeding season when males roost communally at night. Flocks of hundreds to thousands (sometimes hundreds of thousands) of robins forage together in the day and fly to roosting sites to sleep together at night. The composition and distribution of these flocks is highly variable in the winter, as robins mingle with each other in different combinations and move actively over large areas in search of unfrozen ground and crops of berries such as toyon, manzanita, madrone, dogwood, and bitter cherry (on the west side) or juniper (on the east side). Due to their sheer numbers and habit of regurgitating or defecating seeds in new locations, robins play a significant ecological role by dispersing entire crops of seeds across the landscape.

Note: *Superficially similar to robins,* Varied Thrushes *breed from Oregon to Alaska. They are irregular winter visitors to the Sierra Nevada from early October to late May, with most occurring in foothill woodlands and lower elevation mixed conifer forests on the west slope. Some years they are fairly common though thinly dispersed; other times they are absent for one or more years in a row. When present, they are rare on the east slope from early October to mid-December.*

RANGE American Robins are one of the most widely distributed and abundant birds in North America. Breeding birds are common in nearly all forested habitats in the Sierra Nevada from late February to September while wintering birds are irregularly distributed below the snowline in winter. It is thought that most of the breeding and wintering birds are from separate populations but this is poorly understood. WEST SLOPE: Common and widespread breeders, but concentrated in the conifer forests of the Mixed Conifer and Upper Montane Zones, and only locally common at higher and lower elevations. Nonbreeding flocks wander among foothill woodlands, grasslands, and chaparral-covered hillsides, but they are highly mobile and unpredictable; ranging from extremely abundant to absent, but this changes year to year and even month to month. **EAST SLOPE:** Basically follow the same pattern as on the west slope, except that wintering flocks wander in search of juniper crops.

THRASHERS (Mimidae)

SAGE THRASHER *Oreoscoptes montanus*

LIFE HISTORY Once known as Mountain Mockingbirds, these small thrashers of the vast sagebrush flats in the Intermountain West are now more accurately, but less evocatively, named Sage Thrashers. Their entire life, at least in the breeding season, is so closely tied to sagebrush they are considered sagebrush-obligates, and if you want to find these thrashers you will almost certainly be rewarded if you search the flats and valleys along the east side of the Sierra Nevada.

East of the Sierra Nevada they first appear in early March and by the end of the month their lovely, long, melodious songs are carrying far and wide across the sagebrush. Typical of the thrasher family, these songs contain many complex elements, including fragments of other bird songs that thrashers mimic. Sage Thrashers are dully streaked and dusky gray so they can be hard to spot amid the sagebrush, even when males are stridently proclaiming themselves from the tops of tall shrubs, but as soon as they launch into the dramatic flights they use to establish their territories and attract mates, they cannot be missed. Males fly in exaggerated undulating circles repeatedly around their territories, singing as they fly, then landing and flashing their quivering wings over their bodies. Then, if suddenly alarmed, they drop to the ground and run away rather than fly.

Although they are little studied and poorly known, it seems that both sexes help build bulky nests either on the ground or in tall shrubs (nearly always in sagebrush, but occasionally in other locally available shrubs). Both sexes help incubate the 4–5 eggs for about 12 days. Parents catch most of the insects they eat and feed their chicks by foraging on the ground, and when they fly back to their nests with food, they drop to the ground and secretively walk the final stretch. Chicks fledge in 11–14 days, then remain near the nest and are fed by adults for at least another week, but there is no other information on the lives of young birds. Most pairs raise two clutches of eggs, one in May and another in late June. By mid-summer, thrashers may form small flocks that gather to supplement their diets with fruits and berries (such as currants) and as many insects as they can find.

RANGE Sage Thrashers are almost entirely restricted to the interior West during the breeding season, with a short migration south into the Southwest and northern Mexican deserts. Postbreeding and migrating birds are notorious for wandering out of their normal range and can show up as far away as the Pacific and Atlantic coasts. **WEST SLOPE:** Transients are very rarely reported but could show up almost anywhere. Rare in the Kern River Valley in fall and winter, and spring migrants are uncommon in April. **EAST SLOPE:** Possible in any habitat dominated by tall sagebrush but most observations occur in two distinct locations, from Honey Lake to Sierra Valley in the north, and from Mono Lake to Bishop in the south. First arrive in March, then common from April–August, with some birds lingering until mid-October. Normally absent in November and December, but there are a couple January and February sightings from the Owens Valley.

CALIFORNIA THRASHER *Toxostoma redivivum*

LIFE HISTORY Few people ever see or know anything about these secretive thrashers. Except for short bouts of singing from the tops of shrubs, these large thrashers have little reason to reveal themselves or leave the dense cover of impenetrable chaparral thickets. Their very loud, extraordinarily rich songs, full of many musical phrases and fragments of other bird songs, make them one of the most accomplished singers in North America. Both sexes sing frequently, starting with the first winter rains in November, to help defend their territory and if two pairs meet at a territorial boundary, they may sing sternly at each other for a sustained period of time. One early naturalist fittingly rendered their song as *kick'-it-now, kick'-it-now, shut'-up, shut'-up, dor'-o-thy, dor'-o-thy*. They also make a variety of other sounds, including their common *chupp* call.

Pairs probably mate for life and are year-round residents on their territories. They live, nest, and feed exclusively within the confines of low-elevation chaparral thickets on the west slope. In the summer they forage for insects on the ground, using their long, curved bills to sweep back and forth through the leaf litter with vigorous sideways arcs, tossing leaves aside and making a noisy racket. Then they switch to a diet of berries from late summer through winter, feeding on the abundant berries found in chaparral, including many poison oak berries.

By late February, they initiate an extended breeding season in which they raise two clutches of eggs between February and June. Their nests are stout platforms of coarse twigs which are well hidden in dense shrubs. Both sexes construct the nest and help incubate their 3–4 eggs for about 14 days. They are very protective parents, sitting tight on the eggs until closely approached then dropping to the ground and running off at the last second. One of their most feared nest predators are scrub-jays, so they launch strong and fierce attacks, sometimes killing them.

Young birds fledge in about 14 days, and even though they can run immediately, it takes a week before they can fly well. Parents continue to feed their fledglings for up to 3 weeks although females may start a second brood while the males finish caring for the first brood. Young birds remain on their parents' territories for several months until they are chased off.

NOTE: *A few breeding pairs of* Bendire's Thrashers *can be found from April through July along Kelso Valley Road in eastern Kern County, where they occur among Joshua trees and desert shrubs.* Le Conte's Thrashers *are uncommon residents in desert-scrub habitats in the South Fork Kern River Valley and in the Owens Valley as far north as Bishop.*

RANGE California Thrashers are entirely restricted to chaparral habitats of California and northern Baja California. WEST SLOPE: Their exact distribution and numbers are difficult to assess, but they are locally common on chaparral-covered slopes and canyons below 3000 ft. Populations could be patchily distributed because they do not seem to occur in all available habitats. They have been reported as high as 4000 ft but are extremely rare transients at these elevations. In the South Fork Kern River Valley they occur east towards Walker Pass, where they sometimes slip over to the east slope. EAST SLOPE: Very rarely reported on the east side of Walker Pass and on the east side of the Sierra Nevada as far north as Sand Canyon and Ninemile Canyon.

STARLINGS (Sturnidae)

EUROPEAN STARLING *Sturnus vulgaris*

LIFE HISTORY Although they are surprisingly beautiful birds, starlings are a perfect example of what can go wrong when an animal is introduced to a new area. They may have some interesting ecological roles in their native land, but they have proven an unmitigated disaster in the New World. From the 80–100 starlings introduced to New York City's

Central Park in 1890–91, the population has grown to an estimated 200 million starlings in North America. The problem is not their sheer numbers, nor their feeding habits, but the fact that they nest in tree cavities, which are a scarce resource. Many of our native cavity-nesting birds have been massively overwhelmed by the much more aggressive starlings, and in some areas there is hardly a nook or cranny not occupied by noisy, messy starlings.

Starlings have short, stocky bodies and strong, sharp bills to help them forage for invertebrates, berries, fruits, and grains in open, short-grass meadows and pastures. These opportunistic birds do especially well around stables, agricultural fields, and pastures where there are grains and where the grasses have been grazed down. They are often observed in the company of cows and horses.

Most of the year, starlings feed and roost in flocks, often traveling great distances to join other flocks at large communal roosts each night, then traveling back to their favorite feeding areas in the morning. Flocks form at the end of the nesting season, gradually growing in size as juveniles and adults finish nesting. By late fall, flocks start moving toward favorable wintering areas.

Males head back to their breeding locations in March or April, often shifting from agricultural areas and towns into native habitats where they seek out tree cavities and old woodpecker holes. They favor forest edges near meadows and fields, selecting cavities then filling them with nesting materials as they sing to attract newly arriving females. Starlings are extremely talented singers and readily mimic other birds, mixing fragments of other bird songs into a constant mix of whistles, screams, liquid notes, clicks, and rattles. Pet starlings can mimic any household sound, including music and human speech.

The breeding season is highly synchronized within each population, but most eggs are laid from mid-April to mid-May. The 4–5 eggs are incubated for 12 days, with females incubating at night and the pair switching off every 10–30 minutes all day long. Young birds fledge at 21 days of age and after several days of being fed by their parents they leave to join flocks with other young birds and nonbreeding adults. Many pairs immediately raise a second brood.

RANGE European Starlings are native to Europe and Asia, but were introduced to North America in 1890, spreading across the continent and reaching California in 1942. They were found at Mono Lake in 1947 and in Yosemite Valley in 1966, then becoming widespread and common in the Sierra Nevada over the next couple decades. According to Christmas Bird Count data, their winter numbers seem to have stabilized in the region in the last 10–20 years, but it is possible that they continue to expand their breeding range when they move into the mountains each summer. Common to abundant year-round residents in the lower foothills and valley bottoms though some move upslope from April–August. **WEST SLOPE:** Generally common year-round residents below the Mixed Conifer Zone and below 3000 ft, being mainly found around towns, ranches, and agricultural areas rather than in large areas of native habitat. Breeding birds may be locally common during the summer at higher elevations around towns, human settlements, camps, and stables. **EAST SLOPE:** Common to abundant year-round residents on lower slopes and valley bottoms, especially near agricultural areas. Breeding birds are often observed nesting in cottonwood and aspen cavities from April–August, generally below 7000 ft, with those moving upslope to breed returning downslope before winter.

PIPITS (Motacillidae)

AMERICAN PIPIT *Anthus rubescens*

LIFE HISTORY American Pipits have a pretty simple story: They forage for insects and a few seeds on bare open ground and short-grass meadows. In the winter they gather in large, loosely associated flocks on agricultural fields or muddy lakeshores, where they are surprisingly inconspicuous until they dash up and wheel across barren ground with sharp *pip-pit* calls. In the breeding season they make a long distance migration to the Arctic, where they breed on barren tundra that looks almost exactly like the fields where they feed all winter.

But in the Sierra Nevada the pipit story took an unexpected turn in 1975 when the first nest ever found in California was discovered at 10,500 ft near Tioga Pass, and then other nests were discovered throughout the High Sierra soon thereafter. Migrating, but not nesting, pipits had been observed in these same well-studied locations for decades, so biologists hypothesize that after a 5000-year absence (due to an episodic global drying period) a small population of breeding pipits re-colonized the Sierra Nevada in the mid-1970s. It is intriguing that these pipits are the same subspecies that breeds in the Rocky Mountains (*A. r. alticola*), rather than the subspecies that winters in the lowlands around the Sierra Nevada then breed north of California in the summer (*A. r. pacificus*).

Pipits nest at extreme elevations so they have a narrow breeding window. They arrive in late April–early May, with males immediately setting up scattered territories in moist alpine meadows near small tarns and lakes. Males engage in frequent long-distance chases, perching on prominent lookout boulders, and singing fast tinkling *chee* notes during exuberant display flights that involve flying steeply up 100 ft then spiraling back down to their perches with wings and tails fully spread.

Females make shallow scrapes on the ground that they ring and then line with bits of dry grasses and sedges. The 4–6 eggs are generally laid in early to mid-June, and females incubate for 14 days while being fed by males who call them over when they have food to offer. Their summer diet consists of insects and invertebrates collected on the ground, and frequently from the surfaces of snowbanks, as the pipits walk and run, making quick dashes and turns with their strong legs. It is thought that their unusually long hind toe is a useful adaptation that helps them walk on snow.

Both parents feed their nestlings for about 14 days on the nest, and then for another 14 days after the young leave the nest and stay well-hidden among grassy clumps. When family groups break up, the young birds join loose flocks with other juveniles, but the adults become secretive because they spend about a month molting and cannot easily fly until they grow new feathers. As soon as the adults are ready to fly again they all seem to leave the high mountains very quickly in September (though some may linger until November in a mild year). Most nests are built in June in any type of tree standing alone or located on a forest edge. Pairs raising second broods may still be actively nesting in August and September.

RANGE American Pipits are common migrants and wintering birds in open barren areas throughout the western and southern United States, then heading north to the arctic or upslope into alpine meadows to breed. A small and very scattered population breeds at 9000–12,000 ft on alpine peaks from Tower Peak on the northern boundary of Yosemite National Park (and irregularly as far north as Mt. Rose and the Desolation Wilderness at Lake Tahoe), to the southern boundary of Sequoia National Park above Mineral King. **WEST SLOPE:** Abundant in the Central Valley and in grazed fields and agricultural areas at the very lowest edges of the foothills during the winter with peak numbers from late September through February, and very few lingering until May. Breeding birds, consisting of a different subspecies, are found on scattered alpine peaks and meadows (on both sides of the Sierra Nevada crest) from late April to late September, sometimes until November.

EAST SLOPE: Very common fall migrants in agricultural areas and valley bottoms from mid-October to November, then lingering irregularly through the winter depending on snowfall. Migrants and wintering birds mostly found around Honey Lake, Sierra Valley, Mono Lake, and Bishop, with many retreating towards Mono Lake and the Owens Valley during the coldest months. Spring migration in late March–early May involves smaller numbers of pipits than in fall.

WAXWINGS (Bombycillidae)

Cedar Waxwing *Bombycilla cedrorum*

LIFE HISTORY These colorful birds, easily overlooked amid groups of robins, are an ephemeral and irregular presence in the Sierra Nevada. Even when perched in trees, flocks of 30–100 waxwings are surprisingly inconspicuous unless you hear them making their high-pitched *bzeee* whistles. These trilling whistles are hard to hear and to the human ear sound like one uniform call, but waxwings actually have 7 types of *bzeee* calls for different social settings.

Waxwings are unique among North American birds in specializing on a diet of simple sugars that they find in ripe fruits and berries (even hummingbirds that drink flower nectars supplement their diets with many insects). They can survive for two months on a diet of fruit sugars alone and are so specialized that they have a hard time digesting other nutrients. Although fruits and berries are a fairly abundant food source, these crops occur in patches and are unpredictable thus forcing waxwings to wander far and wide. Another disadvantage to this diet is that waxwings are prone to intoxication and even death from eating too many fermented fruits later in the season. It is thought that waxwings may find fruit crops by smell, but this aspect of their life history is little studied.

From September to May small flocks of waxwings roam the lower elevations of the Sierra Nevada in search of toyon, mistletoe, and madrone berries (on the west side) or elderberries and juniper berries (on the east side), as well as many other native fruits and berries, and the fruits of exotic ornamental plants in towns and parks. In early May, they switch to a diet of insects that they flycatch in the air or glean from leaf surfaces in preparation for their breeding season. By the end of May, they leave the Sierra Nevada for their breeding grounds that stretch from coastal northwest California to Canada.

There is a nesting record from Bucks Lake (Plumas County) and a cluster of July sightings around Lake Almanor (a month when all waxwings have left for their breeding grounds) that suggests a small population may be breeding in the far northern Sierra Nevada.

Note: *Nesting in northern Canada and Alaska, then wandering south and roaming unpredictably over vast portions of North America, small flocks of* **Bohemian Waxwings** *are highly irregular winter visitors in the Sierra Nevada from late November into early March, with only a few reports every couple years.*

RANGE Cedar Waxwings are highly irregular in terms of their numbers and distribution; abundant some years and some seasons, but nearly absent in others. They begin to disperse southward from their breeding areas in late August, showing up almost everywhere in California in fairly low numbers by September, then becoming increasingly common at lower elevations in October. From December–April, there is a massive influx of birds into low-lying areas west of the Sierra Nevada. They begin to wander back towards their breeding areas (mostly north of California) in May. Except for breeding birds, and a very few stragglers, they are absent from California in June and July. **WEST SLOPE:** Although transient flocks show up at almost any elevation, wintering waxwings are almost entirely restricted to habitats below the Mixed Conifer Zone, and they are particularly common in oak woodlands and mixed chaparral habitats below 3000 ft. Some might breed around Lake Almanor (see above). **EAST SLOPE:** Fall migrants are often seen below 6000 ft in September and October, then may linger in small numbers through the winter, particularly around homesteads and towns where exotic plants provide dependable supplies of berries. There is a brief, and small, movement of northbound waxwings in May.

SILKY-FLYCATCHERS (Ptilogonatidae)

PHAINOPEPLA *Phainopepla nitens*

LIFE HISTORY Oddly crested, with piercing red eyes and shimmering black feathers (males) or mouse-gray feathers (females), Phainopeplas can be found feasting on mistletoe berries and flying insects in live oak and blue oak woodlands or in oak–chaparral habitats on the west slope. They are widespread, year-round residents in these areas but do not appear to defend territories and are seldom predictable. Often the only way to know they are in an area is to hear their unique, question-ing *wurp* calls from among tangled oak branches and chaparral thickets.

Their nesting season begins in late March at the lowest elevations and a month later at higher elevations, but they can reportedly rear 2–3 broods and nesting activities have been observed as late as Septem-ber in the Sierra Nevada. In the "hot" deserts of Southern California, Phainopeplas may have two nesting seasons: first breeding in desert habitats in February–April then moving into oak woodlands to breed again in May–July, but this behavior has never been documented in the resident Sierra Nevada population.

As part of their courtship, males construct compact, shallow nests, often placing them in loose colonies with about a dozen other pairs that cooperate to chase away nest predators like scrub-jays. These nests have a gray appearance because they are made of plant fibers, spiderwebs, and slender stems, but they are often buried deep inside mistletoe clumps and hard to find. Females may help finish nests as they lay 2–3 eggs that hatch in 14 days, with both parents equally sharing incubation duties. Young birds leave the nest at 20 days of age but noth-ing is known about the lives of immature birds.

RANGE Phainopeplas are widespread residents in southern California, with populations extending north along the Coast Range and west slope of the Sierra Nevada. **WEST SLOPE:** Uncommon year-round resi-dents of the Foothill Oak Zone below 3000 ft, though locally common in some areas. Phainopeplas seem to be generally restricted to the low-est elevations from November to May, then move upslope and wander more widely from June or July to early November (the span of time when they occur in their lowest numbers at many locations); though month-by-month abundance records for every county in the Sierra Ne-vada (as listed on the eBird website) show no consistent patterns, even between neighboring counties. In the Kern River Valley, which is a fair-ly discrete area with many excellent observations, Phainopeplas seem to move eastward and upslope in May and June, are present in fairly low numbers in August–October, then show up in sizable numbers from November to at least February (perhaps due to northern birds moving south for the winter). **EAST SLOPE:** Absent on the east side from late October until early April, when they start moving into the southern end of the Owens Valley. By May they wander north to Bishop, where they are regular though scarce until September (rarely October). A few of these northbound visitors seem to overshoot, with one extraordinary record near Woodfords in late May and several Mono Lake records in

June. There are two breeding records from July at Hogback Creek west of Independence, and they should be looked for elsewhere on the west side of the Owens Valley.

WOOD-WARBLERS (Parulidae)

ORANGE-CROWNED WARBLER *Oreothlypis celata*

LIFE HISTORY In the foothill oak woodlands of the west slope there is a moment when spring arrives, and that moment is marked by the boisterous and sudden appearance of Orange-crowned Warblers. One day there may be a single bird, flitting nervously through the still-bare oak branches while singing its diagnostic trilling song, and within days Orange-crowns are everywhere. They are the first heralds of the coming waves of migrant songbirds that dally behind them. It is almost miraculous but every year they seem to time their arrival almost to the day that the leaves of black oaks and blue oaks begin to break bud and unfurl, and these are the leaves soon covered with millions of newly hatched, green, oak moth caterpillars that will sustain the warblers and their hungry nestlings. As Orange-crowns forage, they rush back and forth snapping up caterpillars, leaning this way and that for better looks, hanging upside down at times, and poking their long, sharp bills into leaf tangles.

Male Orange-crowned Warblers begin arriving in early to mid-March and are followed a few weeks later by females because this crop of easy food fades quickly and Orange-crowns want to raise their nestlings while food is abundant. An added pressure is that the earliest-arriving males will have the best breeding success, but if they arrive too early they may be trapped in late snowstorms.

Females seek out brushy habitats surrounded or overshadowed by oaks and build small cup nests of leaves and twigs that they place on the ground, well hidden under overhanging vegetation, where they incubate 4–5 eggs for 12 days. Both parents feed their nestlings a steady diet of soft caterpillars and the young birds fledge in 11 days. The lives of young birds are largely unknown, but both adults and juveniles continue feeding in the foothills until caterpillar numbers start to decline in late May. At this point they make a quick journey upslope into the high mountains, and perhaps even over the crest, in search of moist montane willow thickets with fresh leaves and abundant insects. From July to mid-August, Orange-crowns outnumber other warblers in nearly every habitat from 6000–11,000 ft.

RANGE Breeding Orange-crowned Warblers are widespread and common across western and northern North America, where they are the most abundant warblers in many locations. During the winter they are fairly common in the lowlands west of the Sierra Nevada. **WEST SLOPE:** Breeding birds are common in brushy, foothill oak woodlands up to 3000 ft, and occasionally into the lower edges of the Mixed Conifer Zone, from early April to late May (or early June), then moving upslope and becoming common in the mountains until late August. Increasingly smaller numbers linger in the high mountains until mid-October. Very small numbers may spend the winter in various habitats below 4000 ft. **EAST SLOPE:** Absent on the east side in winter except for a dozen or so that linger around Bishop. The first northbound stragglers appear in March, clustering around Bishop and venturing north to Mono Lake, and by April they are found along the entire east side and probably breed in many moist canyons north of Bishop. Many move upslope in June but they are commonly seen migrants at all elevations in August-September; most have left by late October.

NASHVILLE WARBLER *Oreothlypis ruficapilla*

LIFE HISTORY Right on the tail of the main rush of Orange-crowned Warblers come Nashville Warblers, slightly delaying their arrival because they nest in cooler and higher elevation forested habitats. Nashvilles occur in two separate populations in North America, but the western population is so little studied that almost everything known about their life history is based on the eastern population.

In the Sierra Nevada they arrive in great numbers during the first week of April and quickly settle on dry wooded slopes where an understory of ceanothus, manzanita, kitkitdizze (mountain misery), and other dense shrubs fill in the open spaces under towering oaks, pines, and firs. Singing males are soon heard everywhere in the upper reaches of the Foothill Oak Zone, throughout the Mixed Conifer Zone, and into the lower reaches of the Upper Montane Zone. At least in the Sierra Nevada, Nashvilles seem to be closely associated with black oaks (almost to the exclusion of elevation or other types of neighboring trees), perhaps because there is an abundant supply of oak moth caterpillars on the newly emerging oak leaves. To some extent, however, they may be generalists because they are also found around willow thickets and montane chaparral though it is not clear if these are preferred nesting habitats.

Songs consist of two-parted phrases that conclude with a trill: *sweet-ah, sweet-ah, sweet-ah, swee swee swee*, and may be followed by dry, chipping call notes. In early May, females spend about 7 days building tidy nests of leaves and moss tucked against plant stems or under low vegetation on flat ground. Males watch closely and sing from nearby perches but typically play no role until the 4–5 eggs hatch in 11 days, then both sexes feed the nestlings until they leave the nest in 9-11 days. The lives of young birds are unknown, but Nashville Warblers seem to remain on their breeding ground through June, then join mixed-species flocks that spend the rest of the summer foraging for insects at higher elevations. They are conspicuous members of foraging songbird flocks seen throughout the Upper Montane and Subalpine Zones during July.

Note: *Looking like pale Nashville Warblers with reduced yellow patches,* **Virginia's Warblers** *are rare visitors to the east slope. Most are seen in May and August and probably represent wandering birds, but they may be irregular breeders south of Mono Lake with a few confirmed nesting records from Lee Vining Canyon and along Onion Valley Road west of Independence.*

RANGE Nashville Warblers breed from the mountains of northern California to southern British Columbia. A few early migrants show up on the west slope in March, but most start arriving in early April. Breeding gets underway by late April, with eggs being laid in early May. Nashvilles seem to remain on their breeding grounds in May and June, but in July they head upslope and are common in brushy habitats and forest edges to treeline on both slopes. Many leave the Sierra Nevada by the end of August, but small numbers linger through September. **WEST SLOPE:** Common breeders in the upper Foothill Oak Zone through the Mixed Conifer Zone, mostly 3000–5000 ft; may be locally common to at least 6700 ft but their upper breeding limits are not clearly understood because it is hard to tell whether a bird has bred locally or moved upslope after breeding. **EAST SLOPE:** Breeding status on the east side is not clear. Spring migrants first arrive in the Owens Valley in April, and during May are at least briefly widespread in lowlands along the entire east side. Clusters of sightings in June, when they should be on breeding territories, suggest that they regularly breed around Mammoth Lakes, June Lake, Lee Vining Canyon, and Lundy Canyon. North of Lake Tahoe they are widespread and common breeders in riparian habitats.

YELLOW WARBLER *Dendroica petechia*

LIFE HISTORY It is somehow fitting that the fast, whispery songs of these intensely yellow warblers are often rendered *sweet-sweet-sweet-I'm-so-sweet*, and that they intersperse their songs with emphatic *chip* notes as if determined to call attention to themselves. Yet their summertime visits to the mountains are all too short, for Yellow Warblers arrive late and depart early, seldom joining mixed flocks with other warblers and songbirds during the summer. Males first arrive in mid- to late April, but their numbers do not increase until May, when they become quite common in cottonwoods, willows, alders, and aspen thickets along streams and wet meadows. Although primarily associated with willows, they can also be surprisingly abundant in patches of dry montane chaparral where they nest among manzanita and ceanothus.

Males spend about a week on their breeding grounds before beginning to sing and defend territories. They may be observed foraging for small insects that they pick from leaf surfaces, catch from the air, or hover to snatch from inaccessible branch tips. Females show up about 10 days later, pairing up with males and beginning to build nests within 2–3 days of arrival. Courtship is apparently a brief affair with males making slow stalling flights in front of potential mates.

Females build deep cup nests of grasses and bark strips lined with hairs and fibers that are located in the upright forks of bushes or small trees, especially willows. The 4–5 eggs are mostly laid in late May to mid-June, but nests with eggs have been found in late June at higher elevations. Many nests are parasitized by Brown-headed Cowbirds, but Yellow Warblers usually detect the foreign eggs and quickly abandon their nest and build a new one on top of the old one, sometimes repeating this process each time they are parasitized and creating multi-tiered nests (nests with 5 tiers have been found).

Successful nests are incubated for 11 days, with the females being very active and making many short trips to forage during the daytime even though males may also feed them at the nest. Nestlings are fed by both parents for about 9 days until they leave the nest, and they remain with their parents for up to 3 more weeks. Nothing is known about the lives of young birds, but in the Sierra Nevada it seems that they start leaving in July.

RANGE Yellow Warblers breed abundantly across the northern United States, Canada, and Alaska, with part of the breeding population extending south along the Sierra Nevada. Perhaps due to their far-northern breeding grounds, they are fairly late migrants with peak numbers moving north in May and some still migrating in early June. Most seem to arrive on their breeding grounds in the Sierra Nevada by mid-May, with the nesting season fully underway by early June. It seems that they breed and then leave because numbers drop off in July and they are relatively scarce in the mountains in August (though still regularly reported at low elevations and at Lake Tahoe). Interestingly enough, numbers seem to increase dramatically in September, which may represent a wave of southbound migrants from the north. Alternately, molting adults may just be highly secretive in August then conspicuous again when they start feeding in preparation for their own migration. In October they are scarce or absent on the west side, but on the east side they linger north of Mono Lake until mid-October, and south of Mono Lake until late October. **WEST SLOPE:** Common and widespread breeders as high as 6500 ft, possibly breeding locally at higher elevations. **EAST SLOPE:** Common and widespread breeders as high as 7500 ft, maybe as high as 9000 ft, and mostly north of Bishop.

YELLOW-RUMPED WARBLER *Dendroica coronata*

LIFE HISTORY As the most resilient and adaptable of all local warblers, Yellow-rumps bring an unexpected bit of cheer to dreary winter days with their bright *chip* calls and lively antics. They have an amazing ability to tolerate cold, and on the east side they may linger far into the winter by hanging out around hot springs. Part of their extraordinary physiology is their ability to digest wax, a rare trait among insect-eating birds, which allows them to supplement their diets with berries and fruits in the absence of insects. On the west side they will eat small berries, like poison oak and honeysuckle, while on the east side they can feed on abundant juniper berries.

In addition to being dietary generalists, Yellow-rumps are not picky about how they find food. They forage in nearly every niche from the highest treetops to ground level, finding insects on almost every surface and crevice, and they are frequently seen flycatching from high perches. On rainy days when the ground and leaves are too wet, they readily cling to tree trunks and probe for hidden insects in the bark. When insects try to avoid the warblers by free-falling from branches Yellow-rumps will often chase them by dropping towards the ground like fluttering leaves in avid pursuit.

Many Yellow-rumps spend the winter in low-lying valleys around the Sierra Nevada, especially on the west side where they freely roam upslope into foothill forests. From late March into April their numbers begin to pick up as migrants move north and breeding birds flock together in anticipation of the snowmelt at higher elevations, but by May even their highest elevation breeding grounds have opened up and they are singing on territories.

Although they are found in every coniferous forest type in the Sierra Nevada (except gray pine on the west side and pinyon pine on the east side), their territories are relatively large so they end up being thinly dispersed. Still, the slow, spiraling warbling songs of males ring out through mountain forests everywhere, making them the most widespread breeding warblers in the Sierra Nevada.

Females arrive about a week later, but even though these hardy birds may be the first warblers on their montane breeding grounds, they do not necessarily breed any earlier because they still have to wait for food supplies to become available. Nesting dates in the Sierra Nevada range from mid-May to late July depending on elevation and snow. Females build loose or compact nests of twigs, needles, and grasses on horizontal branches near the trunk, usually in conifers. Males sing nearby and may occasionally add a few items. Females incubate 4–5 eggs for 12 days, both parents feeding nestlings that leave the nest in 10–14 days, and then feeding the young birds for another two weeks. Little else is known about their breeding biology beyond these few bare facts.

After the breeding season, Yellow-rumps join mixed-species flocks and wander the mountains from 12,000 ft to the lowest valley floors, utilizing every habitat from sagebrush flats, marshes and meadows, to alpine rock fields. They linger in the high mountains until winter storms push them downslope, often descending in great numbers in a single day.

RANGE Yellow-rumped Warblers are common breeding birds in montane coniferous forests throughout western North America; later wintering in coastal and low-lying areas. **WEST SLOPE:** Uncommon to fairly common below 4000 ft from November–March, though their numbers vary from year-to-year. Breed from 4000–10,000 ft. **EAST SLOPE:** Generally rare, or at least irregular, in winter, though they linger until cold weather drives them to warmer regions. Numbers pick up again in late March, and they are common from April–October. Most nest from about 6000–10,000 ft.

Black-throated Gray Warbler
Dendroica nigrescens

LIFE HISTORY Much of the basic life history of these relatively tame and easily observed birds is unknown and unstudied. For example, almost nothing is known of their breeding biology except that females make deep cup nests of twigs, grasses, and feathers and lay 3–4 eggs. Males do not seem to help out but they have been observed following females closely and scolding them continuously.

In the Sierra Nevada, Black-throateds are common breeders on the west slope, where they variously overlap with Orange-crowned, Yellow-rumped, and Hermit Warblers, but seem to favor drier and more open woodlands with a brushy understory. In common with Orange-crowns and Nashvilles, they associate with oaks where they forage tirelessly for the small, green, oak moth caterpillars that are superabundant in April and May.

They arrive on their breeding grounds in early April at lower elevations and by early May at higher elevations, with males immediately announcing their arrival with buzzy *weezy-weezy-weezy-weezy-weet* songs. On the west slope they are common breeders in almost every forest that contains oaks, from canyon live oak or blue oak woodlands, to black oaks mixed with a wide range of conifers. They remain common until late July or early August, but unlike other warblers they seldom join the mixed-species flocks that wander willow thickets and forests near treeline. Most seem to leave the region in late August after making a brief appearance on their former breeding grounds where males may even sing for a few days before departing.

RANGE Black-throated Gray Warblers are common and widespread breeders in dry open woodlands throughout the West, then wintering in Mexico. **WEST SLOPE:** A few early migrants show up in late March-early April, and they become very common and conspicuous in the foothills by mid-April. Most of these males continue north, or head upslope as food becomes available in early May, but many remain to breed at lower elevations, where nesting activity has been observed at 3000 ft in early May. Their prime nesting range is from 3000–5000 ft, but they could be locally common to about 7000 ft. During the summer they are inconspicuous but probably common, though their movements and distribution are not known. Most leave in August, with some lingering until late October. **EAST SLOPE:** Generally uncommon to rare on the east side from April–August, with some lingering until late October. They breed in pinyon pine-juniper woodlands of the Great

Basin and are thought to be local breeders adjacent to or on the slopes of the Sierra Nevada in these same habitats. For example, clusters of sightings around places like Bishop and Sierra Valley suggest local breeding, but there are few confirmed nesting records that could be used to map out their actual breeding distribution.

HERMIT WARBLER *Dendroica occidentalis*

LIFE HISTORY Despite their name, Hermit Warblers are gregarious birds that mingle freely with mixed-species flocks the entire year, even traveling south and spending the winter with flocks of small songbirds. Only when breeding do solitary males and seldom-seen females appear to be hermits, and partly because they forage alone in the canopies of somber coniferous forests where few other birds dwell.

These same remote feeding niches, high overhead where birds are hard to watch, ensure that Hermit Warblers are one of our least-known birds. Nearly all aspects of their life history are poorly documented and virtually everything known about their breeding biology in the Sierra Nevada comes from close study of one nesting pair.

Hermit Warblers nest at the same elevations as Black-throated Gray Warblers but are restricted to moist, shaded conifer forests while Black-throateds seek out dry and sunny oak forests. This is an important distinction because their songs are so similar that it is easy to mistake the two species, but Hermits have a faster and higher-pitched song *seezle seezle seezle seezle zeet-zeet.*

In the spring, Hermits appear within a brief window of time from mid-April to early May, promptly settling on their breeding grounds at lower elevations, or just as quickly moving upslope to higher breeding grounds. Their entire lives revolve around treetops so they are little affected by snow depths. In the Sierra Nevada, they breed in the Mixed Conifer and Upper Montane Zones, showing a strong preference for ponderosa pines but using other conifers as well. They forage almost entirely in the upper canopy and, unlike other warblers, the presence or absence of a shrubby understory has no impact on them.

In the breeding season, males establish territories through persistent song and many active chases, and females make cup nests of fine twigs, needles, and spiderwebs, where they incubate 4–5 eggs. Both parents feed their nestlings then split the brood, with each parent taking half the fledglings and feeding them for an unknown amount of time.

Note: *Hermit Warblers are so closely related and similar to* Townsend's Warblers *that the two species hybridize readily where their ranges overlap in Washington and Oregon. In the Sierra Nevada, Townsend's are only passing migrants, making a fleeting appearance in the spring and a more pronounced appearance in the fall, when they are frequently observed mingling with mixed-species flocks and rarely lingering through the winter.*

RANGE Hermit Warblers have the most restricted breeding range of any local warbler, being found only in a narrow belt of conifer forests from the Sierra Nevada to Washington. In the Sierra Nevada they breed only on the west slope as far south as northern Kern County in moist, shaded conifer forests from 4000–7000 ft. **WEST SLOPE:** Migrants arrive in the foothills in large numbers in mid-April, reaching their breeding grounds by late April to mid-May. There is a sudden increase in numbers at higher elevations in mid- to late July, including young birds, so this probably marks the end of the breeding season. By August nearly all, except for a few stragglers, have moved into the upper montane forests of the west side, or subalpine forests on both sides of the crest, where they favor stands of conifers but mingle with other songbirds on forest edges. Some remain through September, at almost any elevation below treeline, but all leave by early October. **EAST SLOPE:** Stray spring migrants are occasionally observed in valley bottoms in April and May, but fall migration is slightly more pronounced. Most July records are in the north, where postbreeding birds moving upslope from the west side may be spilling over the crest. By August, postbreeding birds drift south to low-lying areas of central and southern Sierra Nevada, where they are rare. A few may linger into September or even October.

MacGillivray's Warbler *Oporornis tolmiei*

LIFE HISTORY Always shy and elusive, MacGillivray's Warblers are dependably conspicuous only when males are singing and chasing each other on their territories. Females remain hidden in the dense bushes where these warblers spend all their time.

Although migrating birds sometimes show up in dry brushy areas, these warblers are usually encountered in riparian or willow thickets near streams and wet meadows. They require not only dense, brushy vegetation but also some degree of tree cover. They forage for insects within the innermost portions of bushes and small trees, usually within three feet of the ground.

Males occasionally ascend onto the tops of bushes or onto the low branches of taller trees, where they sing 6–8 buzzy notes *churry churry churry churry cheery cheery.* Both sexes make distinctive sharp, junco-like *tsik* notes when alarmed by intruders.

Their breeding biology is little studied, but females build loosely constructed nests very low in dense bushes, sometimes on or near the ground, with 3–5 eggs being laid from late May to late June, depending on elevation. Females incubate eggs for 12 days then feed the nestlings until they fledge at 8–9 days of age. Nothing is known of the lives of young birds, but in August both adults and juveniles are regularly found in mixed-species flocks moving through willow thickets in subalpine meadows.

RANGE MacGillivray's Warblers breed widely in riparian habitats west of the Rocky Mountains. Despite their secretive habits, they are surprisingly common and widespread breeders in the Sierra Nevada, occurring in many types of wet, brushy habitats at low to mid-elevations on both slopes. They begin arriving at low elevations in great numbers at the very end of April, then increasingly move upslope to their breeding grounds by late May. Surprisingly, in some areas they may even nest on slopes of dry montane chaparral, at least near water. After breeding, they move further upslope to montane meadow edges, many to treeline, in late July and August. There is a noticeable pulse of southbound migrants in mid- to late August then numbers drop off sharply in September, with a few lingering into the first week of October. **WEST SLOPE:** Widespread breeders in wet, brushy areas from 4000–8000 ft. **EAST SLOPE:** Breeding birds may be narrowly restricted to riparian corridors from 6000–8000 ft, and they are scarce or absent south of Bishop. Both spring (May) and fall (August–early October) migrants are uncommon but regular in valley bottoms along the east side.

WILSON'S WARBLER *Wilsonia pusilla*

LIFE HISTORY Despite their status as one of our most common migrants and one of the Sierra Nevada warblers with the broadest breeding ranges, these colorful, perky warblers are relatively uncommon during the breeding season and are almost entirely restricted to pockets of deciduous trees and shrubs near streams and wet meadows. It is always a pleasure to find them during the breeding season when they appear unexpectedly like radiant, golden-yellow jewels amid green leaves.

They are best known as migrants, both in the lowlands in spring, and around montane meadows in late summer when they are sometimes so abundant they seem to drip from every bush. They are eager, fast-moving little warblers, flitting restlessly from branch to branch in constant search for insects, caterpillars, and spiders. Moving quickly, they focus on conspicuous food items and shun the cryptic insects sought by slow-moving warblers. Not only do they glean insects from surfaces, but they hover around branch tips and dart out to snatch flying insects from the air.

Wilson's Warblers arrive in a sudden rush in mid-April, with numbers picking up even more dramatically east of the crest when numerous northbound migrants sweep up the east side in early May. In mid-May those that intend to stay and breed locally begin establishing territories, settling among thickets of willows, alders, aspens, and other riparian trees and shrubs. Males sing fervently, with 4–15 rapid chattering *chee-chee-chee-chee-chee* notes until they attract mates, then fall silent until nest-building nears completion at which point they sing briefly again. In one Sierra Nevada study, 25 percent of the males secured multiple mates (up to three), and these males sang persistently throughout the entire breeding season.

Males and females stay in contact with sharp *chimp* calls as females construct nests on the ground amid overhanging vegetation and dense bushes, sometime during the first half of June. One biologist counted 2500 items in a Wilsons' nest, everything from grasses, leaves, and bark strips, to hairs. Females lay 3–6 eggs in early to late June (or even in July at the highest elevations), then incubate their eggs for 12 days, feeding during short frenzied breaks they take throughout the day, but remaining tightly on the nest if approached and flushing up only at the last second (sometimes doing a broken-wing display as a distraction). Nestlings leave the nest at 9-11 days and parents split the brood, each feeding half the fledglings for up to 3 weeks.

RANGE Wilson's Warblers breed in boreal forests of northern Canada and Alaska with a smaller population nesting far to the south along the Cascade-Sierra axis. In the Sierra Nevada they are abundant spring migrants in April, showing up in almost any brushy or wooded habitat, then widespread but uncommon breeders May–July in riparian habitats from the lower edges of the Mixed Conifer Zone to treeline; they may be more common in the northern half of the Sierra Nevada. In August they move upslope and are common around the edges of montane meadows with other warblers and songbirds. They are still fairly common at all elevations in September, but most have wandered south of Lake Tahoe by this time of year, and all have left by October. **WEST**

SLOPE: Breed from 4000 ft to treeline. **EAST SLOPE:** Breed from about 5000 ft (in the north) and 7000 ft (in the south) to treeline.

SPARROWS (Emberizidae)

GREEN-TAILED TOWHEE *Pipilo chlorurus*

LIFE HISTORY The loud and lively vocalizations of Green-tailed Towhees are one of summer's most characteristic sounds among expansive scrublands of the east slope. There it is a pleasure to see these otherwise secretive and poorly-known birds in full breeding splendor as they scan the terrain from prominent perches, showing off their cinnamon-red crowns and shimmering yellow-green feathers, and "mewing" fitfully if intruders enter their brushy kingdoms.

Due to their reclusive nature, little is known about the full scope of this species' behavior and movements. In the spring they migrate inconspicuously along both slopes, becoming conspicuous only after stopping to breed. They stick close to dense brush at all times and, except for singing and territorial defense, much of their feeding and life history occurs deep within tangled thickets. They occupy a variety of habitats so long as there are large pockets of densely-packed shrubs with thinly dispersed trees, but they favor a mix of shrubs rather than uniform thickets. In drier areas they can be especially numerous among tall bushes in drainages or along the edges of riparian thickets.

Nesting begins in mid-May but may be delayed until early June at higher elevations. Females build relatively large, thick-walled cups that are well hidden on or near the ground, where they lay 4 eggs that they incubate 12 days. Both parents feed the chicks, which leave the nest about 11 days after hatching.

RANGE Green-tailed Towhees are birds of the arid Intermountain West that range from the Rocky Mountains to the east slope of the Sierra Nevada, where some spill over the crest into brushy habitats on the upper west slope. The first migrants show up in mid-April at lower elevations, but the bulk of the breeding population arrives by the end of May. Numbers generally remain consistent until early September (though they become much harder to find once juveniles fledge in July), but taper off quickly by mid-September, with some lingering through October and an occasional individual staying through winter at lower elevations. **WEST SLOPE:** Seldom reported from lower and middle elevations during migration, but they are locally uncommon breeders in montane chaparral above 6000 ft (where they are far outnumbered by breeding Fox Sparrows). They have been found nesting as low as 2500 ft in Nevada County. **EAST SLOPE:** Common and vocal breeding birds from 6000–9500 ft among the extensive stands of mixed shrubs—especially sagebrush, bitterbrush, wild rose, and mountain mahogany—that are abundant on the east side.

Spotted Towhee *Pipilo maculatus*

LIFE HISTORY Like Green-tailed Towhees, Spotted Towhees reside among dense bushes and ascend onto prominent singing perches in the breeding season. But they differ in being much more confiding and curious, frequently wandering from the cover of protective shrubs and often allowing close approach before retreating. Many are common residents around foothill homes and even become daily visitors to backyard bird feeders, where their lively colors and antics make them popular birds.

These stunningly-attired birds are surprisingly well camouflaged in the dappled shade under shrubs, but they often reveal their location with noisy "double-scratching" among the dry leaf litter. By hopping forward then backwards with a scratching motion of their strong legs and feet, they brush aside loose leaves to reveal the invertebrates, fallen seeds, and fruits that comprise their diet. In the breeding season, they find large numbers of beetles this way, and at all seasons they eat the abundant acorns and berries found in their preferred habitats.

Spotted Towhees are common residents in almost every patch of shrubs on low foothill slopes, where their numbers increase sharply in the winter as towhees from higher elevations or northern regions move into the Sierra Nevada. Breeding birds occur with decreasing frequency at higher elevations, and they are uncommon in brushfields and chaparral habitats in the main forested belts on both slopes, where they linger until pushed downslope by cold weather in October.

During the winter, Spotted Towhees often forage in loose groups along with other brush-loving sparrows. Pairs that nest at lower elevations begin to establish territories in February though their breeding season does not begin until April. Nests and eggs can be found from mid-April to early July, but May and June are the peak months when females build well-made ground nests and incubate 3–4 eggs for 12 days. Both sexes feed young birds on the nest for about 9 days, then for another 30 days off the nest.

RANGE Spotted Towhees are widespread and common residents almost everywhere west of the central Great Plains, where they meet Eastern Towhees, their closest relatives. Populations in the northern parts of their range are often migratory, but those in the Sierra Nevada appear to be year-round residents with some altitudinal migration. **WEST SLOPE:** Common residents in the Foothill Oak and lower Mixed Conifer Zones, especially below 4000 ft; uncommon summer residents in montane chaparral of the Upper Montane Zone. Numerous individuals wander as high as treeline in late summer, and they can become fairly common throughout the Upper Montane Zone in September and October before moving downslope for the winter. **EAST SLOPE:** Common residents on the east side, occurring widely in brushy habitats and streamside thickets up to about 7500 ft. The subspecies found on the east slope occasionally wanders over the crest after breeding, and has been reported on the upper west slope in October.

Rufous-crowned Sparrow *Aimophila ruficeps*

LIFE HISTORY If not for this species' distinctive *Dear-Dear-Dear* calls, sometimes made when mildly alarmed by intruders, Rufous-crowned Sparrows would be rarely detected. At best, these secretive birds may be briefly observed as they pop into view when they are singing or curious about an intruder's location, but in general they remain entirely within the confines of protective shrubs and are poorly known. A few anecdotal sightings appear in the literature but no studies or detailed observations have ever been published on the Sierra Nevada population.

Rufous-crowned Sparrows are diagnostic birds of open grassy hillsides, mostly on south-facing slopes in canyons with clumps of shrubs, rocky outcrops, and scattered trees. They avoid chaparral or oak woodland even though those habitats are far more widespread, and as a result their highly localized distribution gives the appearance that they occur in loose colonies. In fact, pairs are extremely solitary and remain on their territories year-round.

Males have bright, bubbling songs that have been compared to high-pitched House Wrens or muted Lazuli Buntings. They begin singing in March, but their songs are seldom heard or recognized. Sightings of young birds, and adults acting as if they have a nest nearby, suggest that these sparrows nest in April with fledglings becoming increasingly common toward the end of May. Their thick-walled, but loosely constructed nests are placed in small hollows sunk into the dirt. Nests are concealed at the bases of grass clumps or small shrubs, and females sit so tight on their 4 eggs that they wait until the last second to run (rather than fly) from an approaching intruder. Young birds leave the nest when about 9 days old and often remain with their parents as a family group well into winter.

RANGE Rufous-crowned Sparrows are widespread throughout the arid Southwest, from dry hillsides in Oklahoma to sage-covered slopes above the Pacific Ocean. Found in the Sierra Nevada only in a very narrow altitudinal band in the Foothill Oak Zone on the west side. **WEST SLOPE:** Resident on relatively steep grassy slopes with scattered shrubs, well above the Central Valley but seldom higher than 2500 ft. May breed in patches of suitable habitat as high as 3000 ft, and on very rare occasions individuals have been observed up to 4000 ft (as in Yosemite Valley). **EAST SLOPE:** No known records, though they occur within miles of the crest at Walker Pass in Kern County and could conceivably occur on the east slope in the low desert mountains between Walker Pass and Tehachapi Pass.

CALIFORNIA TOWHEE *Melozone crissalis*

LIFE HISTORY In their 1924 book, *Animal Life in the Yosemite,* Joseph Grinnell and Tracy Storer rightly called California Towhees the most characteristic birds of the foothills, and to this day these towhees are still common and easily observed birds in virtually every brushy habitat below the vast conifer belts of the Sierra Nevada. Even more than Spotted Towhees, they are willing to use open areas as long as they have quick escape to nearby shrubs. This habit of feeding on the ground in the open, along with their accommodating acceptance of humans, means they are a conspicuous presence around countless backyards, ranch dwellings, and city parks in the lower foothills. They are particularly easy to find along quiet stretches of roads and trails throughout the foothills, where they take advantage of their favorite combination of open ground and nearby shrubs.

These towhees are notable for their sedentary habits and aggressive territoriality. They are not inclined to wander, and given their preference for a single location, it is no surprise that they fight fiercely, sometimes to bloody conclusions, over territorial boundaries. It is not uncommon, for example, to see males returning repeatedly to fight their own reflections in windows or reflective hubcaps.

Given this species' abundance and easily observed behaviors, it is remarkable how little is known about the details of its life history. Pairs remain together throughout the year and are mostly solitary though they may temporarily join flocks of foraging sparrows that move through their territories in the winter. By early spring their ringing "songs" (little more than energetic bursts of their sharp *chink* calls strung together) can be heard almost everywhere among the open oak woodlands and brushy hillsides of the lower west slope. Nesting activities commence in late April when females lay 4 eggs in bulky, but loosely constructed nests placed in the densest portions of shrubs or low trees. Young birds fledge after 10 days, but may remain with their parents for 4–6 weeks, during which time family groups are noisy and easily located. It is believed that pairs may raise two or more broods.

RANGE California Towhees are almost entirely restricted to open, brushy habitats west of the Sierra Nevada, where they are sedentary, year-round residents from southwestern Oregon to the tip of Baja California. **WEST SLOPE:** Common and conspicuous in open oak woodlands and broken chaparral habitats throughout the Foothill Oak Zone, becoming less common and more local above 2500–3000 ft and rare as high as 5000 ft. A handful of late summer records at higher elevations suggest that there is some upslope movement after the breeding season. **EAST SLOPE:** Seldom thought of as birds of the east slope but locally common on shrubby hillsides and in brushy canyons and oak woodlands as far north as Olancha. The few towhees observed in Big Pine and Lone Pine may wander north from this population or drift over to the Sierra Nevada from the endangered subpopulation at the southern end of the Argus Range (on the east side of the Owens Valley).

CHIPPING SPARROW *Spizella passerina*

LIFE HISTORY It would be hard to guess how many campgrounds and picnic areas in the Sierra Nevada are regularly visited by Chipping Sparrows, but it would be a lot. These dapper little sparrows certainly do not mind human company, and they evidently relish open cleared forests as much as humans do. Everywhere throughout their extensive range, Chipping Sparrows favor habitats with openly spaced trees and relatively open ground where there is a mix of shrubs and grasses (including recently burned areas). They are remarkably cosmopolitan in their choice of habitats and have been found breeding from oak woodlands in the lower foothills to patches of subalpine trees amid snowbanks—an altitudinal span shared by few other Sierra Nevada birds.

Although they hunt for seeds and insects on the ground, Chipping Sparrows lack the strong digging claws of some of their near relatives, so rather than scratching in the leaf litter for buried food, they walk quickly and make short, abrupt flights while scanning the ground surface. They have a lot in common with Dark-eyed Juncos, including having comparable life histories and behavior, and fast-trilling songs that are so similar it takes quite a bit of practice to separate the two species. They are both found in open forests, but Chipping Sparrows prefer drier habitats with fewer grasses and herbs, often on forest edges, and so avoid directly competing with juncos.

Males start singing from prominent perches in mid-April at lower elevations, and mid- to late May at higher elevations. From the end of April through June, females can be found building nests on the outer branches of conifers less than 10 ft above the ground (rarely higher). These nests are distinctive in having an outer structure of neatly interlaced grasses and a smooth-surfaced inner cup of animal hairs so tightly woven that the lining can be lifted out of the nest without losing its shape. Young birds leave the nest when 9–12 days old, and at about 21 days of age depart to join roaming flocks with other juveniles. These flocks are a common sight in the upper Sierra Nevada by late summer, with flocks growing in size as adults finish breeding and band together in preparation for migration.

RANGE Chipping Sparrows are one of the most common and widely distributed migrant songbirds in North America and they are found breeding everywhere in California except the Central Valley and low-lying desert areas. Most leave California by the end of September but some linger until the end of October, and a fair number remain through the winter from the southern end of the San Joaquin Valley south through the warmer portions of southern California. Spring migrants first arrive at lower elevations in early April, with numbers picking up dramatically from mid- to late April and individual birds moving upslope as snow conditions allow. They have been found breeding from the lowest edges of the foothills to timberline on both slopes, but they are particularly abundant in mid-elevation forests. **WEST SLOPE:** Most breeding birds are found in the Upper Montane Zone, generally from 5000–9000 ft, but can be fairly common in ponderosa pine forests and blue oak woodlands down to 2000 ft. During the winter, single birds and small groups are rarely encountered in the low foothills of the central and northern Sierra Nevada; but they are locally uncommon in the southern San Joaquin Valley (around Bakersfied, for example) and occasionally roam into the warmer, low-lying valleys between the Kern River and Tehachapi Pass. **EAST SLOPE:** Widespread breeding birds in a variety of dry, open conifer habitats below treeline. There are only a handful of winter records north of Kern County.

Brewer's Sparrow *Spizella breweri*

LIFE HISTORY Despite their nondescript appearance, Brewer's Sparrows attract a lot of attention from birdwatchers because their distribution in the Sierra Nevada is a bit of a mystery, and they show up in many unexpected locations. They would make an ideal subject for anyone who likes bird puzzles.

Brewer's Sparrows are by far the most abundant birds breeding among unbroken expanses of low-growing sagebrush, bitterbrush, and other desert shrubs (like rabbitbrush and greasewood on alkaline flats). Nearly all these habitats occur on the east side, except for scattered sites along the Sierra Nevada crest where sagebrush spills over onto the upper portions of the west slope and where it has been long suspected there might be small breeding populations of these sparrows.

The life history of Brewer's Sparrows is poorly known and they have never been studied in the Sierra Nevada. They spend most of their time within the confines of dense shrubs, but males frequently ascend onto shrub tops to sing lively buzzy, trilling songs or to scan their surroundings, so they are fairly easy to spot. During the breeding season they search the foliage and bark of sagebrush or other shrubs for insects, and occasionally gather seeds from the ground, but they rarely venture into the open spaces between shrubs. Their nests are located within a few feet of the ground, and the nesting season seems to extend from May to early July (in the high mountains). This species reportedly renests as soon as the first brood fledges, so that may account for mid-summer nesting records. Nothing is known of the fledgling or immature stages in these birds.

RANGE Brewer's Sparrows are common summer residents throughout the arid Intermountain West, where they are the most abundant birds in the vast sagebrush flats between the Rocky Mountains and the Sierra Nevada. In many areas, their numbers are declining due to grazing and the alteration of undisturbed sagebrush habitats. They arrive in California in early April and are abundant from early May–late August. Numbers drop off quickly in late September though some linger into October, and they are casual in winter on the east side from Inyo County south.
WEST SLOPE: Fairly rare transients in the foothills from mid-April through May, and at any elevation in late August and September. Breed at scattered locations well west of the crest, including Butte Meadows in Butte County (on the far northwest boundary of the Sierra Nevada), Mosquito Ridge just east of Foresthill, Placer County, and along the headwaters of the South Fork Kern River around Kennedy Meadows,

Troy Meadows, and the Domelands Wilderness. Many summer records from the west side of the crest in the central and southern Sierra Nevada may represent local breeding populations. **EAST SLOPE:** Common in sagebrush habitats from the desert floor up to the crest (around 10,000 ft), also found in bitterbrush thickets and occasionally in rabbitbrush and greasewood stands on alkali flats.

BLACK-CHINNED SPARROW *Spizella atrogularis*

LIFE HISTORY Loudly trilling birds calling from arid, rocky hillsides of chaparral or sagebrush may be reclusive Black-chinned Sparrows, one of the Sierra Nevada's most enigmatic and highly sought-after birds. Known to occur at only a few obscure, isolated locations and spending their entire lives within the tangled branches of impenetrable shrubs, this is a species whose distribution and life history are largely a matter of conjecture. Their primary habitat consists of rocky slopes covered with stands of mixed shrubs. They avoid densely-packed stands, preferring areas where there are alleyways and small openings between shrubs for quick movements.

Although singing males ascend onto high shrub tops to sing, throwing back their heads to show off their black chins, they mainly sing at sunrise and then remain elusive the rest of the day. Females are seldom observed unless you hear one fiercely chipping if you get too close to her nest.

Very little is known of their foraging or nesting behaviors, all aspects of which occur under the cover of shrubs. Nesting probably begins in May or early June. Nests are located 1–3 ft above the ground, and it is thought that only females incubate the 2–4 light blue eggs. Young are tended by both parents then join flocks with other juveniles in late summer, but little else is known of this species.

RANGE Black-chinned Sparrows favor arid, brushy habitats from central California to eastern New Mexico, with scattered populations on the arid west slope and southern east slope of the Sierra Nevada. Actual distribution may shift on a regular basis because Black-chinned Sparrows appear to seek out brushy habitats 5–10 years after a wildfire, then move on to new locations when the brush becomes tall and dense again. Spring migrants first appear in the southern Sierra Nevada in early April (exceptionally in late March), but the majority of records are from May, when males are singing on territory. Few are reported from June–August, and it would be exceptional to find one in early September. **WEST SLOPE:** Given the vast expanses of suitable habitat below

4000 ft it is likely that there are numerous, small breeding populations waiting to be discovered on the west slope; only a handful are currently known, including Mosquito Ridge Road in Placer County, Ice House Road in El Dorado County, Cherry Lake Road in Tuolumne County, and around Johnsondale in Tulare County; migrants, and possibly breeders, are infrequently found south and east of the South Fork Kern River Valley in Kern County. **EAST SLOPE:** Breed in sagebrush stands below 8000 ft in the Owens Valley south of Independence, but there are a few records from further north including a remarkable sighting from the Tahoe Basin in late August.

VESPER SPARROW *Pooecetes gramineus*

LIFE HISTORY These ground-dwelling sparrows are rather specialized in their habitat preferences and easily overlooked despite being relatively widespread, year-round residents in the region. Although they share sagebrush habitats with Brewer's Sparrows on the east side, and short-grass meadows with Savannah Sparrows and American Pipits on the west side, Vespers are unique in favoring grassy areas with bare, open ground and scattered shrubs. They avoid habitats where grasses become lush or crowded, or where there are dense shrubs, but may become locally numerous where grasses and shrubs are growing back after a recent fire. Numbers decline in areas that are overgrazed.

Despite occurring in open areas, Vespers are generally hard to spot because they stay hidden in available cover and often crouch against the ground rather than flying when disturbed. The exception is when the streaky males ascend onto shrub tops, dirt mounds, or fence posts to sing their rich, melodious songs of clear, long introductory notes combined with flutey trills. Long after other sparrows have stopped singing for the day, Vesper Sparrows may continue singing into the evening twilight, hence their name.

Nests are constructed on the ground in small hollows at the bases of weed or grass tufts. Unlike other sparrows, males may occasionally assist in incubating eggs or brooding the 3–5 chicks. Males tend fledglings for about 3 weeks after they leave the nest while females start a second (or even third) brood; as a result, nesting activity may be observed almost all summer long. Nothing is known of the lives of immature birds once they leave their parents.

RANGE Vesper Sparrows are widely distributed across the northern United States. Populations in the Sierra Nevada are comprised of separate wintering and breeding subspecies though there is some overlap in their timing and distribution. Migrants from the north arrive in October and are found west of the Sierra Nevada until early April. These departing birds are replaced by another subspecies from the south that stays to breed, primarily on the east slope, until September. **WEST SLOPE:** Individual birds and small flocks can be found alone or in the company of pipits and other sparrows in open grasslands and cultivated fields of the lower foothills throughout the winter, mainly south of Placer County. A few Vesper Sparrows linger after mid-April in the foothills; but from May–September most birds on the west slope are breeding in high mountain meadows near the crest, particularly on the Kern Plateau and in the southern Sierra Nevada. **EAST SLOPE:** Widespread breeders from April–September, favoring dry meadows bordered by open desert scrub where they can be fairly common up to 9000 ft, otherwise scarce and hard to find. Some overwinter in the Owens Valley as far north as Bishop.

LARK SPARROW *Chondestes grammacus*

LIFE HISTORY These sparrows are a delightful and colorful presence in the rolling grasslands of the lower west slope, where they sweep up from roadsides and trails into the safety of overhanging oak branches as cars and pedestrians pass by. Unlike other sparrows that dive for cover, these beautifully marked sparrows sit confidently on exposed branches or fences, allowing close inspection of their striking plumage. Lark Sparrows are highly social, even while breeding, and can be found in large groups at almost any season.

These sparrows are inhabitants of grassland–shrub edges, or open grassy woodlands with scattered trees. They readily use fallow fields or areas disturbed by grazing or recent fires. Most of their lives are spent on the ground, walking about in search of insects and seeds (over half of the insects they eat are grasshoppers), but they retire to nearby trees and bushes to rest and sing.

Lark Sparrows are unique among songbirds for their elaborate courtship rituals. Males strut like turkeys in front of prospective mates, cocking their tails to show off their white outer tail feathers and drooping their wings so they brush against the ground. A courting male will present a twig to a female, who holds it in her bill as they copulate. Males later assist in finding potential nest sites, but females make the final choices, sometimes choosing abandoned nests made by other birds (though she will share the nest with the resident female if it is currently occupied). Most nests are located on the ground, in small pits placed against the bases of weed or grass tufts, or rarely a few feet high in trees or shrubs. Females incubate 4–5 eggs for 11–13 days, and both parents help feed the nestlings. Young birds are led to safe, brushy areas as soon as they leave the nest, remaining hidden until they can fly.

RANGE Lark Sparrows are widely distributed breeding birds throughout North America, but their distribution in California is complex. In general they are scarce breeders east of the Sierra Nevada and common or locally common residents on the west side, with additional migrants passing through the state in April–May and August–September. **WEST SLOPE:** Common residents of foothill grasslands and open oak woodlands; sometimes wander upslope towards the Mixed Conifer Zone in the spring, and rarely as high as the Upper Montane Zone in late summer. **EAST SLOPE:** A scarce breeder at scattered locations along the east side (reportedly breed in Inyo County, and at the far northern end of the Sierra Nevada) but primarily known as an uncommon to fairly common migrant, passing through the region relatively quickly from mid-April to mid-May; and more leisurely from July to the end of September, when they can be found in meadows as high as 10,000 ft. Individual birds are occasionally reported during the winter as far north as Honey Lake.

BLACK-THROATED SPARROW *Amphispiza bilineata*

LIFE HISTORY Black-throated Sparrows are so highly adapted to arid desert environments that they can derive the water they need and survive for months solely on a diet of dry seeds. This enables them to breed in some of the region's harshest environments, including sun-baked slopes of the Mojave Desert on the Sierra Nevada's southeastern boundary. They are absent from desert flats but are common in open, shrubby habitats on rocky slopes above the desert floor. Away from their preferred habitats they are irregular and highly localized breeders among sagebrush and pinyon-juniper woodlands on the east slope, or among arid chaparral stands on the west slope.

Black-throated Sparrows forage extensively on the open ground between scattered shrubs but also feed readily among low-lying branches, varying their diet from insects in spring to seeds in summer and winter.

Males are avid songsters and maintain large territories, but as soon as females begin incubating and caring for young, the territorial borders are dramatically reduced to the areas right around their nests. Males are relatively unique among sparrows in occasionally helping build the nest, which is located within a few feet of the ground in low bushes. Females incubate the 3–4 eggs for 12 days. On extremely hot days, females stand over their nests with wings spread to shield the nestlings from the intense sun. Young birds abandon the nest when about 9 days old, before they can even fly, but they continue to be fed by their parents for another two weeks until leaving to join flocks of other immature Black-throated Sparrows. Parents commonly raise second broods in years of abundant food.

RANGE Black-throated Sparrows are widespread and locally common throughout the arid western United States, but in California they are mainly limited to areas east of the Sierra Nevada. Most spring migrants arrive in early April and remain locally common until mid-August, with some lingering into mid-September; irregular and casual through the winter with numbers picking up again in late March. **WEST SLOPE:** Only recently have avid birdwatchers discovered breeding populations on the west slope though the species was long suspected of breeding in the upper valleys of the Kern River and Kern Plateau (where they are now known to be fairly common). In the north, however, breeding populations are quite small, highly local, restricted to arid chaparral, and not found every year; known locations include Cohasset Ridge in Butte County (a few miles west of the Sierra Nevada boundary), Foresthill Divide (including Foresthill Bridge and Mosquito Ridge) in Placer County, and Ice House Road in El Dorado County, with other sites waiting to be discovered. **EAST SLOPE:** Highly local and rare to uncommon breeders north of Bishop with birds frequently observed in the Mono Basin and just east of Woodfords in Alpine County; they might also breed sparingly north of Plumas County. In Inyo and Kern counties they are common breeders and irregular winter visitors on the desert slopes below 7500 ft. In the late summer, they occasionally wander to higher elevations.

Sage Sparrow *Amphispiza belli*

LIFE HISTORY These highly secretive, brush-loving sparrows have a complex and poorly understood distribution in the Sierra Nevada. Part of the problem is that there are 3 subspecies in our region, each distinct enough that they may actually constitute two or 3 species; in addition, there appears to be both resident and migratory populations that further confuse the status of these three forms. The *belli* subspecies on the west slope (formerly known as "Bell's Sparrow") is currently known only from a few locations, where they are resident in impenetrable chaparral thickets dominated by chamise, and vast stretches of this habitat have never been surveyed. The *canescens* subspecies is found in sagebrush, rabbitbrush, and bitterbrush thickets of the southern Sierra Nevada and on low desert slopes of the east side as far north as Mono Lake; in these habitats they may overlap with Black-throated Sparrows although Sage Sparrows also breed on the valley floors and flats avoided by Black-throated Sparrows. And finally, the *nevadensis* subspecies favors sagebrush thickets in the colder, higher deserts from Mono Lake north.

Except when males ascend onto shrub tops to sing, Sage Sparrows remain hidden at all times among extensive stands of low to moderately high shrubs, often in areas that have recently burned. Sage Sparrows are timid and run away like mice when alarmed, rarely taking to the air or leaving the safety of shrub cover, making them difficult to locate or observe even in areas where they are common.

These sparrows have an unusually early breeding season, with nesting already underway in early March around Mono Lake and in full swing throughout Kern County by mid-March. The *belli* populations on the west slope remain in pairs year round, and *nevadensis* populations on the northern east slope arrive on their breeding grounds already paired up. Males follow their mates and sing from exposed perches as the rarely observed females build well-hidden nests within a foot or two of the ground in dense shrubs. Females incubate 3–4 eggs for about 12 days, and both parents feed the nestlings. Fledglings probably fly when they're 9–10 days old, but the juvenile and immature stages are unstudied.

RANGE Sage Sparrows are widespread breeders in sagebrush habitats of the Great Basin from the Rocky Mountains to the Sierra Nevada, with the northernmost populations retreating to the southwest deserts for the winter. They are highly local and irregular to common in the Sierra Nevada, with some populations resident and some migratory, and at least a few individuals remaining to overwinter in most parts of their range. **WEST SLOPE:** The *belli* subspecies are rare and highly local residents in chamise habitats of the Foothill Oak Zone from Placer County (Foresthill Bridge) south to Mariposa County; the *canescens* subspecies are rare residents in sagebrush and shrub habitats of Tulare and Kern counties, in particular around the South Fork Kern River Valley. **EAST SLOPE:** The *canescens* subspecies are rather common residents in desert shrub habitats below 8000 ft in Kern and Inyo counties. The *nevadensis* subspecies are scarce breeders in sagebrush habitats north of Mono Lake, mainly from early April-late August though they are occasionally found outside of the breeding season.

Savannah Sparrow *Passerculus sandwichensis*

LIFE HISTORY These sparrows of wet meadows may be fairly common but are still elusive due to their creeping, mouse-like behavior and reluctance to flush from cover. You may see them leap up in zigzagging flight as you walk across grasslands, fields, or marsh edges, but their all-too brief flights terminate abruptly when the birds quickly drop back into the grasses and sedges where they otherwise remain entirely hidden.

Around marshes, Savannah Sparrows are sometimes seen walking along muddy edges picking up the insects that form their summer diet, but the best way to observe these birds is when males conspicuously chase each other and sing from rocks, grass tufts, and fence wires while establishing breeding territories in May.

Nests are located under protective tufts of vegetation in small hollows excavated by females. The 4–5 eggs are incubated for 8–12 days, with females tending the eggs and both parents feeding nestlings. Young birds remain in the nest up to 13 days but if disturbed can flee the nest when only 8 days old. Parents split the brood evenly, with each taking care of 1–2 fledglings for about 15 days, at which point the young birds leave to join groups with other immature Savannah Sparrows. Many pairs quickly start a second brood.

RANGE Savannah Sparrows are highly variable with as many as 28 subspecies found in North America from Mexico to the Arctic. At least 4 subspecies are found in the Sierra Nevada, but only two are regular and expected: *nevadensis* as a breeding subspecies on the east side, and *alaudinus* as a wintering subspecies on the west side. At all seasons they favor grasslands, fields, and marshes along the base of the Sierra Nevada though on occasion they are observed at high elevations. **WEST SLOPE:** Common winter residents from September–April, mainly in grasslands of the Central Valley and Foothill Oak Zone but occasionally at higher elevations during migration. They have bred at 8600 ft in Tuolumne Meadows and are fairly common breeding birds at similar elevations on the Kern Plateau, but because they nest very locally, other breeding pairs could be found at new locations. **EAST SLOPE:** Generally common along the entire east base of the Sierra Nevada, with local populations breeding as high as 7500 ft from April to end of October; numbers increase notably after mid-August, a time when some wander as high as the Alpine Zone; by November they retreat to low-lying areas where they can be uncommon through the winter.

Fox Sparrow *Passerella iliaca*

LIFE HISTORY Throughout the summer there is scarcely a stand of montane chaparral not dominated by these common brush-loving sparrows. They share these habitats with Green-tailed Towhees on both slopes, but on the west slope they far outnumber towhees, while towhees are far more abundant on the east slope. Although Fox Sparrows are reclusive and hard to find among these dense thickets, often diving deeper into the impenetrable foliage when alarmed, they can be bold and almost belligerent when nesting. Males ascend onto the tops of tall shrubs or into the branches of nearby trees to sing surprisingly loud, musical songs (their heads thrown back and bodies vibrating with each utterance) while both parents make agitated smacking sounds if an intruder nears their nest.

Even in the winter, when visiting sparrows of many different species gather in the foothills, Fox Sparrows remain largely solitary, spending much of their time scratching for seeds and insects in the deep layers of leaf litter that accumulate under brushy thickets. They are so noisy when they kick leaves aside that this frequently gives away their otherwise hidden locations.

Breeding birds arrive sometime in April, and the nesting season hits full stride in May. Nest-building efforts may be observed in May, but in early June it is possible to both find newly fledged young and nests being built at the same time. Surprisingly little is known about the details and life history of these widespread and common birds, leaving many questions about even the most basic aspects of their nesting activities and early development. Females incubate 3–5 eggs for 12–14 days, but both parents feed the nestlings until they leave the nest at 9–11 days. Family groups with fully fledged young have been observed in August, suggesting extended parental care.

RANGE Fox Sparrows are common breeding birds in the boreal forests of Canada and Alaska as well as in the montane forests of western North America, with wintering birds found in California and across the southeastern United States. They are one of the most variable and taxonomically complex birds in North America, with 18 subspecies currently recognized that likely represent 4 separate species. At least 8 subspecies have been observed in the Sierra Nevada, so while they are year-round residents, the breeding and wintering populations consist of different subspecies. Breeding birds from the "Thick-billed" (*megarhyncha*) group, are recognized by their gray heads and reddish-brown wings and tails; while wintering birds are mostly in the "Sooty" (*unalaschcensis*) group, recognized by their overall dark chocolate brown appearance. Gray-headed, small-billed birds from the Rocky Mountains, the "Slate-colored" (*schistacea*) group, are occasionally observed in winter; as are vagrants from the far northern "Red" (*iliaca*) group, recognized by their strongly reddish hue. "Thick-billed" Fox Sparrows breed in montane chaparral and in brushy forest clearings from April–September, with some lingering as late as October or potentially wintering on the west slope. "Sooty" Fox Sparrows begin arriving from their northern breeding grounds in late September, wandering to as high as treeline until pushed downslope by snow, where they remain in foothill brush fields until April. **WEST SLOPE:** "Thick-billed" are common breeding birds of montane chaparral in the Upper Montane and Subalpine Zones. "Sooty" Fox Sparrows are common in winter in brushy thickets below the snowline. **EAST SLOPE:** "Thick-billed" are fairly common and widespread breeding birds in a wide variety of brushy habitats on the east side though they are less common here than on the west slope. In the driest habitats, they may breed in streamside thickets of wild rose or in patches of mountain mahogany as long as there is a deep layer of leaf litter. The other races are scarce fall migrants and extremely rare in winter.

Song Sparrow *Melospiza melodia*

LIFE HISTORY Brisk, cheerful songs and short, jerky flights are the hallmarks of these abundant streaky sparrows that inhabit virtually every pocket of dense, tangled vegetation in the vicinity of wet meadows, streams, lakes, and marshes. Here they remain mostly hidden among leaves and branches but reveal themselves when singing from the tops of bushes, scolding passersby with petulant *chimp* calls, or feeding on the open ground within easy reach of dense vegetation.

During the summer, Song Sparrows pick insects from leaves and grasses, but in the winter they feed almost entirely on berries and seeds that they collect on the ground. This ground-foraging behavior forces Song Sparrows to shift downslope when snow covers the ground although a few hardy individuals may linger at higher elevations.

Song Sparrows conceal their nests in dense patches of low-standing vegetation like willows, wild roses, or blackberry brambles. Nest-building is an active time, especially because females often select nest sites outside of a male's territory, forcing neighboring males to squabble as they struggle to modify their boundary lines in response.

Females incubate 3–5 eggs for 12–13 days. Both parents feed nestlings, but once young birds leave the nest, males may take charge of feeding the fledglings so females can begin another nesting effort. Young birds are independent within a month, and in areas where Song Sparrows are year-round residents, young males begin establishing territories at 4–7 months of age.

RANGE Song Sparrows are widespread and ubiquitous in North America. In the Sierra Nevada they breed from the base of the foothills upslope into mid-elevation forests though birds that nest at higher elevations must retreat below the snowline in winter, joining migrants from the north and pairs that are year-round residents at lower elevations. Even though they can be common in the winter, they do not form flocks. **WEST SLOPE:** Common during the breeding season in a huge variety of habitats below the mixed conifer forests, and uncommon to rare in the Upper Montane Zone, with birds that breed at higher elevations moving upslope in March or early April. In late summer and fall some roam as high as treeline, lingering in the mountains until November, or until snow pushes them downslope. **EAST SLOPE:** Common breeding birds in willow thickets and patches of streamside vegetation at low to mid-elevations but sometimes as high as 9500 ft. North of Bishop they are uncommon and irregular in the winter due to snow and cold temperatures in the high desert, but south of Bishop they remain fairly common.

LINCOLN'S SPARROW *Melospiza lincolnii*

LIFE HISTORY Lincoln's Sparrows are the high-mountain counterparts to lower elevation Song Sparrows, and although they both frequent moist brushy thickets, these two species scarcely overlap during the breeding season. In addition to sharing the same types of habitat, they are remarkably similar in appearance though the bubbling, wrenlike songs of Lincoln's Sparrows are nothing like the cheery songs of Song Sparrows.

Catching a glimpse of Lincoln's Sparrows to look for the subtle visual distinctions that separate the two species is another matter altogether. While Song Sparrows frequently fly conspicuously across the openings between shrubs, Lincoln's Sparrows are extremely furtive and remain almost entirely hidden among dense vegetation except for a very brief time early in the breeding season when males sit on exposed perches to sing. In fact, there is a period in August when Lincoln's Sparrows are apparently molting and highly secretive so it is almost impossible to find one, even in areas where they are known to occur.

Lincoln's Sparrows breed almost exclusively in wet mountain meadows and marshy areas among willow thickets and thick growths of corn lilies, sedges, and other meadow plants. Here they forage for seeds and insects among the dense ground cover, disappearing even further into the vegetation and slinking away like mice if disturbed.

The nesting season seems to be underway in early June, but nests are well hidden on the ground at the bases of willows and tall herbs. Nesting activity often begins when meadows are still covered in melting snowbanks and rushing rivulets, so nests may be built atop mounds of slightly drier ground. Females incubate 4–5 eggs for 13–14 days, and both parents feed nestlings until they leave the nest at 11 days of age. Young birds stay with their parents for 2–3 weeks after leaving the nest but are soon independent, both parents and youngsters leaving before summer's end.

RANGE The bulk of the Lincoln's Sparrow population nests across Alaska, Canada, and the northern United States, with local colonies occurring southward in "islands" of montane habitat along the Cascade-Sierra axis and the Rocky Mountains. They spend their winters in low-lying areas across the southern and far western United States, including low elevations all around the Sierra Nevada. In April–early May most wintering birds head north, creating a rash of sightings in areas that don't otherwise see many Lincoln's Sparrows, while local breeding birds begin to follow the melting snow upslope in the Sierra Nevada. They become fairly common on their breeding grounds in the Upper Montane Zone by the end of May and remain relatively common until the end of August, when breeding birds depart and are replaced by newly arriving migrants from the north who linger in the Upper Montane Zone until late October (rarely into December as weather allows). Lincoln's Sparrows are not known to breed south of southern Tulare County, but further investigation may find them on Breckenridge Mountain or in the Piute Mountains of Kern County. **WEST SLOPE:** Not often reported in winter but they are probably uncommon winter residents in any wet, brushy area in the foothills, with occasional records as high as 4500 ft. During the breeding season they range from 4000–9500 ft, with most birds nesting in upper montane meadows among red fir, mixed conifer, or lodgepole pine forests at 6000–8000 ft; may wander to treeline in late summer, but most leave the mountains with the arrival of cold weather and snow. **EAST SLOPE:** Breeding status is complex but south of the central Sierra Nevada (roughly around Mono Lake) Lincoln's Sparrows appear to be rare and very local breeders around high-mountain meadows, mostly above 8000 ft, while further north they become increasingly regular and common; for example, they are fairly common in high-elevation meadows around the Tahoe Basin and north of Donner Pass. They are often more easily found while migrating in April or September–October, and they are generally uncommon winter residents below 7000 ft along the entire east slope.

WHITE-CROWNED SPARROW *Zonotrichia leucophrys*

LIFE HISTORY It is worth paying close attention to these common and confiding sparrows because there are two distinct and very different races that occur the Sierra Nevada. Summer-time breeders are "Mountain" White-crowned Sparrows (subspecies *oriantha*), identified by their black lores (the area between their eye and bill). These birds arrive in mid-May and breed around high-mountain meadows and lakes near treeline, where they require a combination of surface water, dense shrubby vegetation, and grassy openings where they forage for seeds and insects.

The male's sweet song, which opens with a rising slurred whistle and ends with a buzzy trill, is easily the most characteristic sound of high-mountain meadows in the Sierra Nevada. White-crowned Sparrows in the Sierra Nevada sing at least 5 different dialects, and scientists believe local dialects help birds find other members of their own breeding populations quickly, which is essential because they have such a short nesting season.

As soon as enough snow has melted, females build nests on the ground or in the low branches of dense shrubs and willows, laying 4 eggs in late May to early June. Eggs hatch in 12 days and both parents feed nestlings until they leave the nest at 9–10 days of age. Males stop singing as soon as they start feeding fledglings and begin molting in preparation for their journey south.

These breeding birds quickly disappear by mid-September, and are almost perfectly replaced by newly arriving "Gambel's" White-crowned Sparrows (subspecies *gambelii*) from Canada and Alaska. These wintering birds, recognized by their white lores, arrive in great numbers and wander through open habitats on both slopes as high as treeline. By mid-November, "Gambel's" White-crowneds move downslope into low-lying areas, where they remain common, or even abundant, from October–April. They can be found in any kind of meadow, clearing, or yard with protective shrubs or brush piles, and they frequently mingle in loose flocks with Golden-crowned Sparrows. By late April, they leave and are replaced by newly arriving "Mountain" White-crowneds.

> **Note:** White-throated Sparrows *are rare but regular visitors from mid-September to early May, with most being observed as fall migrants from mid-October to late November, when they frequently mingle with White-crowned Sparrows in shrubby thickets and are easily overlooked. About 10-20 are seen each winter on the west slope; and on the east slope they are uncommon in the desert lowlands of Inyo County, where as many as 10 have been seen in a single October.*

RANGE White-crowned Sparrows breed in the far north, as well as in pockets of montane habitat in the Cascades, Sierra Nevada, and Rocky Mountains; then head south to winter in low-lying areas of the southern United States and Mexico. In the Sierra Nevada, they are fairly common breeders around wet meadows and willow thickets in the Upper Montane and Subalpine Zones, up to and sometimes above treeline, reaching 11,200 ft around Mt. Whitney. On the east slope, they occasionally breed amid stands of sagebrush, rather than willows, around wet meadows. Wintering birds descend below the level of deep snows, where they can be quite common on lower foothill slopes and valleys, only rarely wandering to higher elevations. Distribution patterns are virtually identical on both slopes.

GOLDEN-CROWNED SPARROW *Zonotrichia atricapilla*

LIFE HISTORY Overwintering Golden-crowned Sparrows are tricksters because with the coming spring they gradually acquire their striking gold-and-black breeding plumages, and males begin singing their sad-sounding, 3-note, *oh dear me*, songs. When you see these birds in late April or May it is natural to think they must be breeding nearby, but then they suddenly depart for their true breeding grounds in western Canada and Alaska.

These are by far our most common *Zonotrichia* sparrows in the winter, and loose flocks of Golden-crowneds, White-crowneds, and Dark-eyed Juncos are a familiar sight in foothill clearings, meadows, and yards, especially on the west slope. Golden-crowneds are reputed to have a preference for shady, dense thickets and to be more closely affiliated with chaparral and oak woodlands with a shrubby understory, but in fact they can be found in a wide variety of habitats, both urban and wild, as long as there is a mix of open ground and nearby shrubs or brush piles.

Like all *Zonotrichia* sparrows, Golden-crowneds do nearly all their foraging on the ground, but unlike the others they are particularly fond of newly sprouted weed seeds, to the point that their bills are sometimes stained green from a steady diet of fresh shoots.

RANGE Golden-crowned Sparrows first arrive in mid-September, and by early October there is a major influx into the Sierra Nevada that lasts about a month. During this fall movement they show up, often in significant numbers, almost everywhere in the Sierra Nevada below treeline, including many areas where they are absent the rest of the year. Numbers decline sharply in November as most birds head toward their primary wintering grounds in the lowlands on the west side of the Sierra Nevada. Some stragglers remain at mid-elevations and on the east side until pushed out by snow in late November or December. Nearly all Golden-crowneds depart by early May. **WEST SLOPE:** Uncommon to common winter residents in the Foothill Oak Zone and even into the lower edges of the Mixed Conifer Zone, occasionally straying upslope to the Upper Montane Zone when the weather is mild. **EAST SLOPE:** Although they are uncommon fall migrants in October all along the east slope, most are pushed out of the region as soon as the weather turns cold. However, they regularly overwinter around Honey Lake, in eastern Alpine County, in the Owens Valley, and in the desert portions of the southern Sierra Nevada; they are otherwise rare, but their numbers can vary from year to year.

DARK-EYED JUNCO *Junco hyemalis*

LIFE HISTORY Dark-eyed Juncos are one of the mountain's most commonly encountered and easily recognizable birds. And during the summer, they nest in virtually every conifer habitat of the main forest belt, from ponderosa pine forests to treeline. Their only requirements seem to be open ground where they forage for insects to feed their nestlings, in addition to a few logs or rocks and some trees or shrubs. Most foraging is done on the ground but males readily ascend into trees, even onto the tops of the highest conifers, to sing clear trilling songs.

Their well-hidden nests are built on the ground under overhanging grasses or protective objects. Nesting takes place from late May until late July (females frequently have two broods). Females incubate 3–5 eggs for 12–13 days with both parents feeding nestlings on the nest for about 12 days. Young birds are dependent on their parents for another

3 weeks. In late July, females at high elevations may still be incubating a second batch of eggs but family groups are the rule, soon coalescing into larger flocks that remain together until the following April.

The breeding juncos of the Sierra Nevada (the "Oregon" race, subspecies *thurberi*) are year-round residents, migrating short distances downslope in response to winter snows, then back upslope during mild winters or periods when the snows melt. The early Yosemite naturalists, Joseph Grinnell and Tracy Storer, witnessed an extraordinary event in Yosemite Valley on November 9, the day after the season's first heavy snowfall: huge numbers of juncos (more in one morning than they had seen in the entire preceding month) leaving the high country and streaming down the valley on route to the foothills.

Our local wintering juncos are joined by large numbers of migrants from the north, with as many as 9 subspecies of juncos possible in the foothills. These include the distinctively marked "Slate-colored" and "Gray-headed" forms. Flocks of foraging juncos are abundant at lower elevations in the winter, where they mill about in forest openings, meadows, backyards, and rural neighborhoods in search of the seeds they eat during the nonbreeding season.

RANGE Dark-eyed Juncos are common to abundant year round in the Sierra Nevada although their numbers and distribution vary widely from year to year depending on levels of snows. Local breeding birds begin moving upslope in April, just as winter visitors from the north leave the area. By the time the ground is clear of snow, in May or early June, juncos are widely dispersed in all mid- to high-elevation conifer forests up to treeline (as high as 11,500 ft on Mt. Whitney), with smaller numbers lingering to breed in lower elevation conifer forests. Flocks head downslope again in October though many remain in the mountains until snows force them out. Their status and distribution are almost identical on both slopes, except that on the east slope their winter numbers may vary dramatically month by month and location by location depending on snow levels, while on the west slope wintering birds are consistently abundant below the snowline.

CARDINALS and ALLIES (Cardinalidae)

WESTERN TANAGER *Piranga ludoviciana*

LIFE HISTORY One might think that the Sierra Nevada's showiest birds would be a bundle of energy, but Western Tanagers are notoriously sedate and deliberate in both behavior and song, foraging quietly and staying hidden among conifer needles as much as possible. These stunning flashes of brilliant yellow and fluorescent red-orange look out of place because tanagers are a tropical family and Western Tanagers are one of 4 species that wander north of Mexico.

In the Sierra Nevada, Western Tanagers are fairly common breeders in the open coniferous forests and mixed conifer-deciduous habitats of the main forest belt. Unfortunately, they are very little studied and much of what is known about the species is anecdotal. Arriving by mid-May, males immediately start singing and establishing large territories that later shrink in size as more males show up. Their songs are a huskier, less-sustained version of an American Robin song, at least to human ears. Males may alternately sing and forage in the tops of trees and shrubs, methodically searching for insects in the foliage or darting up to catch large flying insects, occasionally adding fruits and berries to their diets later in the summer. Their other vocalizations are *pit-ick* or *pit-a-dik* calls that are one of the most distinctive sounds of summer in mountain forests.

Females build loosely constructed nests of twigs woven together with finer materials, placed near the ends of branches where they divide into smaller branches, often in trees near meadow edges. Steller's Jays may be the tanagers' biggest nest predators so whenever jays enter their territory tanagers fiercely defend their well-hidden nests. Females incubate 4 eggs for 13 days; eggs have been observed in early June but are probably laid throughout June depending on elevation. Both parents feed nestlings until chicks leave the nest in 11–15 days, but males seem particularly overwhelmed by fatherhood because they try to feed hatching chicks before they are hardly even out of their eggs, then wait nervously nearby holding uneaten food in their bills unsure of what to do next.

Note: *Remarkably, another flamboyant tropical tanager breeds in the Sierra Nevada. Stunning red* **Summer Tanagers** *are fairly common breeders in the Kern River Valley from mid-May to mid-August; a few stragglers and breeding pairs have been recorded at other locations.*

RANGE Widespread summer breeders throughout the western United States and Canada. In the Sierra Nevada a few hardy pioneers arrive in mid-April, but most of our breeding birds are just reaching the southern portions of the Sierra Nevada at the tail end of April. Within a few weeks, however, they are common migrants along the full length of both slopes, appearing at low to mid-elevations in nearly all types of habitats, and soon thereafter moving to breeding territories. It is thought that they remain on these territories until heading south in mid-August. Tanagers observed after mid-August may be migrants from the north, but this has not been studied. Few are observed north of Yosemite National Park after mid-September, and by the end of September they have abandoned even the southern Sierra Nevada. **WEST SLOPE:** Breed in ponderosa pine forests of the foothills to as high as the red fir forests of the Upper Montane Zone, from about 3000–8000 ft. **EAST SLOPE:** Breed in the main timbered belt from about 6000–8000 ft, commonly nesting in Jeffrey, ponderosa, and western white pines, or in white and red firs.

BLACK-HEADED GROSBEAK *Pheucticus melanocephalus*

LIFE HISTORY Bold, gaudy Black-headed Grosbeaks are the loudest and most conspicuous harbingers of spring throughout the West. As soon as they arrive in late April, males begin singing and aggressively defending territories with so much energy and volume that they cannot be missed. Their penetrating songs are a fast jumble of rising and falling notes that sound like a "drunken robin." Thirty percent of the song syllables are shared by multiple neighboring males, being used as a signal that they know each other and do not need to fight, while the other 70 percent are unique to each male and are used to signal his identity. Males sing almost constantly at each other until females have finished laying their eggs, then they dramatically decrease their singing rates and direct songs at their mates instead (even singing as they help incubate eggs and feed nestlings).

Females sing simplified versions of the males' songs and can produce full songs if they want. However, females reserve their singing until young leave the nest then use it as a way of keeping the family group together (along with males, who also start singing again too).

Black-headed Grosbeaks are partial to oaks and will nest in any type of forest that includes oaks or a mix of oaks and conifers, but they are equally drawn to deciduous trees and tall shrubs near water. They avoid dense interior areas and nearly always nest near forest edges. As soon as females arrive, about a week after males, they fight amongst each other for the best territories and then accept whichever male owns that territory. The highest quality territories are those furthest from neighboring Steller's or Western Scrub-Jays; in one study, 60 percent of their nests were predated by jays.

Grosbeaks feed in pretty much the same niches as Western

Tanagers and Yellow-rumped Warblers, searching for insects on leaf surfaces and occasionally snatching flying insects in quick flights. They mostly forage in black oaks and ponderosa pines, and in oaks they feed on the larvae, pupae, and adults of oak moths. In mid-summer, they supplement their diet with ripening berries and fruits such as service-berries, elderberries, dogwoods, blackberries, and poison oak.

Courting males may be observed making spectacular "song-flights" in early May that involve flying up from prominent perches with stiff, shallow wingbeats while singing loudly and fully spreading their wing and tail feathers, followed by gliding back to their original perch-es. Females form pair bonds within hours of their arrival and from late April to mid-May build nests in the outer branches of small deciduous trees or bushes. Their nests are famous for being so loosely constructed that you might see their 2–5 eggs through the twigs.

Both sexes sit on eggs, with females taking the night shift, but because males lack brood patches they are not truly incubating but primarily keeping eggs covered when females take breaks to eat some food. Eggs hatch in 12–14 days and young birds leave the nest at 13 days of age though it takes 15 more days before they can fly. Flightless young birds stay quiet and well hidden, but as soon as they can fly chicks be-come very noisy and both parents start singing as a way of keeping the family group together.

Adult males leave the Sierra Nevada in late July–early August while females and some juveniles depart in mid-August. Other juve-niles leave a few weeks later. Black-headed Grosbeaks in Arizona and New Mexico follow streamcourses downslope in late summer before migrating south, and it seems that they follow the same pattern in the Sierra Nevada because many August sightings are at lower elevations.

Black-headed Grosbeaks males look like females during their first year and do not attain adult plumages until their second year. These first-year males arrive in the spring about two weeks after breed-ing males to avoid aggressive encounters and then gradually molt into their adult plumage as the summer progresses. Reports of adult males in September (and very rarely in October or even in the winter) are al-most certainly first-year birds that linger to gain familiarity with the territories they will try to defend the following spring.

Note: *Small numbers of closely related and very similar* **Rose-breasted Grosbeaks** *occasionally make surprise appearances almost anywhere in the Sierra Nevada, so look carefully at every grosbeak.*

RANGE Black-headed Grosbeaks are widespread and common breeders in deciduous and mixed-conifer forests throughout the Sierra Nevada, especially near open areas or water. Most arrive in late April–early May and remain until August, with decreasing numbers lingering into September. Some wander upslope to treeline after breeding, but many appear to move downslope before departing. **WEST SLOPE:** Nest in foothill oak woodlands and in pockets of black oaks and deciduous trees throughout the Mixed Conifer Zone, mostly 2500–6000 ft. **EAST SLOPE:** Primarily nest in stands of deciduous trees along streams and wet meadows, mainly in cottonwoods, aspens, and willows, from about 5000–8000 ft.

LAZULI BUNTING *Passerina amoena*

LIFE HISTORY Despite their intensely blue, light-reflecting feathers and loud songs, male Lazuli Buntings have an astonishing ability to hide in full view as they sing from prominent perches. Birdwatchers sometimes find themselves scanning bushes over and over again as Lazuli Buntings sing right in front of them. Even more frustrating, they only breed in local clusters, sometimes with miles of unoccupied habitat in between, so it is a pleasure to finally discover a location where they are singing.

Migrants from Mexico begin showing up in mid- to late April, with a trickle of males for the first week, followed by a sudden deluge of males and females, as well as first-year males who arrive not knowing any songs and immediately begin copying one or more adult songs. Early-arriving males hang out in small groups for several days, feeding quietly together but increasingly singing and fighting as they stake out territories. Males sing complex, buzzy twittering songs, taking about two weeks for all territories to be occupied. As soon as males find mates, their singing rates drop dramatically as they spend all their time closely attending the females.

Lazuli Buntings breed in a wide range of relatively open brushy habitats, from dry chaparral slopes to lush streamside thickets. They even nest in open meadows with patches of tall forbs like corn lilies or cow parsnips. Males may provide variable amounts of parental care throughout the entire nesting process, but they mostly just follow females closely as females pick nesting sites, gather nesting material, and forage for seeds and fruits or glean insects and spiders from plants.

Females build small cup nests in dense vegetation within 3 feet of the ground, first weaving grasses and bark strips around supporting branches then lining the cup with finer grasses and hairs. Females incubate the 3–4 eggs for 12 days and feed the nestlings until they leave the nest when 9–11 days old. Males may help feed nestlings, especially if females start a second brood in late June or July (as many are thought to do), in this case males are solely responsible for the fledglings for up to two weeks while females incubate new eggs.

Note: *A very small number of outrageously blue* **Indigo Buntings** *are increasingly regular visitors to the Sierra Nevada, especially along the east side, and in the Owens Valley, with some remaining to breed.*

RANGE Lazuli Buntings are widespread but only locally common in the Sierra Nevada, with breeding birds patchily distributed in clusters across the landscape. Their habitats are difficult to classify, but they breed in many types of brushy areas and meadow edges from the lower foothills to mid-elevations. Postbreeding birds increasingly drift from their territories in July and early August, coalescing into small flocks that wander through an even wider variety of shrubby habitats from the foothills to treeline, feasting on berries and fruits. Most leave the Sierra Nevada by the end of August, but some linger to the end of September. **WEST SLOPE:** Spring migrants first arrive in the southern Sierra Nevada around mid-April, but they become common everywhere on the west slope by the first week of May (though their arrival at higher elevations may be delayed another week or two). Nest as high as the upper Mixed Conifer Zone, from the foothills to about 6000 ft. **EAST SLOPE:** First arrive in the Owens Valley as far north as Bishop by late April, but within two weeks they are widespread along the entire east side. Nest from valley floors to about 8000 ft. Birds that breed at higher elevations may briefly linger on lower slopes then move to their breeding grounds in early June.

BLACKBIRDS (Icteridae)

RED-WINGED BLACKBIRD *Agelaius phoeniceus*

LIFE HISTORY Although they are so abundant and familiar that they might be overlooked, Red-winged Blackbirds still add a lively and evocative flavor to the Sierra Nevada landscape. In the summer, they are the throbbing pulse of energy animating every marsh, and on lonely winter evenings small groups fly overhead in the last sunset rays chattering to each other with *check* notes and heading for hidden roosts. In short, they are a constant year-round presence and display a variety of memorable behaviors.

Red-wingeds spend every season in groups big and small. Winter flocks in low-lying agricultural areas can number in the millions, feeding on seeds and grains in agricultural fields by day, and then returning each evening to sleep in the same patch of dry marsh vegetation. Flocks of wintering birds can be recognized by their habit of flying in long, narrow columns; while blackbirds that are migrating fly side by side. Within these flocks, subgroups may separate out on the basis of age and sex.

As early as February they begin casting longing eyes towards the still-dormant marshes where they will soon begin nesting, lingering nearby in growing numbers and increasingly acting territorial. By mid-March, they are already abundant throughout the Sierra Nevada; either migrating north or settling on territories in local, low-elevation marshes. Breeding blackbirds favor marshes with tall emergent vegetation but will use willow thickets in wet meadows, as well as the brushy margins of lakes and ponds, or even nearby weedy fields and blackberry brambles.

Each male sings up to nine types of *conk-a-ree* songs, combining these with various *chit* or *check* calls and flashing the brilliant red epaulets they have kept hidden all winter. These patches of red feathers are their most diagnostic breeding cues. For example in one scientific study, blackbirds whose red feathers were covered immediately lost their territories.

Red-wingeds have an unusual breeding system, in which each male guards as many as 15 females who nest on his territory. It is thought that females prefer to nest close together on a single male's territory so they can protect each other's nests from Marsh Wrens, the most notorious killers of eggs and baby birds in marshes. Because of this system, breeding blackbirds are often called "colonial," but it is more likely that they simply clump together in any patch of suitable marsh habitat.

Females begin building nests by at least mid-April, but they nest in so many different types of habitats in so many portions of the Sierra Nevada that it is hard to summarize their breeding behavior. In a typical marsh of cattails and bulrushes, they build nests by weaving strips of cattail leaves around several cattail or bulrush stems, making platforms of wet grasses and then shaping cups from mud that they later line with fine grasses.

Females raise two broods over the course of the summer, incubating each set of 4 eggs for 11–13 days, then feeding their nestlings on a diet of insects for 10 days. Each male helps to varying degrees but at nests where males help feed, the nestlings end up fatter and healthier. Young birds are fed another two weeks after leaving the nest, and even for a couple more weeks after that, but as soon as they are independent they join flocks with older females that feed and sleep as a group.

Note: *Ninety-nine percent of the world's population of* Tricolored Blackbirds *occurs in California, where they are highly threatened by significant habitat loss across their range. Most are found in the Central Valley and coastal California but there are nesting colonies in the Kern River Valley, at Honey Lake, and at scattered locations along the lowest edges of the west slope. Except at Honey Lake, where they leave in the winter, they are mainly resident in and around their nesting areas. They are often seen among large Red-winged Blackbird flocks.*

RANGE The lowest numbers of Red-winged Blackbirds in the Sierra Nevada occur November–December, when they are restricted to low-elevation slopes and valley bottoms. Their numbers may increase in January, but it is hard to tell on the west slope, where they are already common. By mid-February their numbers are clearly increasing all around the perimeter of the Sierra Nevada, and then in March they become abundant everywhere, even at higher elevations sites like Lake Tahoe. Breeding activity begins late March–early April and continues until July, when many blackbirds start moving away from the increasingly dry marshes and wetlands where they have been breeding all summer. There may be an increase in numbers as migrants arrive in August but then numbers slowly diminish through September–October as more and more blackbirds head towards prime feeding areas in the Central Valley. Relatively small numbers (flocks of hundreds or thousands) linger through the winter in valleys and foothills.

WESTERN MEADOWLARK *Sturnella neglecta*

LIFE HISTORY It might be a sign of the meadowlark's popularity that at least 6 states have meadowlarks as their state birds, perhaps in recognition of meadowlarks' intense lemon-yellow breasts and bubbling, flutelike songs. These bright colors and loud songs are adaptations for a grassland lifestyle, where courting birds have a hard time being seen among tall grasses. Streaked and well-camouflaged from behind, meadowlarks can choose to perch on prominent fence posts and show off their boldly patterned breasts when they need to attract mates or defend territories.

Meadowlarks are built for life on the ground, with stocky bodies and short tails, strong legs, and long, sturdy bills. Like all members of the blackbird family, their bills are adapted for "gaping," the ability to forcibly open their bills to pry open crevices or dig in the soil. Meadowlarks feed by picking, probing, and gaping to reach under dirt clods and dig for various food items; in winter and early spring they primarily eat grains in agricultural areas; in late spring and summer they seek insects and grubs in native grasslands; and through the fall they roam in search of various weed seeds in any type of open, barren area or dried grassland.

Although they sing sporadically during the winter, this is nothing compared to the exuberant outpourings that open their breeding season. Males each sing 6–9 versions of these complex melodious songs from fence posts and rocks in open grasslands or pastures. Equally familiar are the *chupp* calls they make when mildly alarmed, for instance, if a group of birdwatchers is staring at them through binoculars.

Breeding males are on their territories in March, with females arriving 2–4 weeks later. Females immediately pair up when they arrive, and males typically mate with two females that nest wherever tall grasses provide dense cover. Their grass nests are very well concealed on the ground, with a roof so they cannot be seen from above, and with grassy tunnels so females can sneak to and from their nests.

The nesting season begins in late April-early May and extends through July because many females raise two broods. Males play little role in the nesting activities though some males are more helpful. Females incubate their 5 eggs for 13–14 days, and young birds leave the nest when 10–12 days old. Fledglings are agile runners but cannot fly at first, so they are dependent on their parents for two weeks.

RANGE Western Meadowlarks are common, year-round residents of the expansive grasslands, agricultural areas, and other barren areas that ring the Sierra Nevada. Numbers start increasing in late February and singing birds are a conspicuous presence by March though it is unknown how many remain to breed. At Lake Tahoe, where they are rare breeders in the summer, there is a clear pulse of migrants in March–April that would be obscured if large numbers remained to breed. After breeding, meadowlarks join loosely associated groups that wander widely in August, with a few individuals or small flocks showing up in the high mountains (as high as treeline); in mid-September to mid-October they are joined by waves of migrants. Large and small flocks linger through the winter in any open area that is free of snow and provides abundant food. **WEST SLOPE:** Abundant to locally common in grasslands, agricultural areas, and open oak woodlands from the Central Valley into the lowest edges of the foothills, then increasingly uncommon and patchily distributed to elevations where conifer forests become dense. In the winter they wander irregularly in the foothills, remaining in some areas for short periods of time then moving on. Very small numbers of migrants show up in open or barren areas at almost any elevation. Breeding birds are restricted to large open meadows and grasslands, mostly below 2000 ft, but occasionally as high as 5000 ft. **EAST SLOPE:** Except during migration, when scattered groups wander widely across open sagebrush flats and small patches of barren or grassy ground, meadowlarks are largely restricted to major valley bottoms with extensive meadows and agriculture. For example, they are fairly common migrants, wintering, and breeding birds at places like Honey Lake, Sierra Valley, Bridgeport Valley, Mono Lake, and the northern Owens Valley.

Yellow-headed Blackbird
Xanthocephalus xanthocephalus

LIFE HISTORY Wherever they nest, Yellow-headed Blackbirds are a raucous and conspicuous presence, but it takes work to find them because they breed in colonies at only a few scattered locations. Bigger and heavier than Red-winged Blackbirds, Yellow-headeds are dominant at higher-quality, food-rich marshes, even kicking out Red-wingeds if the smaller birds get there first. In fact, Yellow-headeds are so impressive that even the marshes' most feared nest predators, Marsh Wrens, back away when Yellow-headeds arrive to nest.

Perhaps for this reason, migrating Yellow-headeds arrive relatively late, heading straight for deep-water marshes and wetlands with abundant thickets of tall, dense cattails and bulrushes; they immediately overwhelm their nesting grounds with loud creaking, caterwauling sounds that are hardly reminiscent of "songs." They are a lively presence from May–July, chasing, displaying, calling constantly, and flying back and forth with food. Males have 13 different displays and females another 7, so these highly social birds are continuously posturing and interacting.

Their most common contact calls are a simple *tsheck*, but males also have two types of songs; one type, with liquid notes and a trill, is directed at other males flying overhead or newly arriving females and involves a male spreading his wings while lifting his bill; another type of song is a raucous *kuk—koh-koh-koh—waaaaaaa*, which involves a male turning his head sharply to the left while only slightly lifting his wings and is used for territorial disputes.

They always nest in groups, with harems of 1–6 females on each male's territory. Territories are usually clustered in tight colonies with all the birds feeding in communal areas on nearby fields or muddy shorelines, rather than finding food on their territories. During the breeding season they mostly eat aquatic insects, specializing on newly emerging dragonflies, but they supplement this diet with terrestrial invertebrates and grains. The colony serves as an information hub, with birds watching each other to learn where the best food sources are located.

Females arrive 1–2 weeks after males, and nest from May–June, building nests by weaving long strands of wet cattail leaves to bind together standing cattail or bulrush stems. Nests have saucer-shaped bottoms and after each visit with new materials, females stamp them down with their feet. The finished cup is open, with a smooth, even rim, and holds 3–4 eggs. Males stand guard as females incubate for 12–13 days. Males may help feed chicks unless they have a large harem and are busy trying to attract more females. Young fledge in 9–12 days and are fed for another couple of days before joining groups of adults and juveniles that lurk secretively in dense stands of cattails as they molt their feathers in July–August.

RANGE Yellow-headed Blackbirds have an abbreviated nesting season, when they are nearly always found at low elevations on the east side. **WEST SLOPE:** Transients and stragglers are occasionally observed, mostly in the spring (April–May), when they stop briefly at marshes or wet meadows. Uncommon migrants and rare breeders in the South Fork Kern River Valley, and they might also breed at Lake Almanor. **EAST SLOPE:** Very early migrants begin arriving the last week of March, but most show up, often in good-sized groups, from mid- to late April, with local breeders stopping to breed in suitable habitats from the Owens Valley to Honey Lake. One of the largest and most easily observed colonies is located along Dyson Lane in Sierra Valley. There are other colonies at Truckee, South Lake Tahoe, Bridgeport Reservoir, and Mono Lake. Numbers decline sharply after mid-August though some linger with Red-winged and Brewer's Blackbirds until October. There are records from every month of the year around Bishop and the Owens Valley.

Brewer's Blackbird *Euphagus cyanocephalus*

LIFE HISTORY Brewer's Blackbirds are one of the Sierra Nevada's most ubiquitous and adaptable birds. They obviously favor human company and all over North America their native range has expanded dramatically due to forest clearing, agriculture, railroads, highways, towns, and other developments. Courtesy of parking lots, campgrounds, stables, and roadside attractions, they have even followed humans into the mountains, and now breed as high as 9000 ft. Despite their close human association, it is a pleasant surprise to occasionally find them around remote mountain lakes.

Like other members of their family, Brewer's are highly social throughout the year. They spend the winter in large flocks, often foraging together with Red-winged Blackbirds, starlings, and cowbirds, in search of waste grains, grass seeds, and weed seeds in open fields or on barren ground. Flocks of Brewer's Blackbirds may be seen flying to and from their feeding areas and traditional roosting sites where they sleep together at night, often in great numbers.

In March (or April and May in the mountains) they begin their breeding season, nesting in small colonies (or occasionally in isolated pairs) in almost any kind of situation. They may nest on the ground, in low bushes, on tree branches and sometimes in tree cavities; it seems that their only requirements are access to prime foraging areas, to water, and to trees where males can stand guard against intruders. In the mountains, these conditions are often met in campgrounds, around picnic areas, and next to popular lakes, which probably accounts for the constant presence of these birds all summer. They also utilize a wide variety of native habitats, usually in wooded margins or brushy thickets near lakes and wet meadows.

Within a colony, each pair's territory consists of the area around their nest, which females defend from other females, while males worry about defending females from other males. Pairs are almost always seen together as they forage for insects on the ground, or as females gather nesting materials for their bulky stick nests. Males become excessively attentive and vigilant during egg laying, forcefully chasing away other males and copulating frequently with the females.

Females incubate their 5–6 eggs for 12–13 days. Then both parents feed the chicks until they become independent at just over a month old. Many pairs raise a second brood and are probably actively engaged in some kind of breeding activity for most of the summer. As summer progresses, nonbreeding adults and recently fledged young begin to gather in increasingly larger groups.

RANGE Brewer's Blackbirds are common breeders on both slopes of the Sierra Nevada from the base of the foothills to nearly 9000 ft. Many wander upslope after breeding. Most leave the Sierra Nevada by the end of November, but some linger around open areas, agricultural fields, and towns through the winter. When it snows they descend to lower elevations or, on the east side, they may abandon some areas temporarily.

BROWN-HEADED COWBIRD *Molothrus ater*

LIFE HISTORY It is easy to dismiss or malign these birds as invasive parasites when in fact they have fascinating life histories. While they do have a detrimental impact on highly threatened species, including Willow Flycatchers and Least Bell's Vireos, some scientists make a valid point that the root of the problem is not cowbirds but humans altering the landscape.

Cowbirds were originally restricted to the Great Plains where they followed nomadic buffalo herds. They evolved to lay their eggs in other birds' nests, which allowed the adults to keep moving while their eggs were raised by other birds. When settlers killed off the buffalo herds, the cowbirds switched to following horses and cows instead and have since invaded every corner of the United States, bringing with them their pernicious egg-laying habits.

In their relentless march across the continent, they reached Yosemite Valley in 1934 and within 10–25 years followed humans into all parts of the Sierra Nevada. They are now ubiquitous summer visitors throughout the mountains, and are nearly always found in close proximity to stables, corrals, campgrounds, picnic areas, and backyard bird feeders where they feast on grains, seeds, and insects. From these primary feeding areas they commute up to 10 miles into all types of habitats in search of nesting birds to parasitize.

Cowbirds have unusual and complex breeding behaviors. Between April and July, females fly off each morning to find songbirds that are in the process of building nests, returning day after day to watch them, and then when the time is exactly right they lay an egg in the target nest. Females have particularly large spatial memory centers (the hippocampus), and they are probably watching and plotting the fate of a dozen or more nests at any given moment because over the course of the summer each female can lay as many as 70 eggs (nearly all of them in different nests).

Another fascinating aspect of cowbirds are their vocalizations. Males have two primary songs, a "perch song" which sounds like bubbling, tinkling water, and a "flight whistle." Flight whistles are meant to be heard at a great distance, and males will not sing them near each other because they do not want to divulge the details of their unique version of the song. Each population has its own distinctive flight whistles and females will not mate with males that do not sing the proper local dialect. One well-studied population near Mono Lake and Mammoth Lakes has been singing the same dialect since 1978.

Perch songs on the other hand are meant for close-up communication and males sing them while bowing and spreading their wings, which forces them to show their underwing coverts and reveal their age (younger and older birds show different colors). These songs have the greatest frequency range of any bird vocalization in the world, ascending from a few hundred hertz to 10–12 thousand hertz almost instantly.

Pairs are highly monogamous and use different vocalizations to maintain their pair bonds. For instance, in response to a male's flight whistles a female makes a distinctive chatter that draws him over. When he gets close to his mate, he switches to his perch song. Females may even chatter at other passing males just to attract them and test her male's ability to defend her. Immediately before and after copulation, a male will loudly run through his entire repertoire, both perch songs and flight whistles in quick sequence, which is a blatant mating advertisement that only dominant males have the courage to attempt. These distinctive vocalizations can be heard all summer long because females need to copulate every day in order to lay up to 70 eggs.

After a long and busy summer, adult cowbirds leave the mountains by the end of July. Their chicks, which are laid in the nests of many other species of songbirds and raised by many types of parents, either linger in the mountains into the fall or head downslope to join large flocks of cowbirds and other blackbirds that spend the winter in warmer valleys and coastal areas.

RANGE Brown-headed Cowbirds are common to abundant breeders from the foothills to treeline, but their populations are patchily distributed and mostly clustered around prime feeding areas (such as stables, pastures, towns, and campgrounds). They avoid large areas of dense or unlogged forests, but they will cross these habitats to reach isolated stables, homesteads, or campgrounds. Cowbirds are abundant in the mountains from April–July, with some juveniles lingering into September. WEST SLOPE: In the winter, when most cowbirds head for the Central Valley or the coast, many remain on the west slope in areas below the snowline where there is abundant food. They are most numerous around towns and ranches at the lowest elevations, but occur locally up to about 3000 ft. They may also be concentrated in the central Sierra Nevada because they are far less numerous in the northern and southern foothills. Breeding birds, however, are abundant everywhere, especially because the west slope is so densely settled with ranches, ranchettes, towns, subdivisions, campgrounds, and various recreation destinations. **EAST SLOPE:** Although small numbers linger through the winter in the Owens Valley and in the Sierra Valley–Honey Lake area, most do not show up until the breeding season when they are abundant in valleys and around pack stations all along the east side. In July, and then even more so in August and September, nearly all of the cowbirds reported in the Sierra Nevada are on the east side, though it is not clear if this represents movements of local birds or the arrival of northern migrants (or a lack of reporting from the west side).

Bullock's Oriole *Icterus bullockii*

LIFE HISTORY With their bold colors and loud chattering calls, orioles are a welcome presence each summer. Even better, they spend most of their time and nest in large shade trees near water so they are a familiar backdrop for summer picnics and trips to favorite swimming holes. Bullock's Orioles are particularly fond of cottonwoods, poplars, and oaks, and they arrive as soon as new leaves appear, taking up residence in riparian and oak woodlands, isolated groves of deciduous trees, backyards, and city parks with tall densely-foliaged trees.

Pairs feed together on caterpillars and other insects, supplementing their diets with fruits and flower nectar. Like other blackbirds, they often feed by gaping, spearing their bills into hairy caterpillars then prying them open to avoid the protective hairs, or spearing their bills into soft fruits and opening them so they can lap up the pooling juices with their tongues.

Pairs wait 1–2 weeks before they begin nesting and then spend two more weeks constructing neatly woven, hanging nests made of hairs, fibers, grasses, and string, including colorful pieces of twine or ribbon. They typically place their nests in isolated trees, or small groves of trees, as well as near forest edges, and usually close to water. In the Sierra Nevada, nests are completed from mid-May to mid-June, and 4–5 eggs are laid as soon as the nest is finished.

Females perform most of the nest building and incubation duties alone, but males stand constant guard while uttering harsh rattling *cha-cha-cha-cha* calls to warn of approaching intruders. Pairs cooperate to aggressively chase off potential nest predators, and they readily puncture and toss out cowbird eggs that are laid in their nest. Both males and females sing, especially early in the breeding season—making a jumble of rising and falling whistles mixed with *check* notes and chatters.

Eggs hatch in 11 days, and both parents feed nestlings until they leave the nest at 14 days of age. Young birds often mingle in small groups that are fed equally by all parents, but within a few days they are independent and loose flocks of orioles soon begin their long migration to Mexico.

Note: *All orioles should be carefully examined because other orioles also visit or breed in the Sierra Nevada. For example, eastern* **Baltimore Orioles** *are rare but regular transients, especially from late May-early June in the Owens Valley.* **Hooded Orioles** *are also rare but widespread transients, with a few remaining to breed in exotic fan palms, particularly around neighborhoods on the west slope.* **Scott's Orioles** *are fairly common breeders in Joshua tree and pinyon-juniper woodlands in the Owens Valley and over Walker Pass into the upper Walker Basin, but very few nest within the area covered by this book.*

RANGE Breeding Bullock's Orioles are largely restricted to riparian woodlands or isolated groves of trees at lower elevations all around the Sierra Nevada. Because they time their arrival to the opening of new leaves, they arrive 1–2 weeks earlier on the west slope. A few hardy pioneers arrive the last week of March in the southern Sierra Nevada, but most arrive in early April on the west slope or mid-April on the east slope, becoming abundant and beginning nest construction in early May. Small groups start heading south again in late July, and their overall numbers decline sharply through August. By early September they are absent in the northern Sierra Nevada and very scarce in the south. Individual birds very rarely linger into winter, taking advantage of flowering exotic shrubs and backyard hummingbird feeders. **WEST SLOPE:** Common breeders to 3000 ft, and locally uncommon to just over 4000 ft. **EAST SLOPE:** Common breeders in valley bottoms and on lower slopes though they have been reported as high as 8000 ft at Mammoth Lakes. In the north they primarily breed below 5000 ft.

FINCHES (Fringillidae)

Gray-crowned Rosy-Finch *Leucosticte tephrocotis*

LIFE HISTORY Rosy-finches are one of the Sierra Nevada's most sought-after birds. They are not rare but it takes a lot of work and a bit of luck to access their lofty kingdoms and find them, and even in their prime habitats you have to work hard to hear their buzzy *chew* calls or spot them swooping and swirling across rocky slopes and alpine ice fields. But on the other hand, when you do find them, they can be ridiculously nonchalant, fearlessly foraging right next to observers, even eating out of people's hands at popular destinations like the summit of Mt. Whitney.

Except during the breeding season, rosy-finches are a flocking species and winter flocks of hundreds or even thousands are regularly observed on the east slope below their prime breeding areas in the High Sierra. Here they wander across rocky slopes and sagebrush flats, and through pinyon pine woodlands, often in the company of the distinctive northern subspecies "Hepburn's" Gray-crowned Rosy-Finches which migrate south in the winter. But as soon as there is a break in the wintry weather, or when the snow begins to melt in April, May, or June, local rosy-finches move back upslope to their breeding grounds.

In the summer, rosy-finches have a very patchy and specialized distribution, breeding only on isolated alpine peaks and along the High Sierra crest, from above treeline to over 14,000 ft. They seem unfazed by extremes conditions, even flying almost playfully in high winds and driving snow. It seems nothing short of miraculous that rosy-finches find food on icy snowfields, but swiftly rising air from the lowlands carries an endless supply of insects into the high mountains, where hapless insects "rain" out of the sky and litter snowfields, alive but too numb to fly. While feeding nestlings, adults make long foraging trips to distant snowfields and alpine meadows, literally stuffing their cheeks with insects and the seeds of daisies, buckwheats, grasses, and sedges then flying back to their nests with the storage pouches in their cheeks full of food.

Nests are typically located in the crevices of vertically fractured rocks and are made of bulky gatherings of mosses, lichens, grasses, and sedges lined with hairs, fine grasses, and feathers. Females build the nests in early June–early July and incubate their 3–5 eggs for 14 days, while males feed the females and later help feed the nestlings until they leave the nest at 15–22 days of age. From July into August, parents are regularly observed feeding their loudly begging fledglings around alpine meadows, both in family groups and in increasingly larger flocks that remain in the mountains until October–November.

RANGE Gray-crowned Rosy-Finches are fairly common breeders around peaks, cirques, lakes, and meadows in the Alpine Zone and in exposed areas of the Subalpine and Upper Montane Zones as low as 9000 ft (breeding birds are regularly observed on the summit of Half Dome in Yosemite National Park at 8800 ft). Found from Sierra Buttes in Sierra County (where nesting is not confirmed) south to Cottonwood Lakes near Mt. Whitney, and Florence Peak in Sequoia National Park. Breeding locations are scattered and widely separated except along the High Sierra crest where rosy-finches are more common. Wintering birds are observed on the east side, mostly south of Bridgeport, but because winter flocks are highly nomadic and because the northern subspecies migrates south onto the east side, they can be expected anywhere along the east side in the winter. **WEST SLOPE:** It is thought that most rosy-finches move onto the east slope for the winter, but lack of access makes it difficult to determine how many remain at high elevations on the west side. **EAST SLOPE:** Large winter flocks are sporadically observed on the east side in November–April, but due to their nomadic nature they are nowhere predictable. For periods of time, smaller groups become regular visitors at bird feeders around Mammoth Lakes, Aspendell, and other mountain communities.

PINE GROSBEAK *Pinicola enucleator*

LIFE HISTORY These utterly unique finches live in boreal and montane forests of northern Europe, Russia, and North America—except for one tiny group that lives way down in the Sierra Nevada all by itself, far from their closest relatives. Elusive and restricted to a narrow altitudinal range, these hard-to-find birds are at the top of many people's must-see lists. Do not be confused by their names, as Pine Grosbeaks are not related to Black-headed Grosbeaks or Evening Grosbeaks—they are more closely related to Hawaiian honeycreepers.

Pine Grosbeaks have a confounding and unstudied story in the Sierra Nevada. Months go by without anyone reporting one, and in some areas they seem to be absent for years, yet there is nowhere else these birds could go because this endemic subspecies lives only in a relatively small part of the Sierra Nevada.

Whatever their seasonal patterns are, they appear to breed in upper montane and subalpine conifer forests, including forests dominated by lodgepole pines, mountain hemlocks, whitebark pines, and red firs. They use their short conical bills to snip off tree buds and the growing tips of conifer branches, supplementing their diets with various fruits and seeds when available. They have been observed eating cottonwood buds, fruits of mountain ash, maple seeds, and pine seeds. Nestlings are fed a diet of insects mashed into a paste with seeds, and regurgitated from storage pouches in the parents' cheeks.

Because they are secretive and hard to spot, Pine Grosbeaks are often detected by the male's fluty, warbling song, which is like a loud, richer version of a Purple Finch's song; they are also decent mimics of other bird sounds. Their distinctive flight calls *tee-tee-tew* are used to hold a flock together (in the nonbreeding season they live in small flocks of 5–15 birds), and mated pairs use identical flight calls so they can recognize each other.

Nest-building begins in late May and nests are well-concealed in dense foliage, usually 6–12 ft high on the south side of a conifer near the trunk. The structure is a bulky bunch of twigs with an inner cup lined with soft grasses, conifer needles, and lichens. Females incubate 3–4 eggs for 13–14 days and both parents feed the nestlings until they leave the nest. Young birds follow their parents closely, constantly begging for food, for several weeks.

RANGE Pine Grosbeaks are uncommon residents of montane conifer forests from 7000 ft to treeline; but their numbers vary considerably each season, and even each year. Found on both slopes of the Sierra Nevada from Lakes Basin in Plumas County and Yuba Pass in Sierra County (one of the best places in the Sierra Nevada to see them), south to Jennie Lakes Wilderness and Kings Canyon National Park. Oddly, many records of straying birds (especially at lower elevations) are from June–July, when adults are breeding.

PURPLE FINCH *Carpodacus purpureus*

LIFE HISTORY Anyone who lives in the foothills and feeds backyard birds will be surprised to learn that the seemingly common Purple Finches are little studied and poorly known. This is especially true in regards to their mysterious winter movements when they irregularly disappear from significant portions of their local range and do not seem to show up anywhere else. Purple Finches spend the winter in the lower foothills but they are unpredictable and their numbers seem to vary dramatically as they move between all types of habitats in constant search of seeds, flowers, buds, fruits, and some insects. They may gather in flocks by themselves or mingle with other finches, and are regular visitors to backyard feeders along with goldfinches and siskins.

On warm sunny days in February, males ascend to treetops and practice their delightful warbling songs, one of the first signs that spring is coming to the foothills. In March they begin moving upslope into well-shaded canyons, riparian woodlands, and moist conifer or oak-conifer forests. Many are on their territories by April, but they become even more abundant in May so it seems that their arrival spans several weeks.

Their twiggy nests are built among dense foliage well out on co-nifer branches, sometimes in oaks. It is not known what roles both sexes play in nest construction, but males feed females, on and off the nest, while the females incubate 3–5 eggs for 12 days. Young birds leave the nest when 13–16 days old and remain near the nest for another week, but nothing more is known of their breeding cycle or the lives of im-mature birds.

RANGE Breeding Purple Finches reach their highest densities in mid-elevation forests on the west slope, where they are most common in riparian woodlands and well-shaded conifer forests from 3000-5000 ft. On occasion, they may breed as high as 8000 ft. Wintering birds generally remain in the Foothill Oak Zone below 3000 ft, but they ir-regularly wander into lower portions of the Mixed Conifer Zone up to 5000 ft. **WEST SLOPE:** From October–February they are concentrated at low elevations where they may move around a lot but are generally common most years. Upslope movement begins in March and peaks in May, when they remain on their breeding grounds until late July; then for some reason they are so rarely reported (except for a handful of low-elevation sightings) in August and September that it is almost as if they leave the Sierra Nevada. South of Yosemite National Park they appear to only breed in a relatively narrow altitudinal band, but north of Yosemite they breed across a much broader range of elevations. **EAST SLOPE:** Only rarely encountered on the east side, and mostly north of Alpine County from March–July. However, they have been recorded breeding around Sierra Valley (where they occasionally overwinter) and they may breed elsewhere in the Diamond Mountains and around Honey Lake.

Cassin's Finch *Carpodacus cassinii*

LIFE HISTORY These vivacious finches breed everywhere in the high mountains, but they are not always conspicuous because they spend much of their time near the tops of conifers. In addition, females and young males are brown, streaky birds that blend in with their surroundings. Only breeding males have bright red plumage and lovely rollicking songs, but they sing for a brief period of time then fall silent when they start nesting and are equally hard to find.

Not surprisingly, their life history and seasonal movements are little studied and poorly known. During the nesting season they overlap with Purple Finches at lower elevations, but prefer slightly drier and more open forests, and at higher elevations they are by far the most numerous finches. Some begin gathering at lower elevations in March, but most arrive and move upslope to breed in April or May. They can be found in whitebark pines, mountain hemlocks, white firs, red firs, cottonwoods, and aspens, but favor mature lodgepole, ponderosa, and Jeffrey pines, especially near meadow edges and water.

Both males and females sing, as well as first-year males (who look like females), and they are all excellent mimics of other bird songs. Their own bright warbling songs are so rapid that the notes seem to fall over each other, but their distinctive calls *kee-up* or *ti-di-lip* are heard more often. Early in the nesting season, breeding males may sing while making slow, mothlike flights to show off their plumage.

These finches are semi-colonial, and a fair number may nest in the same stand of trees, with nests built near the tops of conifers spaced about 75 ft apart. Nests may be built in May–June, but there are very few records, and in fact their entire nesting cycle remains virtually unstudied. Females lay 4–5 eggs, and males have been observed guarding and feeding incubating females, with both parents feeding nestlings. Family groups with begging juveniles are a common sight in July, but beyond these anecdotal observations little is known about their breeding biology.

These finches are gregarious birds, even in the nesting season when unmated males hang out in groups together, and then after midsummer, when family groups start coalescing into increasingly larger flocks that wander in search of food. They are often seen on the ground, picking up gravel, seeds, and insects, or visiting mineral deposits to obtain essential salts. When available, they feast heavily on tree buds and various berries and fruits.

RANGE Although it is possible to provide a simple summary, Cassin's Finches actually have complex and poorly understood seasonal movements. The simple story is that they arrive in April, remain on their breeding grounds until August, then move downslope to avoid the coming winter. But in fact, they are scarce and often absent in the winter and no one knows where they go. If anything, there seems to be a late summer and fall movement toward lower elevations on the east slope, but then most leave the Sierra Nevada in December–February (though transients are occasionally observed at bird feeders). Numbers pick up noticeably in April, and by May they can be found everywhere in the mountains again (though perhaps not until early June in the higher portions of the southern Sierra Nevada). **WEST SLOPE:** Irregularly rare to uncommon, and often absent over large areas in the winter. Breeding birds are common to abundant in upper montane and subalpine forests from 6000 ft to treeline, and locally common breeders in mixed conifer forests down to 4500 ft. **EAST SLOPE:** Irregular in winter, but generally more numerous than on west slope. Common to abundant breeders from valley bottoms (as in the Jeffrey pine forests between Mono Lake and Mammoth Lakes) to treeline, occasionally nesting in aspen groves and cottonwoods in addition to conifers.

HOUSE FINCH *Carpodacus mexicanus*

LIFE HISTORY For most people this is "the red finch" of backyards, city parks, suburbs, and farms. Partial to dry, open areas, House Finches are the common finches of lowlands and foothill towns all around the perimeter of the Sierra Nevada, where they seem to relish human company, or at least human-altered landscapes, not to mention free handouts at bird feeders.

They maintain some degree of connection to wild, native habitats, and flocks of House Finches freely wander into riparian and oak woodlands, or into drier open forests and desert-scrub habitats as long as there is water nearby. Virtually their entire diet (even when feeding nestlings) consists of seeds and some buds, fruits, and berries, which they seek on the ground or in bushes and trees.

House Finches do not migrate north or south, and most probably remain in the foothills all year, but some birds obviously move upslope and downslope with the seasons. They may overlap slightly with Purple and Cassin's Finches although those two mountain finches prefer cooler, more shaded forests, especially in the breeding season.

While still in winter flocks, males and females begin to pair up, with females choosing males based on the brilliance of their red feathers. Males may improve their odds by performing "butterfly flights" in which they fly slowly up to heights of 50–100 ft then glide back to their perches while singing. Songs are very similar to those of other finches but are slower and harsher, ending on a distinctive, down-slurred note. Females may sing to solicit courtship feeding or copulations. Even after pairs have formed, flocks remain together until the nesting season begins, with some pairs nesting in loose colonies and others striking off on their own. They may nest in places as well hidden as dense tangles of vines, or as open as porch rafters (they readily nest around houses, barns, and other buildings).

Their breeding season spans much of the year, with egg-laying recorded from late February to early August in California, and females laying multiple clutches (up to 6 clutches have been recorded in some populations). There is almost no data from the Sierra Nevada, but egg-laying occurs in June at Lake Tahoe. When there are multiple clutches, males take charge of feeding one batch of fledglings while females build new nests and begin incubating new eggs. Males feed incubating females as well, and females will abandon a nest if their mates do not provide enough food. Juvenile birds follow their parents, loudly and aggressively begging for food, but as soon as they are independent, they join flocks of juvenile birds that congregate near food sources until adult birds finish the nesting season.

RANGE House Finches are year-round residents in agricultural areas, towns, and open, dry areas around valley bottoms and lower foothill slopes. Most breed at these elevations but their upslope breeding limits are obscure and need study. They may, for instance, breed around mid-elevation mountain towns. There are many June records from a wide range of elevations, but it is not clear whether these are breeding birds, postbreeding wanderers from lower elevations, or misidentified Purple and Cassin's Finches. **WEST SLOPE:** Common to abundant, at least locally around foothill towns and ranches. They generally stay below 2000 ft but also wander upslope into the Mixed Conifer Zone, and rarely higher, from June–September. **EAST SLOPE:** Fairly common in the north, and common to abundant in the south, from April–October. In the winter most retreat short distances into the lowest valley bottoms, where they are numerous. For instance, in mid-winter they are irregular in low numbers at Sierra Valley (5000 ft) but abundant at nearby Honey Lake (4200 ft); they are likewise irregular at Lake Tahoe (6625 ft) and abundant at nearby Carson City (4700 ft).

Red Crossbill *Loxia curvirostra*

LIFE HISTORY Crossbills are the ultimate avian nomads, wandering vast distances in search of abundant cone crops, then settling down and nesting almost any month of the year. Flocks of crossbills are always unpredictable, showing up without warning, lingering for days or months then vanishing in a day. They can be heard passing swiftly overhead, crying out with loud, ringing *kip* calls as they speed toward unknown destinations.

These oddball finches feed almost entirely on conifer seeds, using their crossed bills to pry open the scales of conifer cones so they can hook out hidden seeds with their tongues. Across North America, there are 8 distinct types of crossbills (these may be 8 separate species), with each type concentrating on its own preferred "key conifer" species, having evolved unique bill and palate structures that make them efficient at eating the seeds of their target conifers. Even though these populations overlap frequently during their nomadic wanderings, they have different calls notes and do not breed with each other.

The primary type in the Sierra Nevada ("type 2" birds) favors lodgepole pine cones at high elevations, or Jeffrey pine cones on the east side, where they cross paths with a few "type 4" birds (experts can tell them apart by their vocalizations). Their basic strategy is to wander nomadically May–June, looking for areas where lots of green, unripe cones promise a large fall harvest. Once a promising crop is located, they stay put, clambering around like agile parrots, nibbling on unripe conifer seeds, other seeds, and some insects while waiting for the conifer seeds to ripen in late September–October.

Although most birds lay eggs and raise young when food is abundant, crossbills are unique in using this period of abundant food to fuel their energetically-demanding molt. The advantage of this strategy is that by November–December crossbills have a thick new coat of feathers, while plenty of cones still hang on the trees if they want to start breeding in December.

Their peak breeding season in the Sierra Nevada, however, seems to be in the summer, when they are particularly noisy and conspicuous. This is when males may be observed singing and doing display flights over the forest with slow flapping wings. Courtship feeding and bill-touching are also common behaviors during pair formation. Both sexes help select well-concealed nest sites, high on conifer branches, where females lay 3 eggs and incubate them for 14 days. Young birds grow relatively slowly on a diet of regurgitated seed paste, leaving the nest at 15–25 days of age, then begging for food and closely following their parents for another month. Pairs probably raise a second brood when there are adequate food supplies.

RANGE Due to their nomadic nature, Red Crossbills show up almost anywhere, especially when conifer crops fail to materialize. They may even venture into the lowlands and linger in oak woodlands, but this is a rare occurrence. In the Sierra Nevada they spend most of their time in lodgepole pine and Jeffrey pine forests, or else flying across the landscape in search of these forests. Ponderosa pines on the west slope may also attract some crossbills. Regardless of elevation, they remain near productive cone crops through the winter.

PINE SISKIN *Spinus pinus*

LIFE HISTORY Pine Siskins are often described as wandering birds that come and go with no particular schedule or pattern, but it is just as likely that they have the ability to hide in full view. You can live years in the Sierra Nevada without seeing a single siskin and then within days of putting out a bird feeder they will be abundant, year-round visitors to your yard.

Like other finches they are gregarious, but not entirely amiable, birds. In flocks with other siskins or goldfinches there is a lot of petty squabbling, and siskins are pugnacious enough to chase larger finches away from food. Despite their inclination to roam widely, or to completely abandon a region without warning, they seem to be permanent residents in the Sierra Nevada that simply move upslope and downslope, or north and south. It would be easy to say that they move when the weather gets cold or food scarce, but they are year-round residents in Alaska and Canada so cold temperatures do not seem to bother them, and they eat superabundant weed and grass seeds, as well as an incredibly diverse range of conifer and plant seeds, tree buds, insects, and spiders, so it does not seem like they would ever run out of food.

Although their tiny, sharply pointed bills limit the size of seeds they can handle, siskins are amazingly resourceful. If they cannot break open large, hard-shelled seeds, they may simply eat the scraps left behind by big-billed finches. And siskins are nimble and well-adapted for clinging and hanging from the tips of branches to reach cones, seed heads, and insects that other finches cannot access. Flocks of noisy and very active siskins will swarm all over the canopy of a single tree, constantly chattering with husky whistles and characteristic *zwee-e-eeet* calls that sound like someone running their finger along a comb.

Siskins are also highly social in the breeding season, when they nest in loose colonies and visit each other's nests on a regular basis. Even their courtships are not private affairs since males display their beautiful yellow feathers by singing in front of the whole flock while flying in circles on rapidly beating wings.

Unfortunately, little is known about the timing or location of their nesting season in the Sierra Nevada. Nest building has been observed from March–August, but their nests are well hidden in conifers and hard to find. They seem to nest in all types of conifer, or oak-conifer, forests from the foothills to treeline though most may move upslope in early summer to breed in mid- to high-elevation conifer forests in June and July.

Females incubate 3–4 eggs for 13 days, staying on their nests almost continuously while males feed them a regurgitated paste of seeds and insects. After the eggs hatch, males bring food which females divide and feed to their nestlings. Young birds leave the nest when they are 13 days old but remain dependent on their parents for another 3 weeks.

RANGE Pine Siskins are common residents with complex seasonal movements on both slopes. Most of the population seems to move from foothill woodlands and fields upslope into montane conifer forests from April–September then back downslope again in the winter, but unknown numbers (and probably very different numbers from year to year) linger at lower elevations in the summer and at higher elevations in the winter.

LESSER GOLDFINCH *Spinus psaltria*

LIFE HISTORY A cacophony of squeaky, slurred twittering and chattering notes are enough to announce that a flock of Lesser Goldfinches has arrived. They may be in trees or bushes, or clinging to tall grasses, but there they are, merrily tussling with old flowers to loosen their seeds, hanging upside down from branches and landing on grass stems to bend them down to the ground with their weight. Everywhere in the foothills of the Sierra Nevada, all 3 species of goldfinches (see below) are a familiar and comforting year-round presence.

Goldfinches prefer warm, low-lying slopes and valley bottoms (while siskins may be thought of as their mountain cousins), and they are not picky about the habitat as long as it has some scattered trees and bushes and water nearby. During the winter, large flocks venture into grasslands and agricultural areas but for resting and nesting they retreat to any type of open wooded habitat.

Most Lessers nest in the foothills, but there are also plenty of sunny, open meadows upslope so it is not surprising that they also nest in somber stands of mixed conifers near meadows. True to their finch nature, they are gregarious at all seasons and nest in loose colonies with their fellow flock-mates.

Males start off the nesting season by spacing themselves out among bushes and trees, singing long sequences of seemingly random and jumbled notes, sometimes adding in the songs of other birds they mimic. In the presence of females they switch to *tee-yeer* courtship calls and give chase, finishing up with newly formed pairs sitting side by side and touching their bills while softly vocalizing together.

Their nesting biology and dates are not well documented in the Sierra Nevada, but they are known to lay eggs from early April to early August in California. In locations where they are largely absent in the winter, they arrive in mid-April so it is likely they begin to breed by late April, with 4–5 eggs being laid sometime in May or even June.

Their compact nests are usually made of plant strips and bits of lichen and are well hidden in dense foliage amid forked branches. As females incubate eggs for 12 days, males stand guard and feed them regurgitated seeds, buds, flowers, fruits, and insects. Nestlings are later fed by both parents and leave the nest in 12 days but remain dependent on their parents for several more weeks. Adults and juveniles appear to join growing flocks of postbreeding birds that wander in search of food, some moving as far upslope as treeline, especially in September.

Note: *Of the two other goldfinches in the Sierra Nevada,* **American Goldfinches** *are more common and familiar. They are widespread transients at low elevations, but fairly rare to uncommon breeders at scattered locations in the foothills of the west slope and at Sierra Valley on the east slope. Some pairs of* **Lawrence's Goldfinches** *breed on the west slope of the Sierra Nevada, but they are only common around the Kern River Valley and other southern areas.*

RANGE Lesser Goldfinches are common, year-round residents on foothill slopes and low-lying valleys all around the Sierra Nevada, with their local status changing very little over the course of the year other than a moderate retreat in the face of winter storms and cold weather. During the breeding season (April–September), nesting colonies can be found at scattered outposts to about 5000 ft on the west slope and 7000 ft on the east slope.

EVENING GROSBEAK *Coccothraustes vespertinus*

LIFE HISTORY One day a scientist is going to put radio transmitters on some Evening Grosbeaks and figure out where these bizarre finches spend the year, but in the meantime we can only speculate and wonder why they come and go in so many unpredictable ways. Some have suggested that these finches are year-round residents in the Sierra Nevada, but it is hard to explain why they would disappear over large areas and for long periods of time.

It would be almost impossible to miss Evening Grosbeaks if they were around. They show up in noisy flocks making piercing *clee-ip* and *cheer* calls as they forage in the tops of conifers and deciduous trees for seeds, fruits, and insects that they crush and crack open with their huge bills. They sometimes descend to the ground to eat fallen seeds, and they are famous for scrounging salt along mountain roads; in fact, one of the most dependable places to see them in the Sierra Nevada are roadside shoulders along Hwy 49 at Bassetts Station and Yuba Pass in Sierra County.

Large winter flocks begin to break up in May as they move towards their montane breeding grounds. They nest at lower elevations among black oaks, Jeffrey pines, sugar pines, and white firs, or at higher elevation forests among red firs and lodgepole pines. Courtship is a very simple ritual of males crouching low and quivering open wings with their heads thrown back while females solicit courtship feeding by begging like baby birds. They are one of very few songbirds that do not regularly use songs, and in fact during the nesting season they are quite secretive.

Nests are flimsy, shallow saucers in the upper portions of trees that are loosely assembled and hard to spot because they do not look like nests. Grosbeaks can be observed gathering nesting material in mid- to late June with 3–4 eggs being laid in early July. Females take care of most nesting duties and spend so much time on the nest that they must be fed by males. Young birds leave the nest at 13–14 days of age, but still take 2–3 months to reach adult size and become mobile enough to join adult flocks.

RANGE Although a handful of Evening Grosbeaks may overwinter at lower elevations on both slopes of the Sierra Nevada, they mostly overwinter on the northern California coast. Some coastal birds start moving towards the mountains in February with this movement picking up steam in March as grosbeaks show up throughout the northern two-thirds of the Sierra Nevada. By April they are pretty common in this portion of the mountains and increasingly scarce on the coast, and then in May they become abundant and widely dispersed along the full length of the Sierra Nevada. From June–August, and especially in August, nearly every Evening Grosbeak in California is in the Sierra Nevada and presumably breeding. These birds are concentrated in a fairly narrow band of mixed conifer and upper montane forests running the length of the mountains as far south as southern Tulare County. In September their numbers decline as they trickle back towards the coast; but then they become numerous everywhere in California in October, perhaps due to the arrival of northern migrants. By November, grosbeaks are pretty scarce in the mountains; and in December all the grosbeaks remaining in the Sierra Nevada are concentrated south of Mariposa. On top of this broad, statewide perspective, there is a significant variety of grosbeak movements within the Sierra Nevada region itself; large numbers of grosbeaks can show up almost anywhere, at any time of year, and may even stay to breed or to overwinter.

OLD WORLD SPARROWS (Passeridae)

House Sparrow *Passer domesticus*

LIFE HISTORY These introduced birds might be considered a problem except that they rarely stray from towns, homesteads, or farms. They nest in cavities, which are a scarce resource, but they mostly nest in cavities in and around buildings so they do not compete with many native birds. It is easy to dismiss House Sparrows as pests, or symbols of a spreading human footprint on the land, but in fact they have a curious life history in the United States to the extent that their populations exploded to around 150 million birds in the 1940s then dropped to 700,000 birds by 2002. Their populations now seem relatively stable and in fact they are starting to evolve regional forms, as if they are becoming native to North America. Conversely, in parts of their original range in Europe their populations are seriously declining.

House Sparrows are year-round residents wherever they can live in close association with humans or livestock. Their favored habitats are characterized by the presence of concrete, buildings, and cows though they wander into nearby trees and bushes for shelter, supplemental food, and sometimes to nest. They have short legs and are efficient in foraging on the ground for livestock feed, cereal grains, and weed seeds, but readily eat food scraps in city parks and visit backyard bird feeders.

Small flocks feed together and may even nest in loose colonies, but flock members have complex hierarchies with males dominating in the fall and winter, and females in the spring and summer. Males with larger black bibs have higher ranks and are favorably chosen by females. Songs are a series of simple *cheep* notes, sometimes accompanied by males fanning their tails up, drooping their wings, and hopping sideways in front of females to show of their plumage.

The majority of pairs stay together over several years, and they intensely defend the space around their nests, with males attacking intruding males and females attacking females. Preferred nesting sites are crevices and cavities in buildings and other structures, occasionally in trees or natural objects. Cavities are stuffed full of readily available materials, including bits of paper and string. Nest-building activities peak in February–May but can continue into August, with eggs being laid from March–late August. Each clutch contains 3–6 eggs, and 4 clutches per year are common.

Both parents incubate 10–14 days then feed their nestlings regurgitated insects, later switching to the seeds and grains they will eat for the rest of their lives. A week after leaving the nest, young birds become independent and join flocks with other juveniles.

RANGE House Sparrows are year-round residents around towns and agricultural areas, especially at lower elevations. Wherever they occur they are seen every day and seem common though their total numbers may be small. Distribution is spotty and deserves further documentation because they appear to be absent from many suitable areas. Some groups move downslope in the winter, but this needs to be studied because migration is not known in North American populations. **WEST SLOPE:** Locally common residents as high as 4000 ft; status at higher elevations not known. **EAST SLOPE:** Locally common to 8000 ft in the southern Sierra Nevada, and to 6000 ft in the north; some of these birds may move downslope in the winter.

Appendix 1. Rare and Unusual Birds of the Sierra Nevada

The following 73 species occur annually in the Sierra Nevada (being seen at least once every year), but are generally peripheral to the region and not characteristic of the local avifauna. Some breed in the Sierra Nevada, or occur as common migrants, but only in very limited areas. Others are rare visitors. [*Note: Due to space constraints, it is not possible to fully describe the status and distribution of each of these species.*]

Greater White-fronted Goose Abundant spring migrants in Sierra Valley and Honey Lake from late February to mid-April; very rare spring and fall migrants at other locations on both slopes.

Snow Goose Uncommon spring and fall migrants over the northern Sierra Nevada; usually seen in flight, but flocks or individual birds rarely and irregularly stop at lakes or reservoirs on both slopes.

Ross's Goose Very rarely observed, but possible among large flocks of migrating Snow Geese.

Brant Rare but regular in the late summer and fall; most records from Mono Lake and Lake Crowley.

Tundra Swan Migrating flocks are regularly heard or observed flying over the Sierra Nevada; spring migrants are uncommon and fall migrants are common at Sierra Valley and Lake Almanor; frequently linger into the winter on east-slope lakes and reservoirs.

Harlequin Duck Formerly nested in remote river canyons of the west slope; current status poorly known, but single birds or pairs are occasionally observed on west-slope rivers; have recently nested on the Merced River in Yosemite Valley but are not present every year.

Surf Scoter Rare and irregular spring and fall migrants or winter visitors; single birds have been reported from many large lakes and reservoirs.

White-winged Scoter Rare and irregular spring and fall migrants or winter visitors; single birds have been found on large lakes and reservoirs.

Ring-necked Pheasant Introduced in agricultural areas but generally absent in the Sierra Nevada; uncommon residents in the Kern River Valley and at Honey Lake; small numbers may persist in the Owens Valley.

Greater Sage-Grouse Rarely found away from their known lekking sites at Honey Lake, Bodie Hills, and Long Valley.

Red-necked Grebe Rare fall and winter visitors, most often reported at Lake Tahoe from September to November, but possible at other large lakes and reservoirs.

Least Bittern Rare breeders in marshes in the South Fork Kern River Valley and in the Owens Valley.

Cattle Egret Widespread in the Central Valley and in southern California but very rarely wander to the Sierra Nevada; most records from the Kern River Valley and the Owens Valley.

Green Heron Uncommon to rare around small ponds and marshes at low elevations on the west slope, where their nesting status is uncertain; rarely reported on the east side.

White-faced Ibis Postbreeding birds irregularly wander to lakes and marshes on both slopes; often nest in colonies around marshes north of Lake Tahoe, with the largest colony at Sierra Valley, but not present every year.

White-tailed Kite Uncommon year-round residents below the Foothill Oak Zone on the west slope, absent above the elevation where oaks start to form a continuous cover and scarcely makes it into the western fringe of the Sierra Nevada foothills.

Yellow Rail A handful of nesting birds were discovered around east-side marshes in the early 1900s, but only observed a couple times since.

Black-bellied Plover A few migrants are observed on the east side, especially in the fall from July to mid-October. Rare spring and fall migrants in the Kern River Valley.

Snowy Plover Isolated breeding populations on alkaline mudflats around Honey Lake, Mono Lake, and Owens Lake, but most pairs nest on the eastern shores of these lakes away from the Sierra Nevada. Spring migrants seldom encountered, but fall migrants are more frequent. Occasionally reported from the Kern River Valley in the fall, and at Lake Tahoe from late July to early September.

Semipalmated Plover Uncommon migrants with peak dates from late April to early May, and from late July to early August. Nearly all west-slope records from the Kern River Valley; most east-slope records from Honey Lake, Mono Lake, and Lake Crowley, especially in the spring.

Black-necked Stilt Rare spring and fall migrants at large lakes and reservoirs on the west slope. Small numbers breed at Honey Lake and

Sierra Valley, and possibly at other east-side marshes. Fall migrants at South Lake Tahoe and other east-side locations in July-August.

American Avocet   Migrants are possible on both slopes, especially in the fall (July to mid-September). Small numbers breed at Honey Lake, Sierra Valley, and Mono Lake.

Solitary Sandpiper   Rare spring (mid-April to late May) and fall (late July to late September) migrants around the muddy margins of small, secluded ponds; possible to 11,000 ft during fall migration.

Greater Yellowlegs   Uncommon spring (April) and fall (July–September) migrants at almost any elevation; found around lakes, marshes, and slow-moving rivers on both slopes.

Willet   Irregular and sometimes common spring (early April to mid-May) and fall (late June-early September) migrants on the east slope. Common breeding birds (May–June) at Honey Lake and Sierra Valley; uncommon at Lake Crowley.

Lesser Yellowlegs   Rare spring (April–early May) and fall (late July–September) migrants on both slopes in far lower number than Greater Yellowlegs.

Whimbrel   Rarely reported as spring (mid-April to mid-May) and fall (late July to early October) migrants; most records from Mono Lake.

Long-billed Curlew   Rare spring and fall migrants in the Kern River Valley. Migration on the east side may peak in mid-April and mid-July; small numbers linger to nest in wet meadows around Honey Lake and Sierra Valley.

Marbled Godwit   Rare spring and fall migrants in the Kern River Valley and at Lake Almanor on the west side. Rare in the spring (April) and fall (July–August) on the east side, most records from Honey Lake, Lake Tahoe, and Mono Lake.

Ruddy Turnstone   Rare spring (early to mid-May) and fall (August–early September) migrants at the Kern River Valley; also at Honey Lake, Lake Tahoe, and Mono Lake on the east side.

Red Knot   Most records are of fall migrants (late July to mid–September) on the muddy margins of east-side lakes and reservoirs. Only a few spring records.

Sanderling   Rare fall migrants (mostly August–September) with a handful of records from the Kern River Valley; best found at South Lake Tahoe, Mono Lake, Lake Crowley, and Owens Valley.

Semipalmated Sandpiper   Rare and easily overlooked fall (late July–early September) migrants; most records from Mono Lake and the Owens Valley.

Baird's Sandpiper   Uncommon fall migrants with a few adults seen from mid-July to mid-August and a strong showing of juveniles from mid-August through September. Most often seen in the Kern River Valley and at Lake Almanor on the west side, and south of Mono Lake on the east side (flocks of several hundred possible in the Owens Valley in August).

Pectoral Sandpiper   Rare fall (late August to mid-October) migrants at the Kern River Valley and at Lake Almanor on the west side; most east-side records from Mono Lake.

Dunlin   Rare spring and fall migrants, with a sharp peak in numbers in late April, and an extended passage from mid-August to November; occasionally lingers through the winter on both slopes.

Red Phalarope   Easily overlooked among large flocks of phalaropes, but one or more individuals are seen each fall, especially at Honey Lake and Mono Lake.

Sabine's Gull   Rare fall (mid-September to mid-October) migrants at large lakes and reservoirs on both slopes of the Sierra Nevada; best looked for at Lake Tahoe, Lake Crowley, and in the Owens Valley.

Bonaparte's Gull   Rare spring (April–May) and fall (late September–early November) migrants, with a few mid-summer records. Nearly all reported from the east side, especially at Lake Tahoe, Mono Lake, Lake Crowley, and the Owens Valley; but occasionally in the Kern River Valley as well.

Franklin's Gull   Small numbers of spring (late April–late May) and fall (June-September) migrants or nonbreeding adults are observed at east-side marshes and lakes. Only a few migrants have ever been reported from the west side.

Mew Gull   Very rarely reported from the east side, and only occasionally reported from Lake Almanor and Isabella Lake on the west side. Found in small numbers among the hundreds of gulls at the Nimbus Fish Hatchery (Folsom Lake) anytime from October to December.

Herring Gull   Scattered individuals and small groups observed at low-elevation lakes and reservoirs from mid-October through the winter. Possible on the east side, but mostly found on the west side, with as many as 2800 reported at the Nimbus Fish Hatchery (Folsom Lake). Rare during spring (March–May) migration.

Thayer's Gull   Fairly common at the Nimbus Fish Hatchery (Folsom Lake) in late fall, with some lingering through the winter; occasionally reported from other west-side lakes and reservoirs. Very few east-side records of juveniles from mid-October to mid-November, mostly from the Owens Valley.

Glaucous-winged Gull   Very rare visitors to the Sierra Nevada except for a handful that show up at the Nimbus Fish Hatchery each fall, where as many as a dozen birds may linger to mid-winter. Single birds have been reported a few times at other lakes and reservoirs on both slopes of the Sierra Nevada, mostly from late October to mid-January.

Common Tern   Rare but regular fall (late August–early October) migrants at large lakes and reservoirs on both slopes, but the vast majority of sightings are from Lake Tahoe, Mono Lake, Lake Crowley, and the Owens Valley. At Lake Tahoe they may outnumber Forster's Terns in September. Found as high as 11,000 ft.

Parasitic Jaeger   Rare but regular migrants that appear at east-side lakes and reservoirs from mid-August to late September; most records from Lake Tahoe, but also reported from Mono Lake and Lake Crowley.

Long-tailed Jaeger   Considered by some experts to be the default jaeger at east-side lakes and reservoirs with Parasitic Jaegers being the exception; most records from Lake Tahoe in late August to mid-September, but observed at other large lakes and reservoirs.

Yellow-billed Cuckoo   Uncommon breeders in flooded riparian forests around Isabella Lake and the South Fork Kern River Valley; very rarely reported anywhere else in the Sierra Nevada.

Burrowing Owl   Very small numbers breed (or have bred) around the Kern River Valley, Honey Lake, and Sierra Valley; may breed at a few other locations but are not present every year. Wandering birds are occasionally observed at unexpected locations, and have been seen as high as 12,000 ft.

Short-eared Owl   Rare and sporadic breeders at low-elevation marshes along the east side, absent many years and present in very small numbers other years. Bred in Sierra Valley in summer of 2011. Otherwise they are scarce postbreeding visitors at any elevation and winter visitors at low elevations.

Vermilion Flycatcher   Two to 6 breeding pairs found in the South Fork Kern River Valley from March–August; vagrants occasionally observed in the Owens Valley, especially in October-November.

Brown-crested Flycatcher   A dozen or more pairs breed in the South Fork Kern River Valley from early May to mid-August; best observed at the Canebrake Ecological Reserve and at the Kelso Creek Sanctuary.

Cassin's Kingbird   Several pairs often breed in the South Fork Kern River Valley near the community of Onyx from late March to late

August; vagrants occasionally observed in the Owens Valley, especially in April–May.

Loggerhead Shrike Fairly common residents in the Central Valley, but rarely wander into the lowest reaches of the west-side foothills except in September–October when migrants might be found at higher elevations. Fairly common from April–August in desert shrub habitats along the east side, but often seen well east of the Sierra Nevada slope.

Northern Shrike Rare and irregular winter visitors in valley bottoms along the east side; not present every winter; more common in the north and increasingly rare to the south.

Bell's Vireo Formerly common breeding birds in low-elevation riparian habitats along both slopes, but fewer than a dozen individuals seen in the past decade or so.

Gray Jay This jay of the Cascade Mountains scarcely reaches the Sierra Nevada region at Lake Almanor, where they are only rarely encountered (and nearly always on the north side of the lake, outside of the Sierra Nevada region).

Cactus Wren Resident pairs are found at only a few locations in the upper reaches of the South Fork Kern River Valley along Chimney Creek Road, Kelso Valley Road, and in the Walker Basin on the west side. Found south of Walker Pass on the east side; rarely wanders north into the Owens Valley.

Northern Mockingbird Locally common residents in the Kern River Valley and in the Owens Valley; breed in the Central Valley but scarce in the lower foothills of the west slope, where they may irregularly breed or visit as postbreeding wanderers.

Lapland Longspur Best looked for around Honey Lake in October–November, with numbers diminishing by December; there are also several dozen fall records from the Owens Valley.

Chestnut-collared Longspur Irregular fall (late September–late November) migrants on the east side; rarely linger through the winter (until about April).

Northern Parula Rare spring and fall migrants, mostly on the east side.

Black-and-white Warbler Rare spring migrants on both slopes, mostly in the southern Sierra Nevada; very few fall records.

American Redstart Rare spring and fall migrants; mostly from the Kern River Valley on the west side, or from the Owens Valley and Mono Basin on the east side.

Northern Waterthrush   Rare spring and fall migrants; mostly from Butterbredt Springs, Owens Valley, and the Mono Basin.

Common Yellowthroat   Common breeders in the South Fork Kern River Valley and locally uncommon in very small numbers at a few other scattered marshes along the west side; uncommon to rare from mid-April to mid-October at scattered marshes along the east side, where they probably nest at some locations.

Yellow-breasted Chat   Uncommon breeders at the South Fork Kern River Valley; based on the presence of singing males may breed elsewhere below 3000 ft on the west side, but in very small numbers and at very scattered locations. Singing males occasionally reported along the east side, mostly south of Mono Lake, but breeding is rarely confirmed.

American Tree Sparrow   Rare and irregular winter visitors on the east side from mid-October to early March, with most records from Honey Lake, but also from Mono Lake and the northern Owens Valley.

Grasshopper Sparrow   Thought to be regular and highly local breeders in foothill grasslands on the west side (exceptionally to 4600 ft), but very few confirmed nesting records. Rare spring (May) and fall (September–October) migrants on the east side; with a handful of June records around Sierra Valley that may indicate local breeding.

Swamp Sparrow   Rare fall (mid-September to mid-November) migrants on the east side; with a few records of birds lingering through the winter. Only a couple winter records from the west side.

Harris's Sparrow   Rare winter visitors on both slopes, with most records from the Owens Valley.

Blue Grosbeak   Fairly common breeding birds in the Kern River Valley, and may breed in very small numbers at a few other locations on the west side in the southern Sierra Nevada. Uncommon and local breeding birds in the Owens Valley.

Great-tailed Grackle   Due to their ongoing colonization of California, the status of these newcomers is in flux. Now common in the Owens Valley and in the Kern River Valley, but rapidly expanding their range northward along both slopes of the Sierra Nevada (breeding at least as far north as Nevada County on both slopes). Wandering birds are regularly encountered at low elevations.

Appendix 2. **Glossary of Place Names**

Most places mentioned in this book are familiar locations, or easily found on a map, but some of the more obscure or unfamiliar places are described here to help the reader locate them.

Aspendell   A mountain community on Hwy 168, southwest of Bishop.

Bassetts Station   Listed on some maps as "Bassetts," a small way-station on Hwy 49 west of Yuba Pass in Sierra County.

Breckenridge Mountain   A 7548-ft peak southwest of Lake Isabella in Kern County (southernmost high peak in Sierra Nevada).

Bucks Lake   A large mountain lake west of Quincy in Plumas County.

Butterbredt Springs   A birdwatcher's hotspot on Jawbone Canyon Road in eastern Kern County.

Canebrake Ecological Reserve   A California Department of Fish and Game reserve about 20 miles east of Lake Isabella on Hwy 178 in Kern County.

Carson Pass   The highest point of Hwy 88, south of Lake Tahoe in Alpine County.

Carson Range   A range that defines the eastern shore of Lake Tahoe and the only part of the Sierra Nevada in the state of Nevada.

Chimney Creek Road   Also known as Chimney Peak Road or Canebrake Road, runs north from Hwy 178 in the South Fork Kern River Valley.

Coldstream Canyon   A mountain canyon on the west side of Truckee in Nevada County.

Desolation Wilderness   Part of the Crystal Range west of Lake Tahoe.

Diamond Mountains   A little-known range south of Susanville and west of Honey Lake in Lassen and Plumas counties.

Diamond Valley   A tiny valley east of Woodfords in eastern Alpine County.

Folsom Lake   A large reservoir east of Sacramento and south of Interstate 80 on the Placer and El Dorado county line.

Greenhorn Mountains   A small range west of Isabella Lake.

Grizzly Mountains   A small range east of Quincy, noted on some maps as Grizzly Ridge.

Hartson Reservoir   Also known as Hartson Lake, on the north shore of Honey Lake in Lassen County.

Henness Pass   An obscure pass on Henness Pass/Jackson Meadows Road, west of Hwy 89 in Sierra County.

Hogback Creek   A riparian area 9.5 miles south of Independence in Inyo County.

Isabella Lake   A large reservoir in the Kern River Valley, next to the town of Lake Isabella.

Kelso Creek Sanctuary   This Audubon California preserve is in the South Fork Kern River Valley east of Isabella Lake.

Kelso Valley Road   A rugged back road that heads south from the community of Weldon in the South Fork Kern River Valley, provides access to Butterbredt Springs.

Kern River Valley   A broad term that encompasses the area where the valleys of the Kern River and South Fork Kern River come together at Isabella Lake.

Lake Crowley   Sometimes referred to as Crowley Lake, a large reservoir on the east side of Hwy 395 south of Mammoth Lakes.

Lakes Basin   A collection of mountains lakes along the Gold Lake Highway between Bassetts and Graeagle in Sierra and Plumas counties.

Leavitt Lake   A small lake along the Pacific Crest Trail south of Hwy 108 near Sonora Pass.

Lee Vining Canyon   Drains the Sierra Nevada crest on the southwest shore of Mono Lake, located above Lee Vining along Hwy 120.

Loch Leven Lakes   A popular hiking destination on the south side of Interstate 80 west of Donner Pass.

Long Valley   Parallels the Owens River on the north side of Lake Crowley.

Lundy Canyon   Drains the Sierra Nevada crest on the northwest shore of Mono Lake.

Meiss Lake   A small subalpine lake located north of Carson Pass along the Pacific Crest Trail.

Mineral King   A ranger station and major wilderness trailhead in Sequoia National Park.

Mountain Meadows Reservoir A large reservoir on the east side of Lake Almanor in Lassen County.

Mt Rose   A 10,776-ft peak on the northeast shore of Lake Tahoe, in the state of Nevada.

Nimbus Fish Hatchery   On the American River below Folsom Lake, next to the town of Folsom in Sacramento County.

Ninemile Canyon   A rugged canyon accessed by Nine Mile Canyon Road west of Hwy 395 in southwest Inyo County.

Pine Creek Pass   A remote alpine pass in the John Muir Wilderness west of Bishop.

Piute Mountains   A small desert range south of Isabella Lake and Hwy 178 in northern Kern County.

Red Lake   A small lake on the east side of Carson Pass along Hwy 88.

Sand Canyon   A short rugged canyon accessed by Sand Canyon Road west of Hwy 395 in northern Kern County.

Scodie Mountains   A small desert range south of Hwy 178 near Walker Pass in Kern County.

Shaver Lake   A large lake in the Sierra National Forest along Hwy 168.

South Fork Kern River Valley   The eastern arm of the Kern River Valley along Hwy 178.

Sweetwater Mountains   A rarely-visited range north of Bridgeport in Mono County; on the east side of Hwy 395, but probably a sub-range of the Sierra Nevada.

Tower Peak   A remote 11,755-ft peak on the north boundary of Yosemite National Park east of the Pacific Crest Trail.

Tuolumne Meadows   A large montane meadow system along Hwy 120 in Yosemite National Park.

Twin Lakes   Found on Twin Lakes Road southwest of Bridgeport in Mono County.

Walker Basin   A small area along the Caliente Bodfish Road, south of the town of Lake Isabella in Kern County.

Walker Creek   Located southwest of Olancha on Hwy 395 in Inyo County.

Whitney Portal   The trailhead for the Mt Whitney hike, west of Lone Pine in Inyo County.

Woodfords   A small community in eastern Alpine County at the junction of Hwys 88 and 89.

Yuba Pass   The high point of Hwy 49 in Sierra County, east of Bassetts.

Index

Accipiter, 50–54
  cooperii, 52–53
  gentilis, 53–54
  striatus, 50–52
Accipitridae, 48–58
Actitis macularius, 71–73
Aechmophorus occidentalis, 36–37
Aegithalidae, 174–176
Aegolius acadicus, 99–100
Aeronautes saxatalis, 105–106
Agelaius phoeniceus, 249–251
Aimophila ruficeps, 225–226
Aix sponsa, 3–4
Alaudidae, 160–161
Alcedinidae, 112–113
Alectoris chukar, 27–28
Amphispiza, 233–236
  belli, 234–236
  bilineata, 233–234
Anas, 4–14
  acuta, 11–13
  americana, 6–7
  clypeata, 10–11
  crecca, 13–14
  cyanoptera, 9–10
  platyrhynchos, 7–9
  strepera, 4–6
Anatidae, 1–24
Anthus rubescens, 207–209
Aphelocoma californica, 151–152
Apodidae, 103–106
Aquila chrysaetos, 57–58
Archilochus alexandri, 106–107
Ardea, 41–44
  alba, 42–44
  herodias, 41–42
Ardeidae, 40–45
Asio otus, 97–98
Avocet, American, 276
Aythya, 14–18
  affinis, 17–18
  americana, 14–15
  collaris, 16–17
Baeolophus, 172–174

inornatus, 172–173
  ridgwayi, 173–174
Bittern, 40–41, 275
  American, 40–41
  Least, 275
Blackbird, 187, 249–259
  Brewer's, 255–256
  Red-winged, 249–251
  Tricolored, 251
  Yellow-headed, 187, 253–254
Bluebird, 195–198
  Mountain, 196–198
  Western, 195–196
Bombycilla cedrorum, 209–210
Bombycillidae, 209–210
Botaurus lentiginosus, 40–41
Brant, 274
Branta canadensis, 1–3
Bubo virginianus, 93–94
Bucephala, 18–20
  albeola, 18–19
  clangula, 19–20
Bufflehead, 18–19
Bunting, 248–249
  Indigo, 249
  Lazuli, 248–249
Bushtit, 174–175
Buteo, 55–57
  jamaicensis, 56–57
  lineatus, 55–56
Calidris, 73–74
  mauri, 73
  minutilla, 73–74
Callipepla californica, 26–27
Calypte anna, 107–109
Canvasback, 15
Caprimulgidae, 100–102
Cardinal, 244–249
Cardinalidae, 244–249
Carpodacus, 262–266
  cassinii, 264–265
  mexicanus, 265–266
  purpureus, 262–263
Cathartes aura, 45–46
Cathartidae, 45–46
Catharus guttatus, 199–201

Catherpes mexicanus, 182–183
Certhia americana, 180–181
Certhiidae, 180–181
Chaetura vauxi, 104–105
Chamaea fasciata, 193–195
Charadriidae, 70–71
Charadrius vociferus, 70–71
Chat, Yellow-breasted, 280
Chickadee, 170–172
  Chestnut-backed, 171–172
  Mountain, 170–171
Chlidonias niger, 82–83
Chondestes grammacus, 232–233
Chordeiles minor, 100–101
Chukar, 27–28
Cinclidae, 189–191
Cinclus mexicanus, 189–191
Circus cyaneus, 49–50
Cistothorus palustris, 187–188
Coccothraustes vespertinus, 271–272
Colaptes auratus, 127–128
Columba livia, 84–85
Columbidae, 84–88
Condor, California, 46
Contopus, 130–133
  cooperi, 130–132
  sordidulus, 132–133
Coot, American, 67–69
Cormorant, Double-crested, 37–38
Corvid, 147–159
Corvidae, 147–159
Corvus, 156–159
  brachyrhynchos, 156–158
  corax, 158–159
Cowbird, Brown-headed, 256–258
Crane, Sandhill, 69–70
Creeper, Brown, 180–181
Crossbill, Red, 267–268
Crow, American, 156–158
Cuckoo, Yellow-billed, 278
Cuculidae, 88–89
Curlew, Long-billed, 276

Cyanocitta stelleri, 149–151
Cypseloides niger, 103–104
Dendragapus fuliginosus, 28–29
Dendroica, 215–220
    coronata, 216–217
    nigrescens, 218–219
    occidentalis, 219–220
    petechia, 215–216
Dipper, American, 189–191
Dove, 84–88
    Eurasian Collared-, 88
    Mourning, 87–88
Dowitcher, 74–75
    Long-billed, 75
    Short-billed, 74
Dryocopus pileatus, 128–130
Duck, 1–24, 274
    Harlequin, 274
    Ring-necked, 16–17
    Ruddy, 23–24
    Wood, 3–4
Dunlin, 277
Eagle, 48–58
    Bald, 48–49
    Golden, 57–58
Egret, 40–45, 275
    Cattle, 275
    Great, 42–44
    Snowy, 43
Emberizidae, 223-244
Empidonax, 133–139
    difficilis, 137–138
    hammondii, 134–135
    oberholseri, 136–137
    occidentalis, 138–139
    traillii, 133–134
    wrightii, 135–136
Eremophila alpestris, 160–161
Euphagus cyanocephalus,
    255–256
Falco, 59–62
    columbarius, 60
    mexicanus, 61–62
    peregrinus, 60–61
    sparverius, 59–60
Falcon, 59–62
    Peregrine, 60–61
    Prairie, 61–62

Falconidae, 59–62
Finch, 260–272
    Cassin's, 264–265
    Gray-crowned Rosy-,
      260–261
    House, 265–266
    Purple, 262–263
Flicker, Northern, 127–128
Flycatcher, 130–143, 278
    Ash-throated, 141–142
    Brown-crested, 278
    Cordilleran, 138–139
    Dusky, 136–137
    Gray, 135–136
    Hammond's, 134–135
    Olive-sided, 130–131
    Pacific-slope, 137–138
    Vermilion, 278
    Willow, 133–134
Fringillidae, 260–272
Fulica americana, 67–69
Gadwall, 4–6
Gallinago delicata, 75–76
Gavia immer, 31–32
Gaviidae, 31–32
Geococcyx californianus, 88–89
Glaucidium gnoma, 94–95
Gnatcatcher, Blue-gray,
    188–189
Godwit, Marbled, 276
Goldeneye, 19–20
    Barrow's, 19
    Common, 19–20
Goldfinch, 269–270
    American, 270
    Lawrence's, 270
    Lesser, 269–270
Goose, 1–24
    Cackling, 2
    Canada, 1–3
    Greater White-fronted, 274
    Ross's, 274
    Snow, 274
Goshawk, Northern, 53–54
Grackle, Great-tailed, 280
Grebe, 32–37, 275
    Clark's, 37
    Eared, 34–36

Horned, 34
    Pied-billed, 32–33
    Red-necked, 275
    Western, 36–37
Grosbeak, 246–248,
    261–262, 271–272, 280
    Black-headed, 246–248
    Blue, 280
    Evening, 271–272
    Pine, 261–262
    Rose-breasted, 248
Grouse, 27–31, 275
    Greater Sage-, 275
    Sooty, 28–29
Gruidae, 69–70
Grus canadensis, 69–70
Gull, 79–84, 277–278
    Bonaparte's, 277
    California, 80–81
    Franklin's, 277
    Glaucous-winged, 278
    Herring, 277
    Mew, 277
    Ring-billed, 79–80
    Sabine's, 277
    Thayer's, 277
Gymnorhinus cyanocephalus,
    147–149
Haliaeetus leucocephalus,
    48–49
Harrier, Northern, 49–50
Hawk, 48–58
    Cooper's, 52–53
    Ferruginous, 57
    Red-shouldered, 55–56
    Red-tailed, 56–57
    Rough-legged, 57
    Sharp-shinned, 50–52
    Swainson's, 57
Heron, 40–45, 275
    Black-crowned Night-,
      44–45
    Great Blue, 41–42
    Green, 275
Hirundinidae, 161–170
Hirundo rustica, 168–170
Hummingbird, 106–112
    Allen's, 111

Anna's, 107–109
Black-chinned, 106–107
Broad-tailed, 110
Calliope, 109–110
Costa's, 109
Rufous, 110–112
Hydroprogne caspia, 81–82
Ibis, White-faced, 275
Icteridae, 249–259
Icterus bullockii, 258–259
Jaeger, 278
Long-tailed, 278
Parasitic, 278
Jay, 147–152, 279
Gray, 279
Pinyon, 147–149
Steller's, 149–151
Western Scrub-, 151–152
Junco, Dark-eyed, 243–244
Junco hyemalis, 243–244
Kestrel, American, 59–60
Killdeer, 70–71
Kingbird, 142–143, 278–279
Cassin's, 278–279
Western, 142–143
Kingfisher, Belted, 112–113
Kinglet, 191–193
Golden-crowned, 191–192
Ruby-crowned, 192–193
Kite, White-tailed, 275
Knot, Red, 276
Laridae, 79–84
Lark, Horned, 160–161
Larus, 79–81
californicus, 80–81
delawarensis, 79–80
Laterallus jamaicensis, 63–64
Leucosticte tephrocotis, 260–261
Limnodromus, 74–75
griseus, 74
scolopaceus, 75
Longspur, 279
Chestnut-collared, 279
Lapland, 279
Loon, 31–32
Common, 31–32
Pacific, 31

Lophodytes cucullatus, 20–21
Loxia curvirostra, 267–268
Magpie, 155–156
Black-billed, 155–156
Yellow-billed, 156
Mallard, 7–9
Martin, Purple, 161–162
Meadowlark, Western, 251–253
Megaceryle alcyon, 112–113
Megascops kennicottii, 92–93
Melanerpes, 113–116
formicivorus, 115–116
lewis, 113–115
Meleagris gallopavo, 29–31
Melospiza, 238–241
lincolnii, 239–241
melodia, 238–239
Melozone crissalis, 226–227
Merganser, 20–23
Common, 21–23
Hooded, 20–21
Red-breasted, 22
Mergus merganser, 21–23
Merlin, 60
Mimidae, 203–205
Mockingbird, Northern, 279
Molothrus ater, 256–258
Moorhen, Common, 68
Motacillidae, 207–209
Myadestes townsendi, 198–199
Myiarchus cinerascens, 141–142
Nighthawk, 100–101
Common, 100–101
Lesser, 100–101
Nucifraga columbiana, 152–154
Nutcracker, Clark's, 152–154
Nuthatch, 176–180
Pygmy, 178–180
Red-breasted, 176–177
White-breasted, 177–178
Nycticorax nycticorax, 44–45
Odontophoridae, 24–27
Oporornis tolmiei, 220–221
Oreortyx pictus, 24–26
Oreoscoptes montanus, 203–204
Oreothlypis, 212–214
celata, 212–213

ruficapilla, 213–214
Oriole, 258–259
Baltimore, 259
Bullock's, 258–259
Hooded, 259
Scott's, 259
Osprey, 46–47
Otus flammeolus, 91–92
Owl, 90–100, 278
Barn, 90
Burrowing, 278
Flammulated, 91–92
Great Gray, 96–97
Great Horned, 93–94
Long-eared, 97–98
Northern Pygmy-, 94–95
Northern Saw-whet, 99–100
Short-eared, 278
Spotted, 95–96
Western Screech-, 92–93
Oxyura jamaicensis, 23–24
Pandion haliaetus, 46–47
Pandionidae, 46–47
Paridae, 170–174
Parula, Northern, 279
Parulidae, 212–223
Passer domesticus, 272–273
Passerculus sandwichensis, 236–237
Passerella iliaca, 237–238
Passeridae, 272–273
Passerina amoena, 248–249
Patagioenas fasciata, 86–87
Pelecanidae, 39–40
Pelecanus erythrorhynchos, 39–40
Pelican, American White, 39–40
Petrochelidon pyrrhonota, 167–168
Pewee, Western Wood-, 132–133
Phainopepla, 210–212
Phainopepla nitens, 210–212
Phalacrocoracidae, 37–38
Phalacrocorax auritus, 37–38
Phalaenoptilus nuttallii, 101–102

Phalarope, 71–79, 277
  Red, 277
  Red-necked, 78–79
  Wilson's, 77–78
Phalaropus, 77–79
  lobatus, 78–79
  tricolor, 77–78
Phasianidae, 27–31
Pheasant, Ring-necked, 274
Pheucticus melanocephalus,
  246–248
Phoebe, 138–140
  Black, 138–139
  Say's, 139–140
Pica hudsonia, 155–156
Picidae, 113–130
Picoides, 119–127
  albolarvatus, 124–125
  arcticus, 125–127
  nuttallii, 119–121
  pubescens, 121–122
  villosus, 123–124
Pigeon, 84–88
  Band-tailed, 86–87
  Rock, 84–85
Pinicola enucleator, 261–262
Pintail, Northern, 11–13
Pipilo, 223–225
  chlorurus, 223–224
  maculatus, 224–225
Pipit, American, 207–209
Piranga ludoviciana, 244–246
Plover, 70–71, 275
  Black-bellied, 275
  Semipalmated, 275
  Snowy, 275
Podiceps, 34–36
  auritus, 34
  nigricollis, 34–36
Podicipedidae, 32–37
Podilymbus podiceps, 32–33
Poecile, 170–172
  gambeli, 170–171
  rufescens, 171–172
Polioptila caerulea, 188–189
Polioptilidae, 188–189
Pooecetes gramineus, 231–232
Poorwill, Common, 101–102

Porzana carolina, 66–67
Progne subis, 161–162
Psaltriparus minimus, 174–175
Ptarmigan, White-tailed, 29
Ptilogonatidae, 210–211
Quail, 24–27
  California, 26–27
  Mountain, 24–26
Rail, 63–69, 275
  Black, 63–64
  Virginia, 64–65
  Yellow, 275
Rallidae, 63–69
Rallus limicola, 64–65
Raven, Common, 158–160
Redhead, 14–15
Redstart, American, 279
Regulidae, 191–193
Regulus, 191–193
  calendula, 192–193
  satrapa, 191–192
Riparia riparia, 165–167
Roadrunner, Greater, 88–89
Robin, American, 201–203
Salpinctes obsoletus, 181–182
Sanderling, 276
Sandpiper, 71–79, 276–277
  Baird's, 277
  Least, 73–74
  Pectoral, 277
  Semipalmated, 276
  Solitary, 276
  Spotted, 71–72
  Western, 73
Sapsucker, 117–119
  Red-breasted, 118–119
  Red-naped, 119
  Williamson's, 117–118
Sayornis, 138–140
  nigricans, 138–139
  saya, 139–140
Scaup, 17–18
  Greater, 17
  Lesser, 17–18
Scolopacidae, 71–79
Scoter, 274
  Surf, 274
  White-winged, 274

Selasphorus rufus, 110–112
Shoveler, Northern, 10–11
Shrike, 279
  Loggerhead, 279
  Northern, 279
Sialia, 195–198
  currucoides, 196–198
  mexicana, 195–196
Silky-Flycatcher, 210–211
Siskin, Pine, 268–269
Sitta, 176–180
  canadensis, 176–177
  carolinensis, 177–178
  pygmaea, 178–180
Sittidae, 176–180
Snipe, Wilson's, 75–76
Solitaire, Townsend's, 198–199
Sora, 66–67
Sparrow, 223–244, 272–273,
  280
  American Tree, 280
  Black-chinned, 230–231
  Black-throated, 233–234
  Brewer's, 229–230
  Chipping, 227–228
  Fox, 237–238
  Golden-crowned, 242–243
  Grasshopper, 280
  Harris's, 280
  House, 272–273
  Lark, 232–233
  Lincoln's, 239–241
  Rufous-crowned, 225–226
  Sage, 234–236
  Savannah, 236–237
  Song, 238–239
  Swamp, 280
  Vesper, 231–232
  White-crowned, 241–242
  White-throated, 242
Sphyrapicus, 117–119
  ruber, 118–119
  thyroideus, 117–118
Spinus, 268–270
  pinus, 268–269
  psaltria, 269–270
Spizella, 227–231
  atrogularis, 230–231

breweri, 229–230
passerina, 227–228
Starling, European, 205–207
Stelgidopteryx serripennis, 164–165
Stellula calliope, 109–110
Sterna forsteri, 83–84
Stilt, Black-necked, 275–276
Strigidae, 90–100
Strix, 95–97
  nebulosa, 96–97
  occidentalis, 95–96
Sturnella neglecta, 251–253
Sturnidae, 205–207
Sturnus vulgaris, 205–207
Swallow, 161–170
  Bank, 165–167
  Barn, 168–170
  Cliff, 167–168
  Northern Rough-winged, 164–165
  Tree, 162–163
  Violet-green, 163–164
Swan, Tundra, 274
Swift, 103–106
  Black, 103–104
  Vaux's, 104–105
  White-throated, 105–106
Sylviidae, 193–195
Tachycineta, 162–164
  bicolor, 162–163
  thalassina, 163–164
Tanager, 244–246
  Summer, 245
  Western, 244–246
Teal, 9–14
  Blue-winged, 10
  Cinnamon, 9–10
  Green-winged, 13–14
Tern, 79–84, 278
  Black, 82–83
  Caspian, 81–82
  Common, 278
  Forster's, 83–84
Thrasher, 203–205
  Bendire's, 205
  California, 204–205
  Le Conte's, 205

Sage, 203–204
Thrush, 195–203
  Hermit, 199–201
  Swainson's, 200
  Varied, 202
Thryomanes bewickii, 183–184
Titmouse, 172–174
  Juniper, 173–174
  Oak, 172–173
Towhee, 223–227
  California, 226–227
  Green-tailed, 223–224
  Spotted, 224–225
Toxostoma redivivum, 204–205
Trochilidae, 106–112
Troglodytes, 184–187
  aedon, 184–185
  pacificus, 185–187
Troglodytidae, 181–188
Turdidae, 195–203
Turdus migratorius, 201–203
Turkey, Wild, 29–31
Turnstone, Ruddy, 276
Tyrannidae, 130–143
Tyrannus verticalis, 142–143
Tyto alba, 90
Tytonidae, 90–100
Vireo, 143–147
  Bell's, 279
  Cassin's, 143–145
  Hutton's, 145–146
  Plumbeous, 143
  Red-eyed, 147
  Warbling, 146–147
Vireo, 143–147
  cassinii, 143–145
  gilvus, 146–147
  huttoni, 145–146
  plumbeus, 143
Vireonidae, 143–147
Vulture, Turkey, 45–46
Warbler, 212–223, 279
  Black-and-white, 279
  Black-throated Gray, 218–219
  Hermit, 219–220
  MacGillivray's, 220–221

Nashville, 213–214
  Orange-crowned, 212–213
  Townend's, 220
  Virginia's, 214
  Wilson's, 221–222
  Yellow, 215–216
  Yellow-rumped, 216–217
Waterthrush, Northern, 280
Waxwing, 209–210
  Bohemian, 210
  Cedar, 209–210
Whimbrel, 276
Wigeon, 6–7
  American, 6–7
  Eurasian, 6
Willet, 276
Wilsonia pusilla, 221–222
Woodpecker, 113–130
  Acorn, 115–116
  Black-backed, 125–127
  Downy, 121–122
  Hairy, 123–124
  Ladder-backed, 120
  Lewis's, 113–115
  Nuttall's, 119–121
  Pileated, 128–130
  White-headed, 124–125
Wood-warbler, 212–222
Wren, 181–188, 279
  Bewick's, 183–184
  Cactus, 279
  Canyon, 182–183
  House, 184–185
  Marsh, 187–188
  Pacific, 185–187
  Rock, 181–182
Wrentit, 193–195
Yellowlegs, 276
  Greater, 276
  Lesser, 276
Yellowthroat, Common, 280
Xanthocephalus xanthocephalus, 253–254
Zenaida macroura, 87–88
Zonotrichia, 241–243
  atricapilla, 242–243
  leucophrys, 241–242